Jewish Landmarks of New York

Foreword by
Jacob R. Marcus
Director
American Jewish Archives

Jewish Landmarks of New York

a travel guide and history

by **BERNARD POSTAL** and **LIONEL KOPPMAN**

FLEET PRESS CORPORATION/NEW YORK

Foreword

In this period of the American Bicentennial celebration, I am delighted to welcome the appearance of JEWISH LANDMARKS OF NEW YORK, by Bernard Postal and Lionel Koppman. Like their three-volume AMERICAN JEWISH LANDMARKS: A TRAVEL GUIDE AND HISTORY, they have assembled an invaluable work about the Jews of New York and its suburbs. It is the only guidebook of its kind; there is nothing else like it.

JEWISH LANDMARKS OF NEW YORK is more than a handbook for the tourist; it is an important book for students of the world's largest Jewish community. Historians, both Jews and Gentiles, will want to know more about a community which has made such a great career for itself. This book supplies the information people seek about New York Jewry, the largest in the Diaspora, both past and present. A ready reference book, indexed and replete with an infinity of important detail, it is the kind of work students will keep on their desk next to their Jewish encyclopedia.

It is also fascinating reading and a source of hard-to-find facts about the Jews of New York. It is a must for the Jewish visitor to the city.

In a way, this volume is the only complete history of the Jews of New York—the chronicle of more than three centuries of our people in one of the greatest cities in world history. It is a delightful book, carefully researched and well-written. We are truly grateful for JEWISH LANDMARKS OF NEW YORK.

Jacob R. Marcus

Director,
American Jewish Archives
Cincinnati, Ohio

Introduction

There have been many books about New York, but despite the tremendous impact the Jews have made on the city, there is no single volume covering the entire history of New York Jewry. There are several excellent works dealing with certain periods, with the role of two of the oldest synagogues, and with a number of institutions, but no one source gives an overall picture of the rise of the Jews of New York,

JEWISH LANDMARKS OF NEW YORK assembles for the first time the essential facts about the Jews of New York from their first settlement in 1654 to the present and about all the major places of Jewish interest in the city.

Much detail has been omitted in the interest of readability, but little of consequence has been knowingly ignored. In putting together this historical account, a conscious effort has been made to be informative and informal as well as accurate and concise. Above all, this history is intended to capture the color, flavor, and sense of accomplishment that characterize every area of Jewish life in New York.

The histories preceding each borough and suburb trace the rise of the world's largest Jewish community and its network of religious, cultural, and philanthropic institutions. It describes the influence of Jews on every phase of the city's life.

By answering most of the reader's questions about the *how, when, why,* and *who* of the Jews of New York, the histories will heighten his/her pleasure in using the landmark sections which deal with the *what* and the *where.*

Bernard Postal and Lionel Koppman

About the authors

BERNARD POSTAL, editor, journalist, and author, is associate editor of *The Jewish Week,* editor of *The Jewish Digest,* and co-author of ten other books on travel, Jewish history, and Israel. He was the director of public relations of JWB for 25 years. Prior to that he was national public relations director of B'nai B'rith for eight years. He is a member of the executive council of the American Jewish Historical Society and the Jewish Historical Committee of B'nai B'rith. In 1954 he received the National Jewish Book Award (together with Lionel Koppman) for his contributions to American Jewish history. He was similarly honored by the American Jewish Historical Society.

LIONEL KOPPMAN, editor, writer, and publicist, is director of public information and publications for JWB. He is a former newspaperman in Texas; medical editor for the United States government; and winner of the National Jewish Book Award in 1954 (together with Bernard Postal) for his contributions to American Jewish history. He was also the recipient of the Outstanding Filmstrip of the Year Award for his filmstrip on Sholom Aleichem in 1970. He is the author of a number of manuals and plays on various aspects of American Jewish life. He has received a grant for a textbook in American Jewish history.

Acknowledgments

Years of independent research went into this book, but much of the material in the landmark sections was distilled from correspondence with hundreds of people. We do not pretend to have visited all the places we describe, but we did see large numbers of them through the eyes of good friends and correspondents.

Much material came from the staffs of Federal, state, and municipal agencies, Jewish and non-Jewish organizations, museums, libraries, synagogues, historical societies, universities, scholars, researchers, rabbinical seminaries, Jewish Community Centers, B'nai B'rith Hillel Foundations, United Jewish Appeal, Federation of Jewish Philanthropies, Jewish Community Councils, Board of Jewish Education, Jewish schools, and editors of American Jewish newspapers. The editors were a fertile source both for historic data and contemporary information.

To this group of men and women who cheerfully furnished information, checked data, helpfully undertook local research, and graciously answered our numerous inquiries, we tip our hats and record their names.

Samuel H. Abramson
American Jewish Committee
American Veterans of Israel
Beth El Synagogue
Board of Jewish Education
Brooklyn Museum
Sam Brown
Central Conference of American Rabbis
City College
Columbia University
Rabbi Wayne D. Dosick
Encyclopedia Judaica
Federation Employment and Guidance Service
Federation of Jewish Philanthropies
Dr. Louis Finkelstein
Rabbi Joseph Gelberman
Rabbi Samuel Z. Glaser
Leonard Gold
* Rabbi Harold H. Gordon
Leslie Gottlieb
Harrison School District
Sam Hartstein
*Harry Herbert
Jewish Association for Services for the Aged
Jewish Theological Seminary of America
Mae Koppman

Marian Kramer
Rabbi Yehuda Krinsky
Brenda Leibowitz
Sesil Lissberger
Long Island and Recreation
  Commission
Merchants Association of Sag Harbor
Metropolitan New York
  Coordinating Council of Jewish
  Poverty
Nassau County Museum
National Council of Young Israel
New York University
New York Board of Rabbis
Susan Nueckel
Pace University
Norman Pollay
C. W. Post Center of Long Island
  University
Pound Ridge Public Library
Mrs. Arthur H. Printz
Rabbinical Assembly
Rabbinical Council of America
Ramah Camps

Sagamore Hill National Historic Site
George Salomon
Morris U. Schappes
Mrs. Morris Shimansky
Abner Sideman
Belle Sideman
Henry B. Stern
Rabbi Malcolm Stern
Suffolk County Historical Society
Town of Bedford, Bedford Hills
Town of Huntington
Union of American Hebrew
  Congregations
Union of Orthodox Jewish
  Congregations
United Jewish Council of the East
  Side
United Synagogue of America
Professor Gerard R. Wolfe
Workmen's Circle
Marjorie Wyler
Yonkers Dept. of Parks and
  Recreation

* deceased

Note

A new national program to provide Orthodox Jewish travelers with local information centers for their unique needs while traveling has been instituted by Agudath Israel of America. Information encompassing many areas of the United States, Canada, and Mexico, regarding kosher food, synagogues, and other pertinent information can be obtained by writing: Agudath Israel of America, 5 Beekman Street, New York, N. Y. 10025.

Information on special tours of Jewish sites and landmarks in New York City can be obtained from the following:

1. Sam Brown, 281 Avenue C, Apt. 7C, New York, N. Y. 10009.
2. Professor Gerard R. Wolfe, New York University, School of Continuing Education, 3 Washington Square North, New York, N. Y. 10003.
3. *Tours of Jewish New York*, American Jewish Congress, 180 East 79th Street, New York, N. Y. 10021.

JEWISH LANDMARKS SERIES

Volume I: AMERICAN JEWISH LANDMARKS: The East
Volume II: AMERICAN JEWISH LANDMARKS: The South and the Southwest
Volume III: AMERICAN JEWISH LANDMARKS: The Middle West and the West

JEWISH LANDMARKS OF NEW YORK

TRAVELER'S GUIDE TO JEWISH LANDMARKS OF EUROPE

Contents

NEW YORK CITY

New York Jewry Today

In 1976 there were 1,998,000 Jews in the five boroughs of New York City and the adjacent suburban counties of Nassau, Suffolk, and Westchester. This is a decline of 357,000 since 1963. Once the Jews of Greater New York represented 40 percent of all the Jews in the country but now they represent slightly less than 30 percent of the 5,731,685 in the United States.

In the city proper, the Jewish population in 1975 was reported to be 1,228,000, a drop of 600,000 over the 1963 figure and a loss of 886,000 over the all-time high of 2,115,000 reached in 1957. In the three suburban counties there were 770,000 Jews compared with 500,000 in 1964.

Manhattan has 171,000 Jews, a figure that surpasses only The Bronx's 143,000 and Staten Island's 21,000. The Jewish population of The Bronx, which reached a peak of 585,000 in 1930 when it accounted for 38 percent of all the Jews in the city, fell to 493,000 in 1937, declined again to 396,000 in 1960, and is now only 143,000. Brooklyn, which had 765,000 Jews in 1964, now has 514,000. Queens' Jewish population dropped from 450,000 in 1964 to 379,000 today. Staten Island's Jewish population rose from 13,000 in 1964 to 21,000 today.

Nassau County, with 455,000 Jews, has more Jews than any county except Brooklyn. Suffolk County, east of Nassau County, has 150,000 Jews, while Westchester County, just north of The Bronx, has 165,000 Jews.

Manhattan, the seat of the city's major business establishments and principal governmental, cultural, communications, entertainment, and transportation centers, is also the headquarters of every city-wide Jewish organization and of all national Jewish agencies and institutions located in New York.

15

New York is also the command post of American Jewry. All but three national Jewish organizations have their headquarters there. This concentration enables the national Jewish organizations and their apparatus to exercise a greater influence on the city's Jewish communal agencies than any local Jewish agency except the Federation of Jewish Philanthropies and the United Jewish Appeal of Greater New York.

While American Jewish life relies heavily on the leadership and philanthropic activities of New York Jewry, it is not really a community but more like "a collection of communities—religious, residential, commercial, intellectual—with interlocking ties, a diverse society that pervades and enriches the entire city." Unlike all other American cities with substantial Jewish populations, New York does not have an overall unified fundraising community-planning or representative body acting and speaking for all Jews.

The Federation of Jewish Philanthropies plans and raises funds for some 130 local health, welfare, medical, educational, and recreational agencies affiliated with it. The United Jewish Appeal of Greater New York, operating out of separate offices from the national United Jewish Appeal, is the principal local fundraising agency for overseas needs, and also provides New York's share of the budgets of several national organizations. Since 1974, Federation and the UJA of Greater New York have combined their annual campaigns into a single joint campaign.

The New York Board of Rabbis, with many members outside the Greater New York area, concerns itself with religious and interreligious matters. The Board of Jewish Education of New York is the central service agency for elementary and secondary Jewish education. The metropolitan area council of the National Jewish Welfare Board unites the city's Jewish Community Centers and YM-YWHAs, some of which are part of the Associated YM & YWHAs of Greater New York. A city-wide Jewish Community Relations Council that will coordinate the efforts of local councils in various parts of the city and also coordinate community relations activities of the metropolitan units of some of the national agencies affiliated with the National Jewish Community Relations Advisory Council and a number of other agencies with community relations programs was created in 1976.

There are also a number of city-wide federations, councils, and chapters of national organizations and thousands (the exact figure is unknown), of local voluntary associations ranging from synagogues, schools, and charitable societies to cultural and social clubs and neighborhood branches of national agencies.

Jews outside of New York regard New York Jewry as a prize example of organized chaos. They grumble at the influence it wields in national Jewish affairs and complain that it does not always meet its full share of national communal responsibilities. Virtually all national Jewish organizations were once headed by New Yorkers; today more and more top national Jewish leadership is drawn from other cities. Although New York is a major convention city, few national Jewish conclaves meet here. When Jewish communities beyond the Greater New York area are asked to support a national or international movement or institution, they always make inquiries as to how much New York will give, and usually insist that the city accept one-third of the quota.

Jews represent 2.8 percent of the American population, but they are seven times as numerous in New York as in the country as a whole. They are overwhelmingly English-speaking and native born, economically middle and upper middle-class, with a large proportion college educated. The Jewish birthrate in New York is falling but the percentage of intermarriage is far lower than in other cities.

Jews in New York earn less on the average than their coreligionists elsewhere in the United States but somewhat more than their Catholic fellow townsmen. Twenty-seven out of 100 gainfully employed New Yorkers are Jews. They account for 41 percent of all New Yorkers in trade, 30 percent in amusement, 35 percent in manufacturing, but only 14 percent of construction workers, 13 percent of transportation workers, 12 percent in finance, and 4 percent in public utilities. Not all Jewish businessmen are merchants and not all Jewish professionals are doctors, lawyers, dentists, or accountants; 26.5 percent of them are self-employed.

A 1973 study by Federation found that 15.1 percent of the city's Jews are poor or near poor, with incomes under $6,000 for a family of four, representing 140,000 families including 272,000 individuals. There were 316,800 one-person Jewish families of which 72,900 were below the poverty level. Half of the Jewish poor were aged couples or individuals.

The 1970 census reported that 543,000 New Yorkers still listed Yiddish as their mother tongue, including 189,000 American-born, 600 blacks, and 65 Puerto Ricans. In New York the municipal hospitals all provide kosher food on request. Often mobile synagogues manned by Chasidic rabbinical students are parked at the city's busiest corners and Jewish passersby are urged to try on phylacteries and to accept gift *mezuzahs*.

In New York the public schools are officially closed on Jewish High Holy Days because about half the teachers are Jewish. There are 800 members of the Shomrim, an association of Jewish policemen, about 200 in the Ner Tomid Society, a similar organization of Jewish firemen, and 15,000 Jewish employees in the Post Office. One out of every seven municipal employees is a Jew. New York Jews show a higher percentage of skilled and semi-skilled workers than do Jews in other parts of the country.

In the vast aggregation of New York Jews there are bankers and truck drivers, United Nations officials and kosher butchers, Nobel Prize winners and actors, policemen and professors, labor union leaders and salesmen, teachers and manufacturers, cabbies and bagelmakers, writers and caterers, rabbis and advertising executives, social workers and garment workers, builders and intellectuals, editors and brokers, and employees of Jewish organizations.

They live in duplex apartments on Park and Fifth Avenues and on Sutton Place, in the huge public, private, and cooperative housing developments, in one and two-family houses in the city and the suburbs, in high rise apartments, and in deteriorating tenements. Some commute by railroad and others are part of the daily subway and bus throngs. They are synagogue-goers of every theological belief, agnostics and atheists, weekend golfers, and *payot*-wearing Chasidim. They are successful novelists, playwrights, fashion designers, teenagers wearing yarmulkas in the subway, businessmen planning a real estate deal, cabbies who speak Yiddish and Hebrew, bankers who collect modern art, bearded Chasidim who drive trucks, and students at every college and university.

In New York one may find a Loyal League of Yiddish Sons of Erin which marches in the St. Patrick's Day parade; advertising banners that span main streets from building to building urging contributions to the United Jewish Appeal and Federation, or the purchase of Israel bonds; street solicitors collecting for Jewish schools, homes, and orphanages; full page advertisements in the *New York Times* for major philanthropies; newspaper travel sections crammed with ads of kosher and Jewish-style resorts; Hanukah clubs and Menorahs in banks and Hanukah greetings in railroad stations; extra cars on commuter trains to accommodate Jews rushing home on the eve of Jewish holy days; and kosher food ads containing Hebrew words in the daily newspapers.

The telephone directories require more than 40 pages just to list the Cohens, Levys, and Goldbergs; the social register has its quota of identifiable Jews; telegraph offices provide special blanks to encourage Jews to send holiday greetings by wire; every politician carries a black and white yarmulke in his pocket—black for luncheons and white for dinners and bar mitzvahs; bagels are available in the United Nations cafeteria; cries of "barata, barata" (bargains, bargains) resound on the Lower East Side as Jewish merchants call out to Puerto Rican shoppers; nearly 100,000 Israeli residents make New York "Israel's fourth city;" mini-food trucks bedecked with Hebrew lettering dispense *glatt* kosher hot dogs and snacks on city streets; and the Hebrew calendar can be followed in the window displays of department stores and candy shops.

In New York there are rabbinically supervised kosher Chinese restaurants with such piquant names as Shang-Chai, Moshe Peking, and Jerusalem East; an Irish pub called the "Irish Yarmulke;" the open-air diamond market on West 47th Street where a gem can be bought from bearded Chasidic Jews, the deal closed with a simple *Mazel tov* and perhaps a lunch at the diamond center's *glatt* kosher restaurant; a guide to the Jewish community of New York used by police in neighborhoods with a large Orthodox Jewish population; truck signs that read, "no passing" on the right, and "Happy Passover" on the left; "Wong Fat, Kosher Butcher" in a shop window in Chinatown; and "Se Habla Yiddish" in a fruit market in Spanish Harlem.

The size of the Jewish population and its impact on the city have fascinated, startled, irked, and impressed foreign and domestic observers since the turn of the century. Jew and New Yorker became synonymous in American folklore in the 1880s when New York's Jewish residents first began to excite comment. Widespread Jewish association with the easily identifiable and widely imitated New York products of the world of fashion, entertainment, and ideas sometimes saddled Jews with the envy and ill will the city engendered in other sections of the country.

Henry James wrote in 1907 that he was shocked at "the Hebrew conquest of New York" which he feared would transform the city into "a new Jerusalem." A visiting Englishman in 1910 found that the Jews, along with other non-British stock, constituted the city's chief audience for the offerings of opera and concert music—an observation that is still valid. Some Americans stated that, "New York would be all right if it were not for the damned Jews." A cliche current in the 1920s was that New York was built by the Italians, run by the Irish, and owned by the Jews. What this really meant was that Italian immigrants provided most of the labor for subways and skyscrapers, that Irish immigrants and their descendants dominated the police force and key political offices, and that immigrant or native born Jews were the city's leading merchants and department storeowners.

Ford Madox Ford, the noted British writer, observed in 1926 that New York owes "its intellectual vividness partly to the presence of an immense Jewish population . . . the only people . . . in New York . . . who really loved books with a real passionate yearning that transcended their attention to all terrestrial manifestations." Another foreigner found in the 1920s that "Israelite support of the arts was the difference between hardly supportable indigence and just bearable comfort for the city's creative talents."

The magazine *Fortune*, in a 1960 issue entirely devoted to New York, brought the picture up-to-date when it declared that "the great Jewish population gives New York much of the dynamism and vigor that make the city unique among all the cities on earth . . . Jewish elan has contributed to the city's dramatic character—its excitement, its originality, its stridency, its unexpectedness."

In 1963, the eminent Jewish sociologist, Nathan Glazer, in his book *Beyond the Melting Pot*, described the Jews of New York as "a group that may never act together and that may never feel together, but that does know it is a single group, from which one can be disengaged only by a series of deliberate acts. Only a minority are 'Jews' if we use some concrete defining index. Only a minority belongs to synagogues, is sent to Jewish schools, deals with Jewish welfare agencies, is interested in Jewish culture, speaks a traditional Jewish language, and can be distinguished by dress and custom as Jews. But, added together, the overlapping minorities create a community with a strong self-consciousness and definite character." A song in a Broadway musical put it this way: "When you're in New York, the whole world seems Jewish and the moon is yarmulke high in the sky."

How It All Began

In the first week of September, 1654, four men, two women, and 17 children, landed in the tiny Dutch outpost of New Amsterdam. They were the founders of New York Jewry. These 23 were the first permanent Jewish settlers in North America, although not the first Jews in the American colonies. Perhaps a score of others are known to have been in the English, Dutch, and French settlements before 1650, and even earlier in the Spanish domains in Florida and New Mexico, where they lived as secret Jews.

The journey for the 23 began in May, 1654, in Brazil. Marranos, or secret Jews, had found a tenuous haven in Catholic Brazil for more than a century, after fleeing the inquisition in Spain and Portugal when those lands expelled the Jews at the end of the 15th century. When the Dutch conquered northern Brazil in 1624, the Marranos established the first public Jewish communities in the Americas at Bahia and Recife.

After the Portuguese recaptured northern Brazil in 1654, they gave the Dutch colonists the option of staying and pledging allegiance to Portugal, or leaving within three months. Choosing exile to Portuguese rule, the 600 Jews of Brazil disposed of their property at a huge loss and sought a new refuge. Most of them headed for Holland, where there was an influential colony of Portuguese Jews. A smaller group sailed for the British, French, and Dutch islands in the Caribbean.

One Netherlands bound ship, carrying 23 Jews and a party of Dutch Calvinists, was captured by Spanish pirates. En route to a Spanish port in the West Indies, the buccaneer vessel was seized by a French privateersman and towed to the French West Indies. Stranded in a strange port, the pauperized refugees had only 933 guilders, and some clothing and house furnishings. When the French captain demanded 2,500 guilders for passage to New Amsterdam, the Jews agreed, and pledged themselves to be collectively responsible for the debt, with all their belongings to be forfeited if the full amount was not paid.

Whether they decided to go to New Amsterdam because they knew it was a Dutch colony whose motherland was a haven for religious dissenters, or whether their coming to New Amsterdam was accidental is still a matter of speculation. So is the name of the ship. The Reverend Johannes Polhemus, pastor of the Dutch Reformed Church in Brazil, one of its passengers, referred to it as the *St. Charles*. The old Dutch minutes of New Amsterdam are too faded in some places for a positive identification, but an English translation published in 1884 called the vessel the *Ste. Catherine*.

The "Jewish Mayflower" reached New Amsterdam a year after its incorporation as a city of 800 inhabitants whose houses were clustered at the tip of Manhattan Island. To collect the balance of the passage money, the ship's captain had the Jews' property sold at public auction. Three of the six adults were imprisoned as debtors when the sale left them still owing 495 guilders. Obliged to pay the daily board of the debtors, as well as special court costs, the Frenchman agreed to their release when his crew consented to wait for their share of the debt until the Jews heard from their kinfolk in Holland.

The Dutch burghers who had bought the Jews' belongings at bargain rates returned them to their owners and took some of the Jews into their own homes. But most of them camped in the open. The minister of New Amsterdam's Dutch Reformed Church grumbled about it, but during the bitter winter of 1654-55 he used church funds to feed "some Jews, poor but healthy," who came "several times to my house, weeping and bewailing their misery."

One, and possibly two, Jews preceded the 23 to New Amsterdam. Solomon Pietersen, counsel for the Jews in the ship captain's action against them, was identified as a Jew in the Dutch records, but Jewish historians are skeptical. But Jacob Barsimson, who arrived on July 8, 1654, was a Jew. The Dutch minutes noted his coming on the ship *Peartree* as "Jew, debtor," who owed 36 guilders for passage and board. He was either an agent of the Amsterdam Jews, exploring the possibility of extensive immigration to New Amsterdam, or a trader in the employ of the Dutch West India Company.

New Amsterdam's Governor Peter Stuyvesant made the Jews' impoverishment an excuse to demand that they "be not allowed further to infest and trouble this new colony." The peg-legged tyrant informed the Dutch West India Company that he intended to order the Jews out, "fearing that owing to their present indigence they might become a charge in the coming winter." Repeatedly, he sought to persuade his superiors that since "we have Papists, Mennonites and Lutherans among the Dutch," and "also many Puritans or independents among the English under this government, who conceal themselves under the name of Christians, it would create still greater confusion if the obstinate and immovable Jews came to settle here."

In January, 1655, the Jews appealed to the Dutch West India Company to revoke Stuyvesant's ouster order. In their plea for permission to stay, the Jews predicted that "the more of loyal people that go to live there (New Amsterdam) the better it is in regard to the payment of various excises and taxes which may be imposed there, and in regard to the increase of trade, and also to the importation of all the necessities that may be sent there."

On April 26, 1655, the Company replied to the Jewish plea in a letter of instructions to Stuyvesant. While agreeing with his fear that the presence of the Jews would create difficulties, the Company reminded the governor that the Jews had suffered heavy losses in Brazil out of loyalty to Holland and that their coreligionists were substantial investors in the Company. For these reasons Stuyvesant was told that "these people may travel and trade to and in New Amsterdam and live and remain there, provided the poor among them shall not become a burden to the Company or to the community, but be

NEW YORK CITY — 22

supported by their own nation." A year later the Company also directed Stuyvesant to allow the Jews to trade and buy real estate throughout New Netherland.

Tolerated but never really welcome in New Amsterdam, the Jews remained a tiny handful. In March, 1655, they welcomed the arrival of Abraham de Lucena, who brought the first Torah Scroll, and a few other adults. These newcomers and most of the first 23 were Sephardim, the name given to Jews of Spanish and Portuguese origin. Barsimson was probably of Ashkenazic, or German ancestry, as was Asser Levy, one of those imprisoned for failure to pay the passage debt.

Because most of the first settlers left for Holland or the Dutch West Indies, the Jewish community numbered not more than a dozen families until the 1680s. In 1660, when de Lucena departed, taking his Torah with him, there turned up a family of seven whose four daughters produced many of the Jews of Colonial New York. A few Jews trickled in from London and the British West Indies after the British captured the city and changed its name to New York. Before 1700 a handful of French Jews and a few from Holland arrived. By then the community was about equally divided between Sephardim and Ashkenazim, but the latter became the majority by 1729.

Although the Sephardim spoke Spanish and Portuguese and the language of the Ashkenazim was Yiddish or German, a common religious outlook and close family and business ties bound the two groups into a tightly-knit community. They numbered hardly more than 100 a century after the first settlement out of a total population of less than 25,000. But they had already made an impact on the city's business and civic life, and established the framework of community organization and a tradition of public service on which succeeding generations built.

From its beginnings in Manhattan, one of the five boroughs into which New York is divided, the Jewish community, like the city itself, spilled over into the four other boroughs—Brooklyn, Queens, The Bronx, and Richmond. Jewish settlement in Brooklyn, a separate city prior to its annexation to New York in 1898, began in 1834. In the 1660s and 1670s, however, Asser Levy owned considerable property in "Bruecklen." Kings County (Brooklyn) archives preserve a 1683 record of the purchase of a slave by Peter Strijker of Vlackbos (Flatbush) from "the worthy Abraham Franckfoort, a Jew residing in N. Jorck (New York)," who did business in the village of Mitwout (Midwood). Eighteenth century documents indicate that other Jews also traded in the Brooklyn villages and owned summer estates there.

In the Queens villages of Flushing, Jamaica, and Newton there were at least four Jewish merchants before 1760. Three circumcisions were performed in Jamaica between 1756 and 1781. A Jewish community did not develop until after the Civil War when peddlers, storekeepers, and farmers settled in the communities joined to New York City in 1898. Part of Forest Hills was once "Goldberg's Dairy Farm."

Manhattan Jews also had business interests in what is now The Bronx before 1700 but the permanent Jewish community only dates from the 1840s. It was founded by artisans, peddlers, and shopkeepers attracted to the area during the construction of the Harlem and Hudson River railroads and the High Bridge that carried the Croton Aqueduct across the Harlem River. Jewish settlers first reached Richmond in the 1850s.

All of what is now suburban Long Island, Nassau, and Suffolk Counties, east of Brooklyn and Queens, was familiar country to 18th century New York Jewry. Asser Levy's family settled at Oyster Bay in 1730 on property he had owned there before 1700. Before the Revolution, Jewish merchants and shipowners were well-known at South Haven, Islip, Jericho, Southampton, Sag Harbor, East Hampton, and Montauk. A handful of Jews lived on Long Island all through the 19th century but they did not become numerous enough to create communal institutions until 1890.

In Westchester County, north of The Bronx, there were Jewish farmers and storekeepers around Pleasantville and Rye as early as 1720 but a Jewish community did not develop in this suburban area until 1870.

Ten Generations of Immigration

One of the most remarkable episodes in the growth of New York has been the gathering together within its borders of more Jews than have ever been congregated in one city in the history of the world.

Massive immigration from the Russian and Austro-Hungarian regions of Eastern Europe was the salient factor in the creation of this unprecedented concentration of Jews. Between 1880 and 1924 more than 2,000,000 Jews reached the United States in flight from pogroms, revolution, war and postwar upheavals, economic discrimination, and social degradation. They came by whole families and often by entire communities. Landing in New York, few of them went further because they found in the great city other Jews who shared their religious traditions and social mores, and help in getting their first foothold in the new world.

When the great migration began, the Jews of New York numbered 85,000, the product of earlier but smaller waves of immigration. By 1800 New York was already the largest Jewish community in North America although few Jews migrated to the United States before then. The limited immigration—chiefly French families from Santo Domingo and a sprinkling of individuals from England and Holland—plus natural growth, barely balanced the inroads of intermarriage. So widespread was the defection from Judaism among the early Jewish settlers in the 17th and 18th centuries that there might not have been any Jews in New York today if immigration had been halted at the beginning of the 19th century instead of in the 1920s. There were only 306 Jews in the city in 1806 and barely 500 in 1812.

A trickle from the Polish province of Posen, newly annexed to Prussia, that began during the Napoleonic Wars, swelled into a stream of Yiddish and German-speaking immigrants in the 1820s and 1830s and reached major proportions in the 1840s. Mostly unlearned in Hebrew but

attached to Jewish traditions, the immigrants came chiefly from Bavaria and
Posen, where Jews were subject to galling restrictions and heavy taxes in
the wake of the post-Napoleonic reaction, and from Poland after the abortive
revolt of 1830.

Extremely poor, most of them arrived with only clothing and
household goods. Many had their passage paid by relatives or Jewish
communities abroad. A second wave of Jewish immigrants, including a good
many of culture and means, poured into New York after the collapse of the
1848 revolutions in Germany, Austria, Bohemia, and Hungary.

Of the 6,000 Jews in the United States in 1825, less than 10 percent
lived in New York, but by 1848 New York was the home of more than half the
country's Jewish population of 13,000. Germans and Poles outnumbered the
native-born, but the descendants of the pioneer Sephardim and those
Ashkenazim who had married into Sephardic families constituted the upper
crust of New York Jewish society until the 1850s.

The native-born had few contacts with the German and Polish Jews,
while the Americanized English and Dutch Jews, who had come in the first
decade of the 19th century, looked down on their fellow-Ashkenazim from
Germany. To divert the Germans and Poles from peddling, unsuccessful
attempts were made to settle them in agricultural colonies.

The Bavarians had little in common with the more cultured refugees
from the abortive 1848 revolutions. All the German Jews considered
themselves superior to those from Posen, while Germans and Poles sneered
at the Galicians, Lithuanians, and Romanians, who began coming after 1860.
The Germans, in whose synagogues German was used until the late 1870s,
displayed similar arrogance toward the East Europeans in the 1880s.
Intermarriage between the various groups in the community during the
mid-and-late 19th century was frowned upon, and even burial in the same
cemetery was usually avoided.

The community was predominantly German in origin in 1871 when the
migration of German Jews to the United States virtually ceased, following
their emancipation in the newly-united Germany. Although the German-
Sephardic elite was at first shocked and dismayed by the tremendous influx
from Eastern Europe that began in the 1880s, there had been a steady trickle
since 1865 of Jews from Romania and the Russian provinces bordering on
Germany. Before 1880, 25,000 East European Jews had reached the United
States, and most of them stayed in New York.

But the older community neither recognized nor was prepared to cope
with the beginning of a folk exodus that was to transplant one-third of East
European Jewry to the United States in a generation and a half. The tidal
wave from Eastern Europe swelled New York's Jewish population to
200,000 by 1890, and to 600,000 by the end of the century. By then the Lower
East Side had become "a seething, human sea, fed by streams, rivulets and
rills of immigration fleeing from all the Yiddish-speaking centers of Europe."

Sons and grandsons of German-Jewish peddlers of the 1840s and 1850s who worried lest the newcomers make American Jewry "a nation of peddlers," sought to settle them in other parts of the country. An Industrial Removal Office offered free transportation to families willing to go to smaller towns and cities. A Yiddish-speaking rabbi, who was a popular East Side orator, was employed to meet the newcomers at Ellis Island to persuade them not to remain in New York. A Jewish Immigrants Information Bureau was set up in Europe to encourage immigrants to take passage for Galveston, Texas, rather than for New York, thus facilitating the settlement of some in the South and Middle West. A number of short-lived agricultural colonies were founded in a futile effort to make farmers of the East Europeans. Those who were established as dairy and tobacco farmers in southern New Jersey, Connecticut, and the Catskill Mountain region of New York laid the foundation for the popular Jewish summer resorts in the seashore area and "Borscht Belt."

A second Sephardic immigration brought several thousand Ladino-speaking Jews from Greece, Syria, Turkey, and the Balkans between 1908 and 1914 in the wake of the Balkan Wars. Descendants of 15th century refugees from Spain and Portugal who had found a haven in the Turkish Empire, were kin of the Sephardim who had come to New Amsterdam in 1654.

More than half of the 250,000 Jewish refugees from Germany and Hitler-occupied Europe admitted to the United States between 1933 and 1945 remained in New York, where German was again heard in synagogues and a flourishing German-Jewish weekly appeared. After World War II, 125,000 concentration camp survivors arrived in New York where they became the backbone of the Chasidic community. The Hungarian revolution of 1956, anti-Semitism in Egypt and North Africa, and an exodus of Jews from Castro's Cuba added additional waves of Jewish immigration to the city's population. In the 1970s considerable numbers of Syrian Jews, and some 10,000 Russian Jews arrived in New York. Most of these new immigrants were aided by United HIAS Service in reaching the United States and were assisted in their resettlement in New York by the New York Association for New Americans. The American ORT Federation continued to maintain a trade school for immigrants in New York to provide vocational rehabilitation.

The 1970 census showed a marked decline over the 1960s in the number of New Yorkers of European birth or parentage, but during the 1960-1970 decade the net emigration of 950,000 whites, including many Jews, was offset by the immigration of 450,000 persons of other races. At the beginning of the 1970s, blacks in the city increased from 1,088,000 to 1,668,000 and during the same period the Spanish language population grew from 700,000 to 1,278,000, with the result that blacks and Hispanics together outnumbered Jews in New York City.

Each layer of Jewish immigration either created its own institutions or modified existing ones to meet its special needs of time and place. Out of their diverse origins, traditions, and experiences, each generation of newcomers poured its own quality, variety, color, and unique contribution into the mainstream of the life of New York and its Jewish community. Enriched and influenced by each other, all of the waves of immigration gradually fused to create the present Jewish community of New York.

The Rise of the Jewish Community

Though short of a religious quorum of ten adult males, the founders of New York Jewry conducted the first Rosh Hashanah services in North America on September 12, 1654, worshipping secretly, probably in an attic or in a borrowed room behind a shop. This was the beginning of Congregation Shearith Israel (the Spanish and Portuguese Synagogue), oldest existing Jewish congregation in North America.

The first community act of the Jews of New York was the acquisition of ground for a cemetery in 1656. No trace remains of this earliest Jewish burial ground referred to as a "little hook of land" north of what is now Wall Street. But a second one, originally a plot 52 by 50 feet, opened in 1682, was never completely effaced by the onward march of the city. One of the city's oldest historic sites, the old cemetery just south of Chatham Square is now hemmed in by buildings on three sides. Part of it was leased in 1746 to John Roosevelt, great-great-great-grandfather of Theodore Roosevelt and great-great-great-great-grandfather of Eleanor Roosevelt, at an annual rental of three peppercorns. Franklin D. Roosevelt's great-great-grandfather sold the Jews a piece of ground adjoining the cemetery in 1784 when they began restoring it after the Revolutionary War.

Public services began in 1673 in a rented room on Beaver Street. The existence of a synagogue was first reported in 1682 by the Reverend Henricus Selyns, a Dutch clergyman, who wrote "we have Quakers, Jews, and Labadists, all of whom hold their separate meetings." John Miller's map of New York in 1695 indicated the existence of a synagogue which was described in a real estate deed of 1700 as a house on Mill Street, "commonly known by the name of the Jews' synagogue."

New York Jewry was the only one in America with any community life in 1728 when efforts began to erect the first building constructed for synagogue purposes. The site, just west of the rented wooden frame house then used as a sanctuary, was bought for £100, one loaf of sugar, and a pound of tea. Because the Dutch Reformed Church and Episcopal Trinity Church were still the only religious bodies legally recognized and therefore entitled to own real estate, the lot was acquired in the name of four individual trustees. Appeals for financial help to Jews in the West Indies and Europe brought £223 of the £600 it cost to build the synagogue. Forty-five percent of the balance was contributed by 15 percent of the donors, 70 percent of whom were in the lowest income bracket, proof that the arithmetic of Jewish philanthropy has not essentially changed.

The one-story brick structure, 35 feet square and 11 feet high, was dedicated on Passover, 1730, and remained in use for nearly a century. White lead and "sundries" were bought from John Roosevelt. The bricks were sold by a G. Stuyvesant. Negro slaves provided the unskilled labor. Only the Dutch Reformed Church, Trinity Church, and the Lutheran, French, and Presbyterian churches ante-dated the first synagogue. Its president at the time of dedication was Jacob Franks, a merchant of Ashkenazic origin, one of whose daughters eloped with Oliver deLancey, member of one of New York's most prominent families which gave its name to Delancey Street.

Portuguese was used in the congregational minutes until 1736 and in financial accounts until 1745. After 1735 English was widely used because the Jewish immigrants from central and eastern Europe were mostly Ashkenazim who knew neither Portuguese nor Spanish. In 1757 Shearith Israel sought a *hazzan* (cantor) "who will be able to teach children Hebrew with translation into English and Spanish." After 1762 the *hazzan* (a lay minister), was required to know only Hebrew and English. Spanish was dropped from the curriculum of the congregation's parochial school in 1766.

In the absence of state-supported public schools, the community's Hebrew school, founded in 1728, was expanded in 1755 into a Jewish parochial school, in which secular and Hebrew education were combined.

The city's first Jewish schoolhouse, erected in 1731, was part of a communal shelter that included the residences of the cantor, ritual slaughterer, and beadle, as well as room for occasional visitors. In 1759 the community received its first overseas emissary seeking contributions for the Jews of Palestine. The first national Palestine appeal in America was conducted in 1770 when members of Shearith Israel raised £32 for their coreligionists in Hebron, compared with lesser amounts by the Newport and Philadelphia communities.

Synagogue funds also cared for the local poor, transients, widows and orphans, the sick and victims of epidemics; provided free matzoth, wood, medical care, and burial, interest-free loans; and maintained a pension plan for aged and chronically ill members. The yellow fever epidemic of 1798 so depleted the synagogue's treasury that a separate charity organization was formed by members of the congregration for the first time. This society published the earliest known campaign literature on Jewish philanthropy in New York in 1806—a printed circular appealing for $5,000 to erect a poorhouse and hospital.

Not until the first substantial influx of German and Polish Jews, and smaller numbers from England and Holland, in the early 1820s, was there any great burden on charity funds or the need for additional synagogues. Mostly Ashkenazim, they found Shearith Israel's Sephardic ritual strange, and sought unsuccessfully to organize within the mother synagogue a separate Ashkenazic service. The secession from Shearith Israel that led to the establishment of Congregation B'nai Jeshurun in 1825 (the first rift between the native-born Sephardim and older Ashkenazic families), was led by English and Dutch Jews and supported by some of Polish and German ancestry.

Social and language differences, conflicts over cemeteries, and minor ritual changes, rather than population growth, led to the proliferation of synagogues and their organizational offshoots between 1830 and 1850. Dutch, Polish, and German seceders from B'nai Jeshurun organized Anshe Chesed in 1828. Further splits led to the formation of Ohabei Zedek (1835) by Germans, Shaarey Zedek (1839) by Poles, and Shaarey Hashomayim (1839) by Germans. Other Germans who quit Anshe Chesed and Shaarey Hashomayim organized Rodeph Sholom in 1842. Beth Israel (1843) was founded by Poles withdrawing from Shaarey Zedek. Wealthier Germans moving toward substantial ritual reform founded Emanu-El in 1845. Another secession from B'nai Jeshurun in 1845 created Shaarey Tefilah. Multiplication by division rather than new congregations organized by newly-arrived immigrants gave New York 27 synagogues to serve 50,000 Jews before the Civil War.

Except for their Ashkenazic ritual, all of the synagogues founded before 1850 were at the outset as Orthodox as Shearith Israel. While the latter held fast to the Sephardic form of Orthodoxy, the newer congregations began modifying their practices even before the city's first ordained rabbi, Leo Merzbacher, arrived in 1842. Until then the only religious leaders were *hazzanim*. Merzbacher was called from Germany to serve both Anshe Chesed and Rodeph Sholom at $200 a year.

English preaching, heard only at Shearith Israel before 1840, was introduced at B'nai Jeshurun by its *hazzan*, Samuel Myer Isaacs, an Englishman. Jacques Judah Lyons, Shearith Israel's minister from 1840–1877, was also a *hazzan*. When Isaacs became minister of the new Shaarey Tefilah, he was succeeded at B'nai Jeshurun in 1849 by Morris Raphall, another Englishman, whose fame as an orator brought throngs of Christians and Jews to hear him preach.

Denied reengagement by Anshe Chesed in 1845 because he spoke against women wearing *sheitels* (ritual wigs), Merzbacher helped form Emanu-El, New York's pioneer Reform congregation, where he introduced sweeping changes in ritual and practice that made his synagogue a citadel of Reform Judaism. Max Lilienthal, the city's second ordained rabbi, was brought from Russia in 1845 by the three leading German synagogues to succeed Merzbacher at a salary of $1,000 a year. Lilienthal also broke with tradition by establishing the custom of confirmation both for boys and girls. The first synagogue formed by East European Jews was Beth Hamadresh Hagodol, founded in 1852. Its earliest rabbi was the Russian trained Abraham Joseph Ash, who served without pay because he was a successful manufacturer of hoopskirts until he went bankrupt in the Panic of 1873.

Religious bickering and social and economic differences, reflecting a growing struggle for community leadership between immigrants and native-born Jews, led to the establishment of multiple and rival charities, mutual aid, and cultural societies. This, in turn, gradually shifted leadership of communal affairs from the synagogues to the philanthropic organizations as they became independent of the congregations out of which they were born.

The two principal philanthropic agencies were the Hebrew Benevolent Society, founded in 1822 by leaders of Shearith Israel and dominated by native-born English and Dutch Jews, and the German Hebrew Benevolent Society, organized in 1844. Legend has it that the older group originated with a visit by a committee of synagogue elders to a hospitalized Jewish veteran of the Revolution. The $300 left in the fund raised for his care gave impetus to the formation of the society when he died.

In the 1840s and early 1850s, the Hebrew Benevolent Society was helping 200 people a year. This increased tenfold in 1858 when its expenditures totaled $3,500. Aiding only German Jews, the German society spent three times as much that same year. The first appeal to all Jews to contribute to a fund for needy immigrants started in 1837 when there was a door-to-door solicitation for food, clothing, fuel, and cash. In 1839 a New York Hebrew Assistance Society was created to aid immigrants. Old-line Jews sponsored a benefit concert of Italian opera in a Christian church in 1849 to raise funds for the relief of newly-arriving German Jews. Organization of a Bachelors Hebrew Benevolent Loan Society, a Young Men's Hebrew Benevolent Fuel Association, and a host of other mutual aid societies between 1830 and 1855 demonstrated that the Dutch warning to Jews to take care of their own, had become the bedrock on which Jewish communal life was being built.

The need for an orphanage and a hospital where Jews would be free from conversionist efforts by Christian clergymen as well as the inability of the community to cope with the mounting number of needy and sick immigrants, spurred unification of Jewish charitable efforts in the 1850s. The two major societies, which did not merge until 1859, were planning "an asylum for the aged and sick of the Hebrew persuasion" in 1851, but were by-passed by a group of individuals who incorporated Jews' Hospital in 1852. Opened in 1855 on 28th Street between 7th and 8th Avenues, the hospital admitted only Jews in its early years, except for accident cases. The words "Jews' Hospital" in English, and *Bet Holim* in Hebrew were emblazoned in big letters over the front of the four-story building. The hospital became nonsectarian in 1864 and the name was changed to Mount Sinai Hospital two years later. In the ensuing century it became a great medical center with a decisive role in the development of the city's network of Jewish-sponsored health services, and in the major changes that characterized medical care in the 20th century. An immediate result of the consolidation of the two benevolent societies was the establishment in 1859 of the first Hebrew Orphan Asylum, whose successor is the Jewish Child Care Association.

Forerunner of the women's groups that now raise huge sums annually for Jewish institutions and causes at home and abroad was the Female Hebrew Benevolent Society, founded by the ladies of Shearith Israel in 1820. The Ladies Association for the General Instruction of Children of the Jewish Persuasion was another pioneer among the women's charity societies organized in the 1840s and 1850s. By 1860, New York had 35 Jewish burial, mutual aid, and charitable organizations. These organizations accounted for the fact that Jews were seldom found in the New York Poor House. In 1858, Mayor Tiemann said that in three years he had heard of only three Jews seeking aid at city institutions.

Out of the mutual aid societies grew the first fraternal orders and cultural groups. B'nai B'rith, oldest national Jewish membership organization, was founded in New York in 1843, mostly by German Jews. The latter also established the Free Sons of Israel in 1849, and the United Order of True Sisters, the first women's organization independent of the synagogue, in 1852. These fraternal societies were important instruments for Americanizing the immigrants and in giving them the security of social, economic, and cultural opportunities. The first B'nai B'rith lodges were opened at Covenant Hall on Orchard Street in the 1850s, where they maintained a library and Jewish Community Center. The Harmonie Club, established by German Jews in 1847 on Ludlow Street as a social and cultural headquarters, was the pioneer Jewish town club. Temple Emanu-El was an outgrowth of the Cultus Verein, founded by synagogue dissenters in 1843. Young people's choirs at Shearith Israel in 1818 and B'nai Jeshurun in 1828 were the predecessors of Jewish young men's literary societies and Jewish military companies in the 1850s. These in turn paved the way for New York's first YM and YWHA in 1874.

This growing network of communal institutions was financed largely from the proceeds of fairs, theatrical benefits, Purim and Chanukah balls, and dinners, which were the major social events in the Jewish community calendar.

Elementary Jewish education in New York before 1851 was provided largely by synagogue sponsored all-day or parochial schools. Immigrant and native-born Jews alike were reluctant to expose their children to the strong Protestant influences that pervaded the early free elementary schools, where education was meagre at best. After the State Legislature empowered local school boards to choose their own texts from approved lists, Jewish pupils poured into the free public schools in great numbers as the books objectionable to Jews were eliminated in Jewish neighborhoods. The fee-charging separate Jewish schools then went out of existence. In their place the synagogues opened afternoon Hebrew and Sunday schools. Wealthier Jews sent their children to private Jewish day and boarding schools. Rabbi Lilienthal presided over a "Hebrew, commercial and classical boarding school" and some Christian private schools sought to attract Jewish students by offering Hebrew studies.

Matzoh-baking and the preparation of kosher meat were also under synagogue supervision until the 1840s. This control broke down because of the proliferation of congregations, the increase in the number of Jewish butchers, and the emergence of Jewish matzoh bakeries operating independent of synagogue supervision. Machine matzoh-baking was introduced by Moses S. Cohen, one of the five matzoh-makers in New York in 1855.

The first Hebrew calendar printed in America appeared in New York in 1850. Eight years later the preacher at Beth Hamedresh Hagodol produced the first full Hebrew book published in the United States. Most printed Jewish literature in mid-19th century New York consisted of prayer books, polemics, and speeches. Religious appurtenances, from Torah Scrolls to prayer shawls, were hard to come by, most of them being imported or brought as gifts by the stream of messengers from Palestine seeking funds among the Jews of New York.

New York Jewry established itself as the leader of the American Jewish community in 1840 when it organized the initial public effort on behalf of persecuted coreligionists abroad. Outraged by the arrest and torture of Jews in Damascus used to force them to confess to ritual murder, New York's Jews held a protest rally at which they called upon the United States government to intercede with the Sultan. This meeting led to the first intercession by the United States to succor Jews abroad when President Martin Van Buren instructed the American consul in Damascus to use his good offices to protect the Jews there.

The rally had been held at B'nai Jeshurun because Shearith Israel's trustees opposed it. There was a reluctance on the part of the native-born Jews to participate in joint communal undertakings lest they be swamped by the German, Polish, and English Jews. Emanu-El, a rival of the mother synagogue in status and influence due to the rising power of the German Jews, also stood apart from early efforts to unite the Jewish community. Opposition in New York also blocked later plans, originating in Philadelphia and Cincinnati, to federate American synagogues.

All the New York synagogues, however, supported the protest against the Mortara Affair in Italy. Shocked by the news that a Jewish child named Edgar Mortara had been secretly baptized by a Catholic nurse in the Mortara home in 1854 and then kidnapped in Bologna with the connivance of Papal officials, the Jews of New York staged a giant demonstration in Mozart Hall in 1858. More than 2,000 people attended, including many Protestants who used the occasion to propagandize for the antialien, anti-Catholic Know-Nothing party.

Although the Mozart Hall rally's demand that President James Buchanan intervene with the Vatican was rejected by the State Department, the protest stimulated the organization of the Board of Delegates of American Israelites in 1859. The first national representative body of synagogues, the Board's aim was to protect Jewish rights at home and abroad. Shearith Israel and Emanu-El did not participate and the Reform synagogues outside of New York also boycotted the new body. It survived until 1878 when it merged with the Union of American Hebrew Congregations, the federation of Reform synagogues. New York was "definitely established as the center of Jewish life in America" when the Board made its headquarters there.

Communal affairs were dominated by descendants of the old Sephardic families and by first and second generation Germans in the 1860s and 1870s when the first trickle of Jews from Russia and Romania gave rise to a new array of philanthropic, cultural, and religious institutions. New York's first *landsmanschaft*, a uniquely European Jewish self-help society based on local origin, but unknown among the earlier immigrants from Germany, was chartered in 1864 as the Bialystok Mutual Aid Society. By 1877 there were five more, providing small loans and funeral and cemetery benefits, as well as 22 East European synagogues.

The German-Jewish community made no organized attempt to aid the post-Civil War immigrants until 1870 when a Hebrew Emigrant Aid Society was formed. It was short-lived because of the belief that the new immigration would be temporary. The Hebrew Free School Association, founded in 1864 to counteract proselytizing among immigrant children, survived as part of the city's first Jewish settlement house.

In 1874 the United Hebrew Charities came into being through an amalgamation of the old Hebrew Benevolent Society and four smaller groups. The new organization created the Hebrew Sheltering Guardian Society in 1879 to care for needy children, and a year later established the Hebrew Technical School for Girls. Through subsequent mergers, the United Hebrew Charities emerged in 1917 as the Federation of Jewish Philanthropies, a huge philanthropic and social welfare complex which in the last decade alone has poured $200,000,000 into the maintenance of 130 institutions, plus tens of millions more spent on new facilities.

The first Home for Aged and Infirm Hebrews opened in 1870. Four years later the native-born and German-Jewish leadership founded the 92nd Street YM and YWHA, now the country's oldest existing Jewish Community Center, to provide cultural and recreational activities for young people. Montefiore Hospital, an outgrowth of a home for chronic invalids established by Mt. Sinai and the United Hebrew Charities to cope with the growing number of chronically Jewish sick who refused to go to city institutions, came into being in 1884.

Out of deep-seated religious differences, immense social and cultural cleavages, and wide economic disparities between the older community and the masses of East Europeans who arrived after 1880, there grew up parallel Jewish communities. Many uptowners were contemptuous of and sometimes hostile to the zealous efforts of their Yiddish-speaking downtown coreligionists to recreate old world institutions, to maintain the minutiae of Orthodoxy, and to cling to their own folkways. The East Europeans equated the Reform synagogues and modernized Orthodox congregations with churches and regarded the Americanized Jew as a thinly disguised missionary. Many of the German Jews denigrated the newcomers as "uncouth strangers" who threatened the status of the older community by giving impetus to the rising antialien sentiment. Some repudiated the "miserably darkened Hebrews" with whom "the thoroughly acclimated American Jew . . . has no religious, social, or intellectual ties."

Responsible uptown leaders, recognizing that they could not ignore the plight of fellow Jews without rejecting their own Jewishness, brought all elements of the community together in the Russian Emigrant Relief Society in 1881. Reorganized as the Hebrew Emigrant Aid Society, this group struggled for 18 months to meet the needs of daily shiploads of destitute Jews dumped in the vast domed shed of Castle Garden, New York's old immigration station. Hundreds slept on floors and temporary benches, crowded into narrow, unsanitary quarters, until a former lunatic asylum on Ward's Island was converted into the Schiff Refugee Center, where hot meals and medical care were provided. There the poet Emma Lazarus, who came from an old Sephardic family, had her first contact with the "huddled masses yearning to breathe free," whom she immortalized in her sonnet on the Statue of Liberty.

When the Hebrew Emigrant Aid Society suspended operations in 1884, its work was taken over by the United Hebrew Charities, which was, at first, not too sympathetic to the East Europeans. This prompted the older established Russian Jews to organize their own relief societies. In 1882 they had formed the Hebrew Emigrant Auxiliary Society. A Hebrew Sheltering Society, which opened temporary immigrant shelters in 1882, and the Hebrew Emigrant Aid Society, founded in 1902 as the Voliner Zhitomirer Aid Society to provide burial for Jews from Zhitomir who had died on Ellis Island, became the predecessors of United HIAS Service, the world-wide immigrant agency.

These societies furnished lawyers and interpreters to help the immigrants through the red tape of Ellis Island, which in 1890 replaced Castle Garden as the principal immigration inspection depot. They provided kosher food for steerage passengers who had not eaten any cooked meals since leaving Europe, temporary housing, and employment information. The United Hebrew Charities provided relief for those needing it after clearing Ellis Island. It even outfitted many with new clothing before sending them to their first jobs. The National Council of Jewish Women operated a port and dock department at Ellis Island to curb exploitation of girls and women arriving alone and penniless.

Once the newcomers were housed and provided with jobs, the older community made strenuous efforts to Americanize them through a network of social service agencies, vocational training programs, kindergartens, and classes in English. The most influential Americanization force was the Educational Alliance. Opened in 1883 as the YMHA's downtown branch and then expanded through a merger with the Hebrew Free School Association and the Hebrew Technical Institute, the Alliance was the first settlement house in the United States.

Its volunteer teachers included some of the city's most cultured Jews, among them Emma Lazarus, the poet; Oscar S. Straus, the diplomat; and Julia Richman, first woman assistant superintendent of schools. Henry M. Leipziger, founder of the Board of Education's adult education system, was the first principal of the Educational Alliance's adult classes.

Out of the Alliance's classes came a long line of eminent citizens. David Sarnoff, radio and television tycoon, and Sir Louis Stirling, his British counterpart, learned English there; Eddie Cantor's career began as an amateur entertainer at the Alliance's summer camp; Morris Raphael Cohen tested his philosophic concepts as a youthful Alliance orator; Sir Jacob Epstein, Jo Davidson, Chaim Gross, William Auerbach-Levy, and Abraham Walkowitz paid three cents a lesson at the Alliance's Art School. When Jacob Epstein was knighted, Walkowitz said to the sculptor's brother, "I see Jake is Sir Jake now." "Pfui," retorted the brother, "Jake was knighted at 102 Hester St.," where Epstein found his first models among pushcart peddlers.

Many East European Jewish lawyers, doctors, engineers, and dentists, who fled Russia before getting their degrees, were able to complete their professional education through student loans from the Baron de Hirsch Fund. With the millions bequeathed by Maurice de Hirsch, French railway magnate, the leading New York Jews who managed the Fund created the Baron de Hirsch Trade School, the Clara de Hirsch Home for Immigrant Girls, underwrote the Alliance classes, and opened settlement houses in other parts of the city. Before it was turned over to the Board of Education, the school had graduated more than 9,000 students. The home is now a women's residence dormitory affiliated with the 92nd Street YM & YWHA.

Galled by patronizing philanthropy and denied a voice in the organizations established for their benefit, the East Europeans fashioned their own pattern of communal services while recreating their intense old world religious life. Because kosher food was unavailable at Mt. Sinai Hospital, where Yiddish-speaking physicians were often snubbed, the East Europeans established Beth Israel Hospital in 1890, the first under Orthodox auspices. They also founded the Jewish Maternity Hospital, Lebanon Hospital, in the Bronx, orphanages, old folks homes and, with the backing of uptown leaders, the Hebrew Free Loan Society in 1902.

Hundreds of *landsmanschaften* organized as mutual aid societies also filled important social and cultural needs. Several hundred thousand Jews belonged to these societies before they were outmoded by Americanization, social security, and commercial insurance. Of the 600 new synagogues established in New York between 1880 and 1914, the majority were of the storefront or back-room variety, organized according to old country town of origin. Each little congregation supported its own rebbe brought over from Europe, and struggled to maintain a separate elementary Hebrew school because the Hebrew Free School Association was not considered sufficiently Orthodox. These one-room schools, usually housed in a tenement flat or basement, were gradually replaced by more modern Talmud Torahs and parochial schools, Talmudic academies, Hebrew classes fostered by the early Zionist societies, and Yiddish schools created by secularists.

Itinerant preachers such as Hirsch Masliansky, the "Yiddish Henry Ward Beecher," Chaim Zhitlovsky, a radical Yiddishist, and the modern services at the People's Synagogue in the Alliance attracted large audiences. Breadwinners in hundreds of families earned their livelihoods as religious functionaries—ritual slaughterers, cantors, sextons, scribes, translators, ritual circumcisers, and itinerant preachers. The omnipresent *pushka*, or charity box, reflected the concern of even the poorest household for needy Jews at home and abroad.

Secularism gradually eroded the Orthodoxy of many of the first and second generation immigrants. Under the impact of poverty, sweatshop conditions, and radical political movements, houses of prayer lost ground to trade unions and lodges. The Yiddish press, stage, and lecture platform became more influential than revered rabbis. Even the strict Sabbath closing was breached. By 1913, sixty percent of East Side stores and pushcarts were open on Saturday. The Keepers of the Sabbath Society gave up its boycott of the antireligious *Jewish Daily Forward*, and Yiddish theatres played to standing room only audiences on Friday nights and Saturday matinees.

Immigrants who resisted Americanization as a threat to their way of life found themselves in conflict with American-born or educated children who rejected the customs and values of their parents as obstacles to Americanization. The struggle between German-Jewish manufacturers and the Jewish trade unions was carried over into the communal arena. As a result of the hostility for nearly a generation to the organized Jewish community control by uptowners, the Jewish labor movement formed separate secular Yiddishist cultural institutions, relief societies, and Zionist parties.

The first big influx of Orthodox East Europeans coincided with the split between Reform and Orthodoxy in the United States. Reform had taken root as an essentially German movement under the influence of European-ordained rabbis. The limited changes in ritual and practice they had encouraged in the New York congregations founded by German immigrants broadened into Reform Judaism as it became Americanized under the leadership of Rabbi Isaac Mayer Wise of Cincinnati and Rabbi David Einhorn of New York's Temple Beth El.

Having accepted some innovations, many of the older New York congregations and their rabbis occupied a middle ground between radical Reform and unchanging Orthodoxy. The hope that the Hebrew Union College, opened in Cincinnati in 1873 as a Reform rabbinical seminary, might train rabbis for all congregations, vanished with the final break in 1885. It was precipitated by a radical declaration of principles adopted by a conference of Reform rabbis convened by Dr. Kaufman Kohler, Rabbi Einhorn's son-in-law and successor at Beth El. This platform repudiated Talmudic regulations and most of the Mosaic code, including the dietary regulations, in favor of the prophetic ideals of the Bible, less stringent Sabbath observance, and rejection of the idea of a return to Zion.

Opponents of this course countered in 1886 by establishing the Jewish Theological Seminary in New York to disseminate the tenets of Traditional Judaism, the original name of Conservative Judaism. The Seminary's founders differed from their Orthodox East European coreligionists only in the use of English in pulpit preaching, religious instruction for the young, greater decorum in the service, and some prayer book modifications. The Conservatives even joined the larger East European synagogues in forming the Union of Orthodox Jewish Congregations in 1898.

Convinced that European Orthodoxy could not thrive in America, the majority of second and third generation Orthodox leaders set out to provide American-educated rabbis for the growing number of non-Reform English-speaking synagogues. When the Seminary opened in 1887, there were only 12 American-ordained rabbis—all Reform.

The East Europeans, whose religious leadership came from Yiddish-speaking old world rabbis, rebuffed the Seminary. Although it had graduated 17 English-speaking rabbis by 1902, most of them immigrants or sons of immigrants, the Seminary was in danger of closing because of meagre support from its founding congregations. Reform Jews put it on a sound footing in the hope that the Seminary would "westernize" the Judaism of the immigrants by fostering an Americanized Orthodoxy without Yiddish, among those to whom Reform Judaism was anathema.

A $500,000 endowment fund raised under the leadership of Louis Marshall, president of Temple Emanu-El, and Jacob H. Schiff, head of Kuhn, Loeb & Co., made it possible to invite Dr. Solomon Schechter, world-renowned savant at Cambridge University, to become the Seminary's president. Dr. Schechter surrounded himself with men who not only made enduring contributions to Jewish scholarship but whose teaching and inspiration gave impetus to Conservative Judaism by molding its rabbinic leadership and constituency.

Dr. Mordecai M. Kaplan, ordained by the Seminary in 1903, became perhaps the single most influential force in American Jewish religious life. As dean of the Seminary's Teachers' Institute and for a generation a professor at the Seminary, he became the mentor of thousands of rabbis, educators, social workers, scholars, and laymen. Founder of Reconstructionism, which advocated substantive changes in Jewish life, and author of significant religious works, Dr. Kaplan and his disciples precipitated a great theological ferment which animated creative changes in all branches of American Judaism.

Under Dr. Schechter's successors, Drs. Cyrus Adler, Louis Finkelstein, and Gerson Cohen, the Seminary, as the fountainhead of Conservative

Judaism, and the congregations affiliated with the United Synagogue of America, began an era of great expansion. Some first and second generation East Europeans who had not rejected the synagogue remained with those East European congregations that moved to newer neighborhoods. The majority joined the newer synagogues led by Seminary graduates that sprang up in all parts of the city, as well as the older congregations. There they found less of a break with tradition than in the anti-Zionist Reform temples whose adherents were drawn from the more well-to-do element. As the East Europeans, once regarded as the wards of Conservatism, scaled the economic ladder, they gave strength and permanence to the movement.

The East European Orthodox community at first relied on its preponderant numbers and constant replenishment through immigration to offset heavy losses to secularism and Conservatism. When both of these bulwarks were breached and it became evident that the Talmudic scholarship of European-trained rabbis had little impact on American-born Jews, the Orthodox established the Isaac Eichanan Rabbinical Seminary. Under the guidance of Dr. Bernard Revel, this Seminary expanded into Yeshiva University. Under his successor, the late Dr. Samuel Belkin and the latter's successor, Rabbi Norman Lamm, it has become the focal point of modern Orthodoxy in America.

Reform made little headway among the Jewish masses of New York until well into the 1930s, although much of the Jewish community's leadership was in the hands of wealthy members of Temple Emanu-El. Reform congregations began attracting considerable numbers of East Europeans after 1936 when the Reform rabbinate adopted a new program that repudiated the 1886 platform. Gradually the Reform synagogues reinstituted ceremonials and Friday evening and Saturday morning worship, added more Hebrew to the service, restored the Bar Mitzvah rite, and turned to active support of Palestine. Sons and grandsons of East Europeans ultimately dominated the Reform rabbinate and acquired influence and status among the Reform laity.

Reform achieved its most phenomenal growth in New York after World War II when children and grandchildren of Yiddish-speaking immigrants began a return to the once rejected Jewish folkways. The leap from secularism to membership in Reform synagogues was made easy as Jews, who had never before belonged to a synagogue in the city, moved into the suburbs in great numbers. The removal of the Union of American Hebrew Congregations (Reform synagogue federation) headquarters to New York in 1951, under the leadership of Dr. Maurice Eisendrath, was followed by a merger of the Hebrew Union College with the Jewish Institute of Religion, founded in New York in 1922.

Before Reform altered its course, New York's most eloquent spokesmen of the compatibility between Jewish tradition and Americanism were Judah L. Magnes and Stephen S. Wise, both Reform rabbis. As secretary of the Federation of American Zionists from 1905-1908 and a leader in the protests against Czarist anti-Semitism, Dr. Magnes won the respect and affection of the East Side Jews. As rabbi of Emanu-El, of which his brother-in-law, Louis Marshall, was president, he openly advocated Zionism in the face of congregational hostility. From the pulpit he denounced a temple trustee who had marched down the aisle of St. Patrick's Cathedral to give away his daughter in marriage to a Hungarian count. His insistence on more traditional forms cost him the pulpit and he became rabbi of B'nai Jeshurun.

Stephen S. Wise, who began his career in this same Conservative congregation in 1893, had little contact with the East European masses until he became the first secretary of the Federation of American Zionists in 1898. From the pulpit of the Free Synagogue, which he organized in 1906 after rejecting an invitation from Emanu-El under the conditions laid down by Marshall, Wise's prophetic mood and oratory attracted wealthy Jews who had been flirting with Unitarianism and Ethical Culture, as well as Yiddish-speaking radicals and Zionists who had broken with Orthodoxy.

"God's angry man," Wise excoriated evil in the synagogue, the Jewish community, business, industry, and politics. Preaching a liberal Judaism that rejected the kind of Reform that was the "center of wealth and fashion," he created a social service division to put Jewish teachings into practice as part of congregational life. When Zionism had only a marginal following among the Jews of New York, Wise was its most passionate spokesman. His sermon on "Jesus the Jew" created such a furor in 1925 that the Orthodox rabbinate excommunicated him as a heretic and narrowly failed to oust him as chairman of the United Palestine Appeal. To prepare rabbis for congregations of all denominations, he organized the Jewish Institute of Religion, which became a focus of significant Jewish scholarship and religious experimentation. He also led the American and World Jewish Congresses.

In their efforts to bridge the chasm between the two Jewish communities in New York, Wise, Magnes, and other like-minded rabbis had potent allies among the more understanding German-Jewish spokesmen who respected the traditions of the East Europeans. Jacob H. Schiff and Louis Marshall were the dominant figures of this group. Despite his German ancestry and membership in Emanu-El, the East Side Jews sensed that Schiff was their friend. Though he contributed princely sums to higher education and philanthropic causes, his principal interest was Jews.

Schiff fought vigorously for the protection of Jews overseas. The relief fund for the victims of the 1903 Kishinev pogrom was organized on a private basis by Schiff before he, Oscar S. Straus, and Cyrus L. Sulzberger formed the National Committee for the Relief of Sufferers of Russian Massacres. The Educational Alliance and the Henry Street Settlement were among his earliest beneficiaries. He was the prime mover in the reorganization of the Jewish Theological Seminary, in the underwriting of the Jewish Encyclopedia, in the establishment of the Jewish Division of the New York Public Library, and the Jewish collection in the Library of Congress. Schiff built the first home of the 92nd Street YM & YWHA, helped organize the

National Jewish Welfare Board, and was the key figure in the formation of the American Jewish Joint Distribution Committee.

For more than a generation Kuhn, Loeb partners, like Schiff, were to the Jewish community of New York what the Morgans and Rockefellers were to the non-Jewish community. Schiff's son-in-law and daughter, Mr. and Mrs. Felix M. Warburg, his son, Mortimer, and granddaughter, Dorothy Schiff, continued the tradition of Jewish community leadership. The third generation of Schiffs were less involved and the Warburgs do not play a leading role in Jewish affairs. Jacob Schiff's grandson was married in a Protestant church in 1963, as his father had been before him. Otto H. Kahn, another Kuhn, Loeb partner, though never prominent in Jewish affairs, supported the Yiddish theatre and helped bring the Habimah Theatre to the United States.

The son of Benjamin Buttenweiser, also a Kuhn, Loeb partner, whose family has been actively associated with many Jewish causes, married the daughter of Isidor Lubin, son of an East European immigrant, and one-time United States Commissioner of Labor Statistics. Rear Admiral Lewis L. Strauss, who gave up his Kuhn, Loeb partnership to enter public service, was president of the Jewish Agricultural Society and Temple Emanu-El, and headed the board of the Jewish Theological Seminary.

Louis Marshall was drawn into the conservative German-Jewish circle when he came down from Syracuse in 1898 to join the Guggenheimer and Untermeyer law firm. His membership in a committee in investigate East Side slum conditions and sponsorship of a Yiddish daily shaped his sympathetic attitude toward the problems of the East European Jews. One of the principal founders of the American Jewish Committee in 1906, Marshall headed the successful fight to abrogate Russia's commercial treaty with the United States in protest against the refusal of the Czar's government to recognize American passports held by Jews. When the treaty was allowed to lapse, Marshall emerged as the recognized leader of American Jewry. The years of his dominance were often called "the era of Marshall law," and he was dubbed "Louis XIX."

Marshall endeared himself to the Jewish masses of New York by his vigorous advocacy of civil rights, unrestricted immigration, and Jewish education. He defended the right of the Yiddish press to publish in wartime, spoke up for Negroes and Chinese, and represented the Catholic Church in its legal fight against an Oregon antiparochial school law. Marshall, a native-born Jew, was for years the chief exponent of unrestricted immigration, while Samuel Gompers, an immigrant Jew, was the leading spokesman for immigration curbs. During the "red hysteria" of the 1920s, Marshall championed the five New York City Socialists who had been denied their seats in the State Assembly. Simultaneously president of Temple Emanu-El and the board of the Jewish Theological Seminary, he fought for greater support of Jewish education and scholarship and the establishment of Jewish Community Centers. Although he had led the fight against the World War I

American Jewish Congress, advocated by Zionists and Yiddish nationalists, he was won over and headed the Jewish delegation to the Versailles Peace Conference. After the war, Marshall helped establish the Palestine Survey Commission which brought non-Zionists into cooperation with the World Zionist Organization and created the Jewish Agency for Palestine.

The forceful leadership of Marshall, Schiff, and their associates in the German-Jewish community to halt Czarist persecution and to stem the rising tide of antialienism, helped break down many of the barriers between the East European and German-Jewish communities. The 250th anniversary of Jewish settlement in America, observed in 1905, brought pride and dignity to both elements. The decisive intercession of uptown leaders in the great needle trades strikes before World War I helped draw the Jewish working class masses into the main stream of Jewish community life.

The uproar created in 1908 when Police Commissioner Theodore A. Bingham charged in an article in the *North American Review* that New York's 1,000,000 Jews, representing a fourth of the total population, accounted for half the city's criminals, led to the first citywide agency to represent the totality of Jewish life. Confronted with the facts that disproved his charges, Bingham retracted, apologized, and resigned, but all elements of the Jewish community were so outraged by the incident that they joined forces in creating the New York Kehillah. It was intended to cope with the complex religious, educational, cultural, and community relations of the entire Jewish community. Under the chairmanship of Rabbi Magnes, the Kehillah undertook to supervise kashruth and Sabbath observance, standardize Jewish education, arbitrate disputes between Jewish workers and Jewish employers, combat juvenile delinquency, and compile communal statistics. Despite influential leadership and wide support, the Kehillah went out of existence during World War I, having failed to overcome deep-seated institutional and religious rivalries.

A more enduring consolidation of Jewish forces in New York grew out of common obligations to suffering Jews in the war zones of Europe early in 1914. Three separate agencies at first undertook relief efforts for the stricken Jews of Eastern Europe. The Orthodox and East Europeans set up the Central Relief Committee, the German Jews formed the American Jewish Relief Committee, and the Jewish unions sponsored the People's Relief Committee. Their merger in 1915 into the American Jewish Joint Distribution Committee (JDC), under the chairmanship of Felix M. Warburg, set in motion the machinery for the first united Jewish war relief campaign. Record breaking sums were collected as volunteers and professionals of the two communities forged an unprecedented alliance. What began as an emergency program grew into American Jewry's major overseas relief and rehabilitation agency. From its New York headquarters JDC raised and administered tens of millions of dollars for war and postwar relief, medical care, economic, religious and cultural reconstruction, refugee resettlement, and aid to Israel.

In the process, the JDC produced a galaxy of notable leaders and set new standards of philanthropic giving that contributed immeasurably to the integration of differing points of view in the Jewish community. Under the pressure of unforeseen tragedy for European Jewry, many of the JDC leaders who had opposed Zionism became important factors in the economic and cultural developments in Palestine after 1921.

Until 1914 Zionism was sneered at by the uptown Jews as an "East Side affair" because the bulk of the members of the Zionist Organization of America were immigrants. One of its founders, however, was Dr. Gustav Gottheil, senior rabbi of Emanu-El, whose son, Richard, a Columbia University professor, served as the first president of the American Federation of Zionists. On her return from the second World Zionist Congress, where Theodor Herzl had urged her to mobilize Jewish women of America for the Zionist cause, Mrs. Richard Gottheil joined the Daughters of Zion. This group had been organized as a discussion club by East Side women even before the first World Zionist Congress in 1897. Gradually it developed chapters throughout the city and in 1912 it became the ladies auxiliary of the Zionist Organization of America. Signatories to the invitation to organize a national body included Henrietta Szold and Mrs. N. Taylor Phillips of Congregation Shearith Israel, and the organizing meeting was held in Emanu-El's vestry hall. The New York chapter of the Daughters of Zion took the name Hadassah, later adopted by the national organization of women Zionists.

When the world Zionist movement shifted its headquarters temporarily to New York during World War I and Louis D. Brandeis took over leadership of the American Zionists, Zionism began to grow in stature and membership as it enlisted broader elements of the New York community. Much Zionist history was made in New York. The Biltmore Platform calling for the establishment of a Jewish commonwealth in Palestine was adopted in New York in 1942. The American Jewish Conference, a democratically elected body of delegates from all parts of the country, which convened in New York in 1943, supported this position and mapped a postwar program of Jewish reconstruction. The United Nations' decision to partition Palestine into Jewish and Arab states and the admission of Israel to the United Nations were both voted on in New York.

Until 1939, the principal Zionist fundraising instrument was the United Palestine Appeal, whose headquarters was in New York. Then the JDC, the United Palestine Appeal, and the National Refugee Service united to create the United Jewish Appeal. For the next 35 years, UJA, from its New York headquarters, became the central American Jewish fundraising organization for the settlement of Jews in Israel and elsewhere, and for aid to needy Jews throughout the world. Between 1939 and the Yom Kippur War of 1973, UJA raised over $2 billion. In 1951, the Israel Bond Organization, also headquartered in New York, began its sales effort.

UJA's annual campaign in the spring, and the fall drive of the

Federation of Jewish Philanthropies—which were united in a joint annual campaign in 1974—together with numerous independent appeals for local, national, and overseas causes and institutions, have made fundraising a major enterprise of the New York Jewish community. Sheer numbers and access to a pool of talented volunteers, professionals, and big donors in the headquarters town of American Jewry, combined to make New York the principal source for raising Jewish philanthropic dollars and a potent force in determining where and how they are spent. The Jews of New York have made philanthropy an art and a science. Federation and UJA showed the way in organizing donors on an industry, trade, profession, and neighborhood basis, a technique now widely emulated by all major philanthropic endeavors.

Federation itself is the largest local philanthropic undertaking in the world under private auspices. Founded in 1917 to serve only Manhattan and The Bronx, it later incorporated the Brooklyn Jewish Federation, established in 1909. At the time of the merger, there were 3,637 separate Jewish institutions in New York City—schools, recreation and cultural agencies, multi-service societies, correctional agencies, hospitals, old age homes and orphanages, child care and family agencies all competing for contributions through a maze of wasted effort, time, money, and duplication of service. In the 1970s there were 130 agencies affiliated with Federation in the city proper and in the three adjacent suburban counties. These included hospitals, old age homes, child care agencies, family services, Jewish Community Centers and YM-YWHAs, camps, medical research centers, adoption agencies, Jewish education agencies, and facilities for the care of the mentally ill.

Most Federation-supported institutions and services are an outgrowth of those originally created to meet the needs of an immigrant generation. As the Jewish population of the city became overwhelmingly native-born and its economic status moved strikingly upward, the community's philanthropic agencies changed their emphasis. They became heavily involved in meeting the medical, residential, and social needs of the aged, supporting recreational and cultural services, underwriting Jewish educational programs, foster homes, homemaker and child adoption services, care for the chronically ill and mentally disturbed, and family services. Jewish family agencies that grew out of the special problems of immigrants now serve one-fourth more people than they did in 1946, including the immigrants of the 1970s. Jewish hospitals, opened initially to provide training for Jewish doctors when they were barred from the staffs of most New York hospitals, now have a large proportion of non-Jewish patients while non-Jewish hospitals have as many Jewish doctors on their staffs as do the Jewish hospitals.

In the 1970s, Federation turned its attention to meeting the urgent needs of the Jewish poor, who were estimated to number over 300,000 and to represent some 15 percent of the city's total Jewish population. More than half of the Jewish poor were elderly. The Federation-funded Metropolitan New York Coordinating Council on Jewish Poverty was created to coordinate community services for the Jewish poor and a new Federation agency, the Jewish Association for Services to the Aged, had a key-role in coping with the housing, relocation, legal aid, social, and communal problems of the aged poor. Other Federation agencies intensified their services to families, the poor, and the aged. Federation also established the Jewish Association for College Youth to initiate new programs for college-age young people and to give them an opportunity to serve other Jews, especially the aged. A number of Federation joint service centers were opened in neighborhoods with substantial numbers of Jewish aged and Jewish poor.

The Federation Employment and Guidance Service stepped up its services on behalf of job seeking Jews affected by the depression and for Jewish young people seeking career and vocational counseling. Branch offices of Federation-supported Jewish family and child care agencies were opened in the suburbs and in newly established neighborhoods with large Jewish populations. The Federation's Commission of Synagogue Relations focused action-producing attention on problems of drug and alcohol addiction, divorce, intermarriage, and the special needs of divorced and widowed parents, the unmarried, and other groups of singles. The phenomenon of black Jews, including some who were properly converted, seeking membership in synagogues and the admission of their children in synagogue religious schools and yeshivas was another concern of the Commission on Synagogue Relations. There were said to be some 3,500 black Jews scattered around the city, who worship at one of the ten or 12 black synagogues in Harlem, Brooklyn, and The Bronx.

Institutions and services established for the immigrant generations also gave rise to professional Jewish social work. Children of the immigrants became the first real Jewish social workers. Pioneering in child care, adoption, family relations, juvenile delinquency, mental hygiene, recreation, and rehabilitation, they sowed the seeds for the flowering of the community's philanthropic program.

Unified philanthropic efforts during World War I paved the way for the community's religious forces to combine to provide religious and welfare services to American Jewish soldiers. Setting aside sectarian differences, rabbinical and congregational groups joined the Council of Young Men's Hebrew Associations and Kindred Associations to form the National Jewish Welfare Board in 1917. Under its banner an agreement was reached on a common servicemen's prayer book, a uniform system of selecting Jewish chaplains, and a program of providing cultural activities, religious literature, and kosher food. This collaboration was enlarged during World War II and has continued as a unique manifestation of interdenominational unity coordinated by the secular National Jewish Welfare Board. World War I also brought thousands of Yiddish-speaking draftees from New York into contact for the first time with American Jews of other backgrounds and set in motion a process of amalgamation that was strengthened during World War II and by the subsequent growth of suburban Jewish communities.

Communal unification was also fostered by the Bureau of Jewish Education, set up by the Kehillah in 1910. Under the direction of Drs. Samson Benderly and Israel Chipkin, this Bureau modernized teaching methods in Jewish schools, adapted the Talmud Torah to American life, encouraged professional teacher training, and stimulated communal responsibility for the support of Jewish education. In 1939 the Bureau was absorbed by the new Jewish Education Committee of New York, founded through a legacy of Michael Friedsam, head of B. Altman & Co. An agency of Federation, the JEC (now known as the Bureau of Jewish Education), has been a major influence in improving Jewish elementary and secondary Jewish education.

The Jewish Communal Register of New York City, published in 1918 by the Kehillah, provided the first statistical picture of the community. It listed 3,637 separate organizations for a population of 1,500,000. Of the 858 congregations, 784 occupied their own houses of worship, 730 were Orthodox synagogues on the lower East Side or in the new ghettos of Brooklyn and The Bronx, 32 were Conservative, and 16 Reform. There were also 2,168 mutual aid societies, 164 philanthropic and social service institutions, and 69 Jewish schools.

In 1927 congregations had increased to 1,044, with 656 owning sanctuaries and 575 supporting full-time rabbis. Notwithstanding the synagogue building boom of the 1920s in the newer areas of settlement, less than one-third of the city's Jewish families were synagogue members in the 1930s. Between 1918 and 1930 the second generation of East Europeans, transformed from essentially a working class group to an increasingly middle-class community, had become the "lost generation" of New York Jewish life.

The flight from Judaism was halted and gradually reversed by the surge of religious and communal activity on the part of the third generation East Europeans after World War II. In the 1930s and 1940s the German-Sephardic and Russian communities had begun to fuse into a native-born generation that had shared the dislocations of the depression, the shock of anti-Semitic agitation, the unifying impact of the war, concern for the victims of Nazism, and pride in the rebirth of Israel. This generation's "reassertion and reinforcement of Jewish identity through religious affiliation" was reflected in the return to the synagogue by war veterans and their families, and by the children of antireligious Yiddishists.

In 1963, there were 630 synagogues in the five boroughs and 153 in the adjacent three suburban counties. Of the 494 Orthodox congregations in the city in that year, some 80 percent were tiny congregations, much like those established in the 1880s. Conservative and Reform congregations numbered 91 and 45, respectively, in 1963 in the city. In 1975 the total number of congregations in the city had dropped to 541. Of these, 375 were Orthodox,

100 Conservative, 46 Reform, and one Reconstructionist.

The reduction in the number of synagogues in the five boroughs was due to two developments: heavy population growth in the suburbs and the closing or sale of many synagogues to blacks and Puerto Ricans as a result of the exodus of Jews from such neighborhoods as Brownsville and East New York in Brooklyn, the entire South Bronx and much of the Grand Concourse and Tremont neighborhoods of The Bronx, and in a number of sections of Manhattan. Among the synagogues that went out of existence were a number of small and older Orthodox sanctuaries in the first and second areas of Jewish settlement. On the other hand, new congregations sprang up in and around the high-rise housing projects in Brooklyn (Starrett City), Queens (Lefrak City), The Bronx (Co-Op City), and Manhattan (Lincoln Center). Orthodox groups such as Young Israel were particularly active in creating new congregations of young married couples who were products of the Hebrew Day schools.

While there are no reliable statistics of synagogue membership, about 40 percent of the Jews in New York City and nearly 50 percent of those in the suburbs belonged to congregations in the mid-1970s. The New York Board of Rabbis claimed 700 members but these included some with congregations in nearby New Jersey, Pennsylvania, Connecticut, and upstate New York.

While synagogue membership declined at the beginning of the 1970s, concern for more intensive Jewish education became widely apparent. The Bureau of Jewish Education turned to tested advertising techniques to encourage enrollment in Jewish schools. The synagogue schools of all denominations expanded their curricula and hours of study, experimented with new approaches, updated curricula, developed more effective texts, and used new teaching tools. Federation began to allocate considerably greater sums to Jewish educational agencies, including Hebrew day schools. Travel to and study in Israel by teenagers became increasingly widespread, encouraged and stimulated by Israeli-oriented agencies and the Jewish educational institutions.

Probably the most striking development in Jewish education in New York during the 1960-1970 decade was the growth of the Hebrew day school. Thirty years ago most American Jews regarded the Hebrew all-day school, which combined secular and Jewish educational programs on the elementary and secondary levels, with considerable distaste. In the 1930s Hebrew day schools in New York had only 3,000 pupils. In 1963, there were 179 in New York, with an enrollment of 40,000, out of a total of 154,342 attending all types of Jewish elementary and secondary schools. In 1975 there were 54,000 pupils enrolled in these schools—128 elementary and 73 high schools. All but 17 of these schools were under Orthodox auspices, and many were sponsored by Chasidic groups in Williamsburg, Borough Park, and Crown Heights in Brooklyn. But there were also such schools conducted by Conservative synagogues and one was under the aegis of a Reform congregation. A considerable number of the children in the Hebrew day schools did not come from Orthodox homes. They left the public schools because of parents' uneasiness over attacks on Jewish children and teachers. By 1972, half the city's white children were attending parochial schools—Jewish, Catholic, and Lutheran.

The Hebrew day schools, formerly found only in the older neighborhoods, have penetrated middle-class areas as well as the suburbs. Their growth in numbers and enrollment created growing Jewish sentiment for government support of parochial schools in contradiction to the general opposition to such aid by the national Jewish community relations organizations and most of the congregational bodies. In the 1970s, sponsors of the Hebrew day schools made common cause with Catholics in seeking state and federal funds for their parochial schools. Financial problems continued to plague the Hebrew day schools as unfavorable court decisions banned the use of state and federal funds for parochial schools. All told there were 700 Jewish schools of all types in the metropolitan New York area in the 1970s, and they enrolled 135,000 children. Most of these schools received educational aids, pedagogical material, and counseling from the Board of Jewish Education.

Establishment of the State of Israel spurred greater interest in Hebrew in the city's public schools. Hebrew now ranks fifth in popularity among the languages offered in some 60 junior and senior high schools. Attendance at congregational Jewish high schools and Hebrew-speaking camps sponsored by national agencies has also increased.

Because of its stress on Jewish education in depth, Orthodox Judaism regained some of its lost ground in New York in the 1960s and 1970s. The efforts of Young Israel synagogues, often led by scientists, professors, and highly educated Jewishly laymen, the impact of the immigrants from Hungary, Syria, Russia, and North Africa who are ultra-Orthodox, the leadership of English-speaking American-educated rabbis associated with Yeshiva University's Isaac Eichanan Rabbinical Seminary, and the Rabbinical Council of America have also strengthened Orthodoxy. Yarmulke-wearing young people in public places have become a common sight. Increased observance of kashruth and the greater availability of kosher food products in supermarkets are also manifestations of increased Orthodox feeling and observance. New York also has several ultra-Orthodox seminaries and rabbinical organizations. The world headquarters of the Lubavitcher Movement and a network of social and economic institutions maintained by other Chasidic communities which isolate themselves from the rest of the community, are located in New York. The presence in New York of the national headquarters of the Reform (Union of American Hebrew Congregations), Conservative (United Synagogue of America), and Orthodox (Union of Orthodox Jewish Congregations of America) movements and their related rabbinical seminaries—Hebrew Union College-Jewish Institute of Religion,

Jewish Theological Seminary of America, and Isaac Eichanan Rabbinical Seminary of Yeshiva University—are a great asset to Jewish life in New York City.

Religious differences among New York Jews have become as much economic as theological. Broadly speaking, Jews in the higher income bracket are more likely to be members of either a Conservative or Reform synagogue. While most of New York's Orthodox Jews are in a low-income group (many of them are among the city's thousands of poor and aged Jews), there is a substantial middle-class and well-to-do Orthodox community. Children and grandchildren of Orthodox immigrants constitute the bulk of membership in Reform and Conservative congregations. For the first time, conversion to Judaism is being encouraged by the Jewish community. The Reform group maintains a school for them at the House of Living Judaism, and the Conservatives have a method of dealing with serious-minded Christians seeking to embrace Judaism. Even the Orthodox are no longer entirely hostile to conversion provided it is accomplished in accordance with the Halacha.

GROWTH OF NEW YORK CITY JEWISH POPULATION

Year	Population
1695	100
1760	100
1795	300
1806	380
1812	500
1825	600
1840	15,000
1850	50,000
1860	60,000
1870	75,000
1880	85,000
1890	200,000
1900	600,000
1910	1,252,000
1920	1,643,000
1930	1,825,000
1940	1,785,000
1950	1,996,000
1957	2,114,000
1960	1,836,000
1975	1,228,000

Changing Neighborhoods

Until well after the American Revolution, most of the city's Jews lived within shouting distance of the spot where the refugees from Brazil had landed in 1654. Clustered in the vicinity of the first synagogue on Mill Street, long known as Jews' Street or Jews' Alley (now South William Street), the Jews had their homes and places of business on Stone, Beaver, and Broad Streets, Hanover Square, and lower Broadway, in the heart of what is now the financial district.

As the city began expanding northward, the Jews started moving toward what is now the City Hall area and Greenwich Village. At about 1820, the majority of Jews had settled around West Broadway. The wealthier lived along Greenwich, Laight, Greene, Pearl, Water, Wooster, and Crosby Streets, the poorer on Broome, Houston, Canal, and Franklin Streets. A year before the oldest congregation moved into its second synagogue on Crosby Street in 1834, only one Jewish family was left in the Mill Street neighborhood. When the second congregation was established in 1825, its synagogue was a converted Negro church on Elm Street.

The Lower East Side first became a Jewish neighborhood in the late 1830s and 1840s when German and Polish immigrants settled on Bayard, Canal, Elm, Baxter, and Mott Streets, and Chatham Square, around what is now Chinatown. From there they pushed east into Division, Allen, Christie and Henry Streets, and north to Stanton, Ludlow, Clinton, Attorney, Rivington, Pitt, Ridge, and Houston Streets. By the 1850s Jews had moved as far north as 20th Street on the east side and to 34th Street on the west side.

After the Civil War, the more prosperous German-Jewish families and the remnant of the Sephardim quit the older Jewish neighborhood, moving en masse to the middle east side between 30th and 57th Streets, and to the west side between 59th and 96th Streets, where they occupied the then luxurious brownstones. Working class and lower middle-class German and Hungarian Jews took up residence north of Houston Street, along the numbered streets between Avenue B and the East River, while others began settling in Harlem.

The exodus of the older families and their synagogues from the Lower East Side was virtually ended by 1880 when the Jewish community was still "hardly more than a subject for idle curiosity." Because each new contingent of Jewish immigrants went first to the Lower East Side, where they took over houses and synagogues abandoned by their predecessors, this section remained heavily Jewish until the final break up of the area as the heart of New York Jewry. The 20 city blocks of the Lower East Side, between Houston Street and East Broadway, east of the Bowery, were "an immigrant Jewish cosmopolis," jammed with nearly 600,000 people by 1910. Most all of these were from Eastern Europe except the Levantine Jews, who took root between Allen and Christie Streets.

There was, however, a steady exodus from the Lower East Side. As "those whose lot improved moved out, they were replaced constantly by new arrivals" from Europe. As early as the 1890s the trek was on from the Lower East Side to Yorkville, between 72nd and 100th Streets, east of Lexington (now part of the Barrio of the Puerto Ricans), and then north to Harlem, where the German Jews had preceded them.

Higher wages won by the garment unions and the opening of the subways enabled Jews to leave the East Side tenements for brighter homes in Washington Heights in northern Manhattan, the lower Bronx, and the Brooklyn neighborhoods of Brownsville, East New York, Borough Park, and Bensonhurst. As the East Side sweatshops were eliminated, and the clothing factories began moving north to Madison Square and then towards Times Square, there was no longer any need for Jews who could afford to live elsewhere to remain on the Lower East Side.

The Lower East Side began to fade as the city's principal Jewish quarter in the 1920s about the time when the German Jews and the more successful East Europeans were taking root on Riverside Drive, West End Avenue, and Central Park West. In the 1930s, when Harlem was abandoned to the Negroes, the Lower East Side had fewer Jews than in 1900, while Washington Heights became known as "the fourth Reich" because of an influx of refugees from Nazism. Until the 1940s, the west side, from 70th to 125th Streets, and from Central Park West to Riverside Drive, was the most important Jewish neighborhood. The brownstones on side streets from 72nd to 96th Streets were heavily populated by middle-class Jews until the 1930s. When these residences became economically unviable, the Jews withdrew to the large apartment houses on the main thoroughfares.

In the 1950s a substantial Jewish exodus began from this section to which blacks and Puerto Ricans had been moving in great numbers. Temple Israel and the West End Synagogue, two of the oldest Reform synagogues in the area, shifted to the middle east side. A third, Rodeph Sholom, reported that its west side membership had fallen, while its east side membership accounted for a third of the total. Older members tended to remain, but their children moved. Shearith Israel, the Free Synagogue, B'nai Jeshurun, the Jewish Center, and the Society for the Advancement of Judaism have remained on the west side.

The Columbia University-Jewish Theological Seminary-Union Theological Seminary cultural complex between 116th and 123rd Streets, from Amsterdam Avenue to Riverside Drive, encourages young professionals, academicians, and older families to stay in that neighborhood despite serious problems resulting from ethnic changes in the area. The Jewish Theological Seminary silenced rumors that it might move because it was unable to obtain urgently needed space by completing a new dormitory. The first New York chavurah, founded in 1969, rented a Morningside Drive apartment near Columbia University where its adherents sought to redefine their own Judaism on a personal level through communal sharing, discussion, and prayer. Widows, retired people living on pensions and Social Security, and owners of neighborhood retail businesses also stayed on the west side because they were reluctant to leave rent-controlled apartments, notwithstanding an increase in crime in the area. The major rebuilding around Lincoln Center in the west 60s, and the erection of new middle and low-income housing projects between West 80th and 90th Streets, gave rise to something of a Jewish revival on the west side.

The Jewish middle-class exodus from the west side in the 1950s and 1960s created new Jewish communities on the middle and upper east side. The 92nd Street YM & YWHA had discussed moving until the 2nd and 3rd Avenue elevated lines were razed, and the new high-rise apartment houses that replaced slum dwellings from Madison Avenue to the East River between 34th and 96th Streets, revitalized the entire area. Temple Emanu-El added a large school wing. A new Reform congregation was established on East 35th Street where it shares quarters with the Community Church. The Park East Synagogue on East 67th Street added an eight-story building. The Park Avenue Synagogue added a multi-use structure. The established Orthodox and Conservative synagogues in the area enjoyed new growth. Central Synagogue remained fixed at 55th Street and Lexington Avenue despite the shifting tides of Jewish population, and added a center annex.

The new east side Jewish settlement also drew from residents on upper Fifth and Park Avenues, Beekman and Sutton Place cooperatives, from older families returned from the suburbs who moved into high-rise cooperatives in the 60s, 70s, and 80s between Fifth and Second Avenues, employees at the United Nations, and executives with firms occupying the skyscraper office buildings on 6th and Park Avenues who reside at neighboring apartment houses. A number of national Jewish organizations have headquarters in buildings between East 52nd and East 84th Streets. The Federation building is on East 59th Street.

On the lower west side, where Jews rarely lived, there is a growing Jewish community in the Chelsea area, south of Pennsylvania Station, thanks to new middle-class cooperative and public housing developments. Luxury apartments on lower Fifth Avenue and modernized tenements in Greenwich Village have brought back middle-class families, students, and intellectuals. Several new synagogues have been formed in Greenwich Village in the last five years. Some Jews have moved into SoHo, between Houston and Canal Streets, where artists' studios and apartments have taken root in old warehouses.

There has also been a return of lower and middle-income Jews to the east side, south of 23rd Street. Since the city's first public housing project, Knickerbocker Village, opened in the 1930s, younger families of limited means have gone back to the first area of Jewish settlement. Peter Cooper Village, Stuyvesant Town, and the network of public housing along the East River have given rise to a new Jewish community. There is a YMHA at the corner of 14th Street and Second Avenue. New Reform and Conservative synagogues have been opened in the area, finding members among the residents of new high-rise apartment houses that sprang up along First,

Second, and Third Avenues between 14th and 23rd Streets, after the elevated lines came down. Some of the older Orthodox congregations in this area gained new members from the refugees from Hungary, Cuba, and Syria who first settled there on their arrival.

The old Lower East Side, the portal to America for hundreds of thousands of Jews, with its crowds of pious Jews, Hebrew schools, kosher butchers, colorful cafes, open air pushcarts, and all the "warming images of the Jewish ghetto" are gone forever. There are still some 20,000 Jews left on the Lower East Side, most of whom live in the public and private cooperatives along Delancey Street, Grand Street, and East Broadway. Many of this Jewish remnant are old and poor, some are pensioners living on social security. There is also a younger Jewish element living in the eight residential developments built on the Lower East Side between 1956 and 1966. The neighborhood is now a daily ethnic confrontation of Puerto Ricans, Chinese, and blacks, as well as Jews. There have been bitter struggles between Jews and Puerto Ricans over rights to apartments in new housing complexes, over the appointment of an anti-Semite as local school superintendent, and over the continued vandalism of the remaining synagogues in the area.

Yiddish and Hebrew signs are still evident but are now outnumbered by those in Spanish, Chinese, Italian, and Greek. Whenever a Jewish storekeeper sells out, the buyer is never a Jew. But the neighborhood is still a Jewish marketplace. Along three blocks of Orchard Street, suburban descendants of yesterday's immigrants converge in search of bargains and nostalgia at shops that sell a great variety of merchandise at bargain prices. Some Jewish merchants employ Spanish-speaking salesmen for their Puerto Rican customers. The throngs of buyers are so dense on Sundays that Orchard Street between Delancey and Houston Streets is reserved for pedestrians from 8 A.M. to 6 P.M. The remaining handful of synagogues are architectural relics of the bygone past where worshipers often pray in the dark, lest lights attract vandals and hoodlums. The synagogues that are still in use are badly in need of repair and their worshipers struggle just to keep them open. The Yiddish writers, poets, playwrights, novelists, scholars, labor leaders, and journalists who once wandered in and out of the *Jewish Daily Forward* building on East Broadway have long since vanished. In 1975 the *Forward* too, left East Broadway, moving uptown to East 33rd Street in the new home of the Workmen's Circle, which also departed from the East Side. With their departure a large part of the remnant of the old East Side faded.

The Educational Alliance, founded for the first immigrants of the 1880s era, is still at East Broadway and busier than ever, serving Jews and the minorities that have taken over the East Side. The Henry Street Settlement, founded in 1893 to serve poor Jewish immigrants, now serves mostly Puerto Ricans, but the executive director and many of the board of directors are Jews, as are nearly half of the old people who come to the

Settlement for a variety of programs. The Settlement sponsors a Jewish theatrical group and serves kosher lunches with menus printed in English and Spanish and prepared by a black dietician.

The Washington Heights area, in northwest Manhattan, is another neighborhood where changes have converted a once important Jewish area into one now predominantly black, Puerto Rican, and Cuban. In the 1920s the neighborhood became one of the areas in which Jews leaving the Lower East Side settled in substantial numbers in new elevator apartment houses. In the 1930s Washington Heights became known as "the fourth Reich" because so many Jewish refugees from Hitler Europe settled there, including the family of Henry Kissinger, who grew up there. In the 1970s the Jews numbered less than one-fourth of the 187,000 people who dwell in Washington Heights. In the 1960s they were one-third of the population. Fear of crime and environmental issues such as noise, dirty streets, and deteriorating schools drove families with school age children away. The remaining Jewish residents included a good many aged poor. Washington Heights is the home of the main campus of Yeshiva University, a YM-YWHA, several Hebrew day schools and synagogues, and a Jewish community council. The latter has had a safety patrol cruising the streets after dark to protect Jewish residents.

Forty years of population shifts and urban redevelopment dropped Manhattan from first to third place as the borough with the largest number of Jews. The latest figures for Manhattan's Jewish population was 171,000. Manhattan's loss of Jewish residents first showed up as huge increases in Brooklyn and The Bronx during the 1930s. By the 1960s, Manhattan's continued loss of Jewish residents was reflected in the growth of the Queens, Long Island, and Westchester Jewish settlements.

The Struggle For Equality

The 23 unwanted refugees who arrived in New Amsterdam in 1654 found no freedom. They fought to achieve it for themselves and others.

The first victory over Peter Stuyvesant's bigotry that permitted the Jewish Pilgrim Fathers to stay was more than an entering wedge for the achievement of further civil rights. It also paved the way for other religious sects to assert and win their rights and set a precedent which succeeding generations of New York Jews emulated in supporting the struggle of other disfranchised and oppressed minorities.

In 1655 when Stuyvesant ordered the Jews exempt from military training and guard duty but imposed a special monthly tax on them in lieu of such service, Asser Levy and Jacob Barsimson challenged this discrimination. Told by the city fathers to "go elsewhere" if they did not like it, the two simple workmen successfully appealed to Holland which ordered Stuyvesant to allow them to help defend the city. When Levy stood guard in defiance of the local authorities, he became the first Jewish soldier in America. Three years later, when Barsimson failed to appear in his own defense in a court action, "no default is entered against him as he was summoned on his Sabbath."

In 1655, Abraham de Lucena was fined for violating the ban on retail selling by Jews, but Asser Levy and Moses de Lucena, the first Jews to be licensed as butchers, were excused in 1660 from killing hogs on grounds of their religion. Levy was admitted to the burgher right in 1657.

That same year the Jews won the right to share in the defense of the city and to own property. But public worship, the vote, retail business, and the practice of any trade but that of butcher were not permitted. They could exercise their religion "in all quietness . . . within their houses for which end they must without doubt endeavor to build their houses close together in a convenient place on one or the other side of New Amsterdam—at their choice." This hint to create a ghetto was ignored, but the Jews did settle in the neighborhood of Mill Street where the first synagogue was opened.

The rights wrung from the Dutch permitted the Jewish settlement to enjoy a decade of reasonable security despite the harassment of Stuyvesant and his successors. All economic disabilities against the Jews were lifted by the English. Freedom of religion began in 1674 when the Duke of York instructed his governor in the colony renamed for him "to permit all persons of what religion so ever, quietly to inhabit within the precincts of yo're jurisdictions without giving them any disturbance or disquiet whatsoever for or by reason of their differing opinion in matter of religion." Another governor decreed in 1685 that "publique worship" was a privilege limited to those "that professe faith in Christ," but the earlier order was reaffirmed in 1686.

Until after the Revolution, all sects remained subject to a special assessment by the Colonial Assembly for the support of Trinity Church. As late as 1730 even "the Jew synnagogg" paid four shillings and nine pence for support of the Church of England ministry.

Saturday was the day New York's householders had to clean the street in front of their residences until 1702 when it was changed to Friday. In 1727 the Jews were permitted to omit the words "upon the true faith of a Christian" in taking the loyalty oath. Fifty Colonial Jews, many of them from New York, were recognized as freemen between 1687 and 1769. Samuel Myers Cohen, a butcher, was the first Jew to become a citizen in 1740 when the British Parliament passed a naturalization law that gave aliens of seven years residence all the rights of native-born British subjects. The right of Jews to vote was questioned in 1737 when a defeated candidate for the Colonial Assembly challenged the outcome on the plea that Jews had all voted for his opponent. The protest was upheld by the legislature which declared votes cast by Jews null and void.

With the adoption of New York State's first constitution in 1777 the Jews were granted full citizenship and complete equality. This final emancipation set a precedent for the other states and paved the way for the achievement of similar rights by Catholics.

The right of rabbis to be Army chaplains, the last battle for Jewish religious equality in the United States, first established during the Civil War, was won chiefly through the efforts of the Reverend Arnold Fischel, the Dutch-born reader at Shearith Israel. As the representative of the Board of Delegates of American Israelites, he negotiated with members of Congress and the War Department and persuaded President Abraham Lincoln to recommend that Congress amend the law to permit the appointment of rabbis as chaplains. Rabbi Ferdinand Sarner, chaplain of the 54th New York Volunteers, was the only one of the three rabbis commissioned under the amended act of 1862 to serve at the front.

Before the Civil War discrimination against Jews in employment in New York and sporadic anti-Semitic incidents were not uncommon and "specific individuals were abused as Jews by those who opposed, hated, or envied them." It was, however, "not a common habit to attack all Jews for whatever anyone found wrong with life in the United States. That remained for the Civil War period."

Even some of the most respectable New York City newspapers "spoke as though all the Jewish bankers in the world, with Belmont in the lead, were joined together for the support of the Confederacy." August Belmont, Democratic party spokesman and banker, who married into the family of Commodore Oliver Hazzard Perry, reared his children as Christians and had nothing to do with the Jewish community, was the particular target of the Republican press. But all Jewish businessmen were regularly denounced as gold speculators and war profiteers.

The leading role played in the Confederacy by Judah P. Benjamin, a Jew, and Senator David Yulee of Florida, who had left the Jewish fold, "provided a convenient slur with which all Jews could be defamed." Anti-Semites who attacked Belmont as a Confederate sympathizer ignored the fact that he aided the United States Treasury in securing the support of European capital and that he had recruited and equipped the first German-American regiment in New York.

Anti-Jewish sentiment was further aggravated by General Ulysses Grant's notorious Order No. 11, expelling all Jews "as a class" from the Department of Tennessee. The "most sweeping anti-Jewish regulation in all American history," the Order was in effect from December 11, 1862 until January 7, 1863 when President Lincoln ordered it rescinded. Issued as part of the Union Army's attempt to halt trading with the Confederacy and the ensuing widespread profiteering, the Order created indignation among native-born Jews, alarm among the German immigrants, and blackened the reputation of all Jewish businessmen. It even played a role in the 1868 presidential election when it prompted many ordinarily Republican New York Jewish voters to switch to the Democrats. Grant, who always regretted the Order, sought to make amends when he became president by appointing Benjamin F. Peixotto, a New York attorney and president of B'nai B'rith, as United States consul general to Romania in 1870, in the hope he would be able to halt the anti-Jewish policies of that country.

Grant's order contributed greatly to the postwar American stereotype of the Jew as peddler and profiteer when he also became equated with a parvenu. Coupled with the rising antialien sentiment of 1870-1890 and the agrarian revolt against Wall Street, these prejudices became the seed-bed of American anti-Semitism.

The "no Jews allowed" pattern of restrictions at resorts and hotels, which took form in the 1870s, claimed as its most prominent victim Joseph Seligman, banker, friend of Lincoln, and the leader of the Jewish community. His exclusion from the Grand Union Hotel in Saratoga Springs in 1877, on orders of its owner, Henry Hilton, created a national sensation. A boycott by Jews and non-Jews of A. T. Stewart & Co., of which Hilton was trustee, ruined the firm's wholesale trade, and only a take-over by John Wanamaker saved the retail establishment.

The Reverend Henry Ward Beecher's famous sermon, "Jew and Gentile," preached from Plymouth Church, Brooklyn, in 1877, was not just an attack on Hilton but a classic repudiation of anti-Semitism. Beecher's denunciation was also aimed at Austin Corbin, a real estate promoter, who publicly announced that he wanted no Jewish patrons at his lavish new resort at Manhattan Beach. A. T. Stewart, when he laid out Garden City, on Long Island, as a model village in the 1870s specifically excluded Jewish property owners.

The New York City Bar Association rejected a Jewish applicant in 1877 solely because he was a Jew. Before the Jews swamped the Lower East Side, the principal property owner on Second Avenue would not rent to Jews. Discrimination by insurance companies against Jewish merchants was so widespread during this period that New York Jews seriously considered forming a company that would accept only Jewish policy holders. While some Jews gained entry to high society clubs and exclusive hotels, most Jews sought social outlets in all-Jewish clubs and patronized resorts where Jews were in a majority. The exclusion of Jews from college fraternities at the end of the 19th century gave rise to Jewish Greek letter societies at the New York colleges.

Jew-baiting of a more violent character was fairly common on the Lower East Side, especially where Irish neighborhoods bordered Jewish sections. The worst anti-Semitic incident in the city occurred in 1902 when the funeral procession of Rabbi Jacob Joseph was attacked by workers in the printing press factory of R. Hoe & Co., which employed no Jews. More than 125 Jews were injured.

Biased or sensation-seeking journalists contributed to the rise of anti-Semitism by drawing a distorted picture of the East Side as a neighborhood of squalor, poverty, and pushcarts, peopled by wild-eyed radicals, bizarre foreigners, and ill-kempt children. Henry James spoke of the East Side as "a vast aquarium in which innumerable fish, of over-developed proboscises, were to bump together, forever, amid heaped spoils of

NEW YORK CITY — 56

the sea." Visitors who failed to recognize that on the sidewalks of the East Side was flowering a fertile seed-bed of great talents, translated the sights and sounds and smells of the East Side into subtle anti-Jewish feeling.

Only a few perceptive non-Jewish observers—Jacob Riis, reporter and reformer; Hutchins Hapgood; and Lincoln J. Steffens, whose muckraking articles greatly influenced muncipal reforms—sensed the ferment of progress on the East Side.

At the very time when Czarist persecution was bringing almost daily shiploads of Jews to New York, American racists and anti-Semites began assailing the "Hebrew conquest" of New York. Foes of immigration made the Jews their principal target, denouncing "the great Jewish invasion" of the metropolis, which they said, threatened to make it "a city of Asiatics."

The struggle against overt anti-Semitism first took organized form in New York in 1859 with the establishment of the Board of Delegates of American Israelites. This body was replaced in 1906 by the American Jewish Committee. Differences of opinion over tactics and techniques created other national agencies in this field. The Anti-Defamation League of B'nai B'rith, founded in the midwest in 1913, moved to New York in the 1930s. New York is also the headquarters of the American Jewish Congress, the Jewish Labor Committee, and the National Jewish Community Relations Advisory Council.

A small beginning in outlawing discrimination was made in New York in 1913 with a state law forbidding places of public accommodation from advertising their unwillingness to admit anyone because of race, creed, or color. Before World War I, Adolph S. Ochs, publisher of *The New York Times* wrote to all daily newspapers reminding them that the word "Jew" is a noun, and was not to be used as an adjective or adverb, as in "Jew-down" or "Jew-boy." Similar efforts ended the practice of identifying criminals by religion, nationality, and race, and eliminated offensive Jewish characters from stage and screen. These modest efforts gradually eliminated the coarser manifestations of anti-Semitism but it took another generation of education before the Jews of New York could work, study, live, and play without restrictions.

In the 1920s and 1930s, a quota system sharply curtailed the number of Jewish students in the city's private colleges and universities. It barred all but a handful from the city's five medical colleges, and held down their number at the city's leading law schools. Not until the state outlawed discrimination in higher education did Jewish medical, law, and dental students get a better break in New York's colleges.

This discrimination impelled many New York Jewish students to seek admission to colleges out of the city and even abroad for the first time. One of the first major victories against Jew-baiting came in 1927 when Henry Ford addressed to Louis Marshall a public apology for seven years of vilification of the Jews in *The Dearborn Independent*.

Few white collar or clerical jobs were open to Jews in New York in the

1920s and 1930s. The big downtown law offices seldom engaged Jewish law clerks. Banks, insurance companies, and public utilities turned away Jewish applicants. Jewish graduates of the City's public high schools found their high academic standing meant little in the face of quotas applied by Ivy League colleges and out-of-town medical schools. Even when they could afford it, few Jews could rent or buy housing in the better neighborhoods. Membership in the influential social clubs was closed to them and summer resorts flaunted "Christian only" signs and advertisements.

Beekman Place, Sutton Place, and the Carl Schurz section were resisting Jewish tenants in the 1920s and 1930s as much as Fifth and Park Avenues did just before World War II. Some luxury cooperatives and the Westchester village of Bronxville still continue this practice today. Once no Jew could rent in the exclusive apartments north of Grand Central Station any more than he could in Forest Hills, Queens, or Bay Ridge, Brooklyn. Coney Island, Brighton Beach, Manhattan Beach, and Sheepshead Bay, once exclusive Brooklyn seaside resorts which barred Jews, now have large Jewish populations. Sea Gate, a segment of Coney Island that was once a Gentile millionaire's preserve, became a middle-class Jewish enclave.

As late as 1915, Long Beach, in Nassau County, now about half-Jewish, was dotted with clubs and hotels that refused to admit Jews. Most golf and country clubs or resorts on Long Island and in Westchester were not open to Jews, and a few are still barred to them. Long Island's leading yacht club, which always excluded Jews, reversed its policy just in time to enable its first Jewish member to pilot the yacht that carried the United States to victory in the America Cup race with Great Britain in 1962. In 1963 one of the largest Long Island country clubs publicly asked Jewish organizations to help it enroll more non-Jewish members to create a better balance. Indignant denials were made when the president of Temple Emanu-El charged in 1963 that a Fifth Avenue cooperative was not available to him only because he was a Jew. Zoning ordinances were invoked in efforts to bar the construction of synagogues in some Long Island and Westchester communities in the 1940s and 1950s, and even in the 1970s, and it took some time before Jewish home-buyers broke through unwritten restrictions.

The 1930s also saw Nazi Bundist parades and rallies, Christian Front meetings, and noisy Coughlinites peddling anti-Semitic literature on street corners. Despite great provocation the Jewish community resisted attempts to outlaw such demonstrations because of its deep commitment to civil rights for all. The close association of such New Yorkers as Sidney Hillman, David Dubinsky, Samuel Rosenman, and Benjamin Cohen with Franklin D. Roosevelt led to attacks on the New Deal as "the Jew deal," and inspired campaign slogans with anti-Semitic overtones, such as "clear it with Sidney." More recent anti-Jewish meetings by latter-day Nazis and the rash of swastika daubings on Jewish public buildings in the 1950s created concern but no panic.

Most overt anti-Semitism in New York is now largely a thing of the past, thanks to state and city antidiscrimination and fair employment legislation fought for by the Jewish community relations agencies. Their programs of intergroup action, information, education, research, public opinion, and determined pressure for remedial laws reduced incidents of anti-Semitism to its lowest level in history in the 1950s and early 1960s, while paving the way for the profound changes toward civil rights and equal opportunities for all minorities. Discrimination still exists, of course, but it is confined largely to the executive suite—where great progress has been made in opening the doors to employment for qualified Jews—a few clubs, some luxury cooperative apartments, and occasional employers. The National Jewish Commission on Law and Public Affairs of the Union of Orthodox Jewish Congregations dealt effectively with many cases of discrimination against Jewish Sabbath observers.

The community relations problems of New York's Jews in the 1960s and 1970s grew less out of anti-Semitism as such, and more from differences with Catholics and Negroes. Christmas observances in the public schools, displays of Christological symbols in public places, child adoption policies, abortion, and public funds for parochial schools were issues on which Catholics and Jews did not always see eye-to-eye. Catholic-Jewish relations, however, were greatly improved as a result of numerous joint educational and research projects involving Catholic clergymen and educators. Sunday closing laws aligned some Protestant groups against Jewish merchants as part of a legal struggle that began more than 200 years ago. It started in New Amsterdam in 1665 when Abraham de Lucena was fined for keeping his shop open during the Sunday church sermon. It ended in 1963 when the City Council enacted a Fair Sabbath Law that gave Sabbath-observing Jewish family-operated establishments the right to open their places of business on Sunday.

Anti-Semitism in the black and Puerto Rican communities, a by-product of the militant black and Puerto Rican struggle for employment, housing, and educational opportunity, became a matter of serious concern for the first time in the 1960s. Long the most vigorous champion of minority rights, the Jews of New York were taken aback by the Jew-baiting of the Black Muslims—now a thing of the past—and by the anti-Semitic statements of some black newspapers and leaders. Charges of discrimination against blacks levied against the Jewish leadership of the International Ladies Garment Workers Union were especially disturbing. While similar charges were made against other unions, Jewish unionists were the first targets because of the blacks' feeling that more was to be expected from Jews than from other whites.

Conflicts between black and Puerto Rican advocates of local school control and Jewish teachers during the 1968 school strike led to anti-Semitic outbursts by various black militants and an angry backlash by Jews. Black publications attacked what they called "exploitation" by Jews of blacks and Puerto Ricans in the school system. Anti-Semitism became an issue in the

1969 mayoralty election when Democratic candidate Mario Procaccino accused Mayor John Lindsay of fostering an "upsurge in anti-Semitism" by his actions during the teachers' strike when there were frequent confrontations between black parents and Jewish teachers. A panel of experts appointed by Lindsay to study bigotry in the city concluded that propaganda and threats used by black extremists during the teachers' strike and the struggle over decentralization of the school system contained "a dangerous component of anti-Semitism."

The charges and countercharges of black anti-Semitism and white racism seriously strained the long-time black-Jewish alliance forged during the years of the civil rights struggle. Facing one another across picket lines at schools on the Lower East Side, Brooklyn, and at housing projects in Queens, mutual recriminations and threats seriously exacerbated black-Jewish tensions. Because much of the black-Jewish conflict occurred in communities where blacks were recent arrivals, some sociologists saw the conflict as due in part to the "normal" conflict between the remnants of a departing group and the upwardly mobile efforts of a new group. Ethnic polarizations over school busing in the Ocean-Brownsville and Canarsie areas, anti-Semitism by a Puerto Rican district school superintendent on the Lower East Side, the bitter and partially successful struggle of the Jews of Forest Hills to prevent the building of a massive low-income housing project in their neighborhood, and discrimination against the Jewish poor by black administrators of local antipoverty programs combined to create great bitterness between blacks and whites.

Affirmative action programs that were designed to give minorities a better break in government employment, often turned out to be undermining the idea of merit in public employment, some sectors of private employment, and in the schools and colleges, were regarded as reverse discrimination against Jews. One of the by-products of affirmative action in the public schools was an almost 50 percent loss of jobs by Jewish school supervisors between 1968 and 1973 as a result of the decentralization of school districts. City College, which three generations of New York Jews used as a stepping stone to a better life, became involved in the black-Jewish conflict when its standards of admission were lowered to make room for more minority students. The idea of racial quotas in civil service, further embittered black-Jewish relations.

Blacks and Puerto Ricans resented the flight of Jews from neighborhoods into which they moved and the transfer of thousands of Jewish children from the public to private and Jewish day schools. The Jews, on the other hand, were fleeing the city because of growing crime, deteriorating schools, street violence, and fear. The president of the Rabbinical Council of America, noting the abandonment of Orthodox synagogues and Hebrew schools in various parts of the city, urged the Jews to remain in changing neighborhoods. The Orthodox were usually the last to leave such areas, with the result that there was greater conflict between them and the newly arrived black and Puerto Rican residents. In one year, 75 Orthodox synagogues were abandoned or sold in Brownsville, East New York, Crown Heights, Williamsburg, the lower Bronx, the upper West Side, and Jamaica.

All of this gave rise to a new mood of anger and militancy on the part of rank and file Jews who refused to believe that the decline of old Jewish neighborhoods was not a deliberate policy of the city government during the years of urban renewal. Long-time Jewish activists and supporters of a wide variety of good causes, Jewish organizations, and many liberal movements, suddenly began to look at programs and projects with an eye as to whether they were good or bad for Jews. Jewish ethnicity, long confined to religion, education, and philanthropy, came to the fore in such areas as housing, poverty, public education, and school busing. This previously unknown Jewish militancy nurtured local Jewish security squads such as the Maccabees in Brooklyn. The Jewish Defense League was founded in 1968 for the specific purpose of protecting Jews from physical attack, especially school teachers and yeshiva students. In its early years the JDL went into Harlem to protect Jewish storekeepers from harassment by the Black Panthers.

As a sense of fear and frustration began to pervade growing segments of the Jewish community, they became more parochial in their concerns and adopted more conservative stances on public issues and gave their support to conservative candidates. The Jewish Rights Council was organized as an outgrowth of the Jewish protests against low-income housing in Forest Hills. The new Jewish militancy also expressed itself in strong demands for Jewish rights to a fair share of poverty funds, food stamps, and jobs created with Federal funds. In the 1970s, some 35 local Jewish community councils sprang up in many neighborhoods concerned with local Jewish interests. With the support of Federation, these councils became instruments for preserving the viability of neighborhood Jewish communities, caring for the needs of the elderly left behind by the exodus of younger families to the suburbs, encouraging the Jewish poor to apply for welfare benefits to which they are entitled, and protecting their legal, civil, and cultural rights. Dissatisfied with the Federation-sponsored efforts for the Jewish poor, a small independent group called Association of Jewish Anti-Poverty Workers was founded and they operate a store-front center in Brownsville. In 1975 there were signs of a resumption of close ties between Jews and blacks.

Businessman and Workingman

Jewish enterprise, innovation, and a sense of social justice were potent factors in New York's rise to commercial, business, and financial eminence, and in its unique role in the emancipation of the workingman.

Handicapped by Dutch restrictions, the early Jewish settlers earned their livelihood chiefly as Indian traders or butchers. Asser Levy built an abattoir with a Christian partner in the 1660s on what is now Wall Street and was also engaged in a flourishing business in furs. By 1700, however, Jewish merchants had made their influence felt in the city's trade and commerce.

The governor of the colony wrote the London Board of Trade "that were it not for one Dutch merchant and two or three Jews that have lent me money, I should have been undone." Nevertheless, most Jewish businessmen were still itinerant traders or retailers of such modest means that few were listed as taxpayers.

Hayman Levy, the best known Jewish merchant in Colonial New York, is reputed to have given the fabulous John Jacob Astor, a non-Jewish immigrant, his first job beating peltries at a dollar a day. A hogshead of rum supplied by Levy also launched the mercantile career of Nicholas Low, ancestor of a future mayor and president of Columbia University.

Jacob Franks, Levy's son-in-law, was chief purveyor of goods to the British during the French and Indian Wars. Another son-in-law, Isaac Moses, owned ships that plied the American coast from Montreal to Savannah and sailed to Europe and India. A privateersman whose captains harassed French shipping, Moses was a partner of Robert Morris, Revolutionary patriot, and, with Samson Simson, also a shipowner, was among the founders of the New York Chamber of Commerce in 1768.

New York's Colonial Jews also included a jeweler, Benjamin Franks, who had sailed with Captain Kidd in 1696; three of the signers in 1705 of a mercantile petition seeking the establishment of a fair standard of value for foreign coins; and Lewis Gomez, a dealer in rum, slaves, and furs, in whose Greenwich Village home the Colonial Assembly met in 1746 because of an epidemic in the commercial quarter of the city. A number of Jewish merchants were engaged in the slave trade with the West Indies.

Rodrigo Pacheco was one of the five merchants chosen to voice New York's protest against the Molasses Act of 1733. Every Jewish merchant in the city pledged himself not to import goods subject to the Stamp Act of 1765. Six risked British retaliation by signing the Non-Importation Resolutions of 1770.

Except for a few Loyalists, every Jew left New York when it was occupied by the British during the Revolution. Uriah Hendricks and Barrat Hays were among the Loyalist merchants whose presence kept the British from confiscating the synagogue. Another was Alexander Zuntz, a sutler with the Hessian troops, who later became president of Shearith Israel.

The 60 identifiable Jewish names in the city directory of 1799 included merchants and brokers, a scattering of shipowners, coppersmiths, soap-boilers, harness-makers, carpenters, tobacconists, accountants, auctioneers, a boat pilot, a mantilla-maker, and a bookseller. Shearith Israel's records first mentioned a tailor in 1819. The wealthiest Jew in New York at the beginning of the 19th century was Ephraim Hart, a partner of John Jacob Astor. Hart, Isaac Gomez, Alexander Zuntz, and Benjamin Seixas were among the 24 founders in 1792 of the Stockbrokers Guild, out of which grew the New York Stock Exchange.

Before the first wave of immigration from Germany and Poland early in the 19th century, most of the old line families were in retail business, stock brokerage, manufacturing, the professions, and public service, but there were also a good number of self-employed artisans. Bernard Hart, grandfather of Bret Harte, the writer of western tales, furnished arms and clothing to the citizens' army formed to defend the city during the War of 1812, and served as secretary of the Stock Exchange. Harmon Hendricks owned a pioneer copper smelter which supplied Paul Revere's foundry and provided some of the metal used in building Robert Fulton's steamboat, the *Clermont*, and the historic warship, USS *Constitution*. Isaac Baer Kursheedt, who had led the secession from Shearith Israel that launched Congregation B'nai Jeshurun, was a manufacturer of lace goods as well as the city's most learned Jew.

The immigrants who were not artisans or professionals turned overwhelmingly to petty trade, particularly peddling and the sale of used clothes. Of the 6,000 peddlers in the United States in 1860, most were said to have been Jews.

Chatham Street, center of the second-hand goods trade in the 1830s and 1840s, was sneeringly called "Jerusalem from the fact that the Jews do most if not all the business on this street." Cheaper and of better quality than the shoddy ready-to-wear men's clothing first introduced after 1820, the renovated used apparel sold by the Jewish immigrants not only found a ready market in New York, but was eagerly sought after in the south and west as the discarded fashions of the style-setting east. Moving around the country with hard-to-get merchandise, many of the second-hand dealers and the omnipresent peddlers became the nuclei of new Jewish communities in the south and west—the founders of great mercantile and industrial enterprises and ancestors of eminent Americans. One second-hand dealer, Levi Straus, who failed in the California gold rush, came back to New York to manufacture a special kind of pants for the miners and to add the word Levis to the English language.

From the second-hand trade and peddling it was a short step to retailing, importing, jobbing, wholesaling, and manufacturing of clothing, drygoods, and other consumer goods. From Chatham Street the Jews moved their establishments to Grand Street and the Bowery, and later, further uptown. The eerie silence that today settles over many business sections of New York on Rosh Hashanah and Yom Kippur was already noticeable more than a century ago. In 1847 the *New York Drygoods Reporter* said that because Jewish customers account for 25 percent of all sales by wholesalers, "some suspended business on the Jewish holidays rather than do without this increasingly influential element."

The *New York Commercial List* in 1853 recorded 2,751 wholesale firms, of which 105 were Jewish; half of these were in the clothing, drygoods, or related fields. An 1859 roster of 3,300 wholesalers and bankers contained 141 firms with Jewish names in the garment and affiliated industries.

The German Jews, who first gave the community the strength of numbers, were quickly absorbed into the middle class because the rags-to-riches saga was more common among those who arrived between 1830 and 1850 than among any other previous immigrant group. In the expanding post-Civil War economy, many of the peddlers, second-hand dealers, artisans, and storekeepers of the 1830-1860 era became well-to-do New York merchants, department store owners, real estate investors, bankers, industrialists, and manufacturers.

From the German-Jewish generations came the Lehmans, Guggenheims, Lewisohns, the Strauses of Macys, the Gimbels, Altmans, Sterns, Bloomingdales, Schiffs, Speyers, and Seligmans. Some of the oldest New York banking houses such as Speyer & Co. (1854), J. W. Seligman (1862), Kuhn, Loeb & Co. (1865), and Lehman Bros. (1868), founded on earnings from jobbing, clothing manufacturing, and cotton goods, were established by immigrants with links to German banks eager to invest in the American economy.

The leading figures of this generation were two former pack peddlers, Joseph and Jesse Seligman, who went into banking after clothing the Union Army. Horatio Alger probably got the idea for his "rags to riches" books, while serving as a tutor in the household of Joseph Seligman. The Seligmans, who sold nearly $200,000,000 worth of American bonds through their German branch when French and English bankers were reluctant to buy these securities during the most critical days of the Civil War, also underwrote some of the first railroads in the west and southwest. Joseph, who was instrumental in getting a pension for President Lincoln's widow, was the first chairman of the city's rapid transit commission and declined President Grant's appointment as Secretary of the Treasury. Jesse, who twice refused the Republican nomination for mayor, was the father of the eminent Columbia University professor of economics, Edwin A. Seligman.

James Speyer, whose immigrant father and uncle founded the banking firm of Speyer & Co. in the 1850s, was the moving spirit in the creation of the Museum of the City of New York and the Provident Loan Society. Albert Speyer, broker for James Fisk and Jay Gould when they tried to corner the gold market in 1869, paid off every dollar to his customers while his principals repudiated their debts.

Jacob H. Schiff, who came here from Germany in 1865 and married the daughter of a Kuhn, Loeb founder, was one of the key figures in American banking from 1885 until his death in 1920. As head of Kuhn, Loeb & Co., his influence was second only to that of J. P. Morgan. As part of the Rockefeller combine, Schiff successfully challenged Morgan in the underwriting of vast industrial enterprises and the railroad projects of James P. Hill and E. H. Harriman. In 1905, when other bankers hesitated, Schiff floated a $50 million loan for Japan, which helped bring about Russia's defeat in the Russo-Japanese War.

Lazarus Straus, who came to New York from Georgia in 1865 to pay off long-forgiven ante-bellum debts, was the father of the remarkable Straus brothers—Isidor, Oscar, and Nathan—who built Macy's from a crockery shop on Chambers Street. Oscar, the first Jewish Cabinet member, served as Theodore Roosevelt's Secretary of Commerce and Labor. Nathan was the city's most beloved philanthropist, and Isidor was a member of Congress. Benjamin Altman, the department store magnate who left a multimillion dollar art collection to the Metropolitan Museum, was the son of an immigrant. The Lewisohn Stadium, once famed for its summer concerts, but torn down in the 1970s, was a gift from Adolph Lewisohn, a German immigrant who made a fortune in metal mining.

Emanuel Lehman (father of Herbert H. Lehman, New York's only Jewish governor and former United States Senator), and his brother, Mayer, were immigrants who became Confederate patriots before they established Lehman Bros. in New York. The Guggenheims, celebrated for their art and literary fellowships, art museum, and support of aeronautical research, are the heirs of a 19th century immigrant who struck it rich when he invested the profits from lace manufacturing in silver and copper mines. The first segment of the now torn down 3rd Avenue elevated line was built in 1878 by Henry I. Hart, of English-German ancestry. Andrew Freedman, son of an immigrant, who developed large stretches of upper Fifth Avenue and The Bronx, was extensively involved in the construction of the first subway system.

The late Arthur Hays Sulzberger, publisher of *The New York Times*, was the grandson of a German-Jewish merchant whose son married into one of the old Sephardic families. Robert Morgenthau, Democratic candidate for governor against Nelson Rockefeller in 1962, and United States Attorney in New York in 1975, is the grandson of Henry Morgenthau, Sr., who came from Germany in 1856 and became wealthy in upper Manhattan and Bronx real estate. The elder Morgenthau helped Woodrow Wilson win the presidential nomination in 1912 and served as ambassador to Turkey.

When the wave of East European immigration began in the 1880s, the German Jews dominated the men's clothing and tobacco industries. Of 241 clothing factories in New York in 1888, 234 were Jewish-owned, as was 80 percent of the retail clothing outlets. Jews were also important factors in the manufacture of shirts, hats, hosiery, metal and leather goods, house furnishings, glass and paint products, in the processing of furs and hides, wholesale meat, and the grocery, wine, and liquor trades. German-Jewish manufacturers were also heavily represented in the women's ready-to-wear field when it began to replace the home and custom-made industry.

The need for cheap and docile labor by the expanding needle trades industry and the religious beliefs of the East Europeans combined to lead many of them into the garment trades. Although the earlier arrivals included many skilled craftsmen and artisans, until 1900 nearly one-third of the East Europeans in New York were employed in the clothing industry. Preferring to work where they could observe the Sabbath and kashruth, they sought employment with Jews who might be more sympathetic to demands for time off for afternoon and evening prayers or absences on the Sabbath and holy days.

Some Jewish employers did not scruple to force Jewish workers to accept lower pay for such privileges. Others who were active on immigrant aid committees combined business with philanthropy by leading immigrants directly to their factories. Harry Fischel, a Russian immigrant of 1865 who erected some of the first tenements in Harlem, Brooklyn, and The Bronx, encouraged Jewish workers in the building trades with half pay for no work on Saturday. Reuben Sadowsky's cloak factory acquired a certain fame because the work schedule was arranged to permit prayers three times daily.

From 1880-1900, most clothing manufacturers employed few workers except highly skilled cutters, who were then largely Germans or Irish. Bundles of unfinished cuttings were turned over to petty entrepreneurs, known as contractors, who finished the garments in their own outside shops. Some contractors handed this work over to subcontractors whose savage competition for bundles led to price cutting and exploitation of the workers through wage cuts and longer hours.

The outside shop became the horrible sweatshop, a sunless tenement flat which doubled as living quarters and factory. Until the contractor became prosperous enough to open an inside shop in a loft building, his workers were often members of his own family or fellow-townsmen. Most of the contractors and subcontractors were also East European immigrants who went into business for themselves as soon as they accumulated some capital. At Ellis Island they met and recruited relatives and former neighbors for the sweatshops.

In the front room of tenement flats tailors, basters, and finishers bent over rented sewing machines that covered every inch of floor space. Piles of finished and half-finished garments filled the bedroom. The red hot stove and blazing grate of glowing flat irons in the kitchen, where the pressers sweated, gave birth to the name "sweatshop." Parents and children worked side-by-side. Payment was by the piece and the longer they worked the more they earned. The working day often began at 4 a.m. and did not end until ten at night. Sanitary conditions were appalling, and the sweatshop became synonymous with disease-breeding tenements occupied by exploited workers.

At the turn of the century, the sweatshops and clothing factories had created a chaotic industry in which more than 200,000 Jewish workers depended for their livelihood on enterprises owned and operated by other Jews. The workers lived on the Lower East Side despite its squalor and congestion because of its proximity to the clothing factories and because it offered cheap housing. They also felt at home in the Yiddish-speaking milieu of relatives and fellow-townsmen where they could sustain their religious life.

A far smaller proportion of the post-1880 immigrants took to itinerant peddling than was the case among their German predecessors because the changing economy had narrowed the market for the peddlers' wares. Most numerous were the pushcart peddlers, whose number was estimated at 25,000 in 1900. They "converted whole blocks of the East Side into a street bazaar where their high-piled carts lined the curb," selling everything from tin cups to bananas and from fish to small articles of clothing. With a five dollar stock of shirts, socks, shoes, pots and pans, and a rented pushcart, an immigrant became a budding Wanamaker. Sometimes he went into business with only 75¢ in cash by peddling pickles, roasted sweet potatoes, soda water, Indian nuts, and halvah. These uncovered wagons started many on the road to uptown success and chain store operations.

For more than a generation the old East Side resembled a *yarid*, or old world market. Hester Street was known as the *chazermark*, or pig market, because it was the center of pushcart operations and an open air labor exchange where workers jostled each other every Saturday for hiring by contractors for clothing manufacturers.

While the stereotype of the East Side Jew was that of a pushcart peddler, a study of 135,000 East European Jews in New York in 1890 showed that 75 percent of those gainfully employed were workers and craftsmen. The other 25 percent included not only peddlers but owners of countless kosher butcher shops, bakeries, fish, vegetable and fruit stands, soda kiosks, delicatessens, small clothing and drygoods stores, and vendors of religious articles and Yiddish and Hebrew books.

The mounting demand for kosher meat among the immigrants helped keep New York an important center of the meat slaughtering and packing industry. Half of the city's 4,000 meat retailers and 300 of the wholesalers were Jews in 1890.

There were 500 Jewish bakeries, many of them ritually supervised, on the East Side in 1900. Some grew into the city's largest baking firms, such as Levy's, Messing, Goodman, and Gottfried. The immigrants' nonalcoholic drinking habits were responsible for flourishing sales of seltzer water, "East Side champagne."

Some thrifty sweatshop workers, peddlers, junkdealers, and petty tradesmen pyramided tiny accumulations of capital into successful clothing manufacturing, real estate, and mercantile enterprises. Most of the first generation East Europeans, however, never climbed beyond the wage worker level. The better educated immigrants escaped the sweatshops as real estate, insurance, and Singer sewing machine agents, salesmen, clerks, and teachers. On the whole, however, the East Europeans needed two generations to achieve what the German Jews had accomplished in one.

The most dynamic force to emerge from the sordid conditions under which the East Siders lived and worked was the Jewish labor movement that began with an outburst of "righteous discontent on the tenement-sweatshop frontier" in the early 1880s. From "the corner of pain and anguish," as Morris Rosenfeld, the ghetto's Yiddish poet laureate, called it, came first laments, then protests, and finally unions.

Individual Jews had participated in the New York tailors' strikes in the 1850s. German-Jewish capmakers joined German and Irish girls in the 1873-74 strike against German and Polish-Jewish manufacturers. German, Hungarian, and Galician Jews and the first Russian Jews employed in clothing factories in 1870 helped form Knights of Labor locals in New York. Many of the 2,000 Jews employed in the Keeny Bros. factory took part in the cigarmakers strike of 1877-78, led by Adolph Strasser, a Hungarian Jew. His chief lieutenants in the International Cigarmakers Union were Ludwig Yablonovsky, a Polish Jew, and Samuel Gompers, an English Jew, who was 13 when he came to New York in 1863. A full-fledged union member at 14, Gompers was one of the founders and first president of the American Federation of Labor in 1881. Except for one year, he headed the AFL continuously until his death in 1924.

The Jewish labor movement originated in the Yiddish section of the Socialist Labor party, formed in 1882. Failure of the first spontaneous strikes against the degradation of the sweatshop demonstrated that the party's Russian-speaking intellectuals could make no headway with the Yiddish-speaking masses. Ab Cahan made the first Socialist speech in Yiddish in August, 1882, in a hall behind a German saloon. He also printed the first Yiddish Socialist handbills to recruit party members.

The first Jewish labor organization was formed in 1885 through an alliance of the Socialist Labor party's Russian and Yiddish sections with some Jewish leaders of German-dominated unions. Known as the Jewish Workingmen's Association, it started an "anti-sweating league" and founded 14 different unions in the garment trades and among other workers. It published the first Yiddish leaflet demanding the eight-hour day, sponsored East Side clubs in support of Henry George's mayoralty campaign in 1886, and launched the *Yiddish Folkszeitung*, the first durable Yiddish labor weekly. The Association disbanded in 1887 and its feeble unions disintegrated in the wake of the antilabor hysteria generated by the Haymarket Riot of 1886 in Chicago.

The remnants of the Socialist Labor party's Yiddish section became the nucleus of the United Hebrew Trades, established in 1888 as a federation of Yiddish-speaking locals of the United German Trades and of new unions in trades and industries where Jewish workers predominated. In 1890, when the United Hebrew Trades took part in the first May Day parade in the United States, its 40 affiliates included unions of Jewish clothing workers, actors, musicians, bank clerks, writers, bakers, seltzer bottlers, painters, bookbinders, printers, grave-diggers, chorus girls, and ragpickers. There were also independent unions of Jewish newsboys and bootblacks.

Despite some minor but short-lived strike victories, many of the unions melted away during the depression of 1893. Their early failures were also due to the union's involvement in the efforts of Daniel de Leon (a Jew of Marrano ancestry), who was head of the Socialist Labor party, to capture the

Knights of Labor and the American Federation of Labor. When de Leon ordered members of the Jewish unions to quit the older labor federations and join his separatist Socialist Labor Alliance, the Jewish unions gradually withered. The militant atheism of de Leon's chief Jewish associates, who staged Yom Kippur demonstrations in front of East Side synagogues, undermined the party's influence among the Orthodox masses.

When de Leon's party split in 1899, most of the Jewish Socialists, led by Morris Hillquit, Morris Winchevsky, Meyer London, Louis Miller, Isaac Hourwich, and Ab Cahan, shifted their support to Eugene V. Debs' new Socialist party. This same group founded the *Jewish Daily Forward* in 1897, and in 1900 the Workmen's Circle, a workers' insurance-fraternal order. With the United Hebrew Trades this trio became a principal factor in the rise of the Jewish labor movement. The plight of the exploited East Side workers had aroused wide public sympathy, but it was the victims themselves who broke the sweatshop system by forming stable and powerful unions "born of despair, with poverty as the midwife."

The International Ladies Garment Workers Union was founded in 1900, followed by the Capmakers Union in 1901, the Fur Workers Union in 1904, and the Amalgamated Clothing Workers Union in 1914. The mass strikes of 1909-1914, known as "the great revolt," and the 1911 Triangle Shirtwaist factory fire that took the lives of 143 girls, were the great turning points in the history of the Jewish workers.

The first general strike in the needle trades began November 22, 1909 when 20,000 Jewish factory girls, makers of blouses and skirts, walked out. The city hummed Charles Harris' tune, "Heaven Will Protect the Working Girl," as upper and middle-class women joined the picket lines after strikers were routed by mounted police. The following year the entire garment industry was paralyzed by the city's biggest strike when 60,000 cloakmakers downed their tools. Dismayed by the bitterness of the struggle between Jewish workers and Jewish employers and by the use of Jewish thugs to assault strikers, the uptown Jewish community helped bring about a settlement. Louis Marshall and Jacob H. Schiff enlisted the aid of Louis D. Brandeis who came down from Boston to serve as chairman of the mediation board which drafted "the protocol of peace."

A milestone in the history of industrial relations, the settlement sounded the death knell of the sweatshop by abolishing homework and inside contractors' shops. It also gave the workers shorter hours, higher wages, decent working conditions, and set a precedent for peaceful resolution of labor conflicts in other industries by creating permanent arbitration machinery.

The great outcry of sympathy and protest that followed the Triangle fire brought state legislation that provided for factory fire prevention and building inspection, sanitary working conditions, workmen's compensation and liability insurance, and shortened hours of labor for women and children.

Strike gains and legislative reforms solidified the Jewish unions behind leaders who modified the militant radicalism of their predecessors into industrial democracy and moved the Jewish workers into the mainstream of the American Labor movement. Abraham Rosenberg, Benjamin Schlesinger, Max Pine, Rose Schneiderman, Abraham Shiplacoff, Joseph Schlossberg, Max Zaritsky, and Morris Sigman, principal architects of the 1909-1920 needle trades strikes, anticipated the trailblazing union practices that became part of the social welfare revolution of the 1930s.

Under the later leadership of Sidney Hillman, David Dubinsky, and Jacob Potofsky, the needle trades pioneered the 40-hour, five-day week, paid vacations, unemployment and health insurance, retirement pensions, workers medical care, education and recreation, and cooperative and low-rent housing. The garment workers also raised a generation of trained labor organizers, economic analysts, lawyers, and editors who played significant roles in developing new patterns of collective bargaining and labor-management partnership in all segments of industry. In the 30 years from 1942 to 1972, employers in the once foul sweatshop industry contributed more than one and a half billion dollars to 127 health, welfare, and union benefit funds.

The Jewish unions also had an important political influence in New York. As the backbone of the Socialist party, they elected Meyer London to Congress, seated several Socialists in the state legislature, and enabled Morris Hillquit to make a remarkable showing in the 1917 mayoralty election. Dubinsky, Hillman, Zaritsky, and Alex Rose were the prime movers in the organization of the American Labor party in the 1930s which rallied pro-Roosevelt but anti-Tammany Jewish workers behind the Democratic state ticket. When the Communists captured the American Labor party, the same leadership created the Liberal party, which became a major force in local and state elections. John L. Lewis found his strongest support among the Jewish leaders of the needle trades unions when he began organizing the CIO in the 1930s; they were equally prominent in the CIO-AFL merger. In 1976, the Amalgamated Clothing Workers Union of America merged with the Textile Workers Union of America under the name of the Amalgamated Clothing and Textile Workers Union. Three of the four top officers of the merged group were Jews.

Today, however, the Jewish trade union movement is nearing its end. Once an overwhelming majority of wage workers, the Jewish population of the city is now predominantly middle and upper middle class, despite the large pockets of Jewish poor and near-poor. Children and grandchildren of factory workers are now professionals, retailers, small manufacturers, civil service workers, executives, scientists, professors, editors, artists, entertainers, and school teachers. About half of the city's school teachers are the offspring of garment workers from whom they imbibed trade union tradition. This accounts for the fact that half the leadership of the United Federation of Teachers is Jewish, with Albert Shanker as its best known leader. Barred from banking, insurance, and other major areas of white collar employment in the 1930s and 1940s, the children and grandchildren of the immigrants from Eastern Europe at the turn of the century went into teaching and civil service positions. Recruited just before and during World War II, these public employees now find themselves threatened by affirmative action programs that discriminate against whites.

The garment center, once almost entirely Jewish and Italian in its workers and ownership, now employs mostly blacks, Puerto Ricans, Greeks, Chinese, and Italians. The Jews are a vanishing minority in the needle trades because as older Jewish garment workers retire or die, they are almost always replaced by non-Jews. Highly skilled Jewish and Italian workers have largely left the industry and have been replaced increasingly by semiskilled blacks and Puerto Ricans, as the industry becomes more mechanized. Jews are still a major factor in the ownership of women's clothing firms and in union leadership. But here too change is under way. There are fewer sons taking over from Jewish fathers in the business. Many garment firms are now part of conglomerates. The man elected president of the International Ladies Garment Workers Union in 1975 predicted that he would probably be the last Jew named to that post. Similar ethnic change is under way in the character of the once all-Jewish fur industry. In both industries Jewish workers account for only a tiny fraction of the total. The ILGWU's Yiddish paper, *Gerechtigkeit*, was discontinued as far back as 1957. The United Hebrew Trades still exists but its unions have mostly non-Jewish workers.

The East European Jews were "one generation proletarians, in most cases neither sons nor fathers of workers" who looked to self-employment or education as the escape route from the wage worker class. The majority of them hailed from communities where tailors, shoemakers, bakers, and other artisans were on the lowest rung of the social and communal ladder. Because they considered such occupations a humiliation, they and their children slaved and saved to achieve something better.

Only the steady influx of large numbers of immigrants before 1924 blurred the fact that the East Europeans and their children had always been "graduating out" of the clothing factories and other working class jobs. From the working class they moved into the lower middle-class occupations, retail trade, and the bottom rungs of the professions and white collar employment and then gradually climbed upward into manufacturing, wholesaling, real estate, building construction, and the communication and mass entertainment fields.

The heavy representation of East European Jews in insurance brokerage began when the big insurance companies hired clothing workers as agents in the tenements and factories, where business was transacted in Yiddish. Billposters, ushers, bookkeepers, and booking agents employed in the Yiddish theatre did well in the budding movie industry. Immigrants who had scooped up junk in backyards and alleys accumulated enough capital to become speculative builders. Coal, wood, and kerosene dealers with a one-horse-and-wagon trade expanded into fuel distribution and subway construction. Marcus Loew and Adolph Zukor, a couple of ex-furriers, fashioned an empire of movie palaces and film production out of penny arcades. East Side newsboys, such as the late David Sarnoff of the Radio Corporation of America, and Samuel Newhouse, who owns the country's biggest newspaper chain, had a special penchant for success. Helena Rubenstein and Hattie Carnegie also started on the East Side.

Manhattan's skyline, which began to take form before World War I, reflected, to a considerable extent, the enterprise and daring of former East Siders who learned the construction business by erecting apartment houses and two-family dwellings in Brooklyn and The Bronx. The Jewish builders who dominated the medium-priced apartment building field beginning in the 1920s erected what sociologist Marshall Sklare dubbed "Jewish avenues" along Eastern Parkway and Ocean Parkway in Brooklyn, Grand Concourse in The Bronx, and later on Queens Boulevard in Queens. These were apartments erected by Jews largely for Jews. Louis Horowitz, who came here from Poland at 13, covered Manhattan with $600,000,000 worth of new skyscrapers, including the Woolworth, Chrysler, and Paramount Theatre buildings, and the Waldorf-Astoria Hotel. A. E. Lefcourt, a one-time newsboy, was the prime mover in the relocation of the garment industry north of 34th Street and south of 42nd Street in the 1930s and 1940s. By 1929, Lefcourt, Paul Singer, Henry and Irwin Chanin, Abraham Bricken, George Backer, and Henry Mandel were raising new skyscrapers on Fifth, Madison, Lexington, and Seventh Avenues, and on the side streets where the garment center was growing. The late Abraham Eli Kazan, who grew up on the East Side, helped rebuild its tenements with the first union-backed cooperatives, and pioneered in building middle-income cooperatives such as Co-Op City in The Bronx, Rochdale Village in Queens, and Penn Station South in Manhattan.

A new generation of Jewish builders led the way in the residential and office building boom which altered the face of Manhattan in the 1960s and 1970s, and changed the life of many of the suburbs. William Zeckendorf, responsible for some of the city's biggest private housing projects, assembled the land on which the United Nations buildings were erected. The 18,000 single-family houses built by William J. Levitt between 1947 and 1951 on 4,000 acres of former Long Island potato land grew into the bustling community of Levittown. Samuel J. Lefrak and Marvin Kratter erected many of the huge residential developments in upper Manhattan, Queens, and Brooklyn. Lefrak built Lefrak City in Queens. The Tishman brothers led off the building transformation on Park Avenue. The Uris brothers were the city's leading builders of office skyscrapers, accounting for 13 percent of all those erected in Manhattan since World War II. The 59-story $100,000,000 Pan Am Building is a monument to the late Erwin Wolfson. The Weilers, Fisher brothers, Minskoffs, Richard Ravitch, Saul Horowitz, Jr., and Sol Atlas were other creators of the new city skyline.

The city's biggest industry, the $7 billion women's ready-to-wear trade, is in a sense a monument to the vanishing Jewish needle trades worker. Seventh Avenue, a generic name for the garment center, is the home of the city's women's and children's apparel industry employing 175,000 people. In the enclave between 35th and 40th Streets, and 6th and 9th Avenues, are designed and produced three out of every four women's dresses, coats, suits, children's garments, and women's sportswear made in the United States. The industry is the city's largest private employer. Many of the manufacturers are sons or grandsons of former union members and organizers who now deal with the unions their ancestors founded. On the streets south and the avenues east of the garment center, other Jewish entrepreneurs dominate the processing of the garment industry's raw materials and the manufacture of millinery, textiles, hosiery, furs, leather goods, underwear, and costume jewelry.

The *shmata* (Yiddish for rag) business, as it is jokingly called, has stimulated folklore and fiction that reflects its Yiddish-speaking origin. Plays and novels such as "The Fifth Season," "Seidman and Son," "I Can Get It For You Wholesale," and "Enter Laughing" depicted the industry's impact on Jewish life, the intergeneration squabbles to which it gave rise, and its mordant humor and bitter competitiveness.

Making clothes and setting dress styles for half the nation at prices within reach of all, the garment industry's verve and enterprise are credited with strengthening American democracy by "eliminating differences in dress that were once a mark of class distinction."

Linked to the garment center through retailing and merchandising are some of the liveliest Jewish contributions to the city—the great department stores in the city proper and in the suburbs, the women's speciality shops, and the discount stores. R. H. Macy's, Gimbels, Bloomingdale's, Lord & Taylor, Saks Fifth Avenue, B. Altman, Franklin Simon, Ohrbach's, and Abraham & Straus are shoppers' paradises. Saks Fifth Avenue and Bergdorf Goodman are landmarks among the high-fashion shops, as are the salons of the leading custom designers—Hattie Carnegie, Molly Parnis, and the late Tobe Coller Davis. Lane Bryant, who made maternity clothes big business and stylish, got its name from an error in Lena Bryant's first bank deposit slip.

Gene Ferkauf, whose name in Yiddish means "to sell," fathered the E. J. Korvette discount stores, which began a merchandising revolution. Bargain-hunters thronged to S. Klein, on Union Square, and its suburban branches, until they went out of business, as they do to the neighborhood department stores of the Alexander's, Gertz, and the May chains in Brooklyn, The Bronx, Queens, and the suburbs. Among the success stories of the post-World War II immigration is that of Stephen Klein, who started the Barton's chain of candy shops which are closed on Friday at sundown and remain shut on Saturday and Jewish holy days.

Creators of the City
Inextricably woven into the entire tapestry of New York's history, Jews have had a large hand in shaping the city's civic, cultural, and professional life and in coloring its liberal, social, and political outlook. In every generation they were distinguished for community responsibility, a passion for social and political reform, a zest for culture, and a gift for expressing the city's uniqueness in word, song, and art.

1. *In the People's Service*
The liberal political bent of Jewish voters in New York goes back to the days when Thomas Jefferson coalesced the opponents of the domestic and foreign policies of the Federalist party into a new political alignment. Samson Simson, first Jewish member of the New York Bar, was among the founders and a vice-president of the Jeffersonian Democratic party in 1795. He and Naphtali Judah were early members of the Society of St. Tammany (Tammany Hall), which began as a social group supporting Jefferson. In 1798, the Reverend Gershom Mendes Seixas, first native-born minister of Shearith Israel, preached a sermon sharply at variance with the views of the other clergy who supported the Federalists in their denunciations of the republican regime in France. Mordecai Myers took an active part in helping the Democratic-Republicans win a state election in 1800 that paved the way for Jefferson's presidential victory in the fall.

Mordecai M. Noah, friend and political ally of Presidents Andrew Jackson, Martin Van Buren, and William Harrison, was grand sachem of Tammany in 1820 and the Jewish community's spokesman for more than 40 years. When he was appointed sheriff of New York County in 1822 there were protests against the likelihood that a Jew might have to execute Christians. "Pretty Christians that they should require hanging at anyone's hands," was his retort. Noah's successor in the Tammany hierarchy was Emanuel Hart, a sachem for half a century, who was elected to Congress in 1851. Jonas N. Phillips, president of the City Council in 1857, was acting-mayor for a time.

Because they opposed slavery, many of the native-born and most of the immigrant Jews quit the Democrats in the 1850s to join the new Republican party. In local elections, however, most of the immigrant generation stayed with the Democrats, who were more friendly to immigrants, until the Tweed Ring scandals of 1871.

Jonathan Nathan was one of the founders of the Republican party in New York and J. Solis Ritterband was the first president of the New York Young Men's Republican Club. Sigismund Kaufmann and Dr. Joseph Goldmark, refugees from the 1848 revolutions in Europe, were among the organizers of the Republican party in Brooklyn. In 1856 Kaufman campaigned for John Fremont, first Republican presidential candidate. J. Dittenhoefer was a Lincoln presidential elector in 1860 and 1864. Kaufmann, a Lincoln elector in 1864, was a power in Republican circles because of his

NEW YORK CITY — 74

influence with the German immigrants. This earned him the Republican nomination for lieutenant governor in 1870. Joseph and Jesse Seligman, who declined all municipal and national offices, were among the sponsors of the pro-Lincoln rally at Cooper Union that paved the way for Lincoln's nomination in 1860.

Although there were many prominent Jews in the Democratic party at the time of the Tweed Ring exposures, most of them were associated with the reform group of the party. Joseph Seligman and Joseph Blumenthal served on the Committee of 70 that exposed the Tweed machine, and Simon Sterne was the committee's secretary. Samuel A. Lewis and Adolph Sanger were elected president of the Board of Aldermen as anti-Tammany Democrats in 1874 and 1885, respectively. Sanger was acting-mayor when the Statue of Liberty was accepted by the city in 1886. Anti-Tammanyite Theodore Myers was elected city controller in 1887, and reelected in 1891 as the Democratic and Republican nominee. Oscar S. Straus was secretary of the committee of Democratic reformers that returned William R. Grace as anti-Tammany mayor in 1884. Albert C. Cardozo, the first Jew elected to the State Supreme Court, resigned in 1872 to escape impeachment when he was implicated with the Tweed Ring.

Like other newcomers to the city, the immigrant Jews at first accepted the help of Tammany and gave it their support. Anti-Tammany reformers were regarded as alien uptowners, but Yiddish-speaking saloonkeepers allied with Tammany had the influence needed to do petty favors for those strange to American ways. Petty Jewish politicians could be counted on to provide food baskets, jobs for breadwinners, and help for youngsters in trouble and for peddlers entangled with the law.

De Ate, as the immigrants called the 8th Assembly District, became a Tammany stronghold after 1892 when its Republican assemblyman, "Silver Dollar" Smith, a Jewish saloonkeeper, switched to the Democrats in protest against immigration curbs enacted by a Republican Congress. In the Tammany-controlled wards where the Jewish immigrants were the balance of power, Democrats and Republicans sought Jewish votes by picking Jewish candidates. Henry Goldfogle, Tammany's East Side spokesman for many years, was elected to Congress by the Democrats in 1900, the first Jew from the East Side so honored. The following year Tammany made Jacob Cantor president of the Borough of Manhattan, the first of seven Jews to hold this post, and named Aaron J. Levy as Democratic leader of the State Assembly. The Republicans elevated Otto Rosalsky and Gustav Hartman to the bench, and in 1908 elected Samuel Koenig Secretary of State and New York County chairman. Edward Lauterbach had filled the same office in the 1890s.

As they acquired political sophistication, the Yiddish-speaking masses joined other elements of the Jewish community in supporting political reform movements, regardless of party. The Citizen's Union had a number of Jews among its founders when it was formed in 1897 to war on Tammany corruption. During the 1901 fusion campaign, when the cleanup of East Side graft and rackets was a major goal, William Travers Jerome, anti-Tammany candidate for district attorney, deluged the ghetto neighborhoods with Yiddish circulars and a Yiddish newspaper. Uptown Jewish notables joined forces with sweatshop workers and synagogue leaders to elect Seth Low, president of Columbia University, as fusion mayor. In Low's reelection campaign wealthy uptown Jews and Christians invested a small fortune in an East Side Yiddish daily in a vain attempt to reelect Low. William Randolph Hearst, a champion of the oppressed Jews of Russia, carried the East Side in his unsuccessful race for mayor as an anti-Tammany candidate, and again in his losing the race for governor in 1906. In both elections he employed Yiddish inserts in his newspapers to win Jewish votes.

The fact that no Jew was elected mayor of the city until 1973 despite the large number of Jewish voters, indicated that they usually supported a non-Jewish liberal in preference to a Jewish conservative. A Jew was first nominated for mayor in 1892, when Edwin Einstein, who had served in Congress, was the defeated Republican candidate. Eight years earlier Tammany had tried to clean its house by nominating for mayor the popular philanthropist, Nathan Straus, but he refused to run. Jonah J. Goldstein, a lifelong Democrat, was the losing Republican nominee in 1945. Rudolph Halley and Harold Riegelman, Liberal and Republican standard-bearers, respectively, lost to Robert F. Wagner in 1953 for the office of mayor. The latter defeated a prominent Jew, State Controller Arthur Levitt, in the 1961 Democratic primary, and then defeated State Attorney General Louis Lefkowitz in the election. In 1965, Abraham Beame, the Democrat, was beaten by John Lindsay, the Republican, in a three-man race in which many Jews among the Reform Democrats voted for Lindsay on the Liberal Party line, while many Catholic Democrats voted for the independent candidate, a Catholic. In 1969 Beame was elected City Controller and four years later he became the first Jewish mayor of the world's largest Jewish-populated city.

Until the Socialist party became a major political force on the East Side, its Jewish masses usually voted Democratic locally, divided in state contests, and were partial to Republican candidates for president. Theodore Roosevelt was their particular favorite. As police commissioner, he had assigned a company of Jewish policemen to protect a notorious European anti-Semite during his visit to the city. As President, he fought immigration curbs, intervened with Romania against its anti-Semitic policies, and protested against Russian pogroms. His appointment of Oscar S. Straus, a former ambassador to Turkey and later a judge of the Permanent Court of Arbitration at The Hague, as Secretary of Labor on the eve of the 1906 gubernatorial election probably cost William Randolph Hearst the governorship.

The Straus appointment was an event of great import to all Jews because no Jew had previously sat in the Cabinet, and the immigrant generation swelled with pride at the honor to the son of a pack peddler. William Howard Taft campaigned for president on the East Side before a huge Jewish audience in 1908. In the 1912 gubernatorial election the East Side faced a dilemma. Roosevelt's Progressive party had named Oscar Straus to oppose Tammany's William Sulzer, a non-Jewish Congressman from the East Side who, as chairman of the House Foreign Affairs Committee, led the fight for the abrogation of the Russo-American treaty of commerce. Although Straus lost, he won over Sulzer in the Jewish districts and ran ahead of Roosevelt, the party's presidential candidate, throughout the state.

Sweatshop exploitation that turned many immigrants to socialism, made the Socialist party the strongest on the East Side by 1910. The party's political titans were Morris Hillquit and Meyer London. Both repeatedly scared the Democrats with strong runs for the legislature and Congress before London was elected to the House in 1910. Thereafter the Republicans put up a single Jewish candidate against him, beating him twice. He was reelected in 1916 and 1920 despite bitter opposition from uptown Jews and many downtowners who attacked him as an atheist and an anti-Zionist. Backed by the Jewish unions in 1917, Hillquit made a remarkable showing as an antiwar candidate for mayor in a three-way race during which the most prominent Jewish leaders warned Jewish voters against him.

In 1912 William Howard Taft said that Jews "make the best Republicans," and 40 years later Adlai Stevenson said they make the best Democrats. Each was right, in his own day. Despite their changed economic status, New York's Jewish voters returned to the Democratic party after 1920 because of the liberal social legislation fathered by Alfred E. Smith and Robert F. Wagner, Sr. The progressive program of Governor Franklin D. Roosevelt strengthened the Democrats' hold on the liberal and international-minded Jewish electorate whose socialist residue settled in the New Deal, Fair Deal, and the Liberal Party.

Smith's closest advisors were Mrs. Belle Moskowitz and Joseph Proskauer, who had met Smith while doing settlement house work on the East Side. Proskauer managed Smith's first three gubernatorial campaigns and joined with him in founding the anti-New Deal American Liberty League when Smith broke with Roosevelt. Key figures in the state Democratic party in the 1920s were Henry Morgenthau, Sr. and Bernard M. Baruch, who had helped elect Woodrow Wilson, Max D. Steuer, Samuel Untermyer, Nathan Burkan, and Herbert H. Lehman. Together with Jesse Straus, later ambassador to France, and Laurence Steinhardt, a future ambassador to Russia and Canada, they raised the money that helped James J. Farley line up the delegates for Roosevelt's victory in the 1932 presidential nomination. Baruch, head of the War Industries Board in World War I, held key posts in World War II, and developed America's first position paper on control of the atomic bomb.

When Roosevelt agreed to run for governor in 1928, he insisted on Herbert H. Lehman as the candidate for lieutenant-governor. Lehman had been active in the Democratic party but was better known as a banker and a leader of the Jewish community. Roosevelt's opponent was Albert Ottinger, son of a German-Jewish immigrant, who had twice been elected attorney general in the face of Democratic sweeps. Rabbi Stephen S. Wise's opposition to Ottinger is said to have been a decisive factor in Roosevelt's narrow victory. In this campaign Samuel L. Roseman plied Roosevelt with facts and figures and then became the governor's speech writer and counsel before moving on to Washington as head of the White House "brain trust."

Dr. Wise was a potent force for political reform, although he never held office. A long-time foe of Tammany, in 1930 Wise and Dr. John Haynes Holmes were the prime movers in the action that led to the resignation of Mayor Jimmy Walker. Wise and Holmes teamed up again to back the fusion campaign of 1933 that elected the Yiddish-speaking Fiorello LaGuardia mayor, and Bernard S. Deutsch, president of the City Council. LaGuardia, raised as a Protestant, was, through his mother, a Jew, related to Luigi Luzzatti, Italy's first Jewish prime minister.

In 1932, Lehman succeeded Roosevelt as governor, the first Jew to hold this office in New York. One of the best and most popular chief executives in the state's history, his "little New Deal" put New York in the vanguard of progressive social legislation. Reelected four times, he resigned in 1942 to become the first director of the United Nations Relief and Rehabilitation Administration in war-torn Europe. In 1949 he was elected to the United States Senate where he led the fight for civil rights and sparked the move to condemn Senator Joseph McCarthy. Long actively identified with major Jewish causes, he returned to the sidewalks of New York when he was past 80 to join Eleanor Roosevelt in a successful battle to reform the city's Democratic party. His death in 1963, the day before he was to receive the Medal of Freedom in a White House ceremony, evoked nationwide regret. His funeral was attended by President Lyndon B. Johnson.

Robert Morgenthau, son of the late Secretary of the Treasury Henry Morgenthau, Jr., who was elected District Attorney of New York in 1973, and former Supreme Court Justice Arthur J. Goldberg, were the defeated Democratic candidates for governor in 1968 and 1970, respectively. Robert Moses was the defeated Republican candidate for governor in the 1930s.

When Jacob K. Javits, a liberal Republican, won the Senate seat vacated by Lehman in 1956, he defeated Mayor Wagner in a tight race. Overwhelmingly reelected in 1962, 1968, and 1974, Javits was the first Republican to carry New York City in a statewide campaign. A product of the East Side where his father was a janitor who did petty favors for Tammany, Javits became a Republican because he was outraged by Tammany venality. A popular member of Congress from 1946-1954, Javits gave up his House seat in 1954 when he won an upset victory over Franklin D. Roosevelt, Jr., in the campaign for State Attorney General.

Most Jews prominent in Republican affairs were also aligned with the party's liberal wing. Among these were former Attorney General Nathaniel Goldstein, Manhattan Surrogate George Frankenthaler, the late Stanley

Isaacs, long the only Republican on the City Council, and Judge Caroline Simon, the first woman nominated for citywide office when she ran for president of the City Council. She later served as New York's Secretary of State. Although Jews have been important factors in the Tammany wing of the Democratic party (two Jews headed Tammany Hall), they have been even more prominent in good government and political reform movements in the Democratic party. Among the founders of the Liberal party, which has been allied in most elections with the Reform Democrats, is Alex Rose, a prominent labor union leader, who remains a force in his party's political deals and endorsements. Sanford Garelik, former chief inspector of the Police Department, was elected president of the City Council in 1969 on the Liberal party ticket.

All boroughs of the city except Staten Island have had at least one Jewish borough president. Manhattan Borough Presidents included Jacob Cantor, Marcus Marks, Hugo Rogers, Julius Miller, Stanley Isaacs, Edgar J. Nathan, Jr., and Samuel Levy. Abe Stark was Borough President of Brooklyn and Sidney Leviss was the first Jewish Borough President of Queens. In 1975, Donald Manes and Robert Abrams were serving their second terms as Borough Presidents of Queens and The Bronx, respectively.

While 85 percent of the city's Jewish voters are registered Democrats, they no longer automatically vote for any Democrat or even for a liberal of any party. The first sign of a more conservative vote occurred in 1966 when 55 percent of the Jews voted against the creation of a civilian review board to check on actions of the police. Jews also voted heavily for the conservative Democratic mayoralty candidate in 1969. In the 1972 presidential election there was a 17 percent drop in the Jewish vote for the Democratic candidate, George McGovern, against President Richard Nixon. In New York City, Jewish voters are regularly wooed by politicians of all parties. Mayor John Lindsay was the first mayor to have a full-time Jewish expert attached to his staff. Lindsay also broke precedent by having a sukkah erected on public property for a reception honoring Prime Minister Golda Meir. The Jewish swing to the right was a reaction to an assault on Jewish interests and on Israel by the New Left and by some black militants. Although Jews are now less than one-fourth of the total population, they represent 32 percent of all voters. This is due to the fact that Jews register to vote and actually vote more consistently than other citizens. The polls often find that a large proportion of voters reporting themselves undecided is highest in predominantly Jewish neighborhoods. The Jewish vote "is the ballgame," as one candidate noted. In recent years the Chasidic rabbis have developed considerable political clout in local elections.

2. *In Pursuit of Learning*

The impact of Jews on education and the cultural arts in New York has been compared to "a sort of cosmopolitan galvanic battery" that is always charging up an intellectual ferment.

The fruitful association with learning dates from 1787 when the Reverend Gershom Mendes Seixas, the community's religious leader, was elected a trustee of King's College (Columbia College). One of the 168 citizens who launched New York University in 1831 was Mordecai M. Noah. Annie Nathan Meyer founded Barnard College. The Ethical Cultural movement with its progressive schools was created by Dr. Felix Adler, son of a rabbi, when he broke with organized Judaism in the 1870s. The science of anthropology received its greatest impetus in the United States from Dr. Franz Boas, geographer and explorer, who taught many of the early American specialists in that field at Columbia University.

Dr. Joel Hart was one of the founders of the New York County Medical Society in 1806. In the 1830s, Dr. Daniel L. M. Peixotto edited the *New York Medical and Physical Journal*, and Dr. Isaac Nordheimer taught medicine at New York University. Dr. Abraham Jacobi, one of the first attending physicians at Mt. Sinai Hospital, had a profound influence on the development of pediatrics. Dr. Simon Baruch, father of Bernard M. Baruch, was a pioneer in hydropathic medicine and the earliest exponent of physical medicine. The city's leading 19th century opthalmologist was Dr. Emil Gruening, father of Ernest Gruening, Alaska's first United States Senator.

Although the struggle for an economic foothold and the conflict with rebellious children tarnished the dream of "the goldene medina" (the golden land) for many first generation East Europeans, they took full advantage of every opportunity for the educational advancement of the second generation. As soon as they learned English, East Side youngsters crowded the public elementary schools, the public libraries, and the free lectures of Cooper Union's People's Institute. They did amazingly well in high school and college. An 1889 report noted that for the previous ten years each graduating class at City College had contained 25 percent Jews. One out of five graduates of the New York Normal College for Teachers in 1889 was a Jewish girl. By 1900 children of immigrants were a majority in the city's free institutions of higher learning. A 1907 study of the secondary schools was "struck with the large percentage of Jewish scholars and their relatively high rank."

City College was long known as "the Jewish college of America." From 1900 on Jews heavily outnumbered non-Jews in its student body. Jews once accounted for 95 percent of its student body and its alumni roster reads like a roll call of the country's leading figures in law, business, art, science, literature, and philosophy. In the 1970s the Jewish enrollment dropped to about 40 percent when scholastic standards, once on a par with those at Harvard, plummeted with the inauguration of an open admissions policy for minorities. From Bernard M. Baruch and David B. Steinman, builder of bridges, to Jonas Salk, developer of the anti-polio vaccine, Arthur Kornberg, Nobel Prize winner, and Mayor Abe Beame, the achievements of Jewish New Yorkers who began their higher education at City College are written large in the history of the 20th century.

Henry Leipziger, father of the city's public adult education program, was once acting president of City College, and Moses J. Stroock headed its board of trustees. The first Jewish president of an American college (not under Jewish auspices), was Dr. Paul Klapper, for many years the dean of City College's School of Education. An immigrant from Romania, Klapper became president of Queens College when City College's Queens branch achieved independent status. In the 1970s, Robert E. Marshak was president of City College, and Jews held the number two administrative posts at Columbia University and New York University. A number of the presidents of colleges in the City University of New York system were also Jews.

Perhaps the two most distinguished immigrant alumni of City College were former Supreme Court Justice Felix Frankfurter, who was born in Austria, and Russian-born Professor Morris Raphael Cohen, one of the few original philosophers America has produced. A legal prodigy, and one of the few Jewish law school graduates engaged as a clerk in a major New York law office before World War I, Frankfurter was dean of the Harvard Law School and mentor of a host of public figures before being appointed to the Supreme Court. Cohen, who went hungry as an East Side teenager in order to rent books, read Gibson's *Decline and Fall of the Roman Empire* while working in a pool hall. A student of William James and Josiah Royce at Harvard, Cohen was head of City College's philosophy department for a generation. Brilliant teacher, liberal crusader, and Socratic gadfly, he was one of the most popular and influential of contemporary American thinkers.

Working in sweatshops by day and attending professional schools at night, the East Side Jews turned in great numbers to medicine, dentistry, pharmacy, law, and teaching. Out of the immigrants' ambition for professional careers for their children came the now familiar boast, "my son the doctor" and "my son the lawyer."

Immigrants and their children contributed greatly to early medical research at Mount Sinai and Montefiore Hospitals and made pioneering discoveries. Joseph Goldberger found the cause of pellagra. Drs. Phoebus Levine and Samuel J. Meltzer were part of the original six-man staff of the Rockefeller Institute, opened in 1910. Selman Waksman won the Nobel Prize for isolating streptomycin, and Isidor Rabi received the same honor for his accomplishments in nuclear physics. Dr. Sigismund S. Goldwater, who served as New York's commissioner of health and hospitals, fathered the medical administration profession when he became superintendent of Mt. Sinai in 1904. Many of the first East Side physicians practiced group medicine as lodge doctors, caring for *landsmanschaften* members, and establishing new facilities for Yiddish-speaking patients who refused to go to Bellevue or Blackwell's Island where they would be wardmates of alcoholics. The first new medical school established in New York State in a generation was the Albert Einstein College of Medicine, sponsored by Yeshiva University, which is the oldest liberal arts college under Jewish auspices. Mount Sinai

Hospital also established a medical school in the 1970s. Yeshiva University opened the Benjamin Cardozo Law School and a new and small Jewish college known as Touro College, has announced plans for a law school.

The campuses of New York's public and private colleges and universities as well as the Jewish institutions of higher learning and research are studded with graphic reminders of the generosity of sons and grandsons of Jewish immigrants. The Guggenheim School of Aeronautics at New York University, Bronx campus (now Bronx Community College); Columbia University's School of Mines, a gift of Adolph Lewisohn; Benjamin Javits Hall at Fordham University's Law School; the Loeb Student Center at New York University; and City College's Aaron Davis Hall for Performing Arts, are but a few examples of this generosity.

The New School for Social Research was expanded in the 1930s by Jewish philanthropists to provide academic posts for noted refugee professors from Nazi Europe. Its graduate faculty was known as "the University in Exile." The original endowment fund of $500,000 for Long Island University came from Nathan Jonas, first chairman of the university's board and a founder of Brooklyn College. William Zeckendorf, board chairman in the 1960s, spurred Long Island University's postwar expansion.

3. *The Cultural Ferment*

Eagerness to use talents pent up by centuries of oppression also galvanized and stimulated American culture. The role of Jews in the New York world of the theatre, music, literature, art, and mass entertainment has been described as "sometimes strident, generally exciting and often original and profound."

In 1859 a New York newspaper said that "if any segment of the population makes extensive sacrifices on behalf of newspapers, the theatre and scholarly and artistic efforts, it is first and foremost, among all immigrants, the New York Jews." This referred to the cultural interests of the German Jews, but the older families had set the precedent.

One of the most prominent artists of 18th century New York was Myer Myers, a leading silversmith, whose work is still preserved in museums. Two of the city's late 18th century bookdealers and publishers were Benjamin Gomez and Naphtali Judah. Mordecai M. Noah and Samuel B. H. Judah were successful playwrights in the 1830s and 1840s, and Henry B. Phillips was a popular actor.

The first permanent Italian opera company in the city was established in 1843 by Max Maritzek, who introduced 36 operas. Moritz Strakosch, who conducted for Maritzek, married Amelia Patti and discovered the vocal gift of her sister, Adelina. The New Orleans-born pianist, Louis Gottchalk, was the city's musical sensation between 1853 and 1863.

Leopold Damrosch and Oscar Hammerstein were the pioneers in establishing New York as the musical capital of the world. Damrosch, friend of Wagner and Liszt, came to New York in 1871 as Temple Emanu-El's musical director. In 1873 he founded the Arion Society, predecessor of the New York Philharmonic Society, and later became conductor of the newly-opened Metropolitan Opera House. The Metropolitan's first impresario was Heinrich Conried, a leader of the New York Germania Theatre, founded by Adolf Neundorf, Temple Emanu-El's musical director. Maurice Grau, Conried's successor, made the Metropolitan pay when he hired Damrosch. The latter introduced German opera because his backers did not know the difference between the more costly Italian stars and the lesser-known Germans. Damrosch's son and successor, Walter, persuaded Andrew Carnegie to build Carnegie Hall.

Oscar Hammerstein, grandfather of Oscar Hammerstein II, of Rodgers and Hammerstein fame, first introduced operas in English in his Harlem Opera House. Later he became the king of vaudeville with his celebrated Victoria Theatre and the huge Olympia Hall. When this combined music hall, theatre, and cabaret opened in 1895 on what was then Longacre Square, but is now known as Times Square, the area became the capital of show business. The profits from this venture were put into the new Manhattan Opera House and competed with the Metropolitan for four years. When he agreed to sell out to the Metropolitan, Otto H. Kahn became the chairman of the Metropolitan's board.

What Damrosch and Hammerstein were to the world of music Charles, Daniel, and Gustave Frohman, and David Belasco were to the theatre. The Frohmans produced over 700 plays and introduced some of the stage's greatest stars, while Belasco, the Frohmans' chief competitor, was both producer and playwright.

The East European Jews found their cultural outlet in the Yiddish theatre, organized in 1882 by Boris Thomashefsky, a choir singer in an East Side synagogue. The first production, Abraham Goldfaden's *Koldunya* (The Witch), was staged by an amateur troupe from London in an East 4th Street hall. Four years later he starred in a stock company that staged plays in Bowery Hall. By the turn of the century, he was the most popular actor, playwright, director, and producer in the Yiddish theatre, and the matinee idol of the sweatshop girls. Michael T. Thomas, the rising young orchestra conductor, is Thomashefsky's grandson.

Jacob P. Adler, who brought over the first company of experienced Yiddish actors in 1890, teamed up with playwright Jacob P. Gordin to usher in the most exciting epoch of Yiddish drama. In the heyday of the Yiddish theatre its greatest stars in addition to Adler and Thomashefsky were David Kessler, Bertha Kalish, Morris Moscovitch, Sigmund Mogilescu, Jennie Goldstein, Ludwig Satz, and Rudolph Schildkraut. Adler's children—Stella, Luther, Celia, Francis, and Julia—all began their acting careers in Yiddish plays.

Adler's Grand Theatre, opened in 1904 as the first built especially for Yiddish productions, and Thomashefsky's National Theatre, whose curtain went up in 1911, made Second Avenue the Yiddish Rialto. At the height of its popularity the Yiddish theatre filled four houses Monday through Thursday via a benefit system through which the *landsmanschaften* bought blocks of tickets. Some claim that the modern theatre party, backbone of Broadway hits, was invented by East Side Jews who seldom said they were going to theatre, but always to a benefit.

In its latter years the Yiddish theatre produced such Broadway and Hollywood stars as Molly Picon, Paul Muni, Edward G. Robinson, Joseph Schildkraut, Menashe Skulnik, Hershel Bernardi, and Maurice Schwartz. The latter's Yiddish Art Theatre began a new era of modern plays and productions in 1918. *Eli Eli*, composed by Jacob Sandler for a Thomashefsky Passover production, became the most moving Jewish melody. *Bei Meir Bist du Schoen*, was written by Sholom Secunda for a Yiddish musicale. He sold the song for thirty dollars and it earned millions for the buyers. Not until the copyright came up for renewal did he earn additional money.

The movies, to which the immigrants flocked, dealt the first body blow to the Yiddish stage from which it never recovered. The end of immigration heralded the doom of Yiddish drama. In 1928 there were 11 Yiddish theatres in New York. In the 1970s, there were three Yiddish theatrical companies enjoying a modest revival of interest with its productions housed in Broadway theatres.

Samuel Rothapfel, better known as Roxy, who built the now demolished Roxy Theatre in 1926, and Mitchell Mark, who opened the Strand in 1914 as "a Cathedral of motion pictures," were as much landmarks of the Great White Way as their theatres.

From the earliest days of radio and television in New York those media counted the Sarnoffs, Paleys, Flamms, and Strauses among their most enterprising leaders.

In the heyday of vaudeville and radio and in the early years of television, the most popular headliners were comedians and singers whose roots were on the East Side. Eddie Cantor, George Burns, the Marx Bros., the Ritz Bros., Jack Pearl, Phil Silvers, Sid Caesar, Milton Berle, Joey Bishop, Fannie Brice, Danny Kaye, and those adopted New Yorkers, Al Jolson, Ed Wynn, and Jack Benny, rose to the top without reliance on Jewish gags. Part of Coney Island's fame as the playground of the masses was attributable to the showmanship of Samuel Gumpertz, who has a permanent niche in show business history as the godfather of the sideshow, and more particularly the genuine freak. Unlike P. T. Barnum's frauds, Gumpertz scoured the world for genuine bizarre people.

The ethnic Jew of vaudeville, who disappeared with the "Dutch act" of Joe Weber and Lew Fields, children of the tenements, and the demise of the "Potash and Perlmutter" variety of humor, was replaced by *Abie's Irish Rose*, which charmed audiences in the 1920s. The daily life of the Goldbergs of The Bronx, as recounted by Gertrude Berg, occupied the regular attention of millions of Americans on radio for 25 years, and later on television. Comics like Sam Levenson, Jerry Lewis, Shelly Berman, Danny Kaye, Alan King,

Myron Cohen, and some of the "sickniks" found their humorous foils in the environment out of which they came.

The city's musical life has been enriched in special abundance by Jews. First of the East Side kids to put the spirit of America to music was Irving Berlin. Son of a synagogue cantor, Berlin was a Bowery saloon song plugger whose first tune earned him 37¢. His earliest songs were about immigrants—*Marie from Sunny Italy*, *Oh How That German Could Love*, and *Yiddishe Eyes*. *Alexander's Ragtime Band*, a musical landmark, set him on the road to fame in 1910. Millions of Americans marched off in World Wars I and II singing his *Oh, How I Hate to Get Up in the Morning* and *God Bless America*. The latter, which has become virtually a second national anthem, is one reason why Berlin's more than 1,000 folk tunes have been called "a continuous obbligato to American history."

George Gershwin had the same relationship to jazz and modern American music. The composer of *Porgy and Bess*, *Rhapsody in Blue*, and other notable works was a self-taught pianist whose first job was playing for rehearsals in a Second Avenue Yiddish theatre. Some of the biggest hits to come out of Tin Pan Alley were written by such East Side tunesmiths as Irving Caesar, Gus Kahn, Gerald Marks, Jack Yellen, Wolfie Gilbert, Ira Gershwin, Harold Arlen, Richard Rodgers, Oscar Hammerstein, II, and Burt Bacharach.

The Jewish musicians who began arriving from Russia in large numbers in the 1890s, after the expulsion of Jews from Russia's big cities, paved the way for a flock of Russian-born Jewish virtuosi and later for native-born artists of world-renown. For years the violin was synonymous with Jewish musicianship, as Berlin's 1908 tune, *Yiddle on Your Fiddle, Play Some Ragtime*, indicated. Jewish artists who made their debut in Carnegie Hall constitute a who's who of 20th century musicians. An early product of the Julliard School was Sophie Braslau, a contralto star at the Metropolitan from 1920-1934, whose father was an East Side doctor. Another was the Romanian-born Alma Gluck. Regina Reznik, Rosa Ponselle, Leonard Warren, Richard Tucker, Jan Peerce, and Robert Merrill were all raised on the East Side. Aaron Copland, one of America's great 20th century composers, grew up in Brownsville. Leonard Bernstein, the ex-Bostonian wunderkind, vitalized music in New York as composer, conductor of the New York Philharmonic, and musical director of the Metropolitan Opera. WASPS, however, still predominate in the control of the Metropolitan, whose board has only two or three Jews. But at the New York City Opera, where Beverly Sills became a great star after being denied a chance at the Metropolitan, Jewish board members outnumber WASPS two to one.

The Naumburgs and the John Simon Guggenheim Foundation have done much to encourage the flowering of the city's musical talents. The Guggenheim fellowships, handed out for nearly 40 years, have become a kind of intellectual knighthood to musicians, artists, writers, scholars, and scientists of promise, as the Guggenheim Museum is a mecca for followers of modern art. The New Friends of Music, which provides chamber music concerts, was founded by Ira Hirschman. Julius Bloom, as director of the Brooklyn Academy, turned a white elephant into the borough's cultural and musical oasis. As executive director of Carnegie Hall, Bloom and violinist Isaac Stern were among those who saved Carnegie Hall from the wrecker's ball in the 1960s. Avery Fisher Hall at Lincoln Center, home of the New York Philharmonic, is not only named for a Jew whose money created it, but it is filled night after night with heavily Jewish audiences. George Wein is the impresario who annually brings the Newport Jazz Festival to the city.

Outdoor music first acquired its enormous impact when the Stadium Concerts were started in 1918 in the now razed Lewisohn Stadium by Mrs. Charles S. Guggenheimer. The Goldman band concerts, begun in 1918 by Edward Franko Goldman on the Columbia University Green, and now conducted by his son, Richard Franko Goldman in Central and Prospect Parks, have been supported since 1924 by the Guggenheim family. The late Sol Hurok, the immigrant who first "presented" anybody when he prevailed upon Efraim Zimbalist to appear before a Jewish cultural society in Brownsville, brought to America the greatest names in music, dance, opera, and ballet.

The new American art form called musical theatre owes much to Jewish lyricists and composers. Marc Blitzstein's *The Cradle Will Rock*, and Harold Rome's *Pins and Needles*—first of the musicals of social significance—and Jerome Kern's *Showboat*, paved the way for the musical plays of Lorenz Hart, Oscar Hammerstein, II, Richard Rodgers, Frederick Loewe, and Alan Lerner. These grassroot operas displaced the musical extravaganzas and revues which Florenz Ziegfeld, an adopted New Yorker, had made Broadway's dominant type of entertainment.

As producers, playwrights, directors, and stage designers, Jews have been among Broadway's most important innovators and trailblazers. From the "star factory" era of the Frohmans and the successive hits of the Schuberts, to the present, the theatre has been enriched by a long line of Jewish luminaries: Elmer Rice, George S. Kaufman, Moss Hart, Lillian Hellman, Sidney Kingsley, Arthur Miller, Sam and Bella Spewack, Clifford Odets, Dore Schary, S. N. Behrman, Lee Strasberg, Max Gordon, David Merrick, Kermit Bloomgarden, Neil Simon, and David Susskind, among others. The Theatre Guild and the Group Theatre, directed almost entirely by Jews, were a major force in transforming taste and style in the American theatre. Lawrence Langner, Philip Moeller, Theresa Helburn, and Lee Simonson of the Theatre Guild gave a stage to Eugene O'Neill and introduced the realism of Ibsen, Gorki, Shaw, and Strindberg. The Neighborhood Playhouse, an offshoot of the Henry Street Settlement, which pioneered off-Broadway drama, was backed by Irene and Alice Lewisohn. Shakespeare in Central Park was the brainchild of Joseph Papp, one-time king of the off-Broadway theatre, who did more than anyone else to bring Shakespeare to the masses. In the mid-1970s, he headed the Public Theatre downtown and the two theatres in Lincoln Center. Many of the off- and off-off (sic) Broadway playwrights and producers have been young Jews. Neil Simon, who has authored a long list of Broadway hits, depicted with good humor and perception the character of New York as he first encountered it in his native Bronx.

The 92nd Street YM & YWHA, which marked its 100th year in 1975, continued to be the city's "little cultural center" for concerts, poetry readings, recitals, chamber music, and the modern dance. Allan Ginsburg was the poet of the beat generation whose adherents once crowded Greenwich Village where Maxwell Bodenheim once presided as high priest of the Bohemians. Bob Dylan, born in Minnesota, caught the tone of restless rebelling youth in his music.

When former President Richard Nixon was quoted in the Watergate tapes as warning his daughter Tricia "to stay away from the arts" because "they're Jews," he was quite right so far as New York is concerned. It was Alfred Stieglitz who first championed the new and daring world of modern art. One of the great photographic artists of his time, he fostered and encouraged the modernists. In 1908, Stieglitz introduced Max Weber, whose work bore the stamp of his East Side boyhood. The same was true of Jo Davidson, Sir Jacob Epstein, William Zorach, Ben Shahn, Abraham Walkowitz, and Maurice Becker. Perhaps one third of the city's art galleries are owned or managed by Jews. The Jewish Museum on Fifth Avenue and the new museum on the uptown campus of Yeshiva University, are among the most popular in the city. Joseph Hirshhorn, a former slum kid who became rich mining uranium in Canada, is one of the leading cultural innovators whose purchases stimulated the new school of art. Most of his multimillion dollar collection is now housed in the Hirshhorn Museum in Washington, D. C.

Barney Josephson opened the city's first integrated night club, "Cafe Society," in Greenwich Village in the mid-1930s, and it became an important incubator of musical talent. Upstairs at the Downstairs, the nightclub founded by Irving Haber, was the breeding ground for some of the country's best comedy and musical talents. Many of the Greenwich Village cafes have been the first step on the road to fame for Jewish entertainers. There are now a number of Israeli nightclubs and coffeehouses: El Avram, where the telephone operator greets you with a *shalom* when you call for reservations; Cafe Feenjon, where Israeli, Arab, and Greek music and food are available, and where Puerto Rican youngsters gave birth to shouts of *nochamol, nochamol* (again, again) when they liked a performance; and Cafe Yaffo, in the heart of the old Gashouse district.

New York's Jewish book publishers and critics have long been influential in molding national literary and cultural tastes. Mavericks like Alfred A. Knopf, Benjamin A. Huebsch, Charles Boni, the Guinzbergs of Viking Press, Horace Liveright, Bennett Cerf, and the Max L. Schuster-

Richard L. Simon duo, dynamically changed the book publishing industry after World War I. They introduced European authors, encouraged new American writers, produced books more attractively, and were responsible for enlarging the American reading audience. The first book clubs and the first paperbacks in America were other innovations of Jewish literary entrepreneurs. Literary critics such as Waldo Frank, James Oppenheim, Louis Untermeyer, Babette Deutsch, Alfred Kazin, John Simon, and Paul Rosenfeld, and the philosophic concepts of Horace Kallen, Sidney Hook, Irving Kristol, Irving Howe, Irwin Edman, David Riesman, Daniel Bell, and Nathan Glazer helped shape American literary and cultural taste and thought. Robert Silvers, as founder-editor of the *New York Review of Books*, Jason Epstein as one of its backers, Norman Podhoretz as editor of *Commentary*, and Norman Mailer, were important literary and cultural influences in the 1960s and 1970s.

Max Abramovitz, associate of Wallace Harrison in designing the United Nations headquarters, was the architect of the Lincoln Center for the Performing Arts. The Coliseum, another city landmark, is the work of Lionel and Leon Levy. Robert E. Blum and David Keiser helped bring Lincoln Center into being. The Lehman Children's Zoo and the Wollman Ice Skating Rink are among the many Central Park reminders of the civic responsibility of the city's Jews.

In the public sector of the city's rebuilding no one accomplished more than Robert F. Moses. President of the 1964 New York World's Fair, he masterminded the city's network of new bridges, parkways, tunnels, shorefront parks, and planned the Jones Beach development on Long Island. Descended from one of the Sephardic families and son-in-law of New York's commissioner of education in 1900, Moses was Secretary of State of New York in 1927. In 1934 he was the losing Republican candidate for governor against Herbert H. Lehman.

4. *The Fourth Estate*

Mordecai M. Noah, founder, editor, or publisher of seven different dailies between 1820 and 1840, was the first eminent Jewish figure in New York journalism. On his *Enquirer* he employed James Gordon Bennett, who, according to legend, started the *Herald* with $100 borrowed from Noah.

Noah's uncle by marriage, Solomon H. Jackson, launched *The Jew*, the earliest known English language Jewish publication in the United States in 1823. Married to a Presbyterian minister's daughter, Jackson started his paper to counteract the widespread efforts to convert the Jews. Twenty different groups were trying to convert the Jews of New York to Christianity in the 1820s. From 1825, when *The Jew* suspended publication, until 1849 there were no other Jewish journals in the city. *Israels Herold* had a brief existence as the first German-Jewish weekly. *The Asmonean*, an English language weekly, appeared from 1849 to 1858. *The Jewish Messenger* founded in 1858, was followed by a succession of weeklies in English, or

German and English. Many of them were absorbed by *The American Hebrew*, established in 1879, which itself was merged into the *American Examiner*. The latter, under the new name of *The Jewish Week and American Examiner*, came under new ownership and editorship in 1970, and became the largest, most widely read, and probably the most influential American Jewish weekly. The Greater New York area also had a number of other Jewish weeklies and fortnightlies in English, as well as the weekly English language, Orthodox-oriented *Jewish Press*.

Noah's successor as the city's most controversial newspaperman was Joseph Pulitzer. His innovations and unorthodox methods on *The New York World*, which he acquired in 1883, involved a bitter war with other publishers. Son of a Jewish father but raised as a Protestant, Pulitzer was assailed by Charles A. Dana of *The New York Sun* as a renegade Jew whose "face is repulsive not because the physiognomy is Hebraic but because it is Pulitzeresque." Pulitzer's relentless battle against political corruption and his struggle with Hearst's jingoistic efforts which led to the Spanish-American War have been forgotten. New Yorkers know his name only as the founder of the Pulitzer Prizes and as the donor of Columbia University's School of Journalism.

Adolph S. Ochs, too, has been forgotten by most New Yorkers but he built an enduring memorial in *The New York Times*. A one-time Tennessee printer's devil, Ochs acquired the bankrupt *Times* in 1896 and built it into the country's most influential newspaper. His high standards of journalistic ethics, enormous energy and resourcefulness, and capacity for choosing brilliant associates made the *Times* synonymous with complete and impartial news coverage and a symbol of honest and socially responsible journalism.

The New York Post, the city's oldest daily, is published by Mrs. Dorothy Schiff, a granddaughter of Jacob H. Schiff. The late Herbert Bayard Swope was the managing editor of *The New York World* when it was the city's most exciting paper. One of its most popular features was *The Conning Tower*, conducted by Franklin P. Adams, better known as F.P.A. Much of New York's flavor is savored in the memorable *New York Times* stories of Meyer Berger, a dead end kid who became a newspaperman of legend, and in the slanguage of Walter Winchell and his columnist colleagues, Mark Hellinger, Louis Sobel, and Leonard Lyons.

Frederick B. Opper, political lampoonist for the Hearst press and *Puck*, who created the cartoon characters, "Happy Hooligan" and "Alphonse and Gaston," was the ace newspaper cartoonist of an earlier generation and a forerunner of Rube Goldberg, Milton Gross, and Al Capp.

Walter Lippmann and Walter Weyl, described in a moment of annoyance by President Theodore Roosevelt as "two uncircumcised Jews," helped found *The New Republic*. Alfred A. Knopf published *The American Mercury* when it was the happy hunting grounds of H. L. Mencken and George Jean Nathan. Hugo Gernsbach created the science fiction magazines. *The Reporter* and *The New Leader* were launched by Jewish liberals.

Norman Cousins was the prime factor in the success of *The Saturday Review* and *Variety*, the Bible of show business, was founded by Sime Silverman.

One of the most colorful episodes in New York journalistic history was the rise of the Yiddish press. It began in 1871 when a Jewish politician published *The Jewish News*, in English, German, Yiddish, and Hebrew, to win votes. Two more enduring weeklies, Kasriel Sarasohn's *Yiddish Zeitung* and Henry Gersoni's *Juedische Post*, appeared in 1872. The first daily, *The Yiddishe Tageblatt* (Jewish Daily News), was founded by Sarasohn in 1885. (*Tageblatt* later became a generic term for any Yiddish newspaper.)

The second daily, *The Teglicher Herold* (1891), merged into *The Warheit* in 1905, which was absorbed by *The Day* in 1917. When *The Forward* was launched in 1897 as the third daily, the city boasted of 12 Yiddish journals reflecting viewpoints from anarchism on the left to Orthodox Judaism on the right. The first morning paper, *The Jewish Morning Journal*, appeared in 1901 as the spokesman of the Orthodox, non-radical community. Merged with *The Tageblatt* in 1928, it was consolidated in the 1950s with *The Day*. There were also numerous weeklies, monthlies, and quarterlies published by political parties, unions, *landsmanschaften*, and cultural groups and a few devoted to literature and humor.

Created by and for immigrants, the Yiddish press flourished so long as mass immigration continued. The Yiddish press taught the immigrants about the ideals and traditions of the bewildering new world, kept them in touch with happenings in the old world, and was influential in molding their political, cultural, and social integration.

The Forward, edited by Ab Cahan from 1902-1951, rose to great influence on the tidal waves of immigration. Cahan made *The Forward* the largest and most influential newspaper in the Jewish world and a major weapon in the rise of the Jewish labor movement and in the Americanization of two generations of immigrants. A successful writer in English, he helped America learn about the Jewish immigrant, and as a Yiddish journalist and Socialist organizer taught the immigrant about America. As a mediator between Yiddish and American cultures he "helped infuse the one with the other and thus had a share in creating a Jewish American culture."

When some of Cahan's Socialist colleagues objected to editorials urging mothers to keep their children supplied with clean handkerchiefs, Cahan asked, "Since when is Socialism opposed to clean noses?" He published simple lessons in civics, history, and American government, and through *The Forward's* letter column, "The Bintel Brief " (bunches of letters) created the most popular immigrant open forum.

By opening its columns to old and new writers, the Yiddish press also encouraged and enriched Jewish cultural creativity. *The Forward* published the works of virtually every notable Yiddish author. Working class poets, essayists, and novelists, such as Solomon Bloomgarden (Yehoash), who first translated the Bible into Yiddish, Morris Rosenfeld, Abraham Reisen, and

H. Leivick, poured out their anguished protests against the sweatshops in the Yiddish press. Rosenfeld's poem, *The Machine*, has been compared to Markham's *The Man With the Hoe*. The works of Peretz, Mendele Mocher Seforim, Sholom Aleichem, Sholom Asch, Zalman Schneur, Israel J. Singer, Isaac Bashevis Singer, and Elie Wiesel all first appeared in Yiddish papers.

The Yiddish press was at the acme of its influence in 1915 when New York's five Yiddish dailies reached a peak circulation of 526,000. By 1921 it had dropped to 400,000. To the first generation of East Europeans, the Yiddish paper had been a household necessity but their children had little need for it, particularly when they began to shun Yiddish as the language of greenhorns. Every reader the Yiddish dailies helped Americanize became a lost reader. English pages and columns and English-Yiddish photo captions were added in the late 1920s in a futile effort to halt an irreversible trend.

The postwar Yiddish-speaking DPs from Europe provided only a temporary shot in the arm. During the 1962-63 New York newspaper strike the Yiddish dailies were crammed with advertisements of public events, job opportunities, Civil Service examinations, and Broadway shows. At the end of 1963, the circulation of *The Forward, Day-Morning Journal*, and the Communist *Freiheit* was down to about 100,000, and still falling. In the early 1970s, the *Day-Morning Journal* suspended publication. It was replaced by a Yiddish weekly, *Allgemeine Zeitung*. *The Forward* also encountered difficulties and in 1975 it made a public appeal to Jews for financial support.

The Hebrew press, which never achieved the status of its Yiddish counterpart in New York, antedated it. The first Hebrew journal, *Hatzofeh Baaretz-Hahadashah*, appeared in 1870 when the first Hebraists began arriving from Europe. One of these was Judah D. Eisenstein, who edited the first Hebrew encyclopedia and translated the Declaration of Independence and the Constitution of the United States into Hebrew and Yiddish. Later Hebrew editors, such as Reuben Brainin, Menahem Ribalow, and Chaim Tzchernowitz, gave rise to the Histadruth Ivrith in 1913, which stimulated Hebrew-speaking societies, publications, and programs. *Hadoar*, now the only Hebrew weekly in the United States, started as a New York daily in 1921. One of the early New York Hebraists was Naphtali Herz Imber, a vagabond genius and poet, who wrote *Hatikvah* in 1886 when it was an anthem without a country.

5. *Their Brother's Keeper*

From the days when they were still only a tolerated minority with a precarious foothold in New Amsterdam, Jews have given leadership and support to almost every liberal, humane, and forward-looking movement. It began with Asser Levy, who gave 100 florins to the fund raised to defend New Amsterdam against the British invasion in 1664. Seven years later he advanced money to the Lutherans to help them build their first church. A public subscription taken up in 1711 to complete the Trinity Church steeple included seven Jewish donors. Gershom Mendes Seixas' lectures on Judaism at St. Paul's Church in 1800 set an enduring example of interfaith amity in the city where the National Conference of Christians and Jews was born in the 1920s.

Moses Judah helped liberate 50 slaves as an active member of the New York Manumission Society from 1799-1809. The Society's records contain the names of many Jews who emancipated their own slaves and helped maintain the underground railway for runaway slaves. Ernestine Rose, who came from Poland, was one of the reformers who began the struggle for women's rights in the 1830s. During the Irish famine relief appeal of the 1840s Shearith Israel conducted a fundraising rally among its members.

Most of the Jewish immigrants from Germany, Bohemia, and Austria sided with the abolitionists. Philip J. Joachimsen, an assistant United States District Attorney in New York, secured the first conviction of a slave trader. When Rabbi Morris Raphall preached a sermon from the pulpit of B'nai Jeshurun early in 1861, attempting to justify slavery on Biblical grounds, he was bitterly assailed in Jewish circles.

Felix Adler, who founded the city's first kindergarten on the East Side, joined with Isaac N. Seligman to erect the first model tenement on Cherry Street in 1885. For a generation he warred on firetraps until he persuaded the state to create a tenement house commission. A generation later the Fred L. Lavanburg Foundation anticipated the public housing program by building the city's first low-rent apartments. Dr. Simon Baruch prodded the city into opening the first public baths on the East Side. The free pasteurized milk stations opened by Nathan Straus were credited with saving the lives of thousands of babies and lowering the city's death rate.

The horrible housing, health, and social conditions on the Lower East Side after 1880 impelled dedicated reformers to establish the Henry Street, University and College Settlements, and Clark and Madison Houses. In the house on Henry Street, founded by Lillian D. Wald, and in the other East Side settlements, uptown Jewish volunteers were introduced to practical social welfare and imbued with the liberal concepts that were converted into legislation by Alfred E. Smith, Franklin D. Roosevelt, Robert F. Wagner, Sr., and Herbert H. Lehman. In these islands of hope for the slum dwellers Lehman, Henry Morgenthau, Jr., Belle Moskowitz, Gerard Swope, and Joseph Proskauer, among others, worked side by side with Eleanor Roosevelt, Frances Perkins, and Harry Hopkins in battling for housing reforms, parks, playgrounds, cleaner streets, and public health services. Thousands of Jewish teachers, lawyers, musicians, artists, and public figures came under the wholesome influence of the settlements where they acquired their social, political, and cultural attitudes.

The social idealism that brought uptown Jews to the East Side as settlement house workers and then involved them in wider communal efforts never waned. Dr. Stephen S. Wise, Lillian D. Wald, Joel and Arthur Spingarn, and Dr. Henry Moskowitz were among the founders of the National Association for the Advancement of Colored People. Arthur

Spingarn was for many years president of NAACP. Professor Edwin R. A. Seligman of Columbia University was the first chairman of the Urban League. A recent president was Theodore Kheel, the labor arbitrator. Columbia University's Franz Boas began the struggle against racism in 1911. Pauline Goldmark and Maud Nathan organized the Consumer's League and were pioneers in the women's suffrage movement. Dr. Abraham Jacoby was advocating birth control in 1912. Alice Davis Menken and Anna Moskowitz Kross led the fight for juvenile courts and night courts for women and wayward minors. Felix Adler headed the National Child Labor Committee.

From the pulpit of the Free Synagogue, Dr. Stephen S. Wise defended the 1919 steel strikers. Abraham Epstein and Isaac M. Rubinow were the trailblazing sociologists whose work contributed enormously to the enactment of the Federal social security program. For years Arthur Garfield Hays was chief counsel of the American Civil Liberties Union and was succeeded by Aryeh Neier. Leo Cherne heads the International Rescue Committee for Victims of Political Oppression. In the struggle for better housing and schools, parks, fair employment practices, school and housing desegregation, and social legislation, there were and are no more vigorous fighters than the descendants of peddlers and sweatshop workers who take American democracy seriously.

6. *Defenders of Freedom*

As defenders of the freedoms they fought so hard to establish and enlarge, the Jews of New York distinguished themselves in every war since Asser Levy and Jacob Barsimson insisted on their right to defend New Amsterdam.

The first Jew to bear arms for the British in North America, Joseph Isacks, enlisted in the New York militia in 1689 on the outbreak of King William's War. Isaac Myers organized a company of volunteers in the Rising Sun Inn and led it across the Alleghenies during the French and Indian War.

Almost all the Jews of New York were on the side of independence when the Revolutionary War began. Four, who were in the ranks when George Washington read the Declaration of Independence to his troops in New York, shared the hardships of the Battle of Long Island, which was fought in Brooklyn. Tory neighbors burned the Bedford (Westchester County) farmhouse of one of these soldiers because his wife refused to disclose the hideout of a band of patriots attempting to reach the American camp at White Plains.

Haym Salomon, the patriotic broker, who had come from Poland in 1775, joined the Sons of Liberty in New York and was later imprisoned by the British. Released to serve as an interpreter to the commander of the Hessian troops, Salomon became an underground agent for the Americans in the New York area, risking his life to help French and American prisoners escape British jails and to induce Hessians to desert. The Continental

Congress voted its thanks to Isaac Moses whose privateersmen wrought havoc on British shipping.

The most ardent advocate of independence in the Jewish community was the Reverend Gershom Mendes Seixas. Anticipating the city's occupation by the British, he took Shearith Israel's ritual objects and records and led a majority of the congregation to Stratford, Connecticut, rather than live under the British. At the age of 68, he vainly petitioned Congress for permission to form a military company during the War of 1812, insisting he "could stop a bullet as well as a younger man." His powerful sermons helped rally public support for the war. Samuel Noah, one of the first Jewish graduates of West Point, was one of the builders of the defenses of Brooklyn against an expected British attack in 1812.

More than half of the 6,000 Jews who volunteered for military duty in the Civil War on the Union side were with New York City regiments. Benjamin Levy, who enlisted at 16, won the Congressional Medal of Honor. Colonel Leopold C. Newman, of Brooklyn, who was mortally wounded at Chancellorsville, received a deathbed visit from President Lincoln. Brigadier General Philip J. Joachimsen organized and commanded the 59th N.Y. Volunteers, and Colonel William Mayer recruited the "Perkins Rifles."

New York's synagogues and Jewish charity societies participated actively in fund-raising projects for the United States Sanitary Commission, which distributed medical supplies, food, and clothing to sick and wounded Union troops. To care for the families of Jewish soldiers the Jewish community raised special relief funds. Several of Mt. Sinai Hospital's wards were converted to military purposes. Dr. Israel Moses, attending surgeon at Mt. Sinai, was in the medical corps where he invented the "Moses Wagon," which was used to transport the wounded. The Jewish hospital became a sanctuary for the wounded during the New York draft riots of 1863.

During the brief Spanish-American War many Yiddish-speaking immigrants volunteered for Army duty in the hope of striking a blow against the nation that had driven out its Jews in the 15th century. General John J. Pershing, commander-in-chief of the American Expeditionary Forces in World War I, paid high tribute to the heroism of Jewish doughboys from New York. Representing 40 percent of the 77th Division, which bore the brunt of the Meuse-Argonne battle, they included two Medal of Honor winners, Sydney G. Gumpertz and Benjamin Kaufman.

The World War II story is graphically recorded in *American Jews in World War II*, a book of over 600 pages devoted to listing the names of New York Jews killed, wounded, or missing in action as well as those decorated for bravery. Among these were Colonel David Marcus, a staff officer who later organized Israel's Army; Lieutenant Meyer Levin, bombardier of the plane that almost sank the first Japanese warship; and Solomon Isquith, who directed the rescue of the USS *Utah* at Pearl Harbor. Thousands of New York Jews served in all branches of the armed forces during the Korean and Vietnam wars.

Manners and Mores

In the 322 years since a handful of refugees found a grudging haven in New Amsterdam, the Jews of New York have risen from an immigrant, low income, embattled group to a largely native-born, well-educated, mostly middle-class community accepted as an inseparable element of the nation's greatest city.

More widely dispersed than ever before throughout the city and its suburbs, yet more densely concentrated, Jews have settled in new neighborhoods which are often as distinctly Jewish as the old Lower East Side was 75 years ago. Never dissolved in the melting pot but imbedded in two cultures, Americanism and Judaism, the Jews fully accept Will Herberg's conclusion that "to be a Protestant, a Catholic or a Jew are today the alternative ways of being an American."

In their new city or suburban areas of residence the Jews have adopted the manners and mores of their non-Jewish neighbors but they have also held on to many of the habits of their parents and grandparents. Despite its poverty and wretched living conditions, the Jewish working class of the immigrant generations was middle class in moral and health standards, in its almost worshipful adoration of education and eagerness to escape from the slums.

Exposés of the old East Side always mentioned its disease-breeding tenements, but the 10th ward, an almost 100 percent Jewish neighborhood, had the lowest mortality rate in the city in 1894. Yiddish-speaking mothers took avidly to health education programs, and welcomed the summer camps sponsored by the settlement houses, the penny luncheons of the public schools, and the pasteurized milk stations of Nathan Straus.

Contemporary descriptions of life on the East Side painted a generally accurate picture of the dismal conditions but seldom mentioned the lack of crime or absence of drunkenness, venereal disease, drug addiction, and illiteracy. Jewish paupers were strangers to the New York Almshouse. No Jew was ever buried in Potter's Field. Most crime and violence on the East Side was not committed by immigrants; they were usually its victims. The few Jewish toughs who came to public attention were children of immigrants. It was never dangerous to walk at night through the slum streets inhabited by Jews, even though most East Side kids belonged to gangs. They warred with neighboring Irish and Italian youngsters who attacked and insulted Jews, knocking over pushcarts and tweaking beards. Bearded and caftaned Jews, the favorite prey of Irish toughs, found protectors in the children of greenhorns. Theodore Roosevelt, when he was police commissioner in the 1890s, first encouraged Jews to become policemen by seeking out "the fighting Jewish type."

Some Jewish gangs did become breeding grounds for criminal rings and the Jewish neighborhoods had their share of poolroom operators, brothel-keepers, and petty grafters. Eddie Cantor told how he helped a gang break into a bicycle shop and was paid off "with a cup of coffee and two doughnuts" and "a nickel carfare home." As a "strongarm" member of a gang of strikebreakers, Cantor was once paid "three bucks a day." Irving Berlin recalled being beaten by neighborhood toughs when he ventured beyond Jewish-controlled streets. The settlement houses and strong Jewish family ties, even where strained by American ways, were prime factors in deflecting Jewish youngsters from gang influence.

The first Jewish athletes were prize fighters who learned boxing to defend themselves from Irish kids on the Bowery who invaded the Jewish East Side. Joe Bernstein, first hero of East Side Jewish youth, achieved fame as Joe Choynski when he battled Bob Fitzsimmons for the heavyweight crown. Jewish fighters from the East Side often took Irish names (Al McCoy, Mushy Callahan, Sid Terris, Leach Cross, etc.) because most fight fans were Irish and Jews regarded prizefighters as bums. When East Side fighters with unmistakably Jewish names—Benny Leonard, Abe Attell, Al Singer, Ruby Goldstein, Benny Jeby, and Barney Levinsky—became title contenders and champions, the crowds yelled "kill the kike" or "hit the Hebe." Later, non-Jewish fighters took Jewish names to attract Jewish fans.

John J. McGraw beat the minor league bushes in a vain search for a "Jewish Babe Ruth" on the theory that a Jewish star in a Giants' uniform would be baseball's greatest box office attraction. When he finally found Andy Cohen, in Texas, Jews who had never before seen a baseball game, jammed the Polo Grounds. Hank Greenberg, the first New York Jew to achieve big league stardom, made it in a Detroit uniform, while Sandy Koufax, who grew up in Brooklyn, hit the top with the Dodgers only after they had moved to Los Angeles. Ronnie Blomberg, the slugging New York Yankee who grew up in Atlanta, was cheered as "the kosher boomer" by Yankee fans.

Though Jewish parents frowned on athletics as the pastime of loafers, immigrant kids took to sports with avidity. Hirsch Jacobs, who sent over 3,000 racing thoroughbreds across the winning line at tracks all over the country, began with the only racers that could find moving room in the slums—pigeons. Mike Jacobs rose from the East Side to transform boxing into big business. Lon Myers and Abel Kiviat wore the colors of the old Irish-American A.C. when they represented the United States in Olympic track and field events. Sammy and Joe Renick, who never knew horses were used for anything but delivering milk when they attended a Bronx Hebrew school, became the country's leading jockeys. Sid Luckman, one of the all time greats of collegiate and pro football, learned the game in Brooklyn.

The East Side schools raised a host of basketball players for City College and St. John's University when their teams ruled the collegiate courts, and the Brooklyn and Bronx schools contributed many Jewish stars to college and professional basketball. Nat Holman, "Mr. Basketball," long the City College coach, learned the game at P.S. 62 whose alumni helped make basketball a rival of baseball as the national sport. Maurice Podoloff, an East Side boy, led the National Basketball Association for 16 years and made the professional game a major sport.

New York area Jewish high school kids still star in sports but most of them now come from the suburbs. Jewish parents now encourage their youngsters to compete and are not unhappy when a prowess in sports yields a college scholarship or a professional contract. The city's Jewish parochial high schools have their own basketball league and Yeshiva University fields a fair team in intercollegiate play. In the Orthodox neighborhoods of Brooklyn it is not strange to see youngsters in yarmulkas playing basketball on YMHA courts.

No matter where the Jews have moved in New York, their dietary predilections have influenced the eating habits of the whole city and of a growing segment of the nation as well. Only a minority of New York Jews keep strictly kosher homes, but many buy kosher food. It is easier today than a generation ago when few kosher items were available in stores. The kosher food industry, concentrated in New York, has become a multimillion dollar enterprise, and the demand is rising.

More than 2,000 different kosher products are made by some 400 companies. Most of them have accepted the rabbinical supervision of the Union of Orthodox Jewish Congregations. The Union's kosher certification service, which guarantees the kashrut of a product, is identified by the "U" symbol, available only to firms meeting strict requirements. The sales promotion value of this symbol has encouraged food packers to turn out everything from unsalted kosher margarine, fruit pie fillings and hard cheeses to kosher spaghetti and baby food. The Heinz Company promoted its kosher ketchup in full page newspaper ads headlined "my brother is a schlemihl."

Manufacturers of kosher products that do not subscribe to the UOJC's service label them "K," or identify them by the Star of David or with some Hebrew words. Frozen or precooked kosher foods are available on planes leaving New York airports, and in hospitals which do not have kosher kitchens. All of the city's newer hotels and most of the larger older hostelries have separate sets of dishes and cutlery for use at kosher affairs. The New York Hilton can serve 3,700 from its own Kosher kitchen.

Kosher catering establishments are highly successful with weddings and bar mitzvahs. Some maintain lavish establishments with synagogue-like names. The innumerable "manors" and "mansions," where so many bar mitzvahs and Jewish weddings are held, originated with Clinton Hall and New Irving Hall, where the East Side congregated for major social events, political rallies, *landsmanschaften* meetings, benefit parties, and even dancing classes. Most of the larger synagogues of all denominations depend heavily on income from their official caterers who use synagogue facilities. Some caterers have succeeded in preparing kosher food that is indistinguishable from non-kosher dishes, including a kosher sukiyaki and glazed "kosher ham."

The scope of the kosher food business in New York gave rise to frequent scandals involving rabbis and dealers who falsely certify restaurants, caterers, and products as kosher. Racketeers have offered kosher ritual food tags to non-kosher caterers. Unethical practices and price gouging in the New York kosher poultry business led to one of the most famous decisions of the Supreme Court of the United States. When the Live Poultry Code of NRA (National Recovery Administration), was created in the 1930s to govern the fiercely competitive all-Jewish industry, a wholesaler by the name of Schechter brought suit, and in the "sick chicken case" succeeded in having the whole NRA declared unconstitutional.

In 1944 New York became the first state to set up a separate division to maintain an on-going inspection of meats sold under kosher auspices. The kosher law enforcement bureau handles 2,500 cases a year, and spot checks every place where kosher meat is slaughtered, manufactured, processed, sold, or served. Eight inspectors and supervisors cover New York City to prevent any establishment from claiming or advertising that it sells or serves kosher meat products unless it is supervised by a competent rabbinical authority. In 1975, it became illegal to advertise products or establishments as "kosher style."

Kosher food products crowd supermarket counters in almost every neighborhood. Candy chains feature chocolate matzos for Passover, chocolate *hamantashen* for Purim, candy *dreidels* for Chanukah, and assorted sweets for other Jewish holidays. Radio and television commercials and newspaper ads plug Jewish bread, kosher wine, and a long list of Jewish delicacies, including a herring *maven*. When bagelmakers strike, it is a municipal disaster. Stores offer gefilte fish, lox, and bagels as Lenten substitutes. Kosher Chinese food is available for home delivery and kosher hot dogs can be bought at Yankee Stadium and Madison Square Garden. Popular restaurants include Passover dishes on their menus, together with non-Passover staples. Department stores feature Passover table settings and window displays of Chanukah gift objects. One daily newspaper publishes a special Passover and Rosh Hashanah section devoted largely to kosher recipes and advertisements for kosher foods and Jewish resorts.

The popularity of kosher and Jewish-style food among non-Jews has been attritubed to the city's cosmopolitan tastes and to the fact that many of them tried and liked Jewish delicacies in Jewish homes or as delegates to conventions held in "Borscht-Belt" hotels. The easy availability of ready-to-serve kosher foods, on the other hand, may explain the absence of more than a handful of genuinely kosher restaurants. The city and suburbs are studded with non-kosher eating places that offer Jewish delicacies and dairy restaurants where Runyonesque-type waiters serve traditional non-meat Jewish dishes. None ever acquired the fame of the now vanished Cafe Royale on 2nd Avenue, "the downtown Sardi's," where Yiddish literati and uptown Jewish communal leaders gathered.

Non-Jewish epicures who relish the gastronomic pleasures of what has been called "belly Judaism," also know and use many Yiddish words and expressions. While Yiddish is declining as a spoken and printed language in New York, it has won a place as a piquant element in American "slanguage." The linguistic amalgam known as New Yorkese has spilled into American English through many expressive words and phrases that come straight from the East Side by way of the garment center, Broadway, radio, television, and the columnists.

Little surprise is evoked when New Yorkers of Irish or Italian extraction refer to a *"zaftig"* girl who may be a *"shikse,"* or who describe a legal arrangement as *"kosher"* and identify a fool as a *"shlemihl."* The tunesmiths of Tin Pan Alley have poured Yiddish phrases into the stream of American popular music. Comedians who tested their routines in the "Borscht Belt" made words like *"gelt," "Mazuma," "momser," "kibitzer,"* and *"meshuggah"* part of the lingua franca. Al Capp's "shmoo" is related to the Yiddish *"schmaltz"* and *"shmo,"* and the latter is an abbreviation for a Yiddish obscenity. The Yiddish deprecatory prefix *"shm"* found its way into the New Yorkese in such descriptive phrases as, "cancer schmancer" and "fancy-shmancy," and even a First National City Bank ad that starts with "wampum, schwampum."

In New York, politicians and reporters talk about a political *mishmash* and of situations that are not *kosher*. Policemen refer to jaywalkers as *schlemiehls*. *Kibitzers* flourish everywhere and *shlock* and *shmattas* have become synonyms for junk and rags. Shrewish women are called *yentas*. A *tsimmes* is not a dish but a lot of noise about nothing. A *gontze metziah* is no great bargain. Advertisers cash in on such slogans as "dress British and think Yiddish," and "you don't have to be Jewish" to relish this or that product associated with Jewish palates, such as rye bread, matzoth, borscht, and Passover wine. A manufacturer of heating units advertised that his product worked best when treated with "a Jewish mother's love." A delicatessen asked in a newspaper ad "what's wrong with kosher delicatessen at your Xmas party." A department store used a full page ad to promote a whole line of *mavens*. Most New Yorkers know the meaning of *chutzpa* and do not need a dictionary to get the meaning of *gantze mishpocha, gantze megillah*, and *mishegas* as used by television comedians and the advertising business. Because so many New York Jews still speak Yiddish, the Department of Agriculture printed and distributed 200,000 copies of a leaflet in Yiddish explaining how poor Jews can qualify and apply for food stamps.

Once the language of the vociferous masses, Yiddish is now chiefly the tongue of scholars, researchers, poets, new immigrants from the Soviet Union, and a passing older generation. It is in no immediate danger of dying, however. There are still a number of important Yiddish cultural journals and party organs in New York, besides the two Yiddish dailies. The Sholom Aleichem Schools of the Workmen's Circle report a growing number of American-born children studying Yiddish in suburban classes. Yiddish is being taught in many universities and some New York Jews are first learning Yiddish terms from television comedians.

The amazing success of Allan Sherman's *My Son the Folksinger* among Jews and non-Jews indicated that the city could still be intrigued by the flavor of the East Side when recaptured by playwrights, novelists, and musicians. While immigrant parents and Jewish garment workers have almost vanished from real life, sentimental portraits of their idiosyncracies and relations with American-born children and grandchildren became more common. "Matzo-ball soup operas"—Jewish family situation comedies and dramas—once the chief stock in trade of the Yiddish theatre, became great Broadway successes. Plays and musicals such as *A Majority of One, Dear Me the Sky Is Falling, Enter Laughing, Come Blow Your Horn, The Tenth Man, Milk and Honey,* and *Cafe Crown* resemble in theme and appeal the plays that brought the immigrant generation thronging to the Yiddish theatre. Although nostalgic sentiment characterizes all of these shows, American-born Jewish audiences, and large numbers of non-Jews, too, have made them great hits, as witnessed by the huge success of *Fiddler on the Roof.*

The story of the New York Jewish immigrant and his descendants became a best seller through the novels and short stories of Herman Wouk, Bernard Malamud, Saul Bellow, Philip Roth, Bruce Friedman, Herbert Gold, Chaim Potok, and the translations of Isaac Bashevis Singer. The body of fiction by and about the Jews of New York provides a continuing insight into the changing patterns of Jewish life and history in the city. The East Side and its impact on Jewish and American life have intrigued writers for half a century. Ellis Island and the ghetto as the Jewish immigrant's frontiers were the themes of Ab Cahan's *The Rise of David Levinsky,* and Mary Antin's *The Promised Land.* The tears and whimsy of Fannie Hurst and Montague Glass were succeeded by the idealized clichés of Leonard Q. Ross' *The Education of Hyman Kaplan,* Milt Gross' *Nize Baby,* and Arthur Kober's *Having A Wonderful Time.* The proletarian novels of disenchantment by Mike Gold, Isidor Schneider, Henry Roth, Joseph Freeman, Albert Halper, and Leona Zugsmith presaged the debunking and self-hatred of Ben Hecht, Jerome Weidman, Budd Schulberg, and the novels of wartime anti-Semitism by Irwin Shaw, Arthur Miller, and Norman Mailer. The books of Harry Golden and Sam Levenson of East Side reminiscences and the recent Jewish novels with New York characters completed the cycle in which New York Jews were no longer pathetic strugglers, victims or *schlemiehls,* but ordinary Americans of middle-class status.

The new *Encyclopedia Judaica* summed up the Jewish role in New York in these words: "So complete was the Jewish involvement in New York cultural life in the middle decades of the 20th century that it would be impossible to imagine practically any aspect of the latter without it. Moreover, this involvement was not at all restricted to the realms of 'high' culture and the arts. It made itself felt most heavily in numerous areas of every day New York life, in its impact on local speech, gestures, food, humor and attitudes. It is doubtful, indeed, if anywhere else in the history of the

Diaspora has a large Jewish community existed in so harmonious a symbiosis with a great metropolis without either ghettoizing itself from its surroundings or losing its own distinct sense of character and identity.

"Nor can the relationship be thought of as having been merely one-way. If the Jews gave to New York unstintingly of their experience, energies and talents, they received in return an education in urbanity and a degree of cosmopolitan sophistication unknown to any other Jewish community of similar size in the past. It is little wonder that many Jews developed an attachment to New York that bordered on the devotional. Above all, when 20th century New York Jews thought of the city they lived in, they did not simply consider it a great capital of civilization that had generously taken them in. Rather, they thought of themselves, and with every justification, as joint builders of this greatness and of its main continuing supports. Such a relationship marks a unique moment in Jewish history and one that given the current political, demographic and cultural trends in the U.S. and the world at large is not likely to recur again."

*****

MANHATTAN

LOWER MANHATTAN

BATTERY PARK *(at southern end of Manhattan–east or west side IRT subway local to South Ferry station).* At Whitehall and State Sts., there is a flagpole that commemorates the settlement in 1654 of the first group of Jews in the United States. Set in a small landscaped plot, a stone's throw from the spot where the first Jewish settlers landed, the flagstaff rises from a 7-foot-high granite base on which a bronze commemorative plaque is mounted. The inscription reads:

ERECTED BY THE STATE OF NEW YORK
TO HONOR THE MEMORY
OF THE TWENTY-THREE MEN, WOMEN
& CHILDREN WHO LANDED IN SEPTEMBER
1654 & FOUNDED THE FIRST JEWISH
COMMUNITY IN NORTH AMERICA

A Star of David at the top of the plaque is flanked by the Lions of Judah; the seal of the American Jewish Tercentenary adorns the bottom. The flagpole was presented to the City of New York at a ceremony during which the plaque was unveiled by Judge Edgar J. Nathan, Jr., a descendant of Abraham de Lucena, an early Jewish settler. ●There is another plaque in the Park honoring Emma Lazarus, noted Jewish poetess. The plaque is set in Israeli granite. ●The East Coast Memorial, a war monument, commemorates the 4,596 Christian and Jewish Americans who died in World War II.

FRAUNCES TAVERN, Broad and Pearl Sts., was once the home of Phila Franks, sister of David Franks and aunt of Rebecca Franks of Philadelphia. Phila lived here after she had eloped in 1742 with the socially prominent Oliver deLancey of New York. In 1783, George Washington said farewell to his officers in the tavern's Long Room, which was faithfully restored in 1907 by the Sons of the Revolution.

SITE OF ASSER LEVY HOUSE, Broad and Stone Sts., was the home of Asser Levy, one of the original settlers, who waged a successful fight to stand guard in the defense of New Amsterdam (now New York). Jews at first were prohibited from this duty and were, instead, burdened with a special tax.

SITE OF CONGREGATION SHEARITH ISRAEL, Broad and S. William Sts. (originally Mill St.). A modern garage at 26 S. William St. occupies the site of the first synagogue in North America. This was Congregation Shearith Israel's (Spanish and Portuguese Synagogue) first building. A plaque marking the site of the first synagogue in North America was dedicated on Sept. 12, 1976. Because of the concentration of Jewish population in this area, the street was informally called "Jews' Alley" or "Jews' Street." Nearby is the site of the home of Abraham de Lucena.

NEW YORK STOCK EXCHANGE, Broad and Wall Sts. The Exchange had its beginnings in 1792, when 24 brokers, five of whom were Jewish, drew up a trading agreement under a buttonwood tree at what is now 68 Wall St.

KUHN, LOEB & CO., 40 Wall St., is an investment banking firm that played a role in the financial history of the U.S. Among its partners were Jacob H. Schiff, Otto Kahn, and Felix and Paul Warburg. In 1914, Kuhn, Loeb & Co. and J. P. Morgan & Co. joined forces to come to the rescue of New York City when it found itself unable to meet a $100 million obligation to England, payable in gold. In 1931, the two firms again rescued the city by organizing a banking group to set up a huge revolving credit.

THE STATUE OF LIBERTY *(boats depart from Battery Park to Liberty Island in upper New York Bay daily from 9 a.m. to 4 p.m. The ferry can be reached by taking a Broadway bus or the IRT or BMT subway to South Ferry).*

This world-famous statue has been the symbol of freedom and hope for millions of immigrants. It is 151 feet high and stands on a pedestal of about the same height. Affixed to the base is the sonnet, *The New Colossus*, by the American Jewish poet, Emma Lazarus. The poem, a tribute to liberty and to America as the haven of the oppressed, follows:

Not like the brazen giant of Greek fame,
With conquering limbs astride from land to land;
Here at our sea-washed, sunset gates shall stand
A mighty woman with a torch, whose flame
Is the imprisoned lightning, and her name
Mother of Exiles. From her beacon-hand
Glows world-wide welcome; her mild eyes command
The air-bridged harbor that twin cities frame.
"Keep, ancient lands, your storied pomp!" cries she
With silent lips. "Give me your tired, your poor,
Your huddled masses yearning to breathe free,
The wretched refuse of your teeming shore.
Send these, the homeless, tempest-tost to me,
I lift my lamp beside the golden door!"

In 1885, as the drive to raise $300,000 for the statue's pedestal was faltering, a wide variety of fund-raising methods were used—from penny collections among school children to high-pressure campaigns in Wall St. Artists and writers were invited to donate works which could be auctioned off for the benefit of the pedestal fund. Among those who contributed original manuscripts were Walt Whitman, Mark Twain, and Bret Harte. But Emma Lazarus, then 34 years old and already known for her poetry, essays, and outspoken advocacy of Jewish rights, submitted a special sonnet for the occasion—*The New Colossus*.

It almost went unwritten. Emma at first refused to contribute to the exhibition, saying that she was unable to write to order. But Constance Cary Harrison, a leading citizen who planned to publish the manuscripts and sketches in a portfolio—a 19th century version of a souvenir journal—personally called on the poetess to persuade her with the following argument: "Think of the Goddess of Liberty standing on her pedestal yonder in the bay, and holding the torch out to those refugees you are so fond of visiting at Ward's Island." Two days later Constance Harrison received *The New Colossus*. Emma Lazarus' sonnet yielded $1,500 for the pedestal fund. For 20 years the poem was all but forgotten. In 1903, Georgiana Schuyler, a New York artist, came across a copy of the portfolio and was so taken with the sonnet that she had it inscribed on a bronze tablet and received permission to have it affixed inside the base of the Statue of Liberty. In 1945, the tablet was moved from the second-story landing to the entrance of the statue.

Among Emma Lazarus' relatives were the Rev. Gershom Mendes Seixas, *hazzan* of the Spanish and Portuguese Synagogue and Revolutionary patriot; Maud Nathan, suffragette; Annie Nathan Meyer, a founder of Barnard College; Robert Nathan, poet and novelist; and Supreme Court Justice Benjamin N. Cardozo.

After Emma Lazarus had seen Jewish refugees huddled at Ward's Island in the East River, her works about her people saw new life. *Century Magazine* in May, 1882, published a passionate prose protest against persecution of all kinds, in answer to a previous article by a Madame Ragozin, who tried to whitewash the Russian pogroms against Jews. For the closing exercises of Temple Emanu-El's religious school, Emma wrote the poem *The Banner of the Jew*, a clarion call for a new Ezra to arise and lead his people. In *The Dance of Death*, a poetic drama based on an incident in the persecution of Germany's Jews in the Middle Ages, she wrote, "I have no thought, no passion, no desire, save for my people." Her activity on behalf of Jewry was climaxed in a series of 16 articles called *Epistles to the Hebrews*, appealing for united Jewish action to help the persecuted Jews of Europe, for economic restratification of Jewish life, for changes in Jewish education, and for the restoration of what was then Palestine as the Jewish homeland. The articles were published in the *American Hebrew*. ☐

ELLIS ISLAND, through which millions of immigrant Jews passed en route to American settlement, was proclaimed by President Lyndon B. Johnson a part of the Statue of Liberty National Monument, and it is now open to tourists.

AMERICAN MUSEUM OF IMMIGRATION, located within the walls of old Fort Wood at the outer base of the Statue of Liberty, is dedicated to those Americans who came from other lands and contributed so largely to the country's cultural and physical development. There are 38 permanent exhibit units in a major exhibit hall enclosed within a terrace. The exhibits tell the story of immigration beginning with the Indians, who originally came to America from Asia. There is a small exhibit entitled "The Seed of Abraham." Of special interest is the Torah used at the first Jewish services held at both Dachau and Mathausen after these concentration camps were liberated in 1945. Other exhibits are devoted to the story of the Statue of Liberty itself. The museum includes dioramas, silk-screen enlargements, photographs, audio-visual aids, murals, and other items.

LOWER EAST SIDE

In this area once lived the largest Jewish community in the world. More than 1,562,000 Jews—most of them from East Europe—arrived in America between 1881 and 1910. The vast majority settled here on the Lower East Side, creating what amounted to a voluntary ghetto.

Life for the immigrants was hard. They lived in tenement houses and eked out a living mostly as peddlers or in the expanding needle trades. Workshops set up in the tenements exploited and enslaved whole families; the sweatshop era had begun, with its disease and degradation. Out of these depths the labor movement developed and grew.

In addition to the settlement houses, which were created to help the immigrants adjust to their American environment, the newcomers organized their own societies to meet their varied needs and gave their overwhelming support to the Yiddish press and Yiddish theatre. Most of these are now memories. A few of the institutions, however, are still in business at the same old stands, but the clientele has changed. Nevertheless, there are a number of kosher dairy or meat restaurants serving blintzes, *varnishkes*, *kishke*, gefilte fish, delicatessen, etc. One can still see Hebrew and Yiddish signs, and wander through stores specializing in Jewish books and ceremonial objects.

Though the population has changed, a significant percentage is still Jewish—the rest mostly Puerto Rican, black, Italian, and Chinese. The pushcarts are gone, and the tenements are giving way to modern housing developments. The great Yiddish theatre and its stars are no more.

ESSEX STREET MARKET, Delancey and Essex Sts. *(IND "D" train to Delancey St.).* This market features items of virtually every kind of Jewish cuisine. There are large numbers of kosher butcher shops and fish stands where giant carp are whittled into manageable portions for gefilte fish by capable dissectors, mostly sturdy, Yiddish-speaking women.

CONGREGATION BETH HAMEDRASH HAGODOL, 60 Norfolk St., is the oldest Russian Orthodox synagogue in the country. Founded in 1852, its first building was on Allen St. The present synagogue, formerly a Methodist church, was acquired and remodeled in 1885. It has been designated a landmark by the city's Landmark Preservation Commission.

CANAL STREET AND EAST BROADWAY. This area contains many shops specializing in Jewish books in Hebrew, Yiddish, and English; skullcaps; prayer shawls; phylacteries; Torah Scrolls and covers; Menorahs; Jewish records; prayerbooks; Israeli jewelry; and other items.

EDUCATIONAL ALLIANCE, 197 E. Broadway (corner Jefferson St.), is the famous pioneer Jewish Community Center—Settlement House which helped Americanize three generations of Jewish immigrants. In the lobby are photographs of some of the Alliance's famous alumni. David Sarnoff learned English here and Arthur Murray learned to dance. William Auerbach-Levy, Jo Davidson, and Jacob Epstein paid three cents a week to study art, using pushcart peddlers or bearded patriarchs for models. Work of the students of Moses Soyer, another artist who developed his talents at the Alliance, is also on exhibit in the lobby. Eddie Cantor acted in Alliance-sponsored plays. Chaim Gross, world-famous sculptor, and Isaac Soyer, Moses' brother, also studied here. Morris Raphael Cohen discussed philosophy in the settlement's *Comte Synthetic Circle.* As a member of the Alliance, Sholom Aleichem wrote many of his works here, lectured in the auditorium, and discussed literature and world Jewish themes with other members. In 1906 Sholom Aleichem and Mark Twain appeared together at the Isidor Straus Theatre of the Alliance. It was here that Sholom Aleichem was introduced as the "Jewish Mark Twain," after which Twain replied, "I am the American Sholom Aleichem."

The Alliance was built in 1893 to help Jewish immigrants become integrated into American society. It was also hoped that the settlement house would overcome the activities of conversionist missions on the East Side. Tablets in the Alliance lobby mention philanthropists who helped make the work of the Alliance possible. Here are the names of such distinguished persons as Jacob H. Schiff; Nathan, Isidor, and Ida Straus; Henry Morgenthau; Benjamin Altman; Adolph and Leonard Lewisohn; Isaac J. and Henry Bernheim; Mayer and Babette Lehman; Isaac N. Seligman; and members of the Guggenheim, Bloomingdale, Stern, Loeb, Greenbaum, Bernheimer, Wolff, Lavanburg, and Dreyfuss families. Andrew Carnegie, the Christian multimillionaire, is also listed.

At one time the Educational Alliance had an all-Jewish membership. Today, while its sponsorship and staff are still mostly Jewish, it provides services to substantial numbers of Christians. The Alliance has a new two-story Israel and Leah Cummings Recreation Center and Gymnasium, and a ten-story apartment house for the elderly, known as the David L. Podell Apartment House. □

NATHAN STRAUS SQUARE, diagonally opposite the Alliance, honors the memory of the philanthropist who made it possible for the poor and young to have pastuerized milk, thereby saving thousands of lives. In 1920, there were 300 Nathan Straus milk stations in 36 cities in America.

B'NAI B'RITH'S birthplace at what used to be Sinsheimer's Cafe, 60 Essex St., is permanently marked by a plaque at the site across the street from Seward Park High School, Ludlow St., bet. Broome and Grand Sts. B'nai B'rith was founded there on Oct. 13, 1843.

SEWARD PARK, next to Nathan Straus Square, was for many years the Lower East Side's main social, recreational, and cultural center. Across from Seward Park is the Garden Cafeteria, where Yiddish writers and actors once congregated.

BIALYSTOKER CENTER AND BIKUR CHOLIM and BIALY-STOKER HOME AND INFIRMARY FOR THE AGED, 228 E. Broadway.

BIALYSTOKER SYNAGOGUE, 7 Willet St., is one of the city's few surviving ecclesiastical buildings from the Federal period. It was originally erected as the Willet Street Methodist Church in 1826 and became a synagogue in 1908. It has been designated a city landmark.

CONGREGATION KAHAL ADAS JESHURUN ANSHE LUBETZ, 14 Eldridge St., has an unusual and spectacular interior.

HENRY STREET SETTLEMENT, 265 Henry St. (now known as the Urban Life Center), was founded in 1893 by Lillian D. Wald, pioneer social worker. The agency was originally called the Nurses' Settlement, and Lillian Wald was the head worker. She is credited with having helped to found the Federal Children's Bureau in 1912. Lillian Wald was a nurse as well as a social worker and, together with other nurses, organized what is still known today as the Visiting Nurses' Service, which has treated thousands of sick people in their homes. The Settlement has the Harry DeJur Playhouse, named for a Russian immigrant who was a Henry St. Settlement boy. He died in 1972 and left funds for the theatre. The Settlement is now a national historic landmark.

RABBI JACOB JOSEPH SCHOOL, for years at 165 Henry St. until it moved late in 1976 to Staten Island, is an all-day yeshiva named after the only Chief Rabbi the Jews of New York ever had. The rabbi's great-grandson, a Marine officer who was killed at Guadalcanal in World War II, is memorialized in the Captain Jacob Joseph Playground next to the school.

SCHIFF PARKWAY, Delancey St. from Chrystie to Clinton Sts., is a parkway named for the famed philanthropist, Jacob H. Schiff.

CONGREGATION SHAAREI SHAMAYIM, Rivington St., is the first Romanian congregation in New York.

CONGREGATION ANSHE SLONIM, Norfolk and Stanton Sts., is the oldest synagogue in New York City (1849).

NAPHTALI HERZ IMBER TABLET, 140 E. Second St., is a memorial bronze tablet on the building dedicated to Naphtali Herz Imber, composer of *Hatikvah*, which was the official anthem of the world Zionist movement for more than a generation and is now the national anthem of Israel.

GUSTAVE HARTMAN SQUARE, (a triangle) at Houston St., Ave. D, and Second St., is named for Judge Gustave Hartman, who spent his life on the Lower East Side as teacher, legislator, and humanitarian.

PERETZ SQUARE, Houston St., between First Ave. and Ave. A, is a small park named for the famous Yiddish writer, Isaac Loeb Peretz.

SECOND AVENUE (lower) was once known as the Yiddish Rialto. There are just a few theatres remaining which produce Yiddish plays, (see also ENTERTAINMENT).

CHATHAM SQUARE CEMETERY, St. James Pl. off Chatham Sq., contains the remains of the first cemetery of the Spanish and Portuguese Synagogue, Congregation Shearith Israel. A tablet over the gateway reads, "what remains of the first Jewish cemetery in the United States." The cemetery, which may still be seen, was acquired in 1682 (see also HISTORIC JEWISH CEMETERIES. For places to dine in this area, see DINING OUT).

CITY HALL, has in the Aldermanic Rooms a portrait of Jacob Hays, the last High Constable of New York City, who was often referred to as the first modern detective. From 1802 to 1849 he was in effect chief of police. ●In a side lobby on the main floor there is a collection of Israeli artifacts in two glass cases. ●Room has been made in the Mayor's Reception Room for a portrait of Abraham Beame, who, when elected in 1974, became the city's first Jewish mayor.

CIVIC CENTER SYNAGOGUE, 49 White St., is an Orthodox synagogue.

MIDTOWN

THE NEW YORK PUBLIC LIBRARY, 5th Ave., at 42nd St., has 120,000 volumes of Judaica in its Jewish Division (see also LIBRARIES AND MUSEUMS).

ISRAEL DISCOUNT BANK, 5th Ave. and 43rd St., has bronze doors cast from an original clay relief by Nathan Rapoport, Israeli sculptor. The name of the bank appears in Hebrew over the doorway. Traditional and contemporary fine arts and crafts from Israel are integrated in the bank's interior design, and a wall-length mural depicts the cultural and industrial life of modern Israel. There are also samples of Israeli minerals and other items.

DIAMOND CENTER runs from the lower forties to the lower fifties, east and west of 5th Ave. The main street, however, is 47th Street between 5th and 6th Avenues. Shops specializing in diamonds and expensive jewelry line both sides of the street. Above these shops are the offices of nearly 400 registered diamond dealers and workshops of over 200 diamond-cutting firms, in addition to sawyers, setters, and equipment suppliers. Many of the activities and transactions of the Center are conducted by Hasidim. It is quite an ordinary sight to see these bearded Hasidim, dressed in traditional Jewish garb, carrying a large fortune of diamonds on their person. A robbery occurs infrequently since 47th St. is one of the best protected streets in Manhattan. In addition to police patrols on the street, detectives are employed by each of the jewelry arcades. The main trading centers are the Diamond Trade Association, 15 W. 47th St., and the Diamond Dealers Club, 30 W. 47th St. The Club is almost entirely Jewish, and this is where most, if not all, the Hasidic "curbstone" diamond dealers transact their business. The Association, which is 90 percent Jewish, was founded by Jews from Belgium. Each organization has a central room that provides booths, lockers, tables, telephones, kosher canteen, bullet-proof windows, and burglar-alarm-studded walls. Above the Club is a small synagogue where dealers can go for the afternoon *mincha* service.

AMERICA-ISRAEL CULTURE HOUSE, 4 E. 54th St., is a showcase for Israel's contribution to the arts. It is also the office of the America-Israel Cultural Foundation.

ISRAEL GOVERNMENT TOURIST OFFICE, 488 Madison Ave.

HARMONIE CLUB, 4 E. 60th St., is the oldest Jewish social club in America. It was founded in 1852.

HOUSE OF LIVING JUDAISM, 838 5th Ave., is the headquarters of the Reform lay movement in America. Here are housed the offices of the Union of American Hebrew Congregations; the National Federations of Temple Brotherhoods, Sisterhoods and Youth; and the New York Federation of Reform Synagogues. Across the east wall of the building are the words from the Bible: "Love Thy Neighbor as Thyself," etched in stone. A Magen David is carved in an attractive stone design above the massive oak entrance doors. The limestone façade is capped by the Tablets of the Law with Hebrew abbreviations of the Ten Commandments in bronze letters. Along the south wall of the building are inscribed Micah's words: "Do Justly, Love Mercy and Walk Humbly with thy G-d." A plaque to the left of the entrance notes that this is the home of the Union of American Hebrew Congregations. A plaque on the right reads: "Moritz and Josephine Berg Memorial," commemorating the parents of Dr. Albert A. Berg, noted surgeon and philanthropist. The vestibule is of rose Cassina marble. Twelve marble pillars that symbolize the Twelve Tribes of Israel support the two-story lobby. In the high arches between the pillars, blue and gold wall plaques illustrate the major Jewish holidays. In the center of the lobby in bronze is the Union seal—*Talmud Torah K'neged Kulom* (The Study of Torah Transcends All). Two pieces of sculpture stand in opposite corners. One is by Walter Midener and the other by Moses Ezekiel. Through the archway to the left is the Sisterhood Lounge. A wood sculpture by Erna Weill stands in the corner of the lounge. In the southwest corner of the lobby is the Union Book Shop, with materials published by the Union of American Hebrew Congregations and its affiliates. Books, filmstrips, records, and games are available. There is a small chapel at the far end of the lobby where daily services are conducted by the UAHC staff. Above the doorway is a sculptured replica of *The Hands Raised in Priestly Benediction.* On the doors are small carvings in bronze representing various rituals of Judaism. Four stained glass windows ablaze with light symbolize four phases of Jewish history and the history of the synagogue. The doors of the Ark bear a gold replica of the Tree of Life resting upon the Scrolls of the Law, guarded on either side by the Lions of Judah. The candelabrum is an emblem of the light that devotion to the moral law affords. Above the Ark are tablets with the Ten Commandments surmounted by the crown of the Torah. The Torah Scrolls within the Ark were rescued from a German synagogue destroyed by the Nazis.

TEMPLE EMANU-EL, 5th Ave. and 65th St., is the largest Jewish house of worship in the world. In plan, the temple follows the basilica common in Italy. The exterior walls are of variegated limestone. The dominating feature of the exterior is the great recessed arch on Fifth Ave., enclosing the rose window with its supporting lancets and the three entrance doors. On the exterior the motifs of the carved decorations have been drawn in general from Hebrew symbols. The symbols of the Twelve Tribes of Israel appear on the front of Beth El Chapel, which adjoins the main temple on the north. The chapel is a two-domed structure reminiscent of the Byzantine churches of the Near East (see also HISTORIC SYNAGOGUES).

STEPHEN WISE CONGRESS HOUSE, 15 E. 84th St., is the home of the American Jewish Congress.

YIVO INSTITUTE FOR JEWISH RESEARCH, 1048 5th Ave., housed in the old Vanderbilt Mansion, is the headquarters of YIVO. This worldwide scholarly institution engages in research on various aspects of Jewish life. The building has been designated a landmark by the New York

Community Trust. YIVO's archives include over 2,000,000 items. Its library contains more than 300,000 volumes in 15 languages (see also LIBRARIES AND MUSEUMS).

SOLOMON R. GUGGENHEIM MUSEUM, 5th Ave. and 89th St., is the only museum in New York named for a Jew. A broad vertical band inscribed "The Solomon R. Guggenheim Museum" ties the two parts of the museum together. This unique structure, set in foliage, was called "a little temple in the park" by Frank Lloyd Wright, its eminent architect. Guggenheim was a metallurgist, mining executive, and patron of the arts. When he died in 1949, he left $8 million to the foundation that bears his name, with $2 million of it earmarked for the museum. There is little of intrinsic Jewish interest in the museum, with the exception of a number of Chagall paintings.

THE JEWISH MUSEUM, 5th Ave. and 92nd St., has a three-story wing, the Albert A. List building, and a sculpture garden. An unusual modern structure connects the wing to the museum proper on each of the first three stories, thus binding a modern structure to a Gothic mansion (built in 1908). A glass facade and special lighting enable passers-by to see exhibits in the wing from the street. The sculpture garden is a memorial to Felix M. and Frieda Schiff Warburg. Situated on land adjacent to the Jewish Museum, the garden features a monumental bronze exhibit entitled *Procession*, consisting of four figures observing a religious ceremony. The first figure carries a Torah; two others hold prayerbooks; and the fourth bears a Menorah (see also LIBRARIES AND MUSEUMS).

MOUNT SINAI HOSPITAL, 99th-101st Sts. and 5th Ave. (originally called "Jews' Hospital"). In 1866, the hospital became, by a special act of the legislature, the Mount Sinai, to emphasize its nonsectarian services.

MEMORIAL PLAQUE FOR THE GHETTO RESISTANCE, Riverside Park at 83rd St., honors the memory of the defenseless Jews who rebelled against the Nazi war machine.

HISTORIC SYNAGOGUES

ORTHODOX

SPANISH AND PORTUGUESE SYNAGOGUE (Congregation Shearith Israel), 8 W. 70th St. (*IND local or West Side IRT to 72nd St., Central Park West or Columbus Ave. bus to 70th St.*). Guided tours of groups are conducted but arrangements must be made in advance. Call TR-3-0800. For more than three centuries, Congregation Shearith Israel has been intimately identified with the history of New York. It has also had many connections with other historic American congregations such as Yeshuat Israel (Touro Synagogue), in Newport, R. I., and Mikveh Israel in Philadelphia. To this day, the congregation holds the legal title to Newport's historic Touro Synagogue. For use of the Touro Synagogue, the Newport

Jewish community pays the New York congregation one dollar a year for rent.

The present building was erected in 1897. In the cornerstone, laid in 1896, there are Jewish ritual articles, earth from the Holy Land, and extensive historical information. The cost of the building exceeded $250,000, an impressive sum in those days. At the dedication on May 19, 1897, the doors were ceremoniously opened by Dr. Horatio Gomez, a great-great-grandson of Lewis Moses Gomez, president of the congregation in 1730, when its first synagogue on Mill Street was dedicated. The Greek Revival style of the building was designed by the noted architect Arnold Brunner. In the north entrance hall there are two massive millstones, five inches in thickness, dating back to a mill erected in the latter part of the 17th century where Mill St. became Mill Lane. These were brought to the synagogue in 1894. These stones recall the mill in the spacious quarters above which the Dutch Church of Manhattan held its services from 1628-1633 and in later years, as tradition has it, the earliest synagogue services in the city were held.

The synagogue keeps a separate gallery for women, as has been traditional in Jewish houses of worship since ancient days. In the earliest days of Congregation Shearith Israel in New Amsterdam, it evoked no comment from Dutch Reformed neighbors, who also seated men and women separately. Tribute is paid to women in the present synagogue by the tablets set up in the L. Napoleon Levy Auditorium in memory of Amelia Barnard Lazarus Tobias "whose beneficence knew no creed," said Sara Lyons, principal of the Polonies Talmud Torah School of the congregation from 1898-1934. To assure that the Reader's words will be heard, the reading desk is set near the center of the synagogue. Symbolizing the desire of the congregants to stand in prayer where their forefathers stood, the boards making up the floor of the present reading desk were transferred from the reading desk of the Nineteenth Street Synagogue. They had been brought from the Crosby Street Synagogue of 1834, and it is said, originally from the Mill Street Synagogue building of 1730.

Three of the Torah Scrolls in the Ark come from the Sephardic congregation in The Hague and were rescued from the Nazis. The oldest pair of bells crowning the Scrolls bear the Hebrew date 5497 (1737). Another pair bear the name of Myer Myers (1723-95), the famous Colonial silversmith. Two of the pointers used in reading the Torah are inscribed with the date of 1846, although others may be older than these. The beaten brass lamp that is kindled during Chanukah may well be 300 years old. The four lamps hanging on the eastern wall of the synagogue were rededicated in 1921 to the memory of four men of the congregation who gave up their lives in World War I. Along the western wall of the synagogue auditorium are a number of memorial tablets. One of these, affixed in 1905 on the 250th anniversary of the congregation, commemorates the ministers, as they were then known, from Saul Pardo, who came to New York from Newport in 1685, to Jacques

J. Lyons, who died in 1877. Two other tablets, originally set up in the Crosby Street Synagogue, honor Abraham Touro, "whose practical efforts to cherish the religion of his fathers were only equalled by his munificence which showered his blessings without sectional distinction," and Washington Hendricks, another philanthropist who was one of the principal supporters of the congregation. Another tablet in the L. Napoleon Levy Auditorium below the synagogue recalls Hendricks' "liberal bequests to the Ladies of the Association for the Moral and Religious Instruction of Children of the Jewish Faith." A tablet in the center of the west wall is dedicated to the memory of Jacques J. Lyons, who was *hazzan* of the congregation from 1839-1877. Another was affixed by the Hebra Hasses Va-Amet on its centennial anniversary in 1902 in tribute to its founder, Gershom Mendes Seixas, the *hazzan* of the congregation, a Jewish minister during the American Revolution, and an incorporator of Columbia College.

The Little Synagogue is a Colonial chapel. Known as the Little Synagogue to distinguish it from the main synagogue, it is a composite of the synagogues occupied by Shearith Israel for more than three centuries under three flags: a decade under the Dutch, a century under the British, and since 1783 under the United States. The chapel is 31 x 24 feet, not much smaller than the first American synagogue erected in 1730, the lines of which it closely follows. Here, tangible reminders of our Colonial heritage and ancient religious artifacts come together as symbols of religious freedom. The Reader's desk was used in 1730. The original railing around it, with its exquisite spindles, holds four candlesticks that are the oldest items in the Little Synagogue. The designs on these candlesticks represent a *Havdalah* set. Made of Spanish brass, the candlesticks may date from the 15th century. They have been in use since 1730. The tablet of the Ten Commandments from 1730 is set above the Ark. Next to it are two very old brass urns with the almond blossom motif in their ornamental carving. In Biblical days, almond sprigs were brought to a synagogue and placed in vases on each side of the Ten Commandments. When sprigs were not available, the urns remained empty. Two of the scrolls were damaged during the British occupation of New York during the Revolutionary War. The interior of the Ark is lined with crimson silk damask, as it was in the 1730 Mill Street Synagogue. The *rimmonim* (Torah headpieces) from the first synagogue of Shearith Israel resemble those used by Sephardim in the 13th century. They consist of a turret with open arches in which gold bells hang.

The *Ner Tamid* (Perpetual Light) in front of the Ark has been in continuous use since 1818. The *bancas* (benches) on each side of the Ark were made in 1834 for the congregation's Crosby Street Synagogue. Along the south wall are three pews from the Mill Street Synagogue with full backs edged with mahogany. They are hand-wrought benches with lockers in which books and *taleisim* (prayer shawls) of the congregants are kept. The other benches were made in 1834 for the Crosby Street Synagogue. In those days members provided themselves with individual seat cushions of various shades and materials. Two memorial lamps are in the alcove on the north wall. One was the *Ner Tamid* of the Nineteenth Street Synagogue. It was remodeled slightly during the restoration to make it match the Davis Memorial Lamp next to it. In the center of the west window hangs the Sabbath Lamp of the Seven Wicks, an interesting and lovely lamp from the 1730 synagogue. The two candlesticks on the window sill and the scones are from the Crosby Street Synagogue. The stained glass windows were made by Tiffany in 1896 and are reminiscent of the stained glass windows from Crosby Street. The Omer Board, made before 1730, has a movable parchment scroll that is set daily to count the days of the seven-week period between Passover and Shavuot. The ancient Chanukah Menorah of beaten brass was made in Holland prior to 1730. The four chandeliers were created for the Little Synagogue in 1896, in the design of the Byzantine oil lamps used in old synagogues of Europe and Asia (see also UNIQUE SYNAGOGUES AND SERVICES). ☐

WALL STREET SYNAGOGUE, 47 Beekman St. On the grass-green roof is a replica of the first synagogue in North America which was erected on Mill Street (now South William St.) in 1730. The original synagogue had only one room and resembled a log cabin. Its replica seats 20 persons. Built of fireproof material, it has rustic wood on the inside, as in the original synagogue. At one end of the 12 x 20 foot room stands the *bimah*.

Modern in construction, the synagogue below seats 180 people—110 men on the main floor and 70 women in the balcony. The synagogue has a kosher luncheon club patronized by stockbrokers and insurance executives whose offices are nearby. ☐

JEWISH CENTER, 131 W. 86th St., is an Orthodox synagogue, despite its name. The sanctuary on the second floor has a beautiful marble altar framed by two lovely stained glass windows recessed on either side. The parchment Scrolls of the Torah, some of which are hundreds of years old, have exquisite silver ornamentation. The synagogue is open every day from 8 a.m. to 7 p.m.

CONGREGATION OHAB ZEDEK, 118-124 W. 95th St., was founded on the Lower East Side and incorporated as the First Hungarian Congregation Ohab Zedek. With the migration uptown of many of its members to what was then fashionable Harlem, Ohab Zedek purchased its third building in 1906 at 18 W. 116th St. and built a beautiful synagogue with facilities for an expanded Talmud Torah and social assembly. In 1912 the world-famous Yossele Rosenblatt was engaged as cantor, and he officiated in the Harlem synagogue for many years. On May 9, 1926, the cornerstone of the present building was laid. Several years later Cantor Rosenblatt was reengaged and he served until 1935. Early in 1938 the former Chief Rabbi of Frankfurt-am-Main, Dr. Jacob Hoffman, became the synagogue's spiritual leader. The following year the Beth Hillel Hebrew Institute was dedicated on a site adjoining the synagogue. It is now called the Dr. Hillel Klein Center of Jewish Education.

YOUNG ISRAEL OF THE WEST SIDE, 210 W. 91st St., is in a building formerly occupied by Reform Temple Israel.

CONGREGATION RAMATH ORAH, 550 W. 110th St., had as its rabbi Dr. Robert S. Serebrenik, who was Grand Rabbi of Luxembourg when the Nazis conquered it. Brought in the spring of 1941 to Gestapo headquarters in Berlin, he faced Adolf Eichmann and bargained for the life of the Jewish people of Luxembourg and other communities. He testified at the Eichmann trial in Jerusalem.

CONGREGATION K'HAL ADATH JESHURUN, 85 Bennett Ave., is a prominent congregation composed mostly of Jewish immigrants from Frankfurt-am-Main. The synagogue's social hall is at 90 Bennett Ave. A day school, the Yeshiva Rabbi Samson Raphael Hirsch, is at 91 Bennett Ave., and a *mikveh* is at 536 W. 187th St. The synagogue's Rika Breuer Teachers Seminary for Girls offers a complete course of studies leading to teacher certification and a course of advanced Jewish studies leading to a general certificate.

CONGREGATION SHAARE HATIKVAH, 715 W. 179th St., was organized in 1935 by Jews who fled from Nazi persecution. CONGREGATION BETH HILLEL OF WASHINGTON HEIGHTS, 571 W. 182nd St., was also organized by refugees from Germany.

CONGREGATION EZRATH ISRAEL (better known as the Actors' Temple), 339 W. 47th St. For more than a quarter of a century, actors, directors, and producers made this temple their spiritual headquarters. Orthodox services are held daily.

RADIO CITY SYNAGOGUE, formerly on 6th Ave., is now at 110 W. 48th St. Among its early supporters were Walter Winchell, the late George Sokolsky, and other well-known professionals.

GARMENT CENTER CONGREGATION, 205 W. 40th St. (in the Brotherhood House). Founded in the 1930s in the vicinity of Macy's, Saks, and Gimbels, the congregation took an active interest in the public life of the city.

FUR CENTER SYNAGOGUE, 228 W. 29th St., is in the heart of the city's fur industry. The synagogue has a reading room, the gift of three mink ranchers' organizations.

CONGREGATION ORACH CHAIM, 1459-63 Lexington Ave. Among its rabbis were Simon Langer, who received the Legion of Honor from the French government, and Dr. Joseph Hertz, formerly Chief Rabbi of England.

CONGREGATION KEHILATH JESHURUN, 125 E. 85th St., is the sponsor of Ramaz School, a private Jewish day school that is modern and progressive in its approach. Religious and secular studies are alternated and, when possible, are correlated and integrated. The school was the inspiration of Joseph H. Lookstein, rabbi of Congregation Kehilath Jeshurun and principal of Ramaz. It is named for Moses Zebulun Margolies, grandfather of Mrs. Lookstein and for 31 years the congregation's rabbi. He was known as

Ramaz—a name coined from the Ra-M-Z of Rabbi Moses Zebulun. The school is coeducational, with classes from kindergarten through 12th grade. The "Ramaz Plan" has excited educators across the nation and the school has become a model for many others.

FIFTH AVENUE SYNAGOGUE, 5 E. 62nd St. This is the only Orthodox synagogue in this area. Immanuel Jakobovits, Chief Rabbi of the British Commonwealth, was once its rabbi.

CONGREGATION TALMUD TORAH ADERETH EL, 133-135 E. 29th St., is over 100 years old.

MARINERS' TEMPLE, 3 Henry St. (on the Lower East Side), has been designated a landmark of New York by the New York Community Trust.

PARK EAST SYNAGOGUE (Congregation Zichron Ephraim), 163 East 67th St., directly across the street from the Soviet Mission to the United Nations, is a colorful city landmark of Byzantine-Moorish architecture. Bulbous cupolas, set at different levels, are surmounted by a slender shaft supporting a Star of David. The façade of the main structure rises from behind an elaborately arched portico. At either wing there is a decorative square tower, one higher than the other, each richly carved, arched, and star-crowned. Standing out in bold relief are the synagogue's stained glass windows. There are two circular windows—one above the Ark, rich pink, blue, and silver, called the Moon, and the other, known as the Sun, in the rear wall facing the street. The Ark is intricately carved, with loops and pointed cupolas leading the eye to the vaulted, spangled, and delicately buttressed roof. A large outdoor plaque has inscribed: "Hear the Cry of the Oppressed—the Jewish Community in the Soviet Union." Construction is under way for a $6 million cultural center and day school. The congregation was founded in 1888 by the late Jonas Weil, its first president.

LINCOLN SQUARE SYNAGOGUE, Amsterdam Ave. and 69th St., is in the shape of a Star of David and is designed to recapture the centrality of the Torah.

CONSERVATIVE

PARK AVENUE SYNAGOGUE, 50 E. 87th St., attracts visitors from all over the world. Founded in 1882 by a group of German and Hungarian Jews, the congregation developed out of the amalgamation of Congregation Agudath Jeshorim, an Orthodox synagogue on East 86th Street; a Reform temple on East 82nd Street; and the Congregation Bikur Cholim on 72nd Street and Lexington Avenue. It is now a Conservative congregation. Its members include some of the most distinguished Jewish civic and communal leaders in the city. It was the congregation of the late, beloved Rabbi Milton Steinberg, who is memorialized in the adjoining Milton Steinberg House, a five-story civic and educational center. The current rabbi, Judah Nadich, was General Eisenhower's adviser on Jewish affairs in

Germany. Sabbath services begin at 5:45 p.m. on Fridays and at 10 a.m. on Saturdays. The synagogue is open every day for individual prayer and meditation. The architecture of the Milton Steinberg House is contemporary, yet designed to blend with the traditional design of the adjacent synagogue. The façade of stained glass windows, designed by the eminent artist Adolph Gottlieb, depicts Jewish traditions and holidays in an overall abstract mural. The design embodies 1,300 square feet of glass comprised on 91 individual window panes covering the four floors. One-third of the glass is designed and painted to contain 21 individual abstract paintings portraying the religious holidays and traditions. Each of the paintings is repeated four or five times at different points on the façade, forming a checkerboard pattern against a background of traditional, diamond-shaped stained glass panes that compose the remainder of the façade. The paintings are on antique glass imported from Europe; the diamond-shaped panes are of American marine antique glass. In the lobby is *The Altar,* a painting by Moshe Castel, an Israeli artist. Other interesting features of the building are a uniquely sculptured pair of bronze Ark doors and a beautiful candelabrum executed by the sculptor, Calvin Albert.

THE BROTHERHOOD SYNAGOGUE (Congregation Beth Achim), 28 Gramercy Park South, is located in the former Friends Meeting House, a New York City landmark built in 1859. The interior is of classical, formal elegance and spare simplicity. The building is what the Victorians called the Italianate style—a melange of near-Renaissance motifs strong on cornices, pediments, and round-headed windows. The building was designated a New York landmark in 1965. It has a long record of social as well as religious usefulness. During the Civil War, its members took an active interest in the cause of the Negro or "Freedman," as they were called, by supplying garments from a sewing room on the third floor. The congregation calls itself "Liberal Conservative."

CONGREGATION B'NAI JESHURUN, 257 W. 88th St., is the oldest Ashkenazic congregation in New York City. It was established in November, 1825, as an offshoot of Congregation Shearith Israel, by a group of English and Dutch Jews who wished to follow the Ashkenazic (English and German) rather than the Sephardic (Spanish and Portuguese) ritual. Among the founders of B'nai Jeshurun were John I. Hart, son of the Reverend Judah Hart of Portsmouth, and Abraham Mitchell, one of a handful of Jews who served in the War of 1812. Haym M. Salomon, son of the famous Haym Salomon of Philadelphia, presented a Hebrew Bible when the first house of worship was consecrated in 1827, on Elm Street. As the city grew, the population moved northward. By 1849 the old synagogue had been outgrown, and a new house of worship was dedicated on Greene Street. The period beginning with the dedication of the Greene Street Synagogue ushered in a flourishing career for the congregation, whose members took active parts in the communal agencies that had begun to grow and develop. In 1865, a new synagogue was dedicated on 34th Street, west of Broadway, on the present site of Macy's. Dr. Morris J. Raphall, first of B'nai Jeshurun's famous rabbis, was the son of the banker to the king of Sweden. He was the first Jewish minister to open a session of the United States House of Representatives with prayer. The congregation's fourth house of worship, on Madison Avenue at 65th Street, was erected in 1885. In 1893, Stephen S. Wise, aged 21, became rabbi of the congregation and served it until 1900, when he went to Portland, Oregon. Another distinguished minister was the Reverend Dr. Judah L. Magnes. The present synagogue was erected in 1918. It has been called "an architectural masterpiece embodying the spirit of ancient Semitic art." Its façade is of a striking composition featuring a tall romanesque portal; the interior is decorated with intricate polychrome ornament. Rabbi Israel Goldstein became the rabbi a few months after the dedication of the present building. In 1928, a six-story community building adjoining the synagogue was dedicated. The congregation's Institute of Adult Jewish Studies, under Rabbi William Berkowitz, attracted nationwide attention.

TEMPLE ANSCHE CHESED, 251 W. 110th St., was founded in 1876.

CONGREGATION SHAARE ZEDEK, 212 W. 93rd St., is over 100 years old.

SUTTON PLACE SYNAGOGUE, 225 E. 51st St., is called the Jewish Center for the United Nations. Its façade of rough stone blocks matches that of the adjoining Greenacre minipark. The themes of Judaism, world peace, and universal brotherhood are reflected in the building and particularly in the stained glass windows. Across the front of the red-carpeted sanctuary is a design in the shape of an open Torah Scroll upon which are inscribed the words of Isaiah: "And they shall beat their swords into plowshares."

THE LITTLE SYNAGOGUE, 27 E. 20th St., is a unique congregation which calls itself "modern Hasidic" but follows the Conservative ritual. Its rabbi, the Reverend Joseph Gelberman, is a religious and psychological counselor and a devotee of Martin Buber. Lectures are given Wednesday evenings throughout the year. With the exception of the summer months, services are held every other Friday evening.

MILLINERY CENTER SYNAGOGUE, 1025 6th Ave., conducts services frequently during the day for those who need to say *kaddish*.

REFORM

TEMPLE EMANU-EL, 5th Ave. and 65th St., is open from 10 a.m. to 5 p.m. daily. *(East Side IRT local to 68th St., BMT to 5th Ave., or 65th St. crosstown bus to 5th Ave.)* A guide is available, call RH-4-1400. Friday night services begin at 5:15 p.m. throughout the year, and from the first week in November and the last week in March, additional services are held on Friday evenings at 8:30. On Saturdays, services begin at 10:30 a.m. The temple has a choir and an organ. It also has a special Sunset Service, conducted from Sunday through Thursday at 5:30 p.m., in the Beth El Chapel under the sponsorship of the Men's Club. Its Friday evening services are broadcast from 5:30 to 6:00 over stations WQXR and WQXR-FM.

This imposing edifice, on the site of the old Vincent Astor residence, is the congregation's fourth building. Its first building, which it purchased in 1847 after worshipping in a private home on the Lower East Side for two years, was at 56 Chrystie St. In November, 1862, an imposing structure at 5th Avenue and 43rd Street was selected as Emanu-El's new home. The building was described by The New York Times as the "architectural sensation of the city." Louis Marshall, lawyer, civic leader, and Emanu-El's president, led the fight for a new temple and laid the cornerstone of the present magnificent building in May, 1928. Marshall died in Switzerland on September 11, 1929. His funeral was the first service held in the present structure. Judge Irving Lehman, who succeeded him as president, dedicated Temple Emanu-El on January 10, 1930. It has been a Reform congregation since its beginning in 1845. The temple's vestibule walls and floors are Siena Travertine; the ceiling is walnut. The walls of the building are actually self-supporting, while the buttresses of the exterior and the trusses of the interior are, respectively, the stone and plaster covering the structural steel members necessary to bridge the span of the great nave. The main body of the temple's auditorium is 77 feet wide between piers and 150 feet in length, from the east wall of the vestibule to the sanctuary steps, with a height of 103 feet to the underside of the ridges of the ceiling. The walls of the auditorium are covered from the top of the stone base to the ceiling with acoustic tile. The side galleries are supported by marble columns. French Vaurion stone was used for the flooring of the aisles. The temple seats 2,500 people. The sanctuary is 30 feet in depth and just over 40 feet wide, with a marble floor and marble (and mosaic) wainscot on the sides. Below the arch is the Ark, with columns of French Benou Jaume marble. The Ark doors are bronze, and the frame of the opening is of Siena marble with mosaic insets. The columns are crowned with small bronze tabernacles. The abbreviated version of the Ten Commandments is on the Ark's bronze grille, while on both sides of the Ark are beautiful seven-branched candlesticks. The Shield of David is repeated in the mosaics and windows of the temple; the Lion of Judah and the Royal Crown of the Torah are also pictured. Twenty-five feet above the sanctuary is the choir loft, cut off by a pierced railing surmounted by marble columns of varied colors carrying arches that conceal the organ, part of which is placed over the choir gallery and part above the sanctuary vault. The great organ, located above the chancel, is four manual, having 116 speaking stops, 50 couplers, 7,681 speaking pipes, 32 bell chimes, and 61 celesta bars. Under Temple Emanu-El is the Isaac M. Wise Memorial Hall, which seats 1,500 and has a stage, kitchen, and banquet facilities.

Just outside the Temple, a "Garden of Freedom" was dedicated during the American Bicentennial in 1976. A Vermont marble bench surrounded by plants, a tree, and shrubbery, has the following inscription: "This garden is dedicated to the people of the United States in grateful recognition of 200 years of religious freedom—1776-1976." ▫

BETH EL CHAPEL, which adjoins the temple on the north, is named for Temple Beth El, which merged with Congregation Emanu-El in 1927. Over the door of the chapel is the verse from Genesis: "This is none other than the house of G-d." The inscription in the exterior frieze of the chapel is from Isaiah: "And the work of righteousness, quietness and security forever." The two domes of the chapel are supported by six columns of pink Westerly granite, while the side walls rest on arches springing from columns of Breche Oriental marble. Verdello marble is used for the wainscots and for the pierced side walls. The sanctuary arch, in which blue is the dominant color, has a golden brown mosaic background with the Ten Commandments inscribed in blue, against which the Ark of wrought steel is set. The chapel is lit by two great chandeliers finished in silver and enamel. The seating capacity is 350. An eight-story community house adjoins Temple Emanu-El to the east. Over the grouped entrance doors is a verse from the 78th Psalm: "Give ear, O my people, to my instructions, incline your ear to the words of my mouth which we have heard and know, and which our fathers have related to us." The community house contains the Ivan M. Stettenheim Library, with thousands of volumes of Judaica and other literature; an assembly room that seats 750; the rabbis' studies; a paneled meeting room for the trustees; the temple's offices; smaller assembly rooms; and other facilities. Adjoining the community house is a religious school building. The building contains eight huge stained glass windows, each of which has more than 1,000 pieces of glass. Illustrating the traditional symbols of Judaism, the windows are divided into four groups—the Ten Commandments, the shofar, the Star of David, the Burning Bush, the Eternal Light, the Tree of Life, the Menorah, and the Book of Jewish Laws.

JUDGE IRVING LEHMAN MEMORIAL MUSEUM, in Temple Emanu-El's religious school building foyer, contains a valuable collection of Jewish ceremonial objects that the distinguished jurist and former president of the congregation gathered during his travels in many parts of the world. Judge Irving Lehman was the older brother of Senator Herbert H. Lehman.

CENTRAL SYNAGOGUE, 652 Lexington Ave., was built in 1870. The cornerstone was laid by Dr. Isaac Mayer Wise on December 14, 1870. No other temple in New York in use today has been on its current site that long. In 1846, 18 young men, most of whom had come from Bohemia, met in a hall in Coblenzer's Hotel on Ludlow Street and conducted their own services. They looked to the Book of Micah for their congregation's name and chose Ahawath Chesed—"Love of Mercy," (from "Do Justly, Love Mercy, and Walk Humbly with Thy G-d"). When the little congregation outgrew its home in 1849, it moved seven blocks east, to Ridge Street, having transformed the upper part of two houses into a synagogue at a rental of $100 a year; dues were $1.50. The ritual in those days was Orthodox. In 1854, the congregation bought a house on narrow Columbia Street, which it remodeled. Its next move, in 1864, was to the southwest corner of Fourth Street and Avenue C. Rabbi Isaac Mayer Wise, who was to lay the cornerstone of the congregation's present structure and whose son was to become its rabbi, spoke at the dedication ceremonies. In 1870, with the movement of the population, the congregation decided to acquire the property at 55th Street and Lexington Avenue. This is said to be the second largest synagogue in New York. It was designed by Henry Fernbach, the first Jewish architect in America. The synagogue seats more than 1,300 persons. The Eternal Light above the Ark was lit in 1872 when the building was opened and was not extinguished until 1946 when gas was replaced by electricity during the 100th anniversary restoration. This light has probably burned continuously longer than any other in New York. In 1898 Congregation Shaar Hashomayim merged with Ahawath Chesed and the new name was Congregation Ahawath Chesed Shaar Hashomayim. This name continued in use until 1920, when it was changed to Central Synagogue. One of the synagogue's rabbis was Dr. Alexander Kohut, who had come from Hungary as one of the leading authors, scholars, and religious leaders. In 1925, Rabbi Jonah B. Wise, the son of Rabbi Isaac Mayer Wise, was offered the pulpit, which he served until 1958. Central Synagogue has taken part in interfaith Thanksgiving services with Central Presbyterian Church and the Congregation of Christ Church Methodist. The ministers rotate in preaching the sermons and conducting services. Central Synagogue was designated a landmark of New York by the New York Community Trust. A plaque on the building reads:

LANDMARKS OF NEW YORK
CENTRAL SYNAGOGUE
THIS IS THE OLDEST SYNAGOGUE BUILDING IN
CONTINUOUS USE IN NEW YORK CITY. THE
CONGREGATION WAS ESTABLISHED IN 1846 AND
THIS TEMPLE, DESIGNED BY HENRY FERNBACH,
WAS COMPLETED IN 1872. THE STYLE IS MOORISH
REVIVAL, THE ARRANGEMENT GOTHIC.

More recently, Central Synagogue was designated a National Landmark.
    JONAH B. WISE COMMUNITY HOUSE, 55th St. near Park Ave., is the Central Synagogue's $2,500,000 structure.
    TEMPLE ISRAEL OF NEW YORK CITY, 112 East 75th St., is one of the better known temples in New York. It moved from the West Side after having been there many years and now has a $2 million sanctuary. Among its most impressive features is its huge cylindrical Ark.
    CONGREGATION SHAARAY TEFILA, 250 East 79th St., once familiarly known as the West End Synagogue, has a new temple. The sanctuary grew out of the shell of a Trans-Lux Theatre that occupied the site

when it was purchased by the congregation. While the structure was completely renovated, certain features were retained, such as the sloping auditorium and the airconditioning system. In the building's four stories and mezzanine are classrooms, offices, an assembly hall, and recreation and meeting rooms. Its original name was the name it now uses exclusively— Shaaray Tefila ("Gates of Prayer). It started as an Orthodox congregation in humble circumstances. In 1847, its struggling Wooster Street congregation frequently paid "worshippers" to insure the required *minyan*. After nearly two decades on Wooster Street, the congregation moved to Broadway and 36th Street. In 1869, an imposing new edifice was consecrated on 44th Street west of 6th Avenue. Ten years later, the congregation voted to abandon Orthodoxy in favor of Reform Judaism. In two decades the congregation made another move, to 82nd Street, east of Amsterdam Avenue. There, it became familiarly known as the West End Synagogue, although its corporate name has always been Congregation Shaaray Tefila.

METROPOLITAN SYNAGOGUE (in the Community Church building), 40 E. 35th St., is well-known for its fine music during services. Its cantor, Norman Atkins, has appeared with opera companies throughout the country and with all of the major symphony orchestras. Leonard Bernstein is the synagogue's honorary music consultant. Special events at the synagogue have included the world premiere of *The Golem* by Abraham Ellstein, presented by the New York City Center Opera Company; a coast-to-coast televised brotherhood service conducted by the Metropolitan Synagogue Choir and the Choir of the Church of the Master; a service of music and prayer dedicated to Ernest Bloch; *Gideon*—a dialogue between Arthur Cantor, producer of the play, and the synagogue's spiritual leader, Rabbi Judah Cahn; the recording of Bloch's *Sacred Service*, with Leonard Bernstein conducting the New York Philharmonic and Rabbi Cahn singing with the Metropolitan Synagogue Choir; and joint Thanksgiving services with the Community Church. Outside the synagogue, on the church building, is a large sculpture of the Prophet Isaiah. Isaiah's right arm holds a shard of sword broken off near the haft; his left arm rises straight up, the hand gripping the blade. The plowshare beside him rounds out the line from the Book of Isaiah that inspired the sculpture: ". . . and they shall beat their swords into plowshares." Below the large figure of Isaiah is a smaller piece of sculpture in the form of an open book. On the right-hand side is a smaller figure of Isaiah; on the left is the "swords into plowshares" passage. Friday evening services are held throughout the year at 8:30 p.m. Services on Saturday begin at 10:45 a.m. In addition to the Sabbath service, there is a Saturday morning period of adult education.

THE STEPHEN WISE FREE SYNAGOGUE, 30 W. 68th St. Founded in 1907 by Rabbi Stephen S. Wise, the synagogue uses the word "free" because the pulpit is free—not subject to control. The pews are free since seats are never sold or reserved. Contributions are voluntary, and there are no fixed membership dues. Rabbi Wise founded the Free

Synagogue partially in reaction to a dictum he received when he was offered the pulpit of Temple Emanu-El in New York. Louis Marshall, an officer of the temple, made it clear that "the pulpit should always be subject to and under the control of the board of trustees." Rabbi Wise then rejected the offer, declaring in part:

A free pulpit, worthily filled, must command respect and influence; a pulpit that is not free, howsoever filled, is sure to be without potency or honor. In the pursuit of the duties of his office, the minister may from time to time be under the necessity of giving expression to views at variance with the views of some or even many members of the congregation. Far from such difference proving the pulpit to be wrong, it may be and ofttimes is found to signify that the pulpit has done its duty in calling evil evil and good good, in abhorring the moral wrong of putting light for darkness and darkness for light.

Rabbi Wise founded the Free Synagogue also in reaction to what he saw as a lack of vitality and influence on the part of the Reform movement of his day. In a lecture at the Hudson Theatre on West 47th Street, he declared:

What is a Free Synagogue? A Synagogue! A Synagogue, a Jewish society, for I am a Jew, a Jewish teacher. The Free Synagogue is not to be an indirect or circuitous avenue of approach to Unitarianism; it is not to be a society for the gradual conversion of Jewish men or women to any form of Christianity. We mean to be vitally, intensely, unequivocally Jewish. Jews who would not be Jews will find no place in the Free Synagogue, for we, its founders, wish to be not less Jewish but more Jewish in the highest and noblest sense of the term.

The response was gratifying. Some attended out of curiosity. Some were seeking a kind of Jewish affiliation they could not satisfy in existing institutions. On April 15, 1907, more than a hundred "religious pioneers" met at the Hotel Savoy for the purpose of organizing a Free Synagogue. Henry Morgenthau, Sr., presided, and Charles E. Bloch served as secretary. Morgenthau reported that 192 persons had announced their intention of joining and contributed $9,300. Among those who joined together with Morgenthau and Bloch were Jacob H. Schiff, Adolph Lewisohn, Isaac N. Seligson, M. J. Stroock, and J. B. Greenhut. Services were first held Sunday mornings at the Universalist Church of the Eternal Hope on West 81st Street, and attracted as many as a thousand people. Beginning with Rosh Hashanah eve on October 3, 1910, services were held at Carnegie Hall, giving the Free Synagogue the largest seating capacity of any Jewish congregation in the country. In 1911, the brownstone houses on West 68th Street were bought to accommodate the school, social service department, executive offices, and studies. Branches of the Free Synagogue were organized on the Lower East Side. (Sabbath eve services were conducted at Clinton Hall, near Grand Street; in The Bronx at 929 Southern Blvd.; in Washington Heights at Corrigan Hall; in Flushing, and in Newark, New Jersey.) A synagogue house was built in 1922 at 40 West 68th St., as temporary quarters. When it became apparent that the needs of the congregation could best be served by the more traditional Sabbath eve service, the Sunday morning services at Carnegie Hall were discontinued, and Carnegie Hall was used only for the High Holy Days. The current five-story structure was dedicated on January 20, 1950. The cornerstone is from the Holy of Holies in Jerusalem. It was presented to Rabbi Wise by Brigadier Sir Wyndham Deedes in 1922. The adornments in the interior of the synagogue were designed by the noted Jewish artist, A. Raymond Katz, who was assisted in the execution of the decor by Louis Ross, an expert in the technique of gesso. Above the portals of the entrance are inscribed the words: "Blessed be he who comes in the name of the Lord. We bless you out of the House of the Lord." The proscenium arch, which spans the choir screen, bears Katz's interpretation of the holidays. At the lower left is the letter *shin*, standing for *Shabbat*. Within the letter are the ritual objects of the Sabbath services in the home—the candles, the *kiddush* cup, the *challah*, and the traditional fish. Masks, the crown of Ahasuerus, and the *megillah* depict Purim. Passover is represented by the cup of Elijah, the pyramids the Hebrews built in slavery, the wheat of the matzo, and the four cups of wine. The Tablets of the Law and the blossoms of spring portray the mood of *Shavuot*. The top of the arch bears the Hebrew inscription: "Know before Whom thou standest." At the top of the right-hand side of the arch are the *dreidel* and the eight branched candelabrum, symbols of Chanukah. Succoth is represented by the *lulav* and *etrog*. Yom Kippur is depicted by the Book of Life. The *shofar* is the central symbol of Rosh Hashanah. At the lower right of the arch are the twisted candle, the *kiddush* cup, and the spice box—symbols of the *Havdalah* service, which concludes the Sabbath day. Six panels on either side of the Ark express the ideals of Judaism—gratitude for G-d's goodness, Torah, labor, good deeds, love of neighbor, prayer and praise of the Lord, ethics, joyousness, truth, peace, justice, freedom, the love of Zion, and study. On the Ark doors are carved hands, in the palms of which are the Ten Commandments. The Ark is surmounted by the words that are the heart of Jewish belief: "The Lord is Our G-d, the Lord is One." The Perpetual Light is fashioned of two Hebrew letters—the *zayin* which stands for *zikaron* or "remembrance," and the *shin*, which, in this instance, stands for *Shaddai*, or the Almighty. The design on the pulpit is a variation on the two letters. The form of the Menorah is also the letter *shin*, standing for *Shaddai*; each branch is crowned with the letter *yod*, which again suggests the name of the Lord. There is a chapel under the east balcony that accommodates smaller groups for special services. ☐

CONGREGATION HABONIM (German-Liberal), 44 West 66th St., was founded in 1939 by a group of refugees from Nazi Germany. The sanctuary has 12 stained glass windows created by Robert Sowers. The whole ensemble may be seen as an image of the life cycle, from youth on the left, represented by slender, shoot-like forms thrusting upward out of deep reddish soil; through the vigor of young manhood in the center, where the long, figure-like forms in bronze seem to join hands, and in so doing create the primordial shelter—the Ark, the temple, the family hearth; on to the extreme right, where the simple, white shield-like form of maturity sets off the more somber hues of the firmament. The three panels just to the left of the center window contain symbols that may be read as the torch of knowledge and as covered scrolls standing in a row. The three panels just to the right of the center window contain a series of forms that to some may suggest a star, to others the Cloak of Many Colors, to still others just the laborious effort of the human being to combine simple elements in this precarious world into a durable structure. In the center window's upper right-hand section, there is a form very much like a letter of the Hebrew alphabet. This form, since it is not an actual letter, appears in bronze on both the inside and the outside of the window. Yet it is in the spirit of the actual characters of the alphabet. This same form may also be read as the head, a rather king-like bearded head in profile, of one of the figure-like forms previously mentioned, while these forms may themselves be seen in another sense as forming between them the letter H. At the bottom of the window, where they are most evident from the outside, are two more bronze forms that recall the Tablets of the Law. From the inside, the whole light center area of the window, with its fiery core of color and its bronze forms, grows upward from the Ark. The faceted backgrounds at both ends of the design are based on the form of the Star of David. While the congregation is affiliated with the Reform movement, it calls itself "German-Liberal," and its male congregants wear *taleisim* and head coverings. Fragments of temples destroyed on *Kristalnacht* have gone into a monument which memorializes the Nazi victims. Behind the monument, in the temple's lobby, is a modernistic representation of the Tree of Life.

CONGREGATION RODEPH SHOLOM, 7 W. 83rd St., was founded in 1842. One of its ministers, Rabbi Aaron Wise, who served from 1875-1897, was the father of Rabbi Stephen S. Wise. The current building, erected in 1930, was designed by Charles B. Myers, for many years architect for the City of New York.

EAST END TEMPLE, 398 Second Ave., is in a former bank branch. There are two museum-type window display cases, each about four and a half feet square and a foot deep, facing 23rd Street. The exhibits vary from month to month. The temple has some silver Torah ornaments made by native craftsmen in Mexico. Its library has over 1,700 volumes of Judaica, almost all of them in English. Sabbath evening services are held at 8:40 p.m. the year round.

HEBREW TABERNACLE OF WASHINGTON HEIGHTS, 605 W. 161st St., is a Reform synagogue, although its male congregants wear hats or *yarmulkas* and *taleisim* and it observes two days of Rosh Hashanah and eight days of Passover and Succoth.

THE INTERNATIONAL SYNAGOGUE, Tri-Faith Plaza of John F. Kennedy International Airport (see Queens, New York).

UNIQUE SYNAGOGUES AND SERVICES

SYNAGOGUE OF THE SOCIETY FOR THE ADVANCEMENT OF JUDAISM (Reconstructionist), 15 W. 86th Street. Sabbath services begin at 6 p.m. on Fridays, and at 10:15 a.m. on Saturdays. One of the unique features here is that both men and women are called up to the Torah. In the Society for the Advancement of Judaism, women have complete equality with men not only in the synagogue service but also on the board of trustees and in the bat mitzvah ceremony. Founded in 1922 by Dr. Mordecai M. Kaplan, the society, which is the fountainhead of the Reconstructionist movement, conducts not only a synagogue but also a school, in the Joseph and Nellie Y. Levy Building, at 32 W. 86th St. It cooperates with the Park Avenue Synagogue and Congregation B'nai Jeshurun in the Milton Steinberg Central High School of Jewish Studies and offers a comprehensive adult education program.

Covering the south wall of the synagogue are murals depicting Palestinian life and the story of Israel's rebirth in the Holy Land. The contrast between ancient Jewish life and modern Zionist activity forms the theme of panels covering more than 180 square feet. The central panel, almost 20 feet long and 5 feet high, deals with present-day agricultural aspects of the Holy Land. Two flanking panels are vertical. In the upper right-hand corner of the panel at the right is the old city of Tiberias. Emerging from the city are some Hasidim in their traditional garb, dancing with the Holy Scroll with expressions of joy and ecstasy. Three Jews are shown at prayer by the Wailing Wall. At the bottom and to the left, children of the yeshiva sit at their studies. To the right a diversified crowd is seen passing through the narrow arched streets of the old city of Jerusalem. The vertical, left-handed panel deals with new elements in the Holy Land. The city of Haifa with its new port is in the upper left corner. To the right is Mount Scopus, dotted with olive trees; and there stands the Hebrew University, in all its glory. Below is Technion-Haifa, Israel's great scientific institute. Two mains from the Ruttenberg Electrical Works lead directly to the young worker who is in the center of the panel. Other laborers at the lower right symbolize the building activity in the land. To the left are suggestions of Tel Aviv's modern architecture, and below, a group of enthusiastic, spirited, singing youth. The murals are the work of Temima N. Gezari, a Jewish artist. ☐

CONGREGATION SHEARITH ISRAEL (Spanish and Portuguese Synagogue), 8 W. 70th St. The services and practices at this congregation are rather unique. The prayers are read in Sephardic Hebrew rather than Ashkenazic. Upon entering the synagogue it is customary to bow and to recite the following words in Hebrew: "Lo, in Thy abundant love I enter Thy house; in reverence to Thee I bow toward Thy holy temple." As congregants approach the doors to leave the synagogue, they turn about momentarily, face the Ark, bow and say, "Lord, lead me in Thy righteousness . . . make Thy path straight before me." A suitable head covering is worn at all times. At morning services, the *talis* (prayer shawl) is worn by all males. The congregational services emphasize the participation of all in chanting the prayers of the synagogue. Special prayers are added on Sabbath days that commemorate the consecration of one of the earlier synagogue buildings; the present synagogue is commemorated on Rosh Hodesh, Jewish festivals, and the High Holy Days. On these commemoration days and other special occasions, the Ark is opened before the *Baruh Sheamar* by one of the worshippers, and the scrolls can be seen blanketed with cloaks of different colors. On the seventh day of Passover and on *Shabbat Shirah*—the Sabbath of Song—the *Az Yashir* (Song of Moses), is chanted during the Torah reading. The *Nishmat* (The Soul of Living) is sung by the choir and congregation, after which the services continue in much the same fashion of antiphonal response that characterized the earlier part of the service. The *hashcaboth* are the memorial prayers recited every Sabbath.

The Reader announces the name of those who are called upon to participate in the ceremony of taking the Torah Scroll from the Ark. The honors to be bestowed include those of opening the Ark, carrying the scroll, removing the bells and band after the scroll has been carried to the reading desk, lifting up the scroll, and accompanying the scroll. The *mitzvot* of removing the bells and band from the scroll generally go to two boys, except on festivals and holy days when they are given to young men. One boy removes the bells from the scroll and places them atop the reading desk. The other boy removes the band and returns to his seat. The first boy then removes the cloak from the Torah, and it is then brought forward to the reading desk, and the bells are placed atop the scrolls. The Torah is unrolled so that five or six columns of its writing are seen and held aloft by the *levantador*, who, after raising the scroll, turns counter-clockwise to the four sides of the synagogue. Many worshippers then hold their hands up, point to the Torah, and chant, "This is the Torah that Moses set before the children of Israel. Moses commanded us our Law, the heritage for the congregation of Jacob." The *hazzan* responds with the following: "The way of G-d is perfect, the word of the Lord is true-tested. A shield is He to all who trust in Him." The Torah reading follows. On being called to the Torah, each person bows to the presiding officer as he approaches the reading desk and says the Hebrew words for "the Lord be with you." The congregation responds, "the Lord bless thee." Then the blessing for the Torah is recited. After the blessing and immediately before the *hazzan* begins to read, the one who is called turns and bows to the previous one who had the *mitzvah*, at which point the latter leaves the reading desk. At the close of the Torah portion, the one who is called says the word *emet* ("truth") or *Torat mosheh emet* ("the Law of Moses is truth"), and the concluding blessing is recited.

After the special announcements and the chanting of the section beginning with the words, *Yehi Hasdeha*, the Torah is returned to the Ark. As the Reader says, "Have I not commanded thee?" the *Sefer*-carrier approaches the reading desk and rests the scroll upon it. The *hazzan* chants *Yimloh*, which is sung antiphonally twice by the *hazzan* and the congregants. Then follows what is one of the most beautiful and impressive parts of the service: As the choir chants Psalm 29, the *Sefer*-carrier slowly begins to leave the reading desk followed by the *hazzan*, who bows ceremoniously to the others on the reading platform, before taking leave; the *parnas* also bows to those on the platform, and then the others fall in. All of these proceed in measured pace behind the *Sefer*-carrier, who returns the *Sefer* to the Ark as the closing strains of Psalm 29 are chanted. At this point in the service, anyone who wishes to express a prayer of gratitude or wants to mark the anniversary of one departed can make an offering before the Ark. Services are held daily at 7:30 a.m. and 6 p.m., with certain exceptions.

Services on any of the festivals or holy days are equally interesting. On the eve of Yom Kippur, the congregants arrive just before sunset, and the men, many of whom come in full dress with white tie and tails, cover themselves with the *talis*. Before the *Kol Nidre* is read, the scrolls, covered in cloaks of white, are carried from the Ark to the reading desk by a number of men, dressed in formal attire, in a beautiful and solemn procession.

On Succoth, Shearith Israel erects a beautiful *succah* that embodies within itself the principle of "a beautiful dwelling," and some of the members eat and study there and "do all that would normally be done within the home." On the evening preceding *Hosha'ana Rabbah*, the *Mishmarah*, a special service, is held in the *succah*. Some congregants remain awake throughout the night and continue reading from the Psalms, the *Zohar*, and other religious books for added spiritual uplift in order to merit blessing in the year ahead. On the following morning, the entire synagogue is bedecked in white. At the conclusion of the *Musaf* service, seven scrolls are carried from the Ark to the reading desk and are held there while seven circuits are made about them by men and boys, carrying the *lulav* and the *etrog* in their hands.

Passover is observed in much the same manner as in other Orthodox synagogues. Of special note is the *Tikkun ha-Tal* (the prayer for dew), in which the congregation and the choir participate with the Reader in the chanting of the beautiful prayers set in lovely poetic form.

On Shavuot, the entire synagogue is decorated with greens and the steps leading to the Holy Ark are covered with an abundance of colorful flowers and plants reminiscent of the fruits that were brought as offerings in Temple days.

On the black fast day of *Tisha b'Ab* the synagogue is draped in black and the services are not read from the reading desk but from a table set especially low in front of the reading desk, as a sign of sadness and mourning.

This table is also draped in black and has chairs for the *hazzanim* and the presiding officer. The twelve white tapers that surround the reading desk are covered in black, and the Ark also has a black covering. The reading light permitted for the evening service should come from the candles; however, because of fire hazards, flashlights have been used in recent years. Small candlelights are placed upon the table for the *hazzanim*. There is virtually no other source of light. All is shrouded in darkness to commemorate one of the most mournful events—the destruction of the Temple in Jerusalem. The *hazzan* begins the service with the chant of Psalm 137, "By the rivers of Babylon there we sat, yea, we also wept . . ." The melody with its sorrowful intonation sets the mood for the entire service. One of the unusual aspects of the service is that often the accentuation in the reading is purposely incorrect. This emphasizes all the more the unusually sorrowful occasion and the fact that everything is changed for the worse on this sad day. Before the closing dirge is read, the Reader announces the number of years passed since the destruction of the Temple. The solemnity and the sadness of the occasion are made more vivid on the following day when even the *Sefer* is covered in black, and the beautiful silver bells that normally adorn the scroll are replaced with two black coverings.

Congregation Shearith Israel has held services on Thanksgiving day without interruption since 1781. □

ETHIOPIAN HEBREW CONGREGATION and the COMMAND-MENT KEEPER'S CONGREGATION, 1 West 123rd St., *(7th Ave. IRT to 125th St.).* The congregants claim to be Ethiopian Hebrews who trace their descent to Solomon and Sheba, and who observe *kashruth* and circumcision. As the congregation is unique, so is the synagogue. On the front wall near the Ark hangs a photograph of one of the rabbis with a partially opened Torah in his arms. There is a stained glass window with two Stars of David; the star on top has an eye in the center, while the lower one has a pointing hand. A plaque on a side wall pays honor to the Rev. Matthew and identifies him as "Chief Rabbi of the Ethiopian Hebrews of the Western Hemisphere." The order was founded 46 years ago with eight people. Ethiopian Hebrews now claim to number 350,000 throughout the Western Hemisphere. On the same wall there is a mizrach, a paper with numerous drawings representing a variety of Bible stories. People from all over the world come to see the synagogue and take part in the services, which start mid-morning on Saturdays. The congregation calls itself Orthodox. Men and women sit separately, the first three rows being reserved for men. The Philips' Hebrew Prayer Book, used by many Orthodox congregations, is also used here. Services are conducted in Hebrew and English. The congregation has a choir, composed of both men and women. The women in the choir are all dressed in white with royal blue headdresses. The Hebrew word for Zion is embroidered on their garments, and some of them wear the *Magen David.*

The service itself is interesting. After the opening prayer and response in Hebrew, the prayers are recited antiphonally in English, the rabbi chanting a portion of a sentence and the congregants responding with the following portion, at a quick pace. Instead of ending the prayers with "Amen," the congregants chant fervently, "Halleluyah, Amen!" The chants are punctuated with notes from the piano, which has a harpsichord attachment to give it the effect of an organ. The prayers alternate with hymns sung by the choir. The high point comes when the Torah is read. In Orthodox and Conservative synagogues seven men are called up to the Torah on Saturday mornings; each one recites the opening blessing, the Reader then reads a portion of the Torah, after which each man recites the closing blessing. At the Commandment Keepers' Congregation, however, there is no limit to the number of men who are called up. The rabbi announces their names and tribes, and each man says both blessings as he is called up. The rabbi assigns the tribes, unless the man has already been assigned a tribe or known whether he is a Levi or a Cohayn (generally the tribes mentioned are limited to Levi, Judah, Reuben, Naphtali, and Simeon). Male visitors will be able to go up, too, since after the male members of the Congregation have been called up, the rabbi asks visitors, "Would any of you gentlemen like to be called up? You have that privilege." After all of the men say their blessings, one of the rabbis reads an entire section of the Torah. Then the Torah Scroll is rolled up, tied, and covered. With the Torah in his arms, the Chief Rabbi leads all of the male congregants in a march around the synagogue and everybody sings hymns and claps his hands. After the Torah is put back in the Ark, the rabbi addresses the congregation. Occasionally he is interrupted with shouts of "Halleluyah," "Holy G-d," and "Halleluyah, Amen." After the rabbi's sermon, the mourner's *kaddish* is recited, not by the mourners alone, but by the entire congregation. The rabbi explains: "This is an example of united prayer. We hope that someday there will be united brotherhood." To which the congregation responds, "Halleluyah, Amen!"

The principal beliefs of the Royal Order of Ethiopian Hebrews were codified by Rabbi Matthew and published under the title: *The Twelve Principles of the Doctrines of Israel with Scriptural Proof* about 1940 in the minute book of the Commandment Keepers. This book also includes the curriculum of the Ethiopian Hebrew Rabbinical College and an article, "Anthropology of the Ethopian Hebrews." □

SOCIETY OF JEWISH SCIENCE, Steinway Hall, 113 W. 57th St., holds services every Sunday at 11 a.m. Organ music is played until all are seated. The Reader recites the *Borchu* in Hebrew and the congregants respond; the same procedure is then followed in English. The *Shma* is recited in unison, after which Deuteronomy VI, 4-10 is read in English. Members rise to sing a hymn from the Jewish Science service pamphlet, accompanied by a piano. There is an exposition of a Psalm by the leader, followed by a piano solo and a lecture by the leader on a topic of religious significance. Following this, the group is asked to repeat aloud the following affirmations:

1. "The G-d Consciousness in me expresses itself in health, in

calmness, in peace, in power, and in happiness";
2. "I am calm and cheerful; I hate no one; I envy no one; there is no worry or fear in me; I trust in G-d all the time." An oral exposition by the leader follows each affirmation. A healing period of silence follows the affirmations. The congregants are told to relax, close their eyes, and to concentrate on the one thing they need most. They are told to present a mental picture of this request to G-d. During the healing period there is complete silence. The healing period usually lasts seven or eight minutes and is the outstanding feature of the service. The remainder of the service consists of the singing of another hymn, a discourse by the leader on Judaism, a collection to further the work of the Jewish Science group, the recitation of *kaddish* when the entire congregation is asked to rise, and the playing of organ music as the congregants leave the hall. The entire service lasts about one hour. During the service an Ark containing a Torah Scroll is on the stage of the hall, but it is never opened.

The Society of Jewish Science was founded in 1922 by Rabbi Morris Lichtenstein. Born in Lithuania in 1889, he was raised in an atmosphere of strict Orthodoxy. He came to the United States when he was 17 and enrolled at the Hebrew Union College-Jewish Institute of Religion in Cincinnati. In 1922, he formed the Society to end the movement of Jews to Christian Science, by showing that what they were searching for was available to them in Judaism. Jewish Science preaches that there is no conflict between their beliefs and medicine. "Medical science can effect cures for some diseases; prayer and correct thinking can effect cures for others." They do not claim to be a new faith or creed but an attempt to reawaken the Jewish consciousness in each Jewish person; it draws its material solely from Jewish sources. Among the ten fundamentals of Jewish Science are these: Prayer, when properly offered, never goes without answer; the individual must keep calm at all times, be cheerful, seek to eliminate anger and hate from his heart and not envy others; worry and fear destroy men, and they must never have a place in anyone's psychology; trust in G-d's goodness is to be cultivated; death is not an end to life but merely a state in the development of the human spirit; and G-d is the source of health, and He heals. □

NEW YORK SOCIETY FOR THE DEAF, 344 E. 14th St., conducts worship services in the sign language during the High Holy Days and one Sabbath each month.

LIBRARIES AND MUSEUMS

THE JEWISH MUSEUM of the Jewish Theological Seminary of America, 5th Ave. at 92nd St., is open from noon to 5 p.m., Mondays through Thursdays and from 11 a.m. to 6 p.m., Sundays; Thursday evenings from 7 to 9 o'clock; closed Friday and Saturday.

Starting in 1904 with a collection of 26 ceremonial objects donated by Judge Mayer Sulzberger, the Jewish Museum has become the repository of the largest and most comprehensive collection of Jewish ceremonial objects in the world. First housed on Morningside Heights, the museum moved to its present location on New York's "Museum Row," in 1947, after Mrs. Frieda Warburg, widow of the prominent banker, presented her six-story mansion to the Jewish Theological Seminary of America as a "tribute to the men of my family, my father (Jacob H. Schiff), my husband, and my brother Mortimer, who each in his own way has done so much to build up the Seminary toward its present effective usefulness."

Before entering the museum itself, the visitor can see a sculpture garden and a wing, and the Albert A. List Building, which enables the museum to mount many more major exhibitions than it had in the past. The first floor has a lobby and large exhibition area; a large gallery, which is occasionally used as an auditorium, is on the second floor; the third floor has three exhibition galleries and a storage area. The Tobe Pascher Workshop, where contemporary Jewish ceremonial objects are made, is in the basement.

Among the most interesting items on display are a predominantly blue mosaic wall from a 16th century Persian synagogue; a 17th century gold *kiddush* cup; the "Friedberg Tower"—an unusually fine silver spice container of the 16th century; a large wooden Chanukah Menorah made by a boy in a concentration camp; a Torah Scroll made of deerskin; a spice container of silver filigree; several unique Torah Arks; a Torah Ark curtain with the representation of the vision of the Prophet Zechariah; a Chanukah lamp in the form of a richly decorated Torah Ark; a pewter Chanukah lamp; a *shofar* in the shape of a fish with an open mouth; a Torah wrapper, painted on linen, with glass pearls; a curtain for the Ark, embroidered on a net, from the synagogue of Pitigliano, Italy; marriage contracts *(ketubot)*; panels of the famous frescoes of Dura Europos, Syria; mosaics from ancient synagogues; a variety of Torah crowns, breastplates, and pointers. The museum's collection of Jewish medals is the largest and most comprehensive ever assembled, and the Harry Stein Collection of ancient Hebrew coins is the most outstanding private collection of its kind outside of Israel. The Jewish Museum conducts a varied program of lectures, concerts, courses, and guided tours. ☐

YIVO INSTITUTE FOR JEWISH RESEARCH, 1048 5th Ave., is the only secular Jewish research institute in the world outside of Israel. Founded in Vilna in 1925, YIVO was moved to New York in 1940 to escape the ravages of the Nazis. It is dedicated to the scholarly exploration of historical, sociological, economic, literary, linguistic, and other phases of Jewish life. YIVO maintains the world's largest collection of original documentary material on Jewish life. There are an estimated three million letters, photographs, and manuscripts ranging from Theodor Herzl's diary to former top-secret documents of the Ministry of Foreign Affairs of the Third Reich. The YIVO library has over 300,000 volumes, and the museum contains the most extensive and complete collection of material on the Yiddish theatre, including thousands of photographs, announcements, manuscripts, music sheets, and other memorabilia. Recognized as the world center for Yiddish research, YIVO has the most complete record of Jewish life in Eastern Europe. Among its collections are the S. Niger Collection, the H. Leivick Collection, the Dr. Khayim Zhitlowsky Collection, the Kalman Marmor Collection, the Dr. Joseph Rosen Collection, the HIAS-HICEM Collection, the Joint Reconstruction Collection, the collections of the Lodz and Vilna Ghettoes, the Vilna Collection, the so-called Berlin Collection, and the DP Collection. Among the specific items of interest are a tractate of the Talmud handwritten by Anshel Rothschild in 1722, which was handed down through five generations of Rothschilds; a handwritten manuscript of Sholom Aleichem that gives a rare insight into the technique of a literary genius; a once-secret Nazi document presented by the prosecution at the trial of Adolf Eichmann; 350 memoirs regarding the development of the American Jewish community today; a rare trilingual Jewish periodical published in the United States in 1871; a Bible printed in Mantua, Italy, in 1742; other materials on Eichmann and the Grand Mufti; the files of Rabbi Schneer Zalman Schneerson on the underground rescue activity of the Orthodox movement in Nazi-occupied France; the archives of Meyer Birman dealing with Jewish life in the Far East; the personal archives of the philosopher Dr. Horace M. Kallen; and the archives of the National Conference of Jewish Communal Service. YIVO not only provides documents and other items for researchers and scholars, it also engages in original research, the results of which are printed and circulated, and conducts a training program for students. Visitors and scholars are welcome at the Atran Exhibition Room and the library reading and reference room.

THE NEW YORK PUBLIC LIBRARY, Jewish Division, 5th Ave. at 42nd St., has more than 140,000 volumes dealing with Jewish subjects, including medieval and modern literature, Talmudic and *midrashic* writings and commentaries. The Division has one of the largest collections of Jewish periodicals ever assembled in this country, as well as extensive files of the more important Yiddish newspapers, both American and foreign, available on microfilm. There are also early Hebrew books—the first one printed in 1475 in Hebrew characters. Available also is literature on the Yiddish theatre both here and abroad, and the history and lore of Jewish people in all parts of the world. The Jewish Division was started in November, 1897, when Jacob H. Schiff, the noted philanthropist, donated $10,000 for the purchase of Semitic literature. The A.M. Bank Collection, which incorporated the Leon Mandelstamm Library and the Meyer Lehren Collection, was purchased, and this was the nucleus from which one of the finest collections of Judaica developed.

The Division started as a reference library for scholars. It became a multi-service, multi-level archive used by people from all over the world. Jewish philanthropists, along with others, helped build up the New York Public Library to its present size. Jacob Schiff, Dr. Albert A. Berg, and Louis M. Rabinowitz were among the library's major benefactors. Their names and others are inscribed on the marble pylons in the library's main lobby. In 1940 Dr. Berg, an outstanding surgeon, donated his collection of English and American literature to the library as a memorial to his brother, Dr. Henry W. Berg. Later he bought and donated the collection of W. T. H. Howe of Cincinnati, and then added, by joint gift, the collection of Owen D. Young. The Berg Collection now has more than 50,000 items, dating from the end of the 15th century. These include two of the eleven known copies of Edgar Allan Poe's first published work, *Tamerlane*. Dr. Berg left the library an endowment of $2 million for the care, servicing, and expansion of his original gifts. Portraits of the Bergs are in the Berg Memorial Room. Jacob Schiff gave, in addition to his other contributions, 317 James Tissot's Old Testament paintings. Louis M. Rabinowitz, New York manufacturer, gave the library 79 incunabula (works printed before 1500). The widow of Simon Guggenheim, the industrialist and former senator from Colorado, donated 1,000 19th and 20th century books, letters, and documents, among them a letter from Theodore Roosevelt, written in 1915, expressing some misgivings about the ultimate success of the women's suffrage movement. □

ZIONIST ARCHIVES AND LIBRARY of the Palestine Foundation Fund (Keren Hayesod), 515 Park Ave., is located in the Jewish Agency for Israel building. Here are more than 50,000 books and pamphlets on Israel, the Middle East, Zionism, and Jewish life. The archival collection consists primarily of materials on American Zionism. There are thousands of photographs, slides, films, filmstrips, and microfilms; in addition, there are hundreds of recordings, including Israeli folk music and symphonic scores. The Zionist Archives and Library, which also serves as an information service, has the Herzl, Gottlied, Brandeis, DeHaas, and Friedenwald Collections, as well as the collection of the late President Franklin D. Roosevelt on material related to Zionism.

NEW YORK UNIVERSITY LIBRARY OF JUDAICA AND HEBRAICA, 2 Washington Sq. N. The library contains the Mitchell M. Kaplan Collection of manuscripts, incunabula, and rare editions, including a treatise on Cabbalah; the *Book of Cusari* by Yehuda-ha-Levi, printed in 1594 in Venice; an encyclopedia on Jewish rituals and customs printed in 1489 in Lisbon; Maimonides *Guide to the Perplexed*; and a 13th century manuscript of a Passover *Haggadah*. Also: the William Rosenthal and Israel Matz Collections of Current Judaica and Hebraica; the Lagarde Collection; the Abraham I. Katsh Collection of microfilms of rare Hebrew manuscripts in the Soviet Union—the only collection of its kind in the United States; an exceptional collection of German Judaica; several ancient Torahs, one of which is 3 feet wide and 50 feet long; and the David Kaufmann Collection of Rare Manuscripts—some dating back to the 11th century. There is a portrait of Albert Einstein in the library showing the famous scientist seated in characteristic attire—a sweater and open-collared shirt; with a pencil in his right hand and papers on his lap. The painting was done from life by the artist, Max Westfield.

MORRIS RAPHAEL COHEN LIBRARY of City College, (the north end of the South Campus), 135th St. between St. Nicholas Terrace and Convent Ave. The $3,500,000, three-story, glass-enclosed library is named for the noted philosopher and member of the college's faculty for more than 30 years. It is of a contemporary design of glass blocks and wide expanses of beige masonry outside and subdued tones and simple decor inside. It provides shelf space for the college's collection of 850,000 volumes, including Dr. Cohen's personal library and papers. The Davidson Collection of Judaica contains 7,000 volumes in Hebrew, Yiddish, French, German, Italian, Arabic, and Aramaic. There are many rare works of medieval Hebrew poetry and Talmudic, *midrashic*, and rabbinic lore, liturgy, rites, and folklore. Professor Israel Davidson, for whom the collection is named, was an alumnus of the college and a professor of Medieval Hebrew Literature at the Jewish Theological Seminary from 1905-1939.

BUTLER LIBRARY, THE JUDAICA COLLECTION, Columbia University, 116th St. and Broadway. This collection includes the Temple Emanu-El Library of Biblical and Rabbinic Literature, presented to the university by Emanu-El in 1892, and the library of Professor Richard Gottheil. There are 6,000 Hebrew books and pamphlets, 1,000 manuscripts, 28 incunabula, and 12,000 volumes of Judaica. The university has a three by five inch psalter printed in Hebrew in 1685 at Cambridge University, England. The psalter was used by Samuel Johnson at the graduation of the first seven candidates for bachelor's degrees at King's College on June 21, 1758. The Hebrew psalter is in the King's College Room, as is a 1708 edition of *The History of the Jews, from Jesus Christ to the Present Time*. The Professor Edwin A. Seligman Collection on Economics and the Spinoza Collection are in the Special Collection Department of Butler Library. (For information on the libraries of the Jewish Theological Seminary, Yeshiva University, and the New York branch of the Hebrew Union College-Jewish Institute of Religion, see PLACES TO VISIT—SEMINARIES.)

MUSEUM OF THE CITY OF NEW YORK, 5th Ave. at 104th St., has a tablet, at the right of the entrance, dedicated to James Speyer, German Jewish philanthropist and moving spirit in the creation of the museum. Speyer selected as the museum's motto the following quotation from Lincoln: "I like to see a man proud of the place in which he lives. I like to see a man live so that his place will be proud of him." In the north wing on the first floor there is a portrait of Moses Levy (1665-1728). The museum displays the work of Myer Myers, well-known early American Jewish silversmith. In addition, there is a portrait of Isaac Moses, prominent Jewish merchant and ardent patriot who fitted out, at his own expense and in association with Robert Morris, eight privateersmen to prey on British commerce, and who helped bolster American credit at a crucial point during the American Revolution.

HISPANIC SOCIETY OF AMERICA, Broadway between 155th and 156th Sts., has a tile with a Star of David glazed in white on a black and white background. The tile, made in Toledo, Spain, in the second half of the

15th century, hangs on the west wall of the museum's staircase. It was once part of the decoration in the synagogue of Toledo, which, after the Jews were expelled in 1492, became the Church of El Transito. The museum also has a 15th century Hebrew Bible inscribed in Spanish. The Hispanic Society was established to advance the study of the Spanish and Portuguese languages, literature, history, and culture.

METROPOLITAN MUSEUM OF ART, 5th Ave. between 80th and 84th Sts. Jewish men and women have played an important role in the museum's development. In addition to the bequests left to the museum by Amelia B. Lazarus, Jacob H. Schiff, and Stanley A. Cohen, the museum's priceless collections have been enriched by a number of Jewish patrons of the arts, among them Benjamin Altman, Michael Friedsam, George Blumenthal, who gave $1,000,000 to the museum, and was its president from 1934 until his death in 1941. Among the Jewish artists whose works are in the museum are Jacob H. Lazarus, Josef Israels, Henry Mosler, Max Lieberman, Lewis Cohen, Bernard Karflol, and Leon Kroll. Jacob Epstein, Isadore Konti, and Maurice Sterne are among the Jewish sculptors whose works are represented. ●The Robert Lehman Wing houses the multi-million dollar collection of modern art assembled by the late banker and bequeathed to the Museum. One room in the wing was taken intact from Lehman's townhouse.

NEW YORK PUBLIC LIBRARY, Aguilar Branch, 174 E. 110th St., is an outgrowth of the library established by Jacob Schiff and the 92nd Street YM & YWHA. It is named for Grace Aguilar, Anglo-Jewish novelist of the 19th century. Much of her writing was devoted to explanations of Jewish ritual. She placed particular emphasis on a knowledge of Jewish history and the Hebrew language. Her major works include The Magic Wreath, The Vale of Cedars, and The Women of Israel. For some time before her death at the youthful age of 31, she was mute. Her last words, expressed in sign language, were: "Though He slay me, yet will I trust in Him" (Job 13:15).

NEW YORK PUBLIC LIBRARY, Lincoln Center Branch, 111 Amsterdam Ave., has the Benedict Stambler Archive of Recorded Jewish Music—a collection of some 4,000 Jewish phonograph records. The collection is part of the Rodgers and Hammerstein Archives of Recorded Sound. Included is a disc of Sholom Aleichem reading from his own work. Mr. Stambler devoted the last 20 years of his life to the gathering, preservation, and dissemination of Jewish music on records.

NEW YORK PUBLIC LIBRARY, Nathan Straus Young Adult Library of Donnell Branch, 20 W. 53rd St., is named for the philanthropist and pioneer advocate of pasteurized milk.

NEW YORK PUBLIC LIBRARY, Bloomingdale Branch, 150 W. 100th St., is named for Samuel Bloomingdale, department store owner and philanthropist.

YESHIVA UNIVERSITY MUSEUM, housed in Yeshiva University's Mendel Gottesman Library, at the Main Center, 2520 Amsterdam Ave., is devoted to Jewish art, architecture, and history. Endowed by Erica and Ludwig Jesselson, the Museum's salient feature is its permanent display of scale models of "Synagogues Through the Centuries," which includes 10 synagogue models ranging from the 3rd to the 19th centuries and important for their style and place in history. Other permanent features are a reproduction of the frescoes found in the ruins of the Dura-Europos Synagogue, 3rd century, Syria; a 17-foot long electronic map tracing the migration of Jews since the time of Abraham; and two audio-visual shows, "The Story of the Synagogue" and "The Story of the Temple." Also on exhibit are the Torah Scroll of the Baal Shem Tov; the first book of Psalms written in Hebrew and printed in Barbados, 1742; a book by Menasseh ben Israel, the renowned 17th century Dutch rabbi; and other historic religious appurtenances and artifacts.

NEW YORK ACADEMY OF SCIENCES, 2 East 63rd St., has a bust of Dr. Paul Ehrlich, German-Jewish scientist, in its lobby. Dr. Ehrlich, who was noted for his discoveries in immunology and antibiotics, won the Nobel Prize in 1908.

LEO BAECK INSTITUTE LIBRARY, 129 E. 73rd St., specializes in material about Jewish life and history in Germany, Austria, and other Germanic-speaking areas of Europe. It houses unique collections of documents, books, manuscripts, photographs, letters, memoirs, clippings, and personal papers about the great and near-great among German Jewish authors, scientists, rabbis, communal leaders, statesmen, industrialists, and public figures.

AMERICAN MUSEUM OF NATURAL HISTORY, Warburg Hall, Central Park West at 79th St., which houses the "Man and Nature" exhibit, is named for the noted Jewish philanthropist and banker. (see also SEMINARIES AND OTHER INSTITUTIONS OF HIGHER LEARNING, THE STATUE OF LIBERTY, and the Midtown section.)

HISTORIC JEWISH CEMETERIES

CHATHAM SQUARE CEMETERY, St. James Place below Chatham Sq. A plot of land in lower Manhattan which is the famous cemetery of Congregation Shearith Israel. A plaque over the gateway to the cemetery has the following inscription:

> This Tablet Marks What Remains of
> The First Jewish Cemetery
> In the United States
> Consecrated in the Year
> 1656
> When It Was Described as
> "Outside the City"

The tablet refers to the cemetery that was located on a plot of ground granted to the Jews of New Amsterdam by Peter Stuyvesant in answer to a petition by Abraham de Lucena, Salvador Dandrada, and Jacob Cohen

Henricques. The site of this cemetery can no longer be identified.
The ground of Chatham Square Cemetery, known also as the New
Bowery Cemetery and the Oliver St. Cemetery, was acquired in 1682.
Benjamin Bueno de Mesquita, who died in 1683, was the first person to be
buried there.

The cemetery played a part in the American defense of New York in
1776. General Charles Lee placed several guns in what he called the "Jew
Burying Ground," and the tablet over the gateway states that the cemetery
"during the War of the Revolution" was "fortified by the patriots as one of the
defenses of the city." Among the graves in the cemetery are those of 18
Revolutionary soldiers and patriots. These include Hayman Levy and Jonas
Phillips, signers of the Non-Importation Resolutions of 1770; Isaac Moses,
signer of bills of credit for the Continental Congress; and Gershom Mendes
Seixas, minister of Congregation Shearith Israel, who closed the synagogue
and removed the scrolls of the Torah to Stratford, Connecticut, when British
forces occupied New York.

A second cemetery of the Spanish and Portuguese Synagogue is
located in a small enclosed triangle of land on 11th Street, a few yards east of
6th Avenue. It was consecrated on February 27, 1805, as Beth Haim Sheni
(The Second Cemetery). Shortly after the yellow fever scourge of 1822, it
became the only Jewish cemetery in New York that could be used. In 1830,
the city opened 11th Street to development and condemned the entire burial
ground. The congregation successfully petitioned the city for that part of the
cemetery that would not interfere with the street. Among the few still buried
in this cemetery is the American soldier and patriot, Ephraim Hart, who was
one of the founders of the New York Stock Exchange. ☐

BETH HAIM SHELISHI, West 21st St., west of 6th Ave. is the third
Spanish and Portuguese cemetery. Consecrated on August 17, 1829, the
graveyard served Congregation Shearith Israel for almost 22 years.
Mordecai Manuel Noah, the playwright and colorful character who tried to
found a Jewish colony on Grand Island in the Niagara River, was one of the
last persons to be buried here. Also interred here are three soldiers of the
American Revolution. On Memorial Day each year, the graves of the
Revolutionary soldiers and patriots in all three cemeteries are decorated
with the American flag. (See also Brooklyn and Queens.)

SEMINARIES AND OTHER INSTITUTIONS OF HIGHER LEARNING

Rabbi Isaac Eichanan Theological Seminary, Amsterdam Ave. and
186th St., (Orthodox), is thought of by many as Yeshiva University.
However, Yeshiva University, which is the nation's oldest and largest
university under Jewish auspices, has 17 schools and divisions of which the
seminary is one. At the Main Center are the seminary, the Yeshiva High
School, Yeshiva College for Men, Teachers Institute for Men, the Bernard
Revel Graduate School, Harry Fischel School for Higher Jewish Studies,
Cantorial Training Institute, and the Graduate School of Science. The other

schools are located elsewhere in Manhattan, The Bronx, and Brooklyn.

In September, 1886, a small group of immigrants on the Lower East Side enrolled their children in America's first Jewish day school—Yeshiva Eitz Chaim. Classes were held in a second-floor loft on East Broadway. Ten years later, the Rabbi Isaac Eichanan Theological Seminary was established, and this, too, was a first—the first school on the American continent for the advanced study of Torah. In 1915, Eitz Chaim became part of the seminary setup, and four years later was approved by the New York State Board of Regents as the Eitz Chaim Talmudical Academy, which combined a high school education with the study of the Talmud. Thus Eitz Chaim became the first high school in America under Jewish auspices.

In 1921, the institution moved to larger quarters and merged with the Teachers Institute, which had been founded by the Mizrachi Organization of America in 1917. In 1928, Yeshiva College was established—the first college of liberal arts and sciences under Jewish auspices in America. That same year Yeshiva moved to uptown Manhattan. In 1945, the state of New York granted Yeshiva university status. ☐

YESHIVA UNIVERSITY, 500 West 185th St. The historic Main Building was erected in 1928 at the Main Center at a cost of $2,500,000. It is one of the outstanding examples of Byzantine architecture in Greater New York. Its towering dome has become an upper-Manhattan landmark. •In the Main Building is the Nathan Lamport Auditorium, whose architectural motifs include twelve pillars representing the Tribes of Israel and other themes. •The Harry Fischel Synagogue-Study Hall is also in the Main Building. •The Mendel Gottesman Library, which has a large collection of Judaica, is on the second floor of the Main Building. This library is especially noted for its rabbinic literature. •The Yeshiva University Museum occupies the ground level of the library, with approximately 4,000 square feet of space devoted to the exhibition area. (See also MUSEUMS and LIBRARIES.) •Pollack Library, south of the Main Building, is one of the university's five principal library collections. Other collections are the Aaron Etra Collection of historical, synagogal, and rabbinical documents; the Nathan Isaac, Gitelson, and Peter Wiernik Collections; the Kraus Library; the library of the late Julius Streicher, member of the Nazi's Third Reich government; and the Hershey Collection of Versailles Conference Papers which represents 5,000 documents related to the peace treaties of World War I. •Wurzweiler School of Social Work, 55 5th Ave., is named for Gustav Wurzweiler. •Benjamin F. Cardozo Law School, 55 5th Ave., named in honor of the late justice of the Supreme Court, is the first law school named for a Jew. ☐

HIGH SCHOOL RESIDENCE HALL of Yeshiva University, Amsterdam Ave. and 185th St., is a $3,500,000 seven-story residence hall and student center. •At the corner of Amsterdam Ave. and 185th St. stands the classroom-administration building. Built at a cost of $3,000,000, it has 35 modern classrooms that serve the seminary and colleges, graduate

NEW YORK CITY, MANHATTAN — 138

schools, and institutes at the Main Center. This building also contains an electronic language laboratory that can transmit foreign language tapes to students in three different languages simultaneously while broadcasting hi-fi tapes to the music study room on another floor. ●The graduate center and other facilities are at 55 5th Ave.

LEAH AND JOSEPH RUBIN RESIDENCE HALL of Yeshiva University, Amsterdam Ave. and 185th St., serves as a dormitory for college students. Here is the university's cafeteria which serves more than 10,000 meals a week. ●The residence hall faces the Danciger Campus, traditional site of the university's June graduation ceremonies.

STERN COLLEGE FOR WOMEN and TEACHERS INSTITUTE FOR WOMEN of Yeshiva University, 253 Lexington Ave. The building houses laboratories, lecture halls, an auditorium, library, classrooms, and a cafeteria which is open to the public for lunches.

THE JEWISH THEOLOGICAL SEMINARY OF AMERICA, Broadway between 122nd and 123rd Sts. (Conservative). The library has one of the largest collections of Judaica in the world. Housed temporarily in a pre-fab construction, in what was the Seminary quadrangle (the Tower stacks having been destroyed in the April, 1966 fire), the library will be located in a new academic building.

On either side of the main entrance are carved the names of Sabato Morais and Solomon Schechter. In January, 1886, Morais, an Italian-born Jew who succeeded Isaac Leeser as rabbi of the historic Mikveh Israel Congregation in Philadelphia, and six other rabbis issued a call for "an institution in which Bible and Talmud shall be studied to a religious purpose." This led to the founding, on January 2, 1887, of the Jewish Theological Seminary in the Nineteenth Street Synagogue of Congregation Shearith Israel. Morais became the seminary's first president and professor of Bible. Schechter, a world-renowned Jewish scholar, was the seminary's president from 1902 until his death in 1915. Under Schechter's guidance, the seminary acquired a reputation for leadership and scholarship throughout the world. One of the accomplishments Schechter is particularly famous for is his discovery, in Cairo, Egypt, of a *Genizah* (a special hiding-place where unusable but forbidden-to-be-destroyed Hebrew books, letters, and documents are kept) that had some 100,000 manuscripts and fragments which had been buried for centuries. Schechter's portrait hangs in the seminary's dining hall. The names of other founders and leaders of the seminary are carved on the pier caps of the columns of the arcade leading into the inner court. These include Mayer Sulzberger, Morris Loeb, Abraham P. Mendes, Alexander Kohut, Mortimer L. Schiff, Joseph Blumenthal, Adolphus S. Solomons, Louis Marshall, Newman Cowen, and Sol M. Stroock.

A set of beautifully constructed wrought iron gates guard the large, vaulted passageway leading through the main entrance. There is an inscription noting that "These gates were presented in 1934 by Mrs. Felix M. Warburg in memory of her parents, Jacob H. and Therese Schiff." The inscription is flanked by the Lions of Judah. Directly above the center of the gate is a solidly forged Menorah, copied from one found on the Arch of Titus in Rome, which was a contemporary replica of the Menorah used in the Temple in Jerusalem. ●The Harriet and Mortimer M. Marcus Rare Book and Manuscript Room has 10,000 rare books, 8,000 manuscripts, some 25,000 fragments from the *Genizah*, and thousands of notes, letters, and documents. There is a Chinese translation of one of Sholom Aleichem's books; a Hebrew edition of *Profiles in Courage*, autographed upside-down by the late President John F. Kennedy; a High Holiday *machzor* shaped to fit inside the sleeve of a toga; *The Long Megillah*, an inch-high Purim *megillah* that stretches out like a tape measure; manuscripts, fragments of manuscripts, and letters written in Maimonides' own handwriting; books used in concentration camps; the *Book of Esther* from one of the original Gutenberg Bibles; a Jewish *Code of Laws*, published in Italy in 1475, believed to be the oldest extant book printed in Hebrew; the *Almanac* of Abraham Zacuto (1440-1510), a celebrated Spanish-Jewish astronomer whose astronomical tables helped Columbus frighten the natives of what is now British Jamaica with a "permanent loss of moonlight," thus making them agree to sell the explorers food; Pentateuch leaves written in Egypt in the 10th century and fragments from the Prophets written in Persia; the first edition of the Pentateuch with Targum and Rashi, printed in Bologna in 1482; Avicentna's *Medical Encyclopedia*, printed in Naples in 1491-1492; a treatise on the plague, believed to be the only copy in existence, which was printed about 1510; the ancient French prayer book *Mahzor Vitry*, written in the 13th century; some manuscripts of the *Zohar*, predating the first edition; the first complete 15-volume set of the Babylonian Talmud with commentaries printed by Daniel Bomberg in Venice between 1520 and 1523; five books of Jewish interest from the libraries of Tsars Alexander III and Nicholas II and of the latter's son, Alexei, all bearing the insignia of the imperial dynasty; and other rare books, pamphlets, manuscripts, and prints. ●The Louis Ginzberg Microfilm Collection includes Judaica and Hebraica from the major libraries of the world.

The library has more than 250,000 volumes. Included are books of 16 languages that were transliterated in Hebrew characters: Arabic, English, French, German, Greek, Italian, Persian, Polish, Portuguese, Provencal, Samaritan, Spanish, Syriac, Tataric, Ukrainian, and Yiddish. The library grew from small beginnings. On the 70th birthday of Dr. Morais in 1893, it was decided to set up the Morais Library at the seminary. The library then owned about 1,000 volumes, to which was added the collection of Dr. David Cassel of Berlin. After Morais' death in 1897, the library received his collection of more than 700 volumes. When the seminary was reorganized in 1902, Judge Mayer Sulzberger of Philadelphia donated his collection of 2,400 rare volumes and almost 500 manuscripts. He later donated the library of the bibliophile, Solomon J. Halberstamm of Berlitz, Austria. In 1907, Jacob H. Schiff donated the collection of the bibliographer Moritz Steinschneider, 60 percent of which was lost in the 1966 fire. In 1921 when his son Mortimer L. Schiff gave the library the Israel Solomons Collection, the seminary library had become second only to the Anglo-Judaica collection in the British Museum. The seminary synagogue is an unusual place of interest. It is Conservative, but in many respects its services resemble an Orthodox service. Actually, it has been described as right-wing Conservative. The Reader and cantor face the Ark instead of the audience, and men and women sit separately. One week out of every year, the Seminary *sukkah*—which extends for a full city block—attracts many visitors, and is used by students, faculty members, etc. ●The Mathilde Schechter Residence Hall, 415 W. 120th St., the Seminary's first residence hall for non-rabbinical students, was made necessary by the growing enrollment of students seeking degrees in Jewish education and history. ☐

HEBREW UNION COLLEGE-JEWISH INSTITUTE OF RELIGION (New York Branch), 40 W. 68th St. (Reform). The campus, principal building, library, and museum of the Hebrew Union College-Jewish Institute of Religion are in Cincinnati, Ohio, where the institution was founded. The five-story structure in New York is the local branch of the HUC-JIR. Founded in 1922 as the Jewish Institute of Religion by Rabbi Stephen S. Wise, the school merged with the Hebrew Union College in 1950. ●In the lobby of the New York school are busts of the "Two Wise Men"—Rabbi Isaac Mayer Wise and Rabbi Stephen S. Wise. There is also a large auditorium. ●The Emil Hirsch-Gerson Levi Library on the fifth floor has approximately 75,000 volumes, including valuable Hebrew manuscripts; autographed manuscripts of Italian and German rabbis from the 16th to the 19th centuries; manuscripts and plays by Cantor Isaac Offenbach and a liturgical composition for the High Holy Days by his son, Jacques Offenbach; seven incunabula; 200 volumes of 16th century editions of Hebraica; the best modern Hebrew literature collection; a fine collection of scholarly periodicals from Europe, Israel, and the Jewish press of America; and proceedings and publications of early American Zionist societies. The library was begun in 1922 with Rabbi Stephen S. Wise's own library and that of his father. Added to these were the Brann Collection from the Jewish Theological Seminary of Breslau, part of the Kohut Library, and the Hirsch and Levi Collections. ●The Wise-iana collection has personal letters and documents of Rabbi Stephen S. Wise, including addresses, articles, sermons, statements, and copies of Rabbi Wise's letters to Presidents Woodrow Wilson and Franklin D. Roosevelt. ●The New York branch of HUC-JIR also has a School of Education and Sacred Music for the training of teachers, principals, and cantors.

HERZLIAH-JEWISH TEACHERS SEMINARY, 69 Bank St., consists of the Jewish Teachers Seminary and People's University—the only Yiddish teachers college in America offering diplomas and the degree of Bachelor of Jewish Literature. There is also a Jewish music division training cantors, music teachers, and folk singers; a graduate division offering the degree of Doctor of Jewish Literature; and the training of men and women to teach Yiddish, Hebrew, and Jewish social studies in colleges and universities. ●The Horace Kallen Academy, a nondenominational junior and senior high school teaching English, Hebrew, and Yiddish under the Seminary's auspices, is a pioneering effort in Jewish education. ●The Jewish Teachers Seminary and People's University was established in 1918 and Herzliah Hebrew Teachers Institute in 1921. These strongholds of Yiddish and Hebrew culture combined in 1967, and in 1971 acquired their own building which also houses the Dr. Abraham and Ann Goodman Hebrew-Yiddish-English Library comprising over 40,000 volumes, including the Israel Matz Collection of Haskalah Literature.

NEW SCHOOL FOR SOCIAL RESEARCH, 66 West 12th St., is famous for its "University in Exile." The "University's" faculty was drawn from among the most brilliant scholars, and political and religious exiles from Nazi Germany. It was organized in 1934 by Dr. Alvin Johnson, president of the New School. Through the School's efforts, these renowned figures were rescued and given the opportunity of teaching in America. During the period from 1934 to 1941, scholars from many of the countries conquered by the Nazis were also brought over. The "University in Exile" was the nucleus of the school's Graduate Faculty of Political and Social Science. Endowment funds for this humanitarian effort were provided by Lucius N. Littauer and many other Jewish philanthropists. Dr. Horace Kallen, the well-known American philosopher, taught here for many years.

NEW YORK UNIVERSITY, Washington Sq. The University's graduate program in the Hebrew language, culture, and education is a unique course of studies for the training of teachers and community leaders in Hebraic studies. In 1933, the University introduced courses in modern Hebrew, and that marked the beginning of the Department of Hebrew Culture and Education, the first and only one of its kind in America. The department has both graduate and undergraduate courses. ●The Washington Square College of Arts and Sciences has its own program of Hebrew instruction. ●Courses in the Hebrew and Arabic languages are also taught in the Division of General Education and Extension Services—a non-credit division of the University. ●The Department of Hebrew Culture and Education sponsors summer sessions and summer workshops in Israel. ●The Jewish Culture Foundation, 2 Washington Sq. ●Murry and Leonie Guggenheim Foundation Institute for Dental Research, 339 E. 25th St. ●Samuel Rubin International Hall, 35 5th Ave. ●Salomon Brothers Center for the Study of Financial Institutions, 90 Trinity Pl. ●Weinstein Center for Student Living, 5 University Pl.

One of the founders of New York University in 1831 was Mordecai M. Noah, who was among the 168 prominent citizens who answered a call in 1830 to discuss the establishment of a university in New York "on a liberal and extensive foundation." ☐

LOEB STUDENT CENTER of New York University, Washington

Sq. South. This luxurious $5 million structure is sheathed in aluminum and glass except for a brick-enclosed auditorium wing jutting from the facade. A gift of $1 million toward the construction of the center was made by Mrs. Alan H. Kempner, and John L., Carl M., Jr., and Henry A. Loeb in memory of their parents. The 1,000-seat assembly hall is named the Eisner and Lubin Auditorium for Joseph I. Lubin and the late Joseph Eisner, business partners and alumni of the University.

NEW YORK UNIVERSITY-BELLEVUE MEDICAL CENTER, 550 1st Ave. The Goldberger Memorial Laboratory is named for Dr. Joseph Goldberger, who is noted for his work on pellagra. ●The Henry W. and Albert A. Berg Institute of Experimental Physiology, Surgery, and Pathology adjoins the building on 30th Street, east of 1st Avenue. The Institute's greenhouse is called the Enid A. Haupt Children's Garden, after its donor, Enid Haupt, editor and publisher of *Seventeen* magazine. The plants in the greenhouse are set on benches of graduated heights so that children or adults, in wheelchairs or standing, can work on them. There is a wading pool so designed that even children in wheelchairs can roll themselves to its edge and swing around to dabble their toes without assistance. A special feature is a long plant box, designed for blind children, containing cacti without spines and a patch of a variety of fragrant herbs. The greenhouse also has decorative birds and an aquarium. A children's pavilion at Bellevue was made possible by a $1 million gift from the William J. Wollman Foundation.

ROCKEFELLER UNIVERSITY, 1250 York Ave., one of the world's great medical and scientific institutions, has portraits of and memorial plaques to Dr. Simon Flexner, Dr. Phoebus Levine, and Dr. Samuel J. Meltzer. Flexner, a world-famous authority on epidemiology, was the first director of the Rockefeller Institute, out of which the university grew. Dr. Levine was a noted biologist, and Dr. Meltzer was a celebrated physiologist and pharmacologist. A number of the scientists at Rockefeller University who have won Nobel Prizes in medicine, chemistry, and physics were Jews.

PACE UNIVERSITY, Schimmel Center, Pace Plaza (in downtown Manhattan), is named for Michael Schimmel, who donated what is said to be the only theatre in this district.

COLUMBIA UNIVERSITY, Broadway between 116th and 124th Sts. In 1762, King's College, as Columbia University was then called, was in financial straits and launched a drive to raise £10,000. Phila Franks used her influence in England to obtain money for the struggling college and enlisted the support of her brother, Moses, a leading Philadelphia merchant. Together they raised £4,000. Since then, many Jewish citizens have played an extensive role in the development of the university. These include Gershom Mendes Seixas, one of the incorporators when King's College was reincorporated as Columbia College after the American Revolution, and a trustee from 1787-1815; Sampson Simson; Jesse and Isaac N. Seligman;

James Speyer; Adolph Lewisohn; Arthur Hays Sulzberger, publisher of *The New York Times;* and Herbert Bayard Swope, editor of *The New York World* in the 1920s. In 1887 Temple Emanu-El set up a fund for the salary of a professor of rabbinic literature. This led to the establishment of a Department of Semitics, which was first chaired by Professor Gustav Gottheil and later by his son, Professor Richard J. H. Gottheil.

EARL HALL, Columbia University, is the interfaith center where Jewish student organizations Seixas, Menorah, and the Jewish Graduate Society meet. A portrait of Rev. Gershom Mendes Seixas hangs in Earl Hall, with the following inscription:

Gershom Mendes Seixas
1745
Regent, University of the State of New York 1784-1815
Trustee of Columbia College 1787-1815
Minister of Congregation Shearith Israel

A required part of the fourth year's study at King's College was an intensive course in Hebrew grammar and Biblical Hebrew, and its first president, Samuel Johnson, knew Hebrew. The official seal of Columbia has the word *Adonai* in Hebrew in a triangular glory above the head of a woman seated upon a throne with three nude children at her knees. To the left of her mouth is a ribbon with the Hebrew words *Ori El*—"G-d is my Light."

BARNARD COLLEGE, 606 W. 120th St. Annie Nathan Meyer, a relative of Emma Lazarus and Benjamin Cardozo, is credited with having originated the idea of a college for women under the wing of Columbia University. Her letter proposing the college, which appeared in the January 1, 1888 issue of *The Nation,* was called the "first broadside in the campaign for the founding of Barnard College." As a bride of 20, Annie Meyer pushed doorbells asking for contributions to the first Barnard College budget; her husband, Dr. Alfred Meyer, gave $500 and signed the lease for the original building at 343 Madison Ave. ●Annie Nathan Meyer Drama Library, 3rd Floor, Barnard Hall. Mrs. Meyer's portrait hangs in the College Parlor. An inscription beneath the portrait refers to Annie Meyer as the "Author of the Original Plea for the Establishment of Barnard College (and) Organizer of the First Board of Trustees." She served as a trustee of the college for over half a century. ●A portrait of Jacob Schiff also hangs in the College Parlor. The inscription beneath it states that he was the donor of Barnard Hall, trustee of the college from 1889-1897, and treasurer from 1889-1893. Barnard Hall has been referred to as "Jake." "Meet me on Jake" is a familiar phrase. A round tablet on the floor of the reception area of the Hall bears an inscription stating that the building is the gift of Jacob Schiff. ●Adele Lehman Hall-Wollman Library, Barnard College, was built from funds from the Wollman Foundation, an additional donation from Adele Lehman, and contributions from other individuals.

CITY UNIVERSITY OF NEW YORK, 139th St. and Convent Ave., has the largest enrollment of Jewish students in any institution of higher learning in the world. There are a number of memorials to Jewish individuals, among them Albert Einstein; Rubin Goldmark, composer; Gustave Hartman, jurist; Paul Klapper, educator and administrator; Mark Eisner, educator; Alfred Stieglitz, photographer; David B. Steinman, engineer and bridge builder; Felix S. Cohen, attorney, philosopher, and author; and Henry Leipziger, the pioneer of free public lectures. ●There is also the Davis Center for Performing Arts.

CITY UNIVERSITY OF NEW YORK—BARUCH COLLEGE OF BUSINESS AND PUBLIC ADMINISTRATION, 17 Lexington Ave., is named after Bernard Baruch. There is a black granite park bench bordering the front of the library dedicated to him. ●The Arthur M. Lamport House, 25 E. 22nd St., is a social and recreational center for Baruch students. The college also has a B'nai B'rith Hillel Foundation.

HUNTER COLLEGE, 695 Park Ave., has a valuable collection of Judaica. ●Also: The Samuel J. Silberman School of Social Work, 129 E. 79th St., is named for a former president of the Federation of Jewish Philanthropies.

NEW YORK MEDICAL COLLEGE, 5th Ave. at 106th St., has the Sophie D. and William W. Cohen Research Building which was established through a $2 million bequest from the late Sophie D. Cohen, prominent philanthropist whose husband William has been a stockbroker and Congressman. In her will, she gave as the reason for her bequest, "It has come to my attention that the New York Medical College, Flower and Fifth Avenue Hospitals, in New York City, is an institution that does not discriminate against Jewish students and selects its student body from among those most qualified, and has among it a very large percentage of Jewish students who are fully capable and equipped, and that its faculty is likewise chosen upon the same principles."

FORDHAM UNIVERSITY AT LINCOLN CENTER, 140 W. 62nd St., has the Benjamin A. Javits Halls of Law. The buildings house the university's law school and law library. Benjamin Javits, a 1918 graduate of Fordham University Law School, is a well-known attorney and brother of Senator Jacob K. Javits.

TOURO COLLEGE, 30 W. 44th St., is the newest institution of higher learning in New York under Jewish auspices.

INFORMATION FOR JEWISH LIVING: JEWISH ORGANIZATIONS, THEIR FUNCTIONS AND SERVICES

For the benefit of persons wanting assistance, advice, or information, major organizations are listed in this section according to the area of service for which they are best known. This is not a complete listing. Readers wanting more information about Jewish organizations should consult the *American Jewish Year Book* or *American Organizations Directory*.

MAJOR COMMUNITY RELATIONS AGENCIES

AMERICAN JEWISH COMMITTEE—INSTITUTE OF HUMAN RELATIONS, 165 E. 56th St., is the national headquarters of this pioneer human relations organization. The American Jewish Committee pursues a varied program to combat bigotry, protect the civil and religious rights of Jews in all countries, and aims to improve human relations for all people everywhere. A wall inscription in the lobby reads: "Dedicated to man's understanding of his fellow man." ●The Blaustein Library is named in honor of the industrialist and philanthropist Jacob Blaustein and his wife. Its contents consists of over 40,000 volumes, numerous periodicals, information files, and special collections in the areas of the Committee's current concerns. Though primarily intended for staff use, it is open to qualified researchers and writers, on application. ●The William E. Wiener Oral History Library is an ever-expanding collection of tapes and transcripts which document the American Jewish experience during the 20th century. ●The Joseph M. Proskauer Room is a legal reference library, named after the eminent jurist. ●*Commentary*, the noted monthly opinion journal, and *Present Tense*, the quarterly journal of Jewish world affairs, have their offices here. ●The editorial office of the *American Jewish Year Book* is also located here.

THE ANTI-DEFAMATION LEAGUE OF B'NAI B'RITH, 315 Lexington Ave. The prime objective of this organization is "to counter the defamation of Jews and assaults on their status and rights." Its three major areas of operation are education, legislation, and monitoring of activities of harmful and potentially harmful organizations and individuals. It is also the headquarters of the American Federation of Jewish Fighters, Camp Inmates, and Nazi Victims. This building is also the headquarters of a variety of citywide and regional B'nai B'rith groups and the New York office of national B'nai B'rith projects.

JEWISH LABOR COMMITTEE, 25 E. 78th St., (in the Atran Center for Jewish Culture), seeks to combat anti-Semitism and racial and religious intolerance abroad and in the United States, in cooperation with organized labor.

METROPOLITAN NEW YORK COORDINATING COUNCIL ON JEWISH POVERTY, 21 E. 40th St.

NATIONAL JEWISH COMMUNITY RELATIONS ADVISORY COUNCIL, 55 W. 42nd St., is the national consultative, advisory, and coordinating council of nine national Jewish organizations and some 100 local Jewish councils.

STEPHEN WISE CONGRESS HOUSE, 15 E. 84th St., the former Ogden Reid home, is the headquarters of the American Jewish Congress. This organization fights all forms of racial and religious bigotry and works to defend religious freedom and the separation of church and state. The Martin Steinberg Cultural Center, dedicated in 1976, is separated from Congress

House by a garden. It is designed as a gathering place for young Jewish artists, writers, musicians, and film-makers. It contains the Charles and Bertie Schwartz Jewish Reading Room and Library and the Bernard L. Madoff Jewish Music Library, a screening room for film presentations, and exhibition space for work by Jewish artists and sculptors. Mrs. Betty Ford, wife of the President, participated in the dedication ceremony.

UNITED JEWISH COUNCIL OF THE LOWER EAST SIDE, 235 E. Broadway, is an umbrella organization for all Jewish organizations on the East Side.

AGENCIES RELATED TO ISRAEL

AMERICA-ISRAEL CULTURAL FOUNDATION, 4 E. 54th St., helps support about 40 cultural institutions in Israel. It conducts a two-way program of cultural exchange between the United States and Israel, and awards scholarships in the performing arts to talented young Israelis for study in Israel and abroad. Among the groups it supports are the Israel Philharmonic Orchestra, the Habimah Theatre, the Inbal dancers, Bezalel National Museum, and the Rubin Academy of Music. It conducts an annual "Music Under the Stars" program at Madison Square Garden featuring the top talent of America.

AMERICAN JEWISH JOINT DISTRIBUTION COMMITTEE (JDC), 60 E. 42nd St., organizes and administers welfare, medical, and rehabilitation programs and distributes funds to needy Jews overseas for relief and reconstruction; in Israel, JDC conducts an extensive program, Malben, which includes institutions to help the aged, youth, handicapped, and others.

AMERICAN JEWISH LEAGUE FOR ISRAEL, 595 Madison Ave., is dedicated to the welfare of Israel as a whole. It is not affiliated with any class or party.

AMERICAN MIZRACHI WOMEN, 817 Broadway, sponsors social service, child care, and vocational education programs in Israel—all conducted within the framework of traditional Judaism. It also conducts a program of cultural activities in America geared to spread Zionist ideals and strengthen traditional Judaism.

AMERICAN ZIONIST FEDERATION, 515 Park Avenue.

AMERICAN ZIONIST YOUTH FOUNDATION, 515 Park Avenue.

BNAI ZION, 136 E. 39th St., is a fraternal Zionist organization. It seeks to spread Hebrew culture in America; offers insurance and other benefits to its members; and sponsors settlements, medical clinics, and youth centers in Israel. The building is called the America-Israel Friendship Building.

BRITH ABRAHAM, 853 Broadway, is a fraternal order that sponsors Zionist activities and conducts a program of civic defense, mutual aid, and philanthropy.

CONSULATE GENERAL OF ISRAEL, 800 2nd Ave. The Israeli Mission to the United Nations is located here.

FARBAND HOUSE, 575 6th Ave., is the home of Farband—Labor Zionist Order—an organization that provides members and families with low-cost fraternal benefits, seeks to spread Jewish education and culture, and supports the State of Israel in keeping with the ideals of Labor Zionism.

HADASSAH, 50 W. 58th St., is the women's Zionist organization of America. The building is fronted by four archways. Its interior is blue and white and lined in part with Jerusalem marble.

THEODOR HERZL INSTITUTE, 515 Park Ave.

ISRAEL GOVERNMENT OFFICE, 850 3rd Ave., houses such Israeli government offices as the Office of the Economic Minister, Ministry of Defense, Treasury Department, etc.

JEWISH AGENCY FOR ISRAEL, INC., 515 Park Ave., administers funds for programs in Israel related to immigration, colonization, public health, housing, absorption, labor, and public works. Over the entrance of the building is a Menorah, symbol of modern Israeli and Jewish tradition and culture, which indicates the purpose to which the building is dedicated. The design of the Menorah, which also appears on Israel's tenth anniversary stamps and commemorative coins, is a modern adaptation of a Menorah carved upon the walls of the necropolis of Beth Shearim in the third or fourth century. The murals in the lobby of the building are the work of the Israeli artist Perli Pelzig, who uses the Italian *sgraffito* technique by which the picture is carved out of superimposed layers of cement and lime concrete of different colors. The first panel as you enter is devoted to *aliyah*, the Hebrew term for "ascent," which refers to immigration. In contrast to the other murals, the first panel is dominated by human faces and figures. The second panel depicts the life of the pioneers. The third panel depicts barren soil and stubborn rock giving way to flourishing farm communities. On the fourth panel are symbols of teeming cities and the ships that carry Israel's flag across the seven seas. Israel's artistic, spiritual, and scientific life is the subject of the fifth panel (on the lobby's eastern wall). Another panel by Perli Pelzig in the second-floor auditorium shows a group of young Israeli pioneers dancing the *hora*. Though set apart from the murals in the lobby, the 25-foot panel in a sense completes the cycle of a people who rose from the dispersion to redeem and rebuild itself and its ancient homeland and at last has learned to dance and sing again.

JEWISH NATIONAL FUND, 42 E. 69th St., raises money to buy, develop, and reclaim the soil of Israel.

LABOR ZIONIST ALLIANCE, 575 6th Ave., supports labor and progressive forces in Israel and works for the democratization of American Jewish community life, the expansion of civil rights, and the progress of organized labor. The Alliance includes organizations devoted to Labor Zionism.

NATIONAL COMMITTEE FOR LABOR ISRAEL (Israel Histadrut Campaign), Histadrut House, 33 E. 67th St. The committee, headquartered in the former Vanderbilt mansion provides funds for various social welfare and other services of Histadrut for the benefit of workers and immigrants. It works to promote an understanding among Americans of the aims and achievements of Israel labor. Of special interest to visitors are photo exhibits of Israeli personalities, lectures and films on Labor Israel, and an exhibit of the Afro-Asian Institute.

NATIONAL YOUNG JUDEA, 817 Broadway, is concerned with the development of a Jewish youth movement dedicated to Zionism and Israel and pledged to service on behalf of the Jewish people in America and Israel.

PALESTINE ECONOMIC CORPORATION, 511 5th Ave., promotes the economic development of Israel through investments.

PIONEER WOMEN, 315 5th Ave., is the women's Labor Zionist organization of America. It offers a program of social services to Israeli youth through agricultural training schools; to women and children through vocational training, kindergartens, and day nurseries; and to Arab women through special clubs and vocational training. It also provides guidance and training for new immigrant women.

POALE AGUDATH ISRAEL OF AMERICA, INC., 156 5th Ave., seeks to educate and prepare youth to become Orthodox *halutzim* in Israel.

RELIGIOUS ZIONISTS OF AMERICA *(Mizrachi-Hapoel Hamizrachi)*, 26 West 26th St., seeks to promote a close relationship between religious Jewry of America and Israel; supports, maintains, and establishes schools and yeshivas in Israel; establishes all-day schools in America; and fosters a youth program through the Bnei Akiva and Mizrachi Hatzair.

STATE OF ISRAEL BOND ORGANIZATION, 215 Park Ave., provides investment funds for the economic development of Israel through the sale of Israel bonds.

UNITED JEWISH APPEAL (national), 1290 Ave. of the Americas.

UNITED JEWISH APPEAL OF GREATER NEW YORK, 220 W. 58th St., conducts a joint campaign with Federation of Jewish Philanthropies.

WOMEN'S LEAGUE FOR ISRAEL, 1860 Broadway.

WORLD ZIONIST ORGANIZATION-American Section, 515 Park Avenue.

ZIONIST ARCHIVES AND LIBRARY, 515 Park Ave.

ZIONIST ORGANIZATION OF AMERICA, 4 E. 34th St., assists in the economic development of Israel and works to strengthen a sense of Jewish identity. The building is known as ZOA House.

ORGANIZATIONS WORKING FOR SOVIET JEWRY AND OTHER REFUGEES

GREATER NEW YORK CONFERENCE ON SOVIET JEWRY, 11 W. 42nd St.

HIAS, 200 Park Ave. S., is an international migration agency. Founded in 1884 as the Hebrew Immigrant Aid Society, the organization's original purpose was to provide shelter and assistance in finding employment for Jewish immigrants. It later became international in scope and character, covering all phases of immigrant aid. Since its founding, the organization has helped rescue more than three million Jews from oppression and persecution, resettling them in lands of freedom and security. They help settle Russian Jewish immigrants to the U.S., outside of New York, among other activities.

NATIONAL CONFERENCE ON SOVIET JEWRY, 11 W. 42nd St.

NEW YORK ASSOCIATION FOR NEW AMERICANS, 15 Park Row, settles Jewish immigrants in New York. The most recent immigrants have been from the Soviet Union.

STUDENT STRUGGLE FOR SOVIET JEWRY, 200 W. 72nd St.

THE JEWISH PRESS

ALGEMEINER JOURNAL, 404 Park Ave. South, is a Yiddish weekly.

AUFBAU, 2121 Broadway, is a paper for German Jews.

THE JEWISH DAILY FORWARD, 45 E. 33rd St. (originally on the Lower East Side), has a bust of Abraham (Ab) Cahan in the lobby. Cahan built the *Forward* from a journal of 6,000 readers to a modern, lively Yiddish newspaper with a paid circulation of 200,000. He was responsible for introducing many human interest features, one of which was the "Bintel Brief" (Bundle of Letters), which carried letters describing problems of the East European Jewish immigrants. The *Forward* was credited with being the principal force in organizing thousands of Yiddish-speaking immigrants in the needle trades union. It was also a chief instrument in the Americaniza-tion of the newcomers. Cahan was the author of the novel *The Rise of David Levinsky*. He had many critics and enemies and was an anti-Communist. The Workmen's Circle, a labor-oriented fraternal organization, is housed in this building.

JEWISH TELEGRAPHIC AGENCY, 165 W. 46th St., is a Jewish wire service serving not only Jewish newspapers in America, but throughout the world.

THE JEWISH WEEK, 3 E. 40th St., is one of the liveliest American Jewish weeklies in the country. Lists most important Jewish happenings in the city.

JEWISH EDUCATION AGENCIES

AMERICAN ASSOCIATION FOR JEWISH EDUCATION, 114 5th Ave., coordinates, promotes, and serves Jewish education nationally through community programs and special projects. The National Council on Jewish Audio-Visual Materials, which is sponsored by the AAJE, lists, evaluates, and originates audio-visual materials.

ATRAN CENTER FOR JEWISH CULTURE, 25 E. 78th St., is the headquarters for the women's division of the Jewish Labor Committee, the Central Yiddish Culture Organization, the Congress for Jewish Culture, Inc. and its World Bureau for Jewish Education, and the International Jewish Labor Fund. The Center has art exhibits from time to time and has a cafeteria serving home-cooked Jewish lunches. ●The William Green Human Relations Library contains published and unpublished material on human relations with special emphasis on labor's role in furthering civil rights.

BETH JACOB SCHOOLS, 142 Broome St.

BOARD OF JEWISH EDUCATION OF NEW YORK, 426 W. 58th St., is the city's central bureau of Jewish education, serving well over 700 schools. BJE works for better teacher training and higher standards in religious schools; sponsors the Jewish Theatre for Children, art exhibits, and music and dance festivals; publishes *World Over* and various booklets; promotes the study and appreciation of the Hebrew language, literature, and culture; conducts an intensive program of adult education; and researches and disseminates information about Jewish education. The BJE library is a specialized pedagogic collection for the use of teachers, principals, social group workers, and lay educational leaders. A trained librarian is available for information, reference, and bibliography work. An unusual illuminated mosaic wall decorates the BJE building. The wall, eight by twelve feet, consists of 20 Venetian glass mosaic panels. They were individually designed by students of 17 Jewish schools, unified through color and dedication to a central theme. The 20 panels offer a multi-colored panorama of Jewish history. From about the middle of March to the end of June there is an exhibit of children's artwork from all types of Jewish schools.

DOWNTOWN TALMUD TORAH, 149 E. Broadway.

HEBREW ARTS SCHOOL FOR MUSIC AND DANCE, 15 W. 65th Street.

THE HEBREW ARTS FOUNDATION, 120 W. 16th St. The building which houses this organization and Histadruth Ivrith of America, known as Hebrew House, has a central Hebrew library, an exhibition hall for Israeli books and art objects, and a Hebrew theatre.

HISTADRUTH IVRITH OF AMERICA, 120 W. 16th St., emphasizes the importance of Hebrew in Jewish life, culture, and education; conducts Hebrew courses for adults; publishes Hebrew books; sponsors the

Hebrew-speaking Masad camps, the Hebrew Academy; and Noar Ivri, a youth group on campuses and in cities throughout the United States.

MESIVTA TIFERETH JERUSALEM, 145 E. Broadway.

TORAH UMESORAH (The National Society for Hebrew Day Schools), 229 Park Ave. S., helps set up Jewish day schools throughout the country. It places teachers and administrators in these schools, conducts teaching seminars and workshops, and publishes textbooks and supplementary reading material.

YESHIVA HEICHAL HATALMUD OF TEL-AVIV, 217 E. Broadway.

YESHIVA HEICHAL HATORAH, 630 Riverside Drive.

YESHIVA OHR TORAH, 308 W. 75th St.

YESHIVA RABBI MOSES SOLOVEICHIK, 560 W. 185th St.

YESHIVA RABBI SAMSON RAPHAEL HIRSCH, 91 Bennett Avenue.

HILLEL FOUNDATIONS

BERNARD M. BARUCH COLLEGE, 144 E. 24th St.

CITY COLLEGE OF NEW YORK, 475 W. 140th St.

HUNTER COLLEGE, 49 E. 65th St. This Hillel unit is known as the Roosevelt Memorial because it is housed in the former home of President Franklin D. Roosevelt and his mother, Sara.

COMMITTEES FOR INSTITUTIONS OF HIGHER LEARNING

AMERICAN COMMITTEE FOR WEIZMANN INSTITUTE, 515 Park Ave.

AMERICAN FRIENDS OF BAR-ILAN UNIVERSITY, 641 Lexington Ave.

AMERICAN FRIENDS OF BEN-GURION UNIVERSITY OF THE NEGEV, 342 Madison Ave.

AMERICAN FRIENDS OF HAIFA UNIVERSITY, 500 5th Ave.

AMERICAN FRIENDS OF HEBREW UNIVERSITY, 11 East 69th St.

AMERICAN FRIENDS OF TEL AVIV UNIVERSITY, 342 Madison Ave.

AMERICAN SOCIETY FOR TECHNION-ISRAEL INSTITUTE OF TECHNOLOGY, 271 Madison Ave.

BRANDEIS UNIVERSITY HOUSE, 12 East 77th St.

MOUNT SINAI SCHOOL OF MEDICINE, 5th Ave. and 100th St.

FRATERNAL ORDERS

B'RITH ABRAHAM, 853 Broadway, was founded in 1883.
FREE SONS OF ISRAEL, 932 Broadway, was founded in 1849.
UNITED ORDER OF TRUE SISTERS, 150 West 85th St., was founded in 1846.
WORKMEN'S CIRCLE, 45 East 33rd St., a Yiddish-oriented fraternal order that was founded by East European immigrants in 1900, it now has many English-speaking branches. It sponsors secularist Yiddish schools for children, and a Jewish educational program. In its lobby is a 7½ foot high model of the sculpture to be created by Nathan Rapoport as a memorial to the Holocaust victims and the Warsaw Ghetto partisans. The sculpture is to be dedicated in 1978 on the 35th anniversary of the Warsaw Ghetto Revolt.

COORDINATING AGENCIES

CONFERENCE OF PRESIDENTS OF MAJOR AMERICAN JEWISH ORGANIZATIONS, 515 Park Ave.
COUNCIL OF JEWISH FEDERATIONS AND WELFARE FUNDS, 315 Park Ave. South, provides national and regional services in Jewish community organization, campaigns and interpretation, budgeting, planning for health and welfare, and cooperative action by Jewish welfare funds and federations in the United States and Canada.
COUNCIL OF JEWISH ORGANIZATIONS IN CIVIL SERVICE, 20 W. 43rd St.
FEDERATION OF JEWISH PHILANTHROPIES OF NEW YORK, 130 E. 59th St., is the "community chest" of Jewish-sponsored agencies in the metropolitan New York area, providing philanthropic support to 130 affiliated institutions. Federation occupies five floors of its 17-story modern office building, with 12 floors leased to commercial tenants. •The Warburg Room on the 7th floor has a 50-foot stained glass memorial wall and a scroll of remembrance. The memorial wall, designed by Irv Koons, one of the nation's top artists, and beautifully illuminated, symbolically depicts, in a series of seven nine-foot high panels, various aspects of Federation's philanthropic activity. The scroll of remembrance is of parchment and is engraved with the names of those who have left legacies to Federation. An electrical device turns the giant scrolls to reveal any one of the 2,600 inscribed names •Behind the Warburg Room is the Sulzberger Room, and on the sixth floor, there is the Madeleine Borg Meeting Room. •The Personal Service Department is, in effect, an information center for people who want to know which Federation agency offers the type of help they need. In a sense, Federation can be considered a miniature "Jewish City Hall," for communal planning, consideration of social welfare

legislation, and religious affairs. Federation conducts a joint campaign with the United Jewish Appeal of Greater New York. JEWISH COMMUNITY RELATIONS COUNCIL OF GREATER NEW YORK, 111 W. 40th St., is a citywide agency that seeks to unify the Jewish community's response to critical community relations problems.

VOCATIONAL AGENCIES

AMERICAN ORT FEDERATION (Organization for Rehabilitation Through Training), 222 Park Ave. South, trains Jewish men and women in the technical trades and agriculture, and organizes and maintains vocational training schools throughout the world.

BRAMSON ORT TRADE SCHOOL, 222 Park Ave. South, is the only specifically Jewish vocational training school in the United States. Its purpose is to teach needle-trade skills to Jewish refugees and other newcomers to enable them in obtaining employment.

FEDERATION EMPLOYMENT AND GUIDANCE SERVICE, 28 E. 21st St.

NATIONAL ASSOCIATION OF JEWISH VOCATIONAL SERVICES, 114 5th Ave., is a national body of vocational agencies.

WOMEN'S AMERICAN ORT, 1250 Broadway.

COMMUNITY CENTERS

ASSOCIATED YM & YWHAs OF GREATER NEW YORK, 130 E. 59th St. YM & YWHA branches serve neighborhoods in four of the five boroughs of New York City and Westchester County.

ASSOCIATION OF JEWISH CENTER WORKERS, 15 E. 26th St.

EDUCATIONAL ALLIANCE, 197 E. Broadway, is an agency that has played an important part in the teeming life of one of the fabled communities of the world—the ever changing, ever exciting Lower East Side. The Educational Alliance has been expanded and now maintains an apartment residence for the aged. (See also section on Lower East Side.)

EMANU-EL MIDTOWN YM-YWHA, 344 E. 14th St., includes facilities for the Jewish Society for the Deaf.

JWB, 15 E. 26th St., is the Association of YM & YWHAs and Jewish Community Centers and camps in the United States and Canada. It is the only Jewish agency accredited by the United States government to serve the religious, cultural, social, and recreational needs of Jewish military and naval personnel and their dependents. It also serves hospitalized veterans, and is the Jewish member agency of the United Service Organizations (USO). JWB encourages appreciation of Jewish culture through its Jewish Book Council, Jewish Music Council, and JWB Lecture Bureau, and has a wide variety of Israel-related activities.

92ND STREET YM & YWHA, Lexington Ave. and 92nd St., is the

largest and oldest Jewish Community Center in continuous existence in the United States. The only YMHA in the United States that has dormitory facilities, this Y has the Henry Kaufmann Building with its Clara de Hirsch Residence Hall, providing comfortable living quarters for about 300 girls. Jacob H. Schiff, one of the first to recognize the importance of Jewish Community Centers, gave the Y its first buildings. A bas-relief of Schiff hangs in this lobby. ●In addition, the Y has a new Theresa L. Kaufmann Auditorium, Kaufmann Art Gallery, the Felix M. Warburg Lounge, and Buttenwieser Hall. With its varied program of activities in music, dance, drama, and the arts, the Y is an important cultural center for all New Yorkers.

WORLD FEDERATION OF YMHAs AND JEWISH COMMUNITY CENTERS, 15 E. 26th St.

YM & YWHA OF WASHINGTON HEIGHTS AND INWOOD, 54 Nagle Ave., is a strikingly modern and functional social, recreational, cultural, and educational center serving people of all ages. It rises three stories high at its main entrance and four stories at the rear. A unique feature of its multi-purpose auditorium which seats 400 persons, is a glass wall facing West 196th St. which opens out into a protected garden. The building has a roof play area of approximately 7,000 square feet.

INSTITUTIONS FOR THE AGED AND HOSPITALS

BETH ISRAEL HOSPITAL, 10 Nathan D. Perlman Pl., was founded in 1890 when 40 immigrants each contributed 25¢ to open a clinic for the sick, impoverished people of the Lower East Side. Its present location is its fifth. It is now one of the largest hospitals in New York and one in which dietary laws are observed. ●The $2 million Charles H. Silver Clinic is designed to care for about 100,000 patients annually. ●On the operating-room floor of the hospital is a statue and plaque honoring Dr. Jonas E. Reinthaler, whose contribution to the development of medical education in the United States was primarily in connection with the furthering of nurses training schools. A 300-bed private and semi-private pavilion meets increased demands for beds on the rapidly growing East Side, where other facilities are inadequate or obsolete. ●Nathan D. Perlman Place is named for the late Judge Perlman, who was a Congressman from 1920-1927, and judge of the New York Court of Special Sessions from 1936 until his death in 1952. He was a vice-president of Beth Israel Hospital.

CENTRAL BUREAU FOR THE JEWISH AGED, 31 Union Square W.

HOME FOR AGED AND INFIRM HEBREWS, 121 W. 105th St., is a 410-bed structure with convertible facilities to accommodate the well and the chronically ill aged.

HOME OF THE SAGES OF ISRAEL, 25 Willett St.

HOSPITAL FOR JOINT DISEASES, 1919 Madison Ave., is another Federation agency.

JEWISH ASSOCIATION FOR SERVICES TO THE AGED, 222 Park Ave. S.

JEWISH HOME AND HOSPITAL FOR THE AGED, 120 W. 106th Street.

JEWISH HOME FOR CONVALESCENTS, 853 Broadway.

JEWISH MEMORIAL HOSPITAL, Broadway and 196th St., serves the communities of Washington Heights and Inwood. The hospital includes a two-story laboratory and research building.

MOUNT SINAI HOSPITAL, 5th Ave. from 99th to 101st Sts., was originally known as "Jews' Hospital" and was founded by Sampson Simson, probably the first Jew admitted to the New York Bar; the Rev. Samuel M. Isaacs; John I. Hart; Benjamin Nathan; John M. Davies; Henry Hendricks; Theodore J. Seixas; and Isaac and John D. Phillips. It became the Mount Sinai Hospital in 1866 by a special act of the legislature. Mount Sinai was New York's first great medical center among the non-municipal hospitals to place emphasis on research. •A plaque in the entrance foyer of the hospital's main building at 100th Street pays tribute to George Blumenthal for "his inspired leadership and unparalleled contribution to the development of (Mount Sinai) during forty-six years as trustee and twenty-seven as president." Mr. Blumenthal gave almost $2 million to the hospital. •On Madison Avenue, between 98th Street and 99th Street, stands the seven-story Atran Laboratory. This building is named for Frank Z. Atran, textile manufacturer and philanthropist, whose $1 million gift made completion of the structure possible.

CHILD CARE INSTITUTIONS

JEWISH BOARD OF GUARDIANS, 120 W. 57th St. This mental health agency, headquartered in its own building—The Edwin B. Elson Building—provides a variety of diagnostic and treatment services for emotionally disturbed youngsters and their parents. Jewish Board of Guardians facilities include:

• MADELEINE BORG CHILD GUIDANCE INSTITUTE, pro-vides out-patient service with its licensed mental hygiene clinics in Manhattan, Brooklyn, and The Bronx.

• CHILD DEVELOPMENT CENTER in Manhattan provides out-patient service.

• HAWTHORNE-CEDAR KNOLLS and LINDEN HILL SCHOOLS, Hawthorne, N.Y., serves severely disturbed adolescents.

• HENRY ITTLESON CENTER FOR CHILD RESEARCH, 5050 Iselin Ave., Riverdale, has a day treatment center for severely disturbed boys and girls.

• STUYVESANT RESIDENCE CLUB, 74 St. Marks Place, is for boys from 15 to 18 years of age.

The agency also conducts a children's court and other community services. Volunteers involved in the activities of JBG are called Big Brothers and Big Sisters.

JEWISH CHILD CARE ASSOCIATION, 345 Madison Ave. The agency provides foster home care and foster family day care, and operates two schools—the Pleasantville Cottage School (Pleasantville, Westchester County), and the Edenwald School (The Bronx). One of the first cottage-plan orphanages in the United States and the first such institution under Jewish auspices, The Pleasantville Cottage School today is considered one of the best residential and treatment centers for emotionally disturbed children from eight to sixteen years old. Edenwald, a smaller school, cares for and trains mildly retarded (educable and trainable), and emotionally disturbed children. Edenwald differs from other schools for educable retarded children in that it serves children who would require separation from families even if they were not retarded. Professional persons—doctors, psychologists, social workers, and teachers—may arrange to visit the Pleasantville Cottage School by calling JCCA's community relations department. JCCA also has group residences for boys and girls who, while able to live and attend school in the community, cannot adapt to foster home living. Of the institutions, four are the Hartman-Homecrest residences which consolidated with JCCA in 1962.

AGENCIES FOR THE HANDICAPPED

ALTRO HEALTH AND REHABILITATION SERVICES, 225 Park Ave. South, retrains, under the supervision of doctors and social workers, the post-mentally ill, cardiac, and tubercular patients to return to full-time jobs. The Altro Workshop has been expanded.

JEWISH BRAILLE INSTITUTE OF AMERICA, 110 E. 30th St., seeks to further cultural, educational, and religious welfare of the Jewish blind. It publishes Hebrew and English prayer books in Braille and teaches Hebrew Braille. It has the largest Jewish Braille and talking-book library in the world.

JEWISH GUILD FOR THE BLIND, 15 W. 65th St., maintains a home for the blind at 75 Stratton St., Yonkers. The Guild helps blind and visually handicapped persons, regardless of race, religion, age, or economic status, to participate in the community on a self-supporting basis. Among its services are teaching the skills of daily living, preparing the blind to travel alone, vocational rehabilitation, sheltered workshops, mental health services, Braille library facilities, student training program, and other services.

ASSISTANCE WITH PERSONAL AND FAMILY PROBLEMS

AGUDATH ISRAEL OF AMERICA, 5 Beekman St., has a variety of social and legal services for the poor and elderly.
HEBREW FREE BURIAL ASSOCIATION, 1170 Broadway.
HEBREW FREE LOAN SOCIETY, 205 E. 42nd St., is a unique institution founded in 1892 with a capital of $95. Here, individuals, employed or not, can get interest-free loans of up to $500 without being investigated and without putting up any collateral. All that is required is the endorsement on each loan of one or two responsible persons who have checking accounts and who do business in Greater New York (on loans of $100 or less, only one endorser is required). Loans must be repaid in a maximum of ten months.
JEWISH CONCILIATION BOARD OF AMERICA, 33 W. 60th St., is an agency to which members of Jewish families torn by internal strife take their problems for arbitration. The decisions of this unusual, non-judicial body—made up mostly of rabbis, judges, businessmen, and lawyers—are binding upon the disputants and enforceable in the civil courts. Referred to as "the court of first resort," the Jewish Conciliation Board sits in regular session. A panel of board members hear disputants plead their own cases. The board's work has been praised by Supreme Court Justice William O. Douglas and other prominent persons. Cases are initiated when a complaint is registered at the office of the JCB; it is then arranged that both parties appear at a fixed session of the board. All sessions are private. An arbitration agreement must be signed by both parties before the hearing.
It is interesting to observe why persons would place themselves under the jurisdiction of a board that may rule against them although no legal case exists. Its officers say that it is because "our people have a great moral sense. They want to do the right thing." The board was originally founded to keep quarrels involving Jews out of the courts and to help immigrants avoid costly litigation. The services of JCB are free. It is a descendant of the *Beth Din*, a religious court in which Jews were allowed to resolve their own differences. In addition to marital difficulties, which comprise 80 percent of the board's work, problems are heard involving the support and maintenance of older parents. The JCB sees itself as more than an arbitration tribunal. It is a Jewish communal institution that aims "to carry out the Jewish ideal of justice simply, without the encumbrances of complicated procedure. Its field of service includes the amicable adjustment of disputes arising between Jewish persons and Jewish religious, communal, fraternal, and benevolent organizations as well as differences arising between individual parties; such differences, by mutual consent, are submitted for conciliation." An important adjunct of the board is the Social Service Department where relief, advice, and guidance are provided for those who are in need. As a rule, problems involving marital relationships, aged parents, and rebellious or indifferent children are resolved in private through this department. ☐
JEWISH FAMILY SERVICE, 33 W. 60th St., provides consultation

NEW YORK CITY, MANHATTAN — 158

centers, a homemaker service, a family location and legal service, a family mental health clinic, a family counseling center, a crisis unit, a youth services unit, and other services.

LOUISE WISE SERVICES, 12 E. 94th St., conducts adoption services and the Jewish Unmarried Mothers Service. It was founded by the late Louise Waterman Wise, who was the wife of Rabbi Stephen S. Wise and the mother of Justice Justine Wise Polier of the Domestic Relations Court.

SYNAGOGAL AND RABBINIC BODIES

CENTRAL CONFERENCE OF AMERICAN RABBIS, 790 Madison Ave., represents the Reform movement. (See also: UNION OF AMERICAN HEBREW CONGREGATIONS.)

EDUCATORS ASSEMBLY, 155 5th Ave. (Conservative).

HOUSE OF LIVING JUDAISM (see Midtown section).

NATIONAL CONFERENCE OF SYNAGOGUE YOUTH, 116 E. 27th St. (Orthodox).

NATIONAL COUNCIL OF YOUNG ISRAEL, 3 W. 16th St.

NATIONAL FEDERATION OF TEMPLE YOUTH, 838 5th Ave. (Reform).

NEW YORK BOARD OF RABBIS, 10 E. 73rd St., located in the former Berg Mansion, is a body of Orthodox, Conservative, and Reform rabbis. It provides chaplains for local civilian hospitals, penal institutions, and other agencies. It is also a center for information about Judaism.

RABBINICAL ASSEMBLY OF AMERICA, 3080 Broadway, represents the Conservative body.

RABBINICAL COUNCIL OF AMERICA, 220 Park Ave., S., is a body of Orthodox rabbis.

SYNAGOGUE COUNCIL OF AMERICA, 432 Park Ave., S., represents synagogues and rabbis of all three wings on a national level.

UNION OF ORTHODOX JEWISH CONGREGATIONS OF AMERICA, 116 E. 27th St.

UNITED SYNAGOGUE OF AMERICA, 155 5th Ave., represents Conservative synagogues.

UNITED SYNAGOGUE YOUTH, 155 5th Ave. (Conservative)

JEWISH WOMEN'S ORGANIZATIONS

NATIONAL COUNCIL OF JEWISH WOMEN, 15 East 26th St., conducts a program of service and education for social action in the fields of social legislation, international affairs, contemporary Jewish affairs, community welfare, overseas service, and assistance to the foreign-born.

THE COUNCIL WORKSHOP FOR SENIOR CITIZENS, 915 Broadway, is an agency of the National Council of Jewish Women. The New York Section is located at 9 E. 69th St.

NATIONAL FEDERATION OF TEMPLE SISTERHOODS, 838 5th Ave., is located in the House of Living Judaism.

NEW YORK JEWISH WOMEN'S CENTER, 299 Riverside Dr., (Apt. 3D), sponsors a women's school in Judaica, a monthly minyan, an outreach campus program, and a monthly Sunday seminar.

UNITED ORDER TRUE SISTERS, INC., 150 W. 85th St., is a fraternal, philanthropic women's organization providing a cancer-treatment program.

WOMEN'S AMERICAN ORT, 1250 Broadway.

WOMEN'S BRANCH, UNION OF ORTHODOX JEWISH CONGREGATIONS OF AMERICA, 84 5th Ave.

WOMEN'S LEAGUE FOR CONSERVATIVE JUDAISM, 48 E. 74th St.

(For other women's organizations, see listing under other categories.)

JEWISH COMMUNAL PROFESSIONAL ORGANIZATIONS

NATIONAL CONFERENCE OF JEWISH COMMUNAL SERVICE, 15 E. 26th St., conducts an annual meeting for professionals in various fields of Jewish communal service and publishes the *Journal of Jewish Communal Service*. Affiliated with it are: Association of Jewish Center Workers, National Council of Jewish Education, National Association of Jewish Family, Children's and Health Professionals, Association of Jewish Community Relations Workers, Association of Jewish Community Organization Personnel, National Association of Synagogue Administrators, and National Association of Jewish Homes for the Aged.

HOUSING DEVELOPMENTS

AMALGAMATED DWELLINGS, 570 Grand St., the first housing development built in Manhattan under the pioneer State Housing Law of 1926, is a cooperative built by the Amalgamated Clothing Workers of America. Within the complex are houses named for Louis D. Brandeis (see Louisville), Edward Filene (see Boston), and Meyer London, who was elected to Congress as a Socialist in 1914 from the Lower East Side.

BARUCH HOUSES, 100 Columbia St., is named for Bernard M. Baruch, advisor to Presidents and chairman of the War Industries Board during World War I, and for his father, Dr. Simon Baruch, a physician in the Confederate Army who later devoted himself to improving public health facilities in N.Y.C.

GOMPERS HOUSES, 50 Pitt St., is named for Samuel Gompers, one of the founders and first president of the American Federation of Labor.

HOLMES-ISAACS HOUSES, 403 East 93rd St., memorializes in part Stanley Isaacs, a leading advocate of public housing and one-time president of the Borough of Manhattan.

LEHMAN VILLAGE, 1605 Madison Ave., is named for the late

Senator and former Governor, Herbert H. Lehman.

STRAUS HOUSES, 228 East 28th St., is named for Nathan Straus, philanthropist, whose milk fund was credited with saving the lives of thousands of babies and lowering the city's death rate.

VLADECK HOUSES, 366 Madison St., is named for B. Charney Vladeck, general manager for many years of the *Jewish Daily Forward* and a member of the first N.Y.C. Housing Authority.

WALD HOUSES, 54 Avenue D, is named for Lillian Wald, founder of Henry Street Settlement and the pioneer of public nursing.

WISE TOWERS, 124 West 91st St., is named for Dr. Stephen S. Wise, noted rabbi, Zionist leader, civic reformer, and president of the American and World Jewish Congresses.

ENTERTAINMENT

THEATRE, MUSIC, AND ART

Although the Yiddish theatre has long passed its peak productions and attendance, it is by no means dead. The following are a number of groups which stage productions from time to time:

THE ANDERSON YIDDISH THEATRE, 66 2nd Ave.

THE EDEN THEATER, 189 2nd Ave.

FOLKSBIENE PLAYHOUSE (in the auditorium of the Central Synagogue), 123 E. 55th St.

THE MAYFAIR THEATER, 235 W. 46th St.

ROOSEVELT YIDDISH THEATRE, 100 W. 17th St.

For the past several years there have been four shows a season. Some of these are shown daily, while others are seen on weekends only. Some of the plays use a musical comedy format with English and Yiddish mixed, and some are modernized versions of old Jewish stage hits by such masters as Abraham Goldfaden, Jacob Gordon, and Z. Libin. The Folksbiene Theatre features an earnest group of amateur performers with professional polish who have been putting on plays for a half century. It is the oldest organization of its kind and is devoted to serious theatre. The Folksbeine season starts in November and performances run for 20 weekends: Saturdays at 8 p.m., Sundays at 2 p.m. and 5:30 p.m. □

EDUCATIONAL ALLIANCE, 197 East Broadway, offers concerts, plays, dance recitals, operas, film programs, forums, and festival activities in its Isidor Straus Theatre.

THEODOR HERZL INSTITUTE, 515 Park Ave., provides lectures and forums on virtually all aspects of Judaism. The institute holds both morning and evening programs with the exception of Friday evenings and Saturdays. In addition to the lectures, there are courses, public functions, conferences, audio-visual presentations, and special events. During the summer months, the institute conducts the Ulpan course in Hebrew, but most other activities are suspended. The institute's art exhibits are always interesting.

JEWISH THEATRE FOR CHILDREN, Franklin Playhouse, 154 W. 93rd St. This group is sponsored by the Board of Jewish Education of New York. It produces original full-length plays based on Jewish themes. Productions can be seen every Sunday afternoon from November through March.

YM & YWHA, 92nd St. and Lexington Ave., features a variety of programs, such as dance recitals, lectures, seminars, concerts, plays, and poetry readings. Some programs are of specifically Jewish interest; most are of interest to all New Yorkers, who frequently visit the Y auditorium.

NIGHTCLUBS

CLUB CAESAREA, 2 E. 86th St., is an Israeli nightclub, featuring *glatt* kosher cuisine. There are two shows nightly and dancing. (Open every evening except Friday). Papa Lou's, a kosher Italian restaurant, is located here.

CAFE FEENJON, 117 Macdougal St., is a nightclub featuring Middle-Eastern, Jewish, and Israeli entertainment.

CAFE YAFFO, 450 W. 42nd St., is a restaurant and night spot designed to give its patrons a taste of Israel. It has experimented with full-length Israeli films shown to diners at no extra charge.

DAVID'S HARP, 131 W. 3rd St., is an Israeli nightclub featuring Middle-Eastern food.

EL AVRAM, 80 Grove St., is an Israeli kosher nightclub and restaurant featuring American-Israeli cuisine and Russian, Yiddish, and Israeli entertainment. In addition to its Israeli owner, Avram Grobard (a singer and accordionist), there is an Armenian oud-player and an Israeli-Arab chef. (Open every night but Monday).

GOLDA'S NIGHTCLUB, near Bleecker and Jones Sts., off 7th Ave.

SABRA EAST, 232 E. 43rd St., is an Israeli supper club. There is a choice of Middle Eastern or traditional *glatt* kosher cuisine. It also features entertainment and dancing.

SIROCCO, 29 E. 29th St., is an Israeli-Greek nightclub.

TEL-AVIV CAFE, 100 W. 72nd St., has nightly entertainment.

DINING OUT

The opportunity to get "a good Jewish meal" to suit every palate and pocketbook makes eating out one of New York's principal pleasures for Jews and non-Jews alike. Whether one's taste runs to blintzes with sour cream, *varnishkes, pirogen,* cream cheese and lox, *maatjes* herring, gefilte fish, *matzo-brei,* hot pastrami or corned beef, chopped liver, *flanken,* stuffed derma, *tzimmes,* stuffed *miltz, lungen* stew, *kreplach* soup, *pitcha,* or any other kind of Jewish food—all are available in New York. There are even restaurants specializing in kosher Chinese food. In recent years a number of Israeli restaurants have opened.

The listing that follows includes not only kosher and Israeli restaurants, but also those with a history of Jewish interest, special atmosphere, or particular Jewish clientele. Prices and hours of some of these restaurants are listed, but these are subject to change. It is wise to check by phone prior to planning a visit to these restaurants.

MEAT RESTAURANTS—MIDTOWN

In an area where 25 to 30 percent of the population is Jewish, it is inevitable that many restaurants will serve dishes with a special appeal to Jews such as gefilte fish, chopped liver, chicken soup, delicatessen, cheese blintzes, etc. Among the many restaurants in this area offering these and other dishes, some of the best known are:

DIAMOND CENTER DELICATESSEN AND LUN-CHEONETTE, 71 W. 47th St.

DUBROW'S CAFETERIA, 515 7th Ave., is a garment center landmark, where a wide selection of Jewish specialties are part of the daily menu.

ESKOW'S, 225 W. 57th St.

HECTOR'S, 1506 Broadway.

HELLO DELI, 460 W. 42nd St., features kosher delicatessen.

KOSHER WORLD, Broadway at 32nd St., sells pizza and falafel and other Middle Eastern dishes. *Shomer Shabbat. Cholov Yisroel.*

LA DIFFERENCE (Roosevelt Hotel), Madison Ave. and 45th St., has a French menu.

MACCABEEM, 147 W. 47th St., has a Middle East menu.

MIDTOWN, 52 W. 47th St., is a *glatt* kosher restaurant.

MOSHE PEKING, 40 W. 37th St., serves *glatt* kosher Chinese and Continental cuisine.

NATHAN'S JEWELRY CENTER RESTAURANT, 36 W. 47th St.

PAPA LOU'S, 2 E. 86th St., is a kosher Italian restaurant, which is also where Club Caesarea is located.

ROSOFF'S, 147 W. 43rd St.

LOU G. SIEGEL, 209 W. 38th St. (near Broadway, open Sunday through Friday, 12 noon to 8:45 p.m., kosher). The specialty of this restaurant, located in the heart of the garment center, is delicatessen, served in generous portions, Hungarian stuffed cabbage is also a specialty. They also feature stuffed derma, *tzimmes*, meat *lungen*, and *miltz* stew. Known since 1917, Siegel's attracts patronage from all over the world. The firm provides kosher catering to TWA and Pan Am Airways. It is one of the few Jewish restaurants open during Passover.

SOLOWEY'S, 431-433 7th Ave.

STAGE DELICATESSEN AND RESTAURANT, 834 7th Ave. (north of Shubert Alley), is frequented by actors, dancers, and musicians.

TIP TOP, 491 7th Ave., is a *glatt* kosher restaurant.

MANNY WOLF'S CHOP HOUSE, 49th St. and 3rd Ave.

YAHALOM, 49-55 W. 47th St., is a *glatt* kosher restaurant and cafeteria. It is in the heart of the Diamond Center. It features American and Hungarian cuisine.

MEAT RESTAURANTS—UPPER WEST SIDE

FASS' RESTAURANT AND DELICATESSEN, 4179 Broadway, is a *glatt* kosher restaurant.

FINE AND SCHAPIRO, 138 W. 72nd St., (open 7 days a week, from 11 a.m. to midnight). The restaurant is kosher, although it does not have rabbinical supervision, as does Lou Siegel's. Their specialties are gefilte fish, boiled beef flanken, stuffed cabbage, potato *kugel*, stuffed derma, and prune *tzimmes*. Also: mushroom and barley soup or lentil soup with frankfurters. They are known for their hot strudel for dessert. The restaurant is conveniently located near the Spanish and Portuguese Synagogue, Temple Emanu-El, etc.

STERN'S RESTAURANT AND CATERERS, 666 West End Ave., (in Hotel Windermere, is open daily from 5 to 8:30 p.m.; Sundays, from 4:30 to 8:30 p.m.). This restaurant is open Friday, but closed Saturday. Money is not handled on the Sabbath. After reservations are made, the Sabbath meals must be paid for in advance.

TOV M'OD LUNCHEONETTE, 2549 Amsterdam Ave.

MEAT RESTAURANTS—LOWER EAST SIDE

BERNSTEIN-ON-ESSEX-STREET, 135 Essex St. (open 12 noon to 10 p.m., except Friday night and Saturday.) This was the first kosher Chinese restaurant in New York and claims to be the originator of kosher Chinese foods. The diner will be served by Chinese waiters wearing black *yarmulkas*. Specialties are won ton soup (Chinese *kreplach*); egg rolls; spare ribs; sweet and pungent veal; Chicken Bernstein (chicken stuffed with minced bamboo shoots and water chestnuts); and pastrami and Chinese vegetables. They also feature a choice of non-Chinese food such as hot corned beef, pastrami, or frankfurters—all of which come from the factory of the owner's famous father, Schmulka Bernstein. The factory is located at 107 Rivington St.

CROWN KOSHER RESTAURANT AND DELICATESSEN, 157 E. Houston St.

G & M KOSHER CATERERS, 41 Essex St., serves kosher meats and spaghetti, as well as the traditional *cholent, kishke,* and *kreplach.*

GLUCKSTERN'S STRICTLY KOSHER RESTAURANT, 135 Delancey St., (open seven days a week, 11 A.M. to midnight). This restaurant specializes in boiled beef *flanken*, steaks, and chops. Pollack's is now an annex to Gluckstern's.

HENRY'S KOSHER DELICATESSEN AND RESTAURANT, 195 E. Houston St. A sign in the window calls attention to the fact that "this is the only kosher restaurant in the vicinity."

KATZ'S DELI, 205 East Houston St., is a popular kosher-style establishment.

MIFGOSH, 830 8th Ave., specializing in Israeli-Yemenite cooking, serves Israeli-American kosher food. *Mifgosh* in Hebrew means a "meeting place where friends meet."

SAM'S KOSHER DELICATESSEN, 158 E. Broadway (closed Saturday).

SECOND AVENUE KOSHER DELICATESSEN AND RESTAURANT, INC. 156 2nd Ave.

Since it is not possible to list all the kosher delicatessen shops in Manhattan, look for the following to ascertain whether the eating establishment is truly kosher:

1. The word "kosher" should be printed in Hebrew; however, this may mean that only the delicatessen is kosher.

2. Check whether milk or milk products are served.

3. For the especially observant, inquire whether the establishment is closed on Saturday.

DAIRY RESTAURANTS—MIDTOWN

BLUM'S KOSHER DAIRY RESTAURANT, 10 W. 47th St.

DIAMOND KOSHER DAIRY LUNCHEONETTE, 4 W. 47th St., on the mezzanine in the Jeweler's Exchange. *Cholov Yisroel*. Full-course suppers are served from 5 to 7 p.m.

ESTHER'S KOSHER DAIRY RESTAURANT, 165 Madison Ave.

FARMFOOD RESTAURANT, 142 W. 49th St., emphasizes health and vegetable salads, but also serves a variety of fish and soups.

GEFEN'S KOSHER DAIRY RESTAURANT, 297 7th Ave., serves *Cholov Yisroel* upon request. (*Cholov Yisroel* is milk that has been produced and tested under the supervision of a recognized Jewish authority.) *Mehadrin* ("zealous") cream available. All cooking and baking are done on the premises. Full-course dinners are served from 4:30 to 8:30 P.M.; special club breakfasts are served from 6 to 10 a.m. (Closed Friday night, Saturday, and Jewish holidays).

R. GROSS DAIRY AND VEGETARIAN RESTAURANT, 1372 Broadway.

HAMIZNON KOSHER DAIRY RESTAURANT, 44 W. 30th St.

DAIRY RESTAURANTS—UPPER WEST SIDE

FAMOUS DAIRY RESTAURANT, 222 W. 72nd St., specializes in blintzes or vegetables with sour cream, soups, fish, and salads.

DAIRY RESTAURANTS—BELOW 23rd STREET

BROWNIE'S, 21 E. 16th St., is a fish and vegetarian restaurant.
CALDRON RESTAURANT, 308 E. 6th St., serves natural foods and has a bakery and natural food store featuring their specialties, *(Shomer Shabbos)*.
HAMMER DAIRY RESTAURANT, 243 E. 14th St.
RATNER'S, 138 Delancey St., is one of the best-known dairy restaurants in New York. They serve a variety of different types of blintzes as well as *kasha varnishkes*, soups and fishes. The tables are laden with a variety of rolls and breads and the bold waiters will undertake to advise the diner on what to order.
YONAH SCHIMMEL KNISHERY, 137 E. Houston St., is an interesting place to visit. There are over a dozen varieties of knishes available, as well as *potatoniks (kugel)*, strudel, *latkes*, sour milk, borsht, cheese bagels, and coffee. They advertise that it is the original Yonah Schimmel's Knishery and a picture of the founder is in the window. They are open from 7 a.m. to 10 p.m.

INSTITUTIONAL RESTAURANTS

ATRAN CENTER FOR JEWISH CULTURE, 25 E. 78th St., has a cafeteria which serves Jewish lunches.
B'NAI B'RITH BUILDING, 315 Lexington Ave., has a kosher counter service.
JEWISH THEOLOGICAL SEMINARY OF AMERICA, 3080 Broadway, and Rubin Hall at YESHIVA UNIVERSITY, 185th St. and Amsterdam Ave., both maintain cafeterias.
STERN COLLEGE FOR WOMEN, 253 Lexington Ave., an affiliate of Yeshiva University, has a kosher cafeteria where lunch is served.
WALL STREET SYNAGOGUE, 47 Beekman St., has a kosher restaurant that serves meals from 11 a.m. to 3 p.m.; also Passover meals.

SHOPPING

BOOKS AND RELIGIOUS OBJECTS

BEN ARI ARTS, LTD., 11 Ave. A, trades in Jewish art, antique Judaica, Israeli gift items, and synagogue supplies and decorations.
BEHRMAN HOUSE, 1261 Broadway. The visitor to this publishing

house will find a homey atmosphere, replete with a large comfortable library in which to browse leisurely while sipping coffee. Behrman House stocks almost every book of Jewish interest. It caters to professional people in Jewish life—rabbis, student rabbis, Jewish teachers and principals, cantors, administrators, writers, etc.

JAKER BIEGELEISEN, 83 Division St., carries a supply of Hebrew books, but his specialty is Hasidism. He also has books on Judaica and Jewish religious articles.

BLOCH PUBLISHING CO., 915 Broadway. This firm was founded in Cincinnati in 1854 by Rabbi Isaac Mayer Wise and his brother-in-law, Edward Bloch. Rabbi Wise had always been eager to address a nationwide audience, and when he moved to Cincinnati, he took steps the very first month to start a newspaper. His young brother-in-law, who had experience in printing was seeking a similar job in Cincinnati, and thus was born Bloch and Company, Publishers and Printers. They published in several languages and distributed their material. Their first publication, the *American Israelite*, a weekly printed in English, was the counterpart of *Die Deborah* in German. In 1901 the firm moved to New York. Charles Bloch, present publisher, is the fourth generation Bloch in the business. The firm publishes and distributes a wide variety of English Judaica and Hebraica and also sells ritual objects and religious novelties made in America and Israel. Though the firm began under Reform Jewish auspices, it has become prominent in the publication of *Haggadahs* and daily and holiday prayer books.

EASTERN JEWELRY MFG. CO., 39 West 19th St., carries Jewish religious goods, gold charms and novelties.

RABBI MOSES EISENBACH, 13 Essex St., carries *Sifrei* Torah, books, *tefilin*, and *taleisim*.

PHILIPP FELDHEIM, 96 East Broadway, has a large stock of German Judaica, and a collection of rare and old volumes. Mr. Feldheim is also a publisher as well as a bookseller.

GIMBEL'S DEPARTMENT STORE, Broadway and 33rd St., has an unusually large display of Israeli stamps, coins, covers, and albums.

HEBREW PUBLISHING CO. AND BOOKSTORE, 314 Grand St., prints a large percentage of Hebrew and English books in the United States and Jewish greeting cards. The firm has monotype machines in Hebrew and groups may arrange in advance for a tour of the premises to see how Hebrew is set into type. The store is spacious, and contains a large variety of books in English, Yiddish, and Hebrew. There are also greeting cards, Torah covers and ornaments, Ark curtains, *kiddush* cups, pointers, original paintings from Israel, spice boxes, candlesticks, *taleisim*, *tefilin*, and an assortment of other items rarely found elsewhere (also: 80 5th Ave.)

NISSIM HIZME HEBREW JEWELRY, INC. 37 Eldridge St. Hizme, a Yemenite Jew, is noted for his original, hand-crafted Hebrew jewelry and religious items. He also designs original Hebrew monograms that may be made into pins or used on personal stationery, or wedding and bar mitzvah invitations. The firm carries an assortment of charms, cufflinks, *kiddush* cups, *talis* clips, *mezuzahs*, etc.

ISRAEL ART DESIGN IMPORT CORP., 21½ Essex St., has Torahs and other Scrolls, *taleisim*, *tefilin*, and unusual arts and crafts.

ISRAEL RELIGIOUS ART, INC., 32 W. 61st St., imports ancient and modern art and carries other items such as Sephardi Torahs from Egypt.

THE JEWISH ART GALLERY, 11 Essex St., has Jewish oil paintings, lithographs, and prints.

KTAV PUBLISHING HOUSE, 75 Varick St., corner Canal St., publishes juvenile books and textbooks, and manufactures an array of articles. It is the world's largest manufacturer of *dreidels*.

J. LEVINE CO., 58 Eldridge St., calls itself "The Synagogue Beautiful" Department Store. It manufactures flexible hooked Torah binders with interlocking woods, scrolls of remembrance, Torah covers, and other religious regalia. It is the sole agent in the United States and Canada for the Yad Vashem Memorial Lights. Once a neighborhood store, its business now is largely mail-order, with customers all over the world. It specializes in synagogue essentials and general Judaica.

MIRIAM RELIGIOUS SUPPLIES MANUFACTURING CO., 54 Canal St., makes pure linen "eternal cloths," *parochet* (Ark Curtains), matzo and *challah* covers, Torah mantles, *yarmulkas*, and gowns. They sell bronze tablets and "earth from Israel" for the use of religious Jews at burial rites.

MOSES PARNES, 41 Essex St., sells scrolls, *tefilin*, and books (both retail and wholesale).

POLLAK'S BOOK STORE, 54 Canal St., sells *taleisim*, *tefilin*, books, and Israeli goods.

SOLOMON RABINOWITZ HEBREW BOOK STORE, 30 Canal St.

REINMAN'S SEFORIM CENTER, INC., 29 Essex St., is a center for copies of the Talmud and other Judaica.

SEPHARDIC PUBLISHING CO., 7 Rivington St.

ASHER SHALLER, 1495 St. Nicholas Ave., sells bar mitzvah sets, books, records, Ark curtains, book bindings, jewelry and Israeli imports.

LOUIS STAVSKY, 147 Essex St., specializes in religious articles for homes, congregations, and schools. They also carry a large selection of books of Jewish interest.

STM SCRIBES, INC. 220 W. 80th St., specializes in Hebrew lettering, invitation, etc., and has *Sifrei* Torah, *tefilin*, and bar mitzvah sets.

TIV TOV EMBROIDERY CO., 48 Eldridge St., carries Torah covers, *yarmulkas*, and *taleisim*.

UNITED NATIONS GIFT SHOP stocks items from Israel.

EMANUEL WEISBERG, 45 Essex St., sells bar mitzvah sets, Hebrew religious articles and antique Judaica (wholesale and retail).

M. WOLOZIN, INC. 38 Eldridge St., manufactures and sells *taleisim* and Hebrew religious articles and books.

YANKEE TALLIT WORKS, 175 5th Ave., produces and sells denim

prayer shawls, *yarmelkes*, and *tallit* bags. The *tallit* is both uniquely American and 100% kosher. Inspired by the American Bicentennial, they appeal to young people who believe that prayer can and should be a less formal experience without having to deviate from tradition or *halacha*. ZION TALIS MANUFACTURING CO., 48 Eldridge St., is probably the leading manufacturer of silk, woolen, and rayon prayer shawls. It also imports and distributes Hebrew religious regalia for synagogue and home use. In its retail store it carries a large selection of items ranging from skullcaps to a *Sefer* Torah. Conducted tours through its plant where the *taleisim* are made can be arranged. Religious school students can visit the plant and see how the actual *talis* is made and the *sofrim* at work repairing or retracing parts of the Torah.

The following specialize in Israeli jewelry, gifts, and other imports:
ABADA CHEN HEBRON LTD. ISRAEL, 94 Canal St.
ARTISTIC ISRAELI JEWELRY MFG. CO., 4 W. 37th St.
EASTERN ORIGINS, 435 Park Ave. South.
FAR-N-WIDE, INC., 175 E. 86th St.
FINKELSTEIN ENTERPRISES, 350 Hudson St.
ILAN IMPORTS, 342 Madison Ave., features handmade silver jewelry.
MEDITERRANEAN TRADING CO., 9 W. 57th St.
THE UNDERGROUND JEWELER, 147 E. 86th St.

JEWISH MUSIC

LOUIS STAVSKY, 147 Essex St., has the largest selection of music and recordings of Jewish interest in the city. Included are popular and folk music; theatrical, art, liturgical, and ethnic music; dances; Hasidic music; language instruction; stories and Biblical readings for children; dramatic works; and solo, choral and instrumental classical music.

(Jewish records can also be purchased at stores selling Judaica, several department stores, and record shops.)

KOSHER CANDIES AND BAKE GOODS

BARRICINI'S AND LOFTS, with branches throughout the Metropolitan area, sell candy and cookies designed for some of the Jewish holidays.
BARTON'S BONBONNIER, (executive offices at 80 DeKalb Ave., Brooklyn, N.Y.), has 21 stores in Manhattan, 14 in Brooklyn, 3 in The Bronx, 8 in Queens, and 4 in Nassau, Suffolk, and Westchester Counties. (Some of these stores are franchised and do not observe the Sabbath.) Barton's

manufactures a full line of candies, cakes, pastries, and other confections for Rosh Hashanah, Chanukah, Purim, and Passover. All of these are packaged in specially designed holiday boxes containing an illustrated explanation of the symbols and customs of the particular holiday. Copies of these leaflets and others explaining various aspects of the Jewish heritage are available without charge at the stores. Most stores also carry a selections of gifts made in Israel. All Barton products are manufactured under the supervision of the Union of Orthodox Jewish Congregations of America and carry the organization's seal of *kashruth*.

GERTEL'S BAKE SHOPPE, 53 Hester St., has cake and other baked goods for the Sabbath and Jewish holidays, in addition to their regular bakery products. There are tables in the shop where coffee and tea are served. (Closed Saturdays and Jewish holidays.)

MOISHE'S HOMEMADE KOSHER BAKERY, 181 E. Houston St.

STERN'S KOSHER PASTRY SHOP, INC., 490 Amsterdam Ave., specializes in wedding cakes.

STREIT MATZOTH CO., 150 Rivington St.

KOSHER CHEESES

CHEESE UNLIMITED, 1263 Lexington Ave., is a small store carrying kosher and non-kosher cheeses. They also carry cheeses from Israel, Poland, Romania, Czechoslovakia, etc.

CHEESES OF ALL NATIONS, 153 Chambers St., carries kosher and Israeli cheeses, as well as non-kosher varieties. Most of the Israeli cheeses are made from sheep's milk with the exception of feta, which is made from goat's milk. The kosher cheeses are made under rabbinical supervision. They also carry gift boxes of kosher cheeses for Passover and Chanukah.

LEIBELS' KOSHER SPECIALITIES, INC. 27½ Essex St., carries kosher cheeses.

MILLER'S CHEESE, 13 Essex St., sells only kosher cheese and is under the supervision of the Union of Orthodox Jewish Congregations of America. They carry eight different varieties of cheese—all made from sheep's milk.

MISCELLANEOUS PUBLIC PLACES

CENTRAL PARK, which runs from 59th to 110th Sts., from 5th Ave. to Central Park W., has among its many recreational attractions the following:

• Herbert H. Lehman Children's Zoo, named for the former senator and governor.

• Wollman Memorial Rink, a popular ice skating area, was a gift of Kate Wollman.

• Michael Friedsam Merry-Go-Round, named for the merchant, art patron, and philanthropist.

- Elkan Naumburg Bandstand, is named for the philanthropist.
- 72nd St. Boathouse and Restaurant was a gift of Mr. and Mrs. Carl M. Loeb, Sr.
- The Sophie Irene Loeb Fountain in the Heckscher Playground.
- The Lionel Sutro Playground is named for a friend of the park system.
- Pulitzer Memorial Fountain, is named for Joseph Pulitzer, famed journalist whose father was Jewish. ☐

CHAPELL MUSIC PUBLISHING CO., 810 7th Ave., has in the lobby of its building a large photo collage depicting such noted Jewish composers as George and Ira Gershwin, Richard Rodgers, Bob Dylan, Julie Styne, and Maurice Hamlisch.

DAMROSCH PARK, (in front of Lincoln Center), is named for the later Walter Damrosch, conductor of the New York Philharmonic, whose father was the music director at New York's Temple Emanu-El.

FELT FORUM, Madison Square Garden's 5,000-seat amphitheatre, 8th Ave. and 33rd St., is named for Irving Mitchell Felt, one-time campaign chairman of the Federation of Jewish Philanthropies, board chairman of Madison Square Garden, and board chairman of the National Conference of Christians and Jews.

AVERY FISHER HALL, Lincoln Center, is named for a one-time book designer who acquired an international reputation as founder of Fisher Radio, maker of high quality high fidelity instruments. He donated $4 million for the Center's main auditorium, the home of the New York Philharmonic.

HADASSAH'S BIRTHPLACE is marked by a plaque in the lobby of the building at 521 5th Ave., which occupies the site of the old Temple Emanu-El at 5th Ave. and 43rd St., in whose vestry room Hadassah was founded in 1912.

JERUSALEM GROVE, adjoining Castle Clinton National Monument, in Battery Park, is a collection of 15 Atlas cedars, similar to those grown in Israel. It was planted by the City of Jerusalem in 1976 as a gift to New York City on the American Bicentennial.

CAPTAIN JACOB JOSEPH PLAYGROUND, next to school at 165 Henry St., is named for a Marine who was killed in action at Guadalcanal during World War II. Captain Joseph was the grandson of Chief Rabbi Jacob Joseph, and the son of Lazarus Joseph, City Comptroller.

LOEB PLAYGROUND, E. Broadway, Market, and Henry Sts., is named for Sophie Irene Loeb, pioneer social worker.

SOPHIE IRENE LOEB FOUNTAIN, Heckscher Playground, 63rd St. and West Drive.

MENORAHS in Cathedral of St. John the Divine, Amsterdam Ave. from Cathedral Pkwy. to 113th St. Each is 12 feet high, following the design of those that stood in King Solomon's Temple. The first of their kind to be used in a Christian cathedral, the Menorahs were a gift of the late Adolph S. Ochs in 1930. One of the Cathedral's two great bronze doors contain tableaux depicting the exploits of Jewish prophets and patriarchs of the Bible.

PALEY PARK, (east of) 5th Ave. at 53rd St., one of the city's growing number of vest-pocket parks, was established by William Paley, chairman of the board of Columbia Broadcasting System, and named for his father, Samuel, a Philadelphia cigar manufacturer and owner of one of the city's first radio stations.

PERLMAN PLACE, (off) 2nd Ave. near 17th St., where Beth Israel Medical Center is located, is named for the late Congressman and Supreme Court Justice, Nathan D. Perlman.

ADOLPH S. OCHS BUST, in the lobby of *The New York Times*, 229 W. 43rd St., memorializes the man who, as publisher, built the *Times* into one of the world's greatest newspapers.

The following schools were named after prominent Jews:

• Louis D. Brandeis High School, 151 W. 84th St., is named for the first Jew appointed to the U.S. Supreme Court.

• Simon Baruch Intermediate High School, 330 E. 21st St., is named for Dr. Simon Baruch, physician, surgeon in the Confederate Army, and pioneer in public health and cardiac therapy. He was the father of Bernard M. Baruch.

• William Ettinger High School, Madison Ave. at 106th St.

• Julia Richman High School, 317 E. 67th St., is named for the first woman to be appointed district supervisor in New York City's school system. She is credited with the establishment of the first P.T.A. in New York and with setting up classes for mentally retarded children.

• Arthur A. Schomburg High School, 2005 Madison Ave.

• Robert E. Simon High School, 600 E. 6th St. □

STATUE OF MOSES is one of the heroic-sized statues of famous lawgivers that ring the top of the exterior of the building of the Appellate Division of the State Supreme Court, Madison Ave. and 25th St. The Moses statue is in the center on the 25th St. side.

STRAUS PARK, 106 St. and West End Ave., is a triangular area containing a fountain in memory of Ida and Isidor Straus, philanthropist husband and wife who went down with the *Titanic*. Mrs. Straus remained with her husband after refusing to leave with the other women and children.

HENRIETTA SZOLD PL., at right angles with East 11th St., is named for Henrietta Szold, founder of Hadassah (see Baltimore, Md.).

The following theatres are named for prominent Jews:

Vivian Beaumont Theatre, Lincoln Center, is named for a daughter of Commodore Beaumont, philanthropist and department store tycoon, whose father was a pioneer merchant in Leadville, Colo.

Martin Beck Theater

Belasco Theater

Billy Rose Theatre

Brandt Theater chain
Loew Theater chain
Minskoff Theatre
Morosco Theatre
Mitzi E. Newhouse Theatre, Lincoln Center, is named for the wife of
Samuel Newhouse, newspaper publisher.
Morton Robbins Theatre
Rugoff Theatre chain
Selwyn Theater
Shubert Theatre
Uris Theater chain

LILLIAN WALD PLAYGROUND, Monroe St., east of Montgom-
ery, is named for the social work pioneer and founder of the Visiting Nurse
Service.

UNITED NATIONS

UNITED NATIONS, 42nd to 48th Sts., from 1st Ave. to the East
River. The permanent headquarters of the United Nations occupies 18 acres.
The glass Secretariat building houses offices of approximately 4,000
employees of member nations. The shallow-domed General Assembly is the
meeting place of the representatives to the organization. A limited number of
tickets to various meetings are available on a first-come, first-served basis on
the day of the meeting. Guided tours are conducted daily from 9:15 A.M. to
4:45 P.M.

Few visitors to the United Nations do not see the connection between
the international peace organization and Jewish contributions to world
civilization, but inscribed on the wall of the Plaza stairway (43rd St. and 1st
Ave.), across the street from the UN enclave, are the words of the Prophet
Isaiah: "They shall beat their swords into plowshares and their spears into
pruning hooks. Nation shall not lift up sword against nation, neither shall
they learn war any more." Only recently was Isaiah's name added to the
inscription, largely due to the efforts of Sam Brown, who conducts tours to
New York sites of Jewish interest. Isaiah's vision of a war-free world has
become a universal ideal; so universal, in fact, that the same idea is expressed
on the base of a statue the Soviet Union donated to the UN. The statue, an
impressive nine-foot sculpture of a man beating a sword into a plowshare,
stands on a broad, granite base in the rose garden north of the General
Assembly building. The work of Russian sculptor Evgeniy Vuchetich, the
statue won the "Grand Prix" diploma at the Brussels World Exhibition in
1958. On the base is inscribed part of the same verse from Isaiah, "We shall
beat our swords into plowshares." The late Secretary General Dag Hammarskjöld, in accepting the statue from the Soviet representative, said that
the "dream of world peace" was Isaiah's and that the statue "gives symbolic
expression" to Isaiah's words. □

• UNITED NATIONS ABRAHAM H. FELLER READING ROOM, UN Building, 42nd St., has a 7,000-volume legal library of the United Nations, named after the first principal director of the organization's legal department—the late Abraham H. Feller. It contains Feller's collection of books on international organization and international law. There is also a portrait of Feller and a bronze commemorative plaque with a quotation from his last book, *The United Nations and World Community:* "The Charter bears the seeds of a greater growth, which, if nourished by governments and peoples, can be made to give forth the fruit of deliverance from our age-long perils." Abraham Feller was one of the principal architects of the UN Relief and Rehabilitation Administration (UNRRA). In 1944-45, he served as general counsel and as UNRRA representative to the International Labor Organization Conference, and to the Bretton Woods Monetary Conference in 1944; in 1949 he became the first American lawyer to appear before the International Court of Justice at The Hague. He was General Counsel of the UN from February 1946 until his death on November 13, 1952.

• Drawing the attention of the thousands of visitors to the UN is the gift of Israel—4,000 square feet of stone slabs from the Kastel Hills near Jerusalem. The stones are in a special garden patio within the open area that connects the UN's three major structures: the Secretariat building, the Conference building, and the General Assembly building.

• The United Nations Meditation Room is a darkened room where people of all faiths can enter, sit on a stone bench and meditate in silence. Just outside the door is a bronze plaque commemorating the 37,000 servicemen who died while fighting under the United Nations' unified command.

• In front of the Secretariat building stands a 21-foot bronze sculpture memorializing the late Dag Hammarskjöld, Secretary General of the UN. It was a gift of the Jacob and Hilda Blaustein Foundation. Jacob Blaustein, a former member of the American delegation to the UN and honorary president of the American Jewish Committee, was a close friend of Hammarskjöld. The sculpture, titled *Single Form,* is the work of the well-known British sculptress, Barbara Hepworth. It is mounted on a granite plinth. □

BROOKLYN

The 514,000 Jews who lived in the 88.8 square miles of Brooklyn in 1976 accounted for 42 percent of the city's total Jewish population and more than the combined total in 42 states. Brooklyn has more Jews than all of Europe excluding the Soviet Union, France, and Great Britain. A few square blocks of Brooklyn house as many Jews as there are in Detroit, St. Louis, or Cleveland.

In 1923 Brooklyn became the borough with the largest Jewish population, reaching 740,000 while Manhattan's fell to 706,000. A peak of 920,000 was reached in 1950 after which Brooklyn's Jewish population began to decline as the tide of Jewish settlement shifted to Queens and the suburban counties. By 1958 it had declined to 854,000, and in 1963 to 765,000.

Permanent Jewish settlement in Brooklyn can only be traced to 1834, the year it received its municipal charter as a separate city, but the history of Brooklyn Jewry begins much earlier. Asser Levy owned substantial property in the 1660s and 1670s in what used to be called Bruecklen. The archives of Kings County preserve a document dated August 15, 1683, recording the purchase of a slave by Peter Strijker of Vlackebos (Flatbush) from "the worthy Abraham Franckfoort, a Jew residing in N. Jorck (New York)." The sale was made in the village of Midwout (Midwood) and the seller signed himself "Aberham Franckfort."

Town records of New Utrecht, New Lots, Gravesend, Williamsburg, and other villages later incorporated into Brooklyn indicate that other Jews also did business there in the early 18th century. Jacob Franks, one of the presidents of Manhattan's Shearith Israel, owned a summer estate in Flatbush in the mid-1700s. Several Jews from New York and Philadelphia shared the hardships of the Continental Army during the Battle of Long Island, which was fought in Brooklyn. Samuel Noah, a kinsman of Mordecai M. Noah and a graduate of the 1807 class at West Point, helped build the defenses of Brooklyn against an anticipated British attack during the War of 1812.

The Jewish community began in the 1830s with separate but almost simultaneous settlements around lower Fulton Street, in what is now the Borough Hall section, and in Williamsburg, then an independent town north of Brooklyn. The founding fathers were immigrants from Bavaria and Alsace who set up small retail establishments. The 1838 Brooklyn directory lists Benjamin Levy as owner of a variety store; Daniel Levy, cartman; another Benjamin Levy, auctioneer; and a Moses family—all with Fulton Street addresses. The first known Jewish settler in Williamsburg was Adolph Baker, who arrived in 1837. By the middle 1840s, there was a good-sized Jewish settlement around Grand Street. Emanuel Pike, a Dutch Jew who had a haberdashery shop in downtown Brooklyn in the late 1840s, was the father of Lipman Pike, the first professional baseball player.

The 1850 census showed Jews prominent in the feed business, tailoring, dry goods, cigarmaking, and meat packing, as well as a scattering of laborers, machinists, watchmakers, ropemakers, pharmacists, and junk dealers. The 1850s saw the establishment of Samuel Liebman's brewery, now Rheingold, the Katz brewery, and the Eagle Fireworks Co., founded in Williamsburg in 1856 by Philip Licht, who made signal rockets for the Union Army during the Civil War. The meat packing industry along Bushwick Avenue was started when a kosher slaughtering house was opened there in 1851 by Ernest Nathan. The dry goods emporium founded in 1865 by Abraham Abraham and Joseph Wechsler became Abraham & Straus, Brooklyn's largest department store. The present name was adopted in 1893 when Isidore and Nathan Straus, who built Macy's, joined the firm. The Namm and Loeser stores, now out of business, both began in the late 1870s. By then, half of Brooklyn's clothing manufacturers were Jews. They also dominated the dry goods field and were important factors in tobacco manufacturing and baking.

An apocryphal tale made up by a couple of Jewish newspapermen in the 1930s gave rise to the legend that Jews from the Borough Hall and Williamsburg sections used to row across the East River to New York on Friday afternoon for worship services and return to Brooklyn on Sunday. Private services in homes or stores began in the 1840s. Public worship by Jews was unknown in Brooklyn until 1851. In that year, Kahal Kodesh Beth Elohim, the first Jewish congregation in Brooklyn and in all Long Island, was organized by Louis Reinhardt, Elias Adler, Isaac Mayer, Moses Kessel, and Isaac Eisman. New York's Congregation Anshe Chesed loaned the Brooklyn group its first Torah. David Barnard, Beth Elohim's first cantor, was listed in Williamsburg's 1849 directory as "Hebrew teacher" and "fancy grocer." Brooklyn's earliest Jewish school was opened behind Barnard's grocery on Grand Street.

A rented hall on what is now Marcy Avenue was Beth Elohim's first house of worship after it outgrew Kessel's home. Its first synagogue, erected on Keap Street in 1876, was Brooklyn's second synagogue. The first was dedicated in 1862 at the corner of Boerum Place and State Street by Congregation Baith Israel, formed by a Borough Hall group in 1854 under the leadership of Morris Ehrlich, Solomon Furth, Morris Hess, and Mark Marks.

Most of the other congregations founded in Brooklyn before the 1880s were offshoots of Beth Elohim and Baith Israel. Williamsburg's Beth Elohim was consolidated in 1921 with Temple Israel, established in 1869, to form Union Temple. In 1861 secessionists from Beth Israel created another Beth Elohim—Brooklyn's first Reform congregation. It is now known as the Garfield Place Temple. Beth Israel's first rabbi was Aaron Wise, father of Dr. Stephen S. Wise. The municipal traffic court at Lafayette and Bedford

Avenues is the former synagogue of Temple Israel, two of whose rabbis, Judah L. Magnes and Nathan Krass, were "promoted" to the pulpit of Emanu-El in New York. Congregation Ahabath Achim, founded in 1868, and Beth Jacob, formed in 1867 in Williamsburg and later merged with Anshe Sholom, were also offshoots of Beth Israel.

A Jewish community also developed around 1850 in Greenpoint where the established settlers were hostile. Jewish funeral processions going through Greenpoint and Williamsburg before the Civil War were frequently attacked by hoodlums. The first Jewish cemetery in Brooklyn, Union Fields in Cypress Hills, was opened in 1848 by the pioneer congregation in Williamsburg. When burials were banned in Manhattan, Congregation Shearith Israel of New York bought a seven-acre tract on the heights of Cypress Hills overlooking Jamaica Bay, about five miles from Williamsburg. Many New York Jews first visited Brooklyn to attend funerals. The huge Washington Jewish Cemetery, on the edge of Bensonhurst, was originally a nondenominational burying ground but later became exclusively Jewish. The oldest section of the Jewish cemetery at Cypress Hills has a monument to Jewish Civil War veterans. Nearby are the graves of Supreme Court Justice Benjamin N. Cardozo, Emma Lazarus, Commodore Uriah P. Levy, and Rabbi Judah L. Magnes. In a newer section, owned by the Workmen's Circle, is a pantheon of Jewish labor leaders and literary figures. Side by side lie Sholom Aleichem, Meyer London, Max Pine, general secretary of the United Hebrew Trades; Morris Rosenfeld, poet of the sweatshops; and Benjamin Schlesinger, one of the founders of the International Ladies Garment Workers Union.

Several of the pre-Civil War Jewish residents of Brooklyn were important personalities. Sigismund Kaufmann, a refugee from the 1848 revolutions in Europe, who settled in Brooklyn in 1849, taught French and German and studied law while working in a pocketbook factory. He and Dr. Joseph Goldmark, also a '48er, helped organize the Republican party in Brooklyn. Goldmark owned a Brooklyn factory that made percussion caps and cartridges. When draft rioters set the factory on fire in 1863, one of those detailed to protect the premises, where ammunition for the Union Army was being produced, was Solomon Furth, Beth Israel's first president, who was a member of a National Guard cavalry regiment. Goldmark's daughters married Dr. Felix Adler, founder of the Ethical Culture movement, and Louis D. Brandeis. Kaufmann, who campaigned for John Fremont in the 1856 presidential election, was one of the draft board judges in 1863 when New York and Brooklyn were bedeviled by antidraft riots. A Lincoln presidential elector, Kaufmann lost a race for the State Senate from Brooklyn in 1869. He presided over the meeting that led to the formation of the Brooklyn Hebrew Orphan Asylum in 1878. Michael Heilprin, a political refugee from Hungary and a foe of slavery; Col. Leopold C. Newman, who lost a foot at the Battle of Chancellorsville in 1863 and who is said to have received a deathbed visit from Lincoln; and Morris Hess were among

Brooklyn's leading supporters of Lincoln.

When Brooklyn still had only a handful of Jews, the Reverend Henry Ward Beecher, whose sister, Harriet Beecher Stowe, wrote *Uncle Tom's Cabin*, created a national stir by defending them from the anti-Semitism of Judge Henry Hilton, the department store king. Beecher's sermon in Plymouth Church, Brooklyn, in 1877, entitled "Jew and Gentile," remains a classic of philo-Semitism. Beecher's denunciation of anti-Semitism was also aimed at Austin Corbin, a real estate promoter who had publicly proclaimed a wish that Jews would not patronize his new and lavish resort at Manhattan Beach, which he hoped would become "the most fashionable and magnificent watering place in the world." But, he added, "we cannot bring the highest social element to Manhattan Beach if the Jews persist in coming." Many Christian patrons of Corbin's hotel, led by the celebrated atheist orator, Robert G. Ingersoll, bitterly assailed Corbin.

A piece of doggerel popular at the time indicates that Coney Island and Manhattan Beach were not only attractive to middle-class Jews from New York but also to Jewish peddlers:

> *On ev'ry path, by almost every turn,*
> *Industrious Israelites a living earn,*
> *By selling colored specs to screen the eye,*
> *Which would not serve an idiot to disguise.*

Corbin hated Jews, but he thought it good business to lure away Jules Levy, cornetist in the rival Oriental Hotel, by raising his salary from $350 to $750 a week to get him to play at the Manhattan Beach Hotel. Levy was adored by the ladies who swooned over him as teenagers of later generations did over crooners.

After the turn of the century, when Coney Island became the summer playground of the masses of New York, part of its fame was attributable to the showmanship of Samuel Gumpertz, who has a permanent niche in show business history as the godfather of the sideshow, and more particularly the freak. From 1906-1930, Gumpertz brought to Coney Island countless oddities and outlandish human beings he found all over the world. Unlike P. T. Barnum's frauds, Gumpertz located genuinely bizarre people on trips to Borneo, Java, and Africa. He was also the organizer of midget sideshows and performances by child acrobats, staged Buffalo Bill's Wild West exposition, and exploited the talents of Harry Houdini.

When the famous Dreamland burned before World War I, Gumpertz put together the Dreamland sideshow, developed the Surf Avenue concessions, bought Barnum's Eden Musee on 23rd Street in New York, and set up the Coney Island waxworks. Later, he was managing director of the Barnum & Bailey Circus. Dr. Moses Bluestone, the first Jewish doctor in the Coney Island area, was for years the personal physician to Gumpertz's freaks. Robert Moses and Paul Moss, the New York City license commissioner, wrote finis in 1938 to Coney Island's ballyhoo artists by outlawing the spielers and ending its raucous era.

In the summer of 1915, Nathan Handwerker, who managed a small downtown Manhattan restaurant, went to work for Feltman's famous shore restaurant at Coney Island. Within a year, Handwerker had opened his own stand, pioneering the nickel hot dog. Until the subway reached Coney Island, he almost went broke. He made his fortune when he picked a choice location between the new boardwalk and the subway terminal. The "follow the crowd to Nathan's" sign became a landmark. At first Handwerker had to hire ten bums clothed in white suits and carrying stethoscopes to line up at the stand, above which was a sign, "If doctors eat our hot dogs, you know they're good." From then on Nathan's was an institution. "Make mine Nathan's" became a national slogan and the hot dog became a national habit. Campaigning for the governorship of New York in 1958, Nelson Rockefeller, while eating a hot dog at Nathan's, blurted out, "no one can hope to be elected in this state without being photographed eating a hot dog at Nathan's Famous." Since then scores of candidates for city, state, and even national office have included Nathan's in their New York vote-gathering itinerary.

Corbin's old domain ultimately became almost as solidly Jewish as the old East Side. In the 1960s more than half the residents of Coney Island, Brighton Beach, and Manhattan Beach, once fashionable resort areas and the meccas of the sporting world, were Jewish. Sea Gate, that portion of Coney Island, west of 37th Street, once a millionaire's preserve and where non-Jews made their last stand on New York's beaches, became a middle-class enclave of 8,000 residents. Most of them were Jewish professionals and business people who lived behind a 12-foot high wire fence and maintained their own synagogue and center. Today Sea Gate is a polyglot middle-class community, still largely white, whose fence has become "a fortification of chain link and barbed wire," and where many fewer Jewish families now reside. The Coney Island beach area, once a rival of Atlantic City as the nation's summer entertainment capital, is now but a shell of its past glory. Central Coney Island, which once housed a predominantly white Jewish population, is now a mixed community of blacks and Puerto Ricans, second generation Italians, and a remnant of poor and elderly Jews seeking to live out their years in familiar but increasingly hostile surroundings. New high rise housing projects are occupied largely by low income families, but Coney Island as a whole is a poverty area and one of the most dilapidated in the city. The Jewish senior citizens fear to go out at night, but in the day time and in good weather they crowd the boardwalk benches. The Jewish Association for Services to the Aged has built the Scheuer House, a residence for elderly Jews, a block from the boardwalk.

Brighton Beach, which is adjacent to Coney Island, has the largest elderly population in the city. While persons over 65 account for 12 percent of the city's population, in Brighton Beach they are 35 percent of the 27,300 residents, almost all of whom are Jews. Many have lived there for 35 to 40 years. They live for the most part in apartment houses of 1930 vintage, rooming houses, one and two-family houses, and winterized bungalows. The quarter of a mile from Brighton First Street to Coney Island Avenue is a tiny Yiddish-speaking shtetl where the old sit day after day in good weather on folding chairs or benches and talk about yesterday.

The Brighton Beach community has been called "the Fort Lauderdale of the senior set" because it is a community of aged and retired former shopkeepers, garment workers, union activists, Yiddishists, widowed housewives, and widowers, all living on Social Security and small pensions. The Shorefront YM & YWHA has 1,400 senior citizens in its programs. The Jewish Association for Services to Aged maintains a community service there which collaborates with the Y in serving the aged. The area has recently been nicknamed "Odessa-by-the-sea" because it has attracted many of the newly-arrived Russian Jews who settled in New York. The Brighton Beach community is very Orthodox, so much so that its pizza parlors have signs assuring patrons that the tomato sauce and ersatz pepperoni are prepared under strict rabbinical supervision.

On the other hand, the Brighton Beach Baths, a private club, is the Rose Bowl and World Series of handball, because its courts have produced an endless number of national champions, most of them Jewish. Manhattan Beach, once described as the Newport of the city's bathing areas, has many high rise apartment houses where large numbers of middle-class Jews live. The same is true of Sheepshead Bay, just east of Manhattan and Brighton Beaches.

Brooklyn attracted few East European Jews until the late 1880s. Right after the Civil War, Greenpoint, a largely German and Irish neighborhood, had as its Republican boss Benjamin Raphael. Half a mile away, in Williamsburg, Ernest Nathan and Jacob Brenner, both German Jews, held the same office. Abraham Oppenheimer succeeded Nathan and was in turn succeeded by Israel Fisher, who in 1894 became the first Jew elected to Congress from Brooklyn. One of the last German Jews of influence was the late Meir Steinbrink, Kings County Republican leader in the 1920s, subsequently a State Supreme Court judge and national chairman of the Anti-Defamation League of B'nai B'rith.

While the older German-Jewish settlement was still concentrated in Williamsburg, Borough Hall, and Greenpoint, the flood of East European immigrants to New York began to spill over into Brooklyn for the first time. Hundreds of refugees from Czarist pogroms were temporarily sheltered in 1881 at hastily erected barracks in Greenpoint.

The earliest large-scale Jewish settlement was in Brownsville. It began when Jacob Cohen, a New York clothing manufacturer, bought a house in Brown's Village in 1885 because his wife needed the fresh country air. A tiny farm village beyond Brooklyn's city limits, its bucolic quiet was broken forever when Cohen moved his factory to Brown's Village and was followed by many of his Jewish workers. After the opening of the Fulton

Street elevated line, other East Side sweatshop operators moved to Brownsville and thousands of their workers followed suit. Farmers cut up their land into building lots which were sold to speculators who in turn sold to realtors and builders. Tailors became landlords and some early Jewish fortunes were based on the Brownsville real estate boom. Louis Horowitz and the Chanin brothers, who later helped change the New York skyline, did their first building in Brownsville and Williamsburg.

By 1900, Brownsville was a worse slum than the East Side. Unpaved streets and walks, homes without drains and sewers, only one public bathhouse, and streets that were morasses in wet weather, made the area unhealthy. Yet, between 1890 and 1900 more than 15,000 Jewish sweatshop workers lived there, attracted by cheap rents and the accessibility of work in a rural atmosphere. The Jewish peddlers of Brownsville formed the American Hebrew League of Brooklyn in the 1890s to protect themselves from neighboring toughs. The same labor union ferment that stirred the East Side boiled up in Brownsville. Abraham Shiplacoff, a Brownsville sweatshop worker, who studied law at night, became secretary of the United Hebrew Trades and labor editor of the *Jewish Daily Forward*. In 1916, Brownsville sent him to the State Legislature as the first Socialist assemblyman. A leader of the 1921-22 clothing workers' strike, Shiplacoff was general manager of the Amalgamated Clothing Workers of America. In his last years, he managed the Brownsville Labor Lyceum.

The most influential civic factor in Brownsville was the Hebrew Educational Society, founded in 1899 with the aid of the Baron de Hirsch Fund. The first Jewish Community Center in Brooklyn, the HES opened milk stations, baby clinics and manual training classes, established farm gardens, organized a branch of the Public Library, and promoted the public evening school system. Patterned after the East Side's Educational Alliance, the Brownsville center encouraged Jewish traditions and cultural activities while furthering Americanization.

By 1917, Brownsville rivaled the East Side as an almost all-Jewish community. On the eve of World War I, over 150,000 Jews lived there. Isolated from the rest of the city, Brownsville not only had its own synagogues and Jewish educational institutions, but a growing class of professional men, educators, merchants, and artists. Except for public school teachers and policemen, the average Jew in Brownsville rarely encountered non-Jews. The area even had a flourishing Yiddish theatre, now a black Baptist church.

Out of this milieu came a notable array of eminent American Jews. Among the teachers in Brownsville's Hebrew schools were the late Rabbi Solomon Goldman of Cleveland and Chicago; Dr. Solomon Grayzel, for many years editor of the Jewish Publication Society of America; and Dr. Louis Finkelstein, for a generation chancellor of the Jewish Theological Seminary of America, whose father was a Brownsville *shochet*. On the teeming streets of the Brownsville ghetto there grew up David Kominsky, known to the world as Danny Kaye; Max Weber, the noted sculptor; Aaron Copland, one of the creators of modern American music; Alfred Kazin, the literary critic; Sol Hurok, whose first presentation occurred when he prevailed upon Efrem Zimbalist to play before a Jewish cultural society in Brownsville; Mortimer Caplin, later United States Collector of Internal Revenue, whose father peddled brushes and second hand shoes from a pushcart; and Joseph H. Hirshhorn, uranium king and art collector, whose collection is housed in the Hirshhorn Museum in Washington.

"Murder, Inc." also came out of the Brownsville slums, but the majority of the immigrant children raised in Brownsville were a credit to the city and nation, just as their contemporaries on the East Side were. A Brownsville cloakmaker was the father of Dr. Arthur Kornberg, who shared the 1955 Nobel Prize in medicine. Sylvia Porter, widely syndicated columnist, was born in Brownsville. So were Colonel David "Mickey" Marcus, the West Pointer who organized and led Israel's army; Lt. Commander Solomon Esquith, who won the Navy Cross for directing the rescue of the USS *Utah* at Pearl Harbor; and Meyer Berger, the *New York Times'* legendary reporter who had a love affair with New York.

Other well-known figures from Brownsville were Sid Luckman, one of the all-time greats of college and pro football; Vic Hershkowitz, the greatest all-around handball player of the century, who learned the game at the Hebrew Educational Society; Sid Gordon, who starred for the New York Giants baseball team at the Polo Grounds; and Al McCoy, neé Al Rudolph, who shared the middleweight boxing title in 1914-17. Abe Stark, long the unofficial mayor of Brownsville, was elected Borough President of Brooklyn, the first Jew to hold this office. He had previously served as president of the New York City Council. The Brownsville Boys Club which Stark built is now part of the city park system. New York's first Jewish mayor, Abraham Beame, is also a native of Brownsville.

That Brownsville is no more. In the 1970s, the historic Jewish neighborhood had become a four-mile area of blight that resembled a bombed-out city. When younger Jewish families began moving out in the mid-1960s, private houses and tenements fell into disrepair and poor blacks and Puerto Ricans began moving in. Gradually, the area became a dumping ground for evicted tenement dwellers from urban renewal projects elsewhere, and for welfare clients. The last Jewish institution to close in Brownsville was the Stone Avenue Talmud Torah, the last of 200 synagogues in the area. Of the 400,000 Jews who once lived in Brownsville, only a tiny remnant of some 1,500 were left in 1976. They had been trapped by age, illness, extreme poverty, and the inability to cope with bureaucratic systems. Federation's Coordinating Council on Jewish Poverty sought to aid the remaining Jews in Brownsville through a variety of projects involving a volunteer escort service manned by college volunteers, a transportation service operated by the Jewish Association for Service to the Aged, and other activities. The independent Council for the Jewish Poor set up a store-front center as a combined meeting place and synagogue. The Hebrew Educational Society, for so long the principal cultural agency of the Jewish community, relocated to Canarsie.

The arrival of hundreds of thousands of additional East European Jews after 1900 and the razing of whole blocks of East Side slums to make way for the Williamsburg Bridge in 1903 and the Manhattan Bridge in 1909, caused a great surge of Jewish migration to Williamsburg, directly across the river from the East Side. While the German Jews gradually retreated to Greenpoint, the Bedford-Stuyvesant area, and the streets around Prospect Park, the newcomers established their own synagogues and Jewish schools. Newly-built elevated and subway lines that brought Williamsburg and other close-in sections of Brooklyn within easy reach of Manhattan's factories and the erection of inexpensive one and two-family dwellings and modern apartment houses in the period between 1910 and 1920, gave impetus to recurring waves of Jewish migration from Manhattan and the older sections of Brooklyn. The move to Williamsburg, and later to Borough Park, Crown Heights, and Bensonhurst was often the first step up the ladder from the East Side tenements.

Each population shift created new institutions as the larger synagogues followed their congregants to the new neighborhoods, but in each old neighborhood there always remained a substantial community, flourishing synagogues, and Jewish schools. The middle-class Jews were the first to quit Williamsburg, their exodus having begun in the 1930s. The more Orthodox Jews stayed on despite rapid neighborhood changes. When the ultra-Orthodox Chasidim, survivors of the Holocaust, arrived after World War II, most of them settled in Williamsburg and later in nearby Crown Heights, both of which became Chasidic strongholds. The older Orthodox residents of Williamsburg, not considered Orthodox enough by the Chasidic newcomers, moved out as blacks and Puerto Ricans moved in, transferring their Orthodox institutions to Queens and Long Island. A mile-square area of Williamsburg, on the edge of the almost all-black Bedford-Stuyvesant area, became known as the "Jerusalem of America." There the Chasidim under the rule of rabbinic dynasties tried to "make paths of heaven out of grimy streets."

The replacement of slum dwellings with public housing projects, where the Chasidim would not live because they would not use elevators on the Sabbath, and the increasing influx of blacks and Puerto Ricans pushed some of the Chasidim out of Williamsburg and into Crown Heights and Borough Park. The Chasidim who remained in Brooklyn—two groups established separate colonies in upstate New York (see New York)—erected their own community buildings, established their own medical services, opened their own stores, and organized an ambulance and bus service, in addition to synagogues, yeshivas, and *glatt* kosher butchers. Many of the Chasidim were counted among the city's poor Jews, and on their behalf Federation created a Commission on Chasidic Affairs to help this community achieve its legitimate health and welfare needs.

A three-story red brick house on Eastern Parkway in Crown Heights is the world headquarters of the Lubavitcher Chasidim, who first established themselves in Williamsburg, in 1941, with the arrival of Rabbi Joseph Isaac Schneersohn, a direct descendant of the founder of Chasidism. To anchor the Chasidic community in Crown Heights, the Lubavitchers bought houses in their neighborhood with the aid of loans from the Hebrew Free Loan Society. During the early 1960s, many of the Jews of Crown Heights abandoned the area, those remaining decided to stand fast in the neighborhood. The Lubavitcher Rebbe called on his followers and other Jews to stay in the neighborhood. Many listened and some even moved back from other areas. Because the Lubavitcher Chasidim have not sealed themselves off from secular activities, they have acquired political clout in the neighborhood. In the 1970s, the police began diverting vehicular traffic on Saturdays between 9 A.M. and 9 P.M. from Crown Heights streets on which Lubavitcher synagogues are located and where there is heavy foot traffic by Chasidim.

The Crown Heights Community Corporation, an anti-poverty center financed by public funds, was headed by a rabbi in the 1970s, staffed by Orthodox youths, served both Jews and blacks, and was professionally directed by Simon Levine, a non-Jewish black. Although there has been some conflict between the Chasidim and blacks in Crown Heights, on the whole, both groups have accommodated themselves to each other. For a time police dressed in Chasidic garb were assigned to Crown Heights, Borough Park, and Williamsburg in an effort to apprehend hoodlums who specialized in molesting Chasidic rabbis and students. In the 1960s, Rabbi Samuel Schrage organized the Maccabees as a Jewish auxiliary patrol manned by bearded Jews and armed only with large flashlights in an effort to fight a crime wave against Jews in Crown Heights and to protect Jewish schools and synagogues from vandals.

An even more important Jewish neighborhood in Brooklyn is Borough Park, which has been a major area of Jewish residence since the 1920s. Nearly 60 to 75 percent of the 80,000 to 90,000 people there are Jewish and the rest are of Italian and Hispanic origin. There were 140 Jewish organizations in the area in 1976. Dozens of stores display signs announcing that they are closed on Saturdays. *Glatt* kosher establishments are common. Many stores advertise "Sabbath clocks" that control electrical appliances on the Sabbath. Borough Park's 13th Avenue from the 30s to 50th Street is a mile of lower middle-class Jewish businesses reminiscent of a shtetl. Though many younger Jews have moved to Queens and the suburbs, this loss has been balanced by Orthodox Jews from Williamsburg and Crown Heights. Thirteenth Avenue is crowded with stores that sell prayer shawls, black hats for rabbinical students, *kiddush* cups, Yiddish and Hebrew records, and kosher food stores of all kinds. A bus line operated by Sabbath-observing drivers links the Jewish communities of Williamsburg, Crown Heights, and Borough Park. It does not run on Saturdays or Jewish holidays. Borough

Park's Jewish community is diversified. There are settlements of Yemenite, Lebanese, Egyptian, and Syrian Jews there, although the latter are more numerous in adjacent Bensonhurst and in Forest Hills, Queens. The Yemenites have their own synagogue, restaurants, and social clubs. Some of them have recently moved to Queens. Borough Park's kosher pizza parlors are run by Yemenites.

East Flatbush, once a solid middle-class Jewish neighborhood, underwent rapid change in the early 1970s as the area became about 15 percent black and Puerto Rican. Flatbush and East Flatbush had been settled before World War I by the children of Jewish immigrants who were raised in the tenements of the East Side, Brownsville, and Williamsburg, and who followed the new subway lines into the farmlands of eastern Brooklyn. When people in Brooklyn referred to Flatbush in the 1970s, they meant a neighborhood into which blacks had not yet moved. However, by 1976, there were blacks in Flatbush and some Jews began leaving. A mosque for Albanian Moslems was opened in Flatbush in the 1970s. The exodus of middle-class Jews from East Flatbush to Canarsie, Queens, and the suburbs, left behind a large elderly Jewish population. Black, Puerto Rican, and Haitian families filled the vacancies left by the departing Jews. Bensonhurst, with its thousands of private homes, remained a largely lower middle-class area, 85 percent white, and equally divided between Jews and Italians.

East New York, once the home of 80,000 Jews, numerous synagogues, societies, and Jewish owned retail businesses, now has only a tiny pocket of old and poor Jews left. The former Jewish residents were largely working people, mostly Orthodox, who moved away under the impact of blockbusting by unscrupulous real estate brokers who panicked Jewish home owners into selling their property with stories that the "blacks are coming." In 1972, the East New York YM-YWHA, the area's major Jewish institution, moved to Queens.

Since World War II, the Jewish population of Brooklyn has shifted several times. Thousands of new households established by war veterans filled the middle-income apartments along the ocean front from Fort Hamilton to Canarsie and from Manhattan Beach to Coney Island, where new clusters of high rise buildings and one and two-family dwellings were heavily tenanted by Jews. Some Jews also began moving back to downtown Brooklyn, Brooklyn Heights, and to the civic center area, either as tenants in new co-ops or as owners of remodeled town houses.

Canarsie, once a sparsely settled marshland, became the center of a fast growing new Jewish community in the 1960s and 1970s. In 1976 there were 75,000 Jews in the area which had ten synagogues and the Hebrew Educational Society. Part Italian and part Jewish, Canarsie exploded in the 1970s over accepting minority students bussed in from East Flatbush. The opening of the new Starrett City housing development for middle-income families, stretching along both sides of Pennsylvania Avenue, between Flatlands Avenue and Shore Parkway, gave rise to a brand new Jewish community. A tent city synagogue opened by Congregation B'nai Israel was the first Jewish organization in this new complex. It was established in 1975, but since then a number of other Jewish groups have been formed to serve the needs of Jewish residents in the 46-building housing development.

Much of the postwar new building in Brooklyn was by Jewish developers, notably the Lefraks, who replaced Luna Park and Steeplechase Park in Coney Island with giant apartment houses, and Marvin Kratter who bought and tore down Ebbets Field, once a Brooklyn sports shrine, and built the Ebbets Houses on the site. George Klein of the Barton Candy Corp. is helping to rebuild Brooklyn's downtown shopping area. A number of new shopping malls in Brooklyn were built by Jewish entrepreneurs.

Although Brooklyn has been part of New York City since 1898, Jewish communal institutions developed independently of those in Manhattan. A Hebrew Benevolent Society organized by the German Jews of Williamsburg in 1868 to care for the local needy, became an important instrument in providing social welfare needs in Brownsville after 1890. Out of this society grew the Brooklyn Federation of Jewish Philanthropies in 1909. During the depression, the New York Federation of Jewish Philanthropies came to the aid of the older Brooklyn agency in order to preserve its service, and in 1937 the latter was merged into the New York Federation. There are a number of local Jewish community councils, as well as a borough-wide Jewish Community Council, and Brooklyn federations of the local units of national Jewish organizations. The Jewish Hospital, an outgrowth of the Hebrew Hospital Dispensary founded in 1895, is Brooklyn's oldest Jewish medical institution. The first Hebrew Home for the Aged was established in 1907, a year after the first YMHA was organized.

After World War I, the synagogue-center movement gained great impetus in Brooklyn among Conservative Jews. The largest of such institutions is the Brooklyn Jewish Center on Eastern Parkway. About half of all the synagogues in New York City are located in Brooklyn, and the great majority of them are Orthodox. There are over 100 Hebrew day schools and elementary and secondary yeshivas in Brooklyn, and a number of ultra-Orthodox rabbinical seminaries.

Jewish voters played an important part in making Brooklyn one of the most heavily Democratic voting areas in the state. Abraham D. Beame, who had served as City Controller before his election in 1973 as the city's first Jewish mayor, was for many years one of the key leaders of the Democratic Party in Kings County. Arthur Levitt, a Brooklynite who has been elected State Controller five times, twice winning reelection as the only Democratic to gain state office during gubernatorial victories by Nelson Rockefeller, failed to win the Democratic mayoralty nomination in 1961 against Robert F. Wagner, Jr. Stanley Steingut, who was elected speaker of the State Assembly, a post previously held by his father, the late Irwin Steingut, was Kings County Democratic leader in the 1960s. Emanuel Celler, who served in Congress from Brooklyn for 50 years, lost his seat in 1972 when he was defeated in the Democratic primary by Elizabeth Holtzman, who in 1976 was one of the two Jewish women serving in Congress, the other being Bella Abzug of Manhattan.

Some of Brooklyn's principal cultural institutions owe much to the leadership of Jews. The late Nathan Jonas was one of the founders of Long Island University. His $500,000 gift constituted the university's original endowment fund. He was the first chairman of the university's board of trustees and played a key role in the establishment of the Brooklyn branch of City College, now Brooklyn College. Jonas' contribution of $1 million fostered the merger of the Brooklyn and New York Federations. William Zeckendorf, Long Island University's board chairman in the 1960s, was a key factor in its postwar expansion into Long Island.

Simon Rothschild, of the Abraham & Straus Department Store, and his son, Walter Rothschild, were among Brooklyn's most influential civic leaders. The late Joe Weinstein, an immigrant who built a tiny Fulton Street store into the Mays department store chain, was known as "Mr. Brooklyn" because of the millions he gave to educational, religious, and philanthropic institutions. Julius Bloom, former director of the Brooklyn Academy of Music, the city's oldest performing complex, turned this perennial white elephant into the borough's cultural and artistic mecca. In his capacity as executive director of the Academy during the 1970s, he was mainly responsible for its renaissance. Under his direction, the Academy became Brooklyn's principal center for all the arts—from ballet to theatre and jazz. Siegfried Landau was director and conductor of the Brooklyn Philharmonic, the borough's only professional symphony orchestra, from 1955-1972.

New York sees, hears, enjoys, and reads the products of an unusually talented group of Jews who were raised in Brooklyn—playwright Arthur Miller, singer Barbra Streisand, writer Norman Mailer, novelist Bernard Malamud, actor Zero Mostel, opera star Beverly Sills, and a long list of vaudeville, radio, television, and nightclub comics such as Henny Youngman, Alan King, Sam Levenson, Phil Foster, Abe Burrows, Buddy Hackett, and Phil Silvers.

* * * * *

Of the many places of Jewish interest in New York City, Williamsburg in Brooklyn is perhaps one of the most fascinating, though it too, like other sections, has undergone vast changes. *(BMT Broadway subway to Hewes Street or Marcy Avenue; by car: across the Williamsburg Bridge to Keap or Hooper Streets.)*

The area is no longer the Williamsburg of yesteryear—it is run down but still unique in many respects. There are the Hasidic Jews, more Orthodox than those of a generation ago; there is also a large number of

Christians. Between the Hasidim and the non-Jewish community, there is a non-Hasidic Jewish community that serves as a "social wall" to deflect the values of the outside world before they can penetrate to the Hasidim.

In the Hasidic neighborhoods, there is no blare of the television set or the radio from any of the Jewish homes, since the Hasidim are not allowed to own a set. They do not read any of the regular Yiddish newspapers. They are frowned upon because the Hasidim feel "the editors are unsympathetic toward the Hasidic Jews and spread lies about them," and "the Yiddish papers are published on the Sabbath, and what can a religious Jew expect from desecrators of the Holy Sabbath?"

The visitor to the area can see Hasidic men with beards, *payot*, long black coats, and broad-brimmed hats; little boys with side-curls and *yarmulkas*; married women—all wearing wigs. Unmarried women and girls are not distinguishable from other single girls with the exception that they dress more modestly. Their dresses are high-necked and long-sleeved, and they always wear hose. Boys and girls are segregated from each other at a very early age, and they never attend any school or participate in activities in which the sexes are mixed.

The Hasidic Jews consider the garments they wear to be the traditional Jewish garments that were once the apparel of all Jews. The types of Hasidic clothing and the appearance of the Hasidim change from class to class, and serve as identifying symbols of social rank. The Hasidic garments vary from *zehr Hasidish* (extremely Hasidic) to *modernish* (modern). Those whose religious observances are less frequent and less intense, wear *modernish* clothing. This may be a long-outmoded dark double-breasted western suit that buttons from right to left.

To recognize the rank of a Hasid, the visitor must note the following: the *yiden* have the fewest Hasidic status symbols and wear *modernish* clothing; the *balebatishe yiden* have, in addition to the clothing, beards and side-locks (some beards are never cut or trimmed and some sidelocks are never cut or shaved, a symbol of still higher status); the *talmidei hachamim*, in addition to having beards and side-locks, also wear *biber* hats (large-brimmed black hats made of beaver); the *sheine yiden*, the next highest in rank, have all of these plus the *kapote*, a long overcoat, usually black, worn instead of a jacket; one rung higher is the *shtickel rebbes* who wear, in addition, the *shtreimel* (a fur hat made of sable) and the *bekecher*, a long Hasidic coat made of silk or a silky material in which the pockets are in the back; and highest are the *rebbes*, whose attire includes that of all the others plus *shich*, slipper-like shoes, and *zocken*, white knee socks into which the breeches are folded.

There are a profusion of Hasidic synagogues in Williamsburg, the most prominent of which is the Congregation Yetev Lev D'Satmar, 152 Rodney Street, headed by the renowned Satmar Rebbe. Within a radius of 40 square blocks there are 32 synagogues of varying sizes. Some of these are

Hasidic and others are non-Hasidic *(Mitnagid)*. The contrast is striking and interesting. Among these are the following:

ADAS YEREIM, Lee Ave., corner of Roebling St.
AHAVATH TORA BEIT YITZCHOK, 657 Bedford Ave.
CONG. AGUDATH ISRAEL, 240 Keap St.
CONG. AHAVATH ISRAEL, 240 Keap St.
CONG. ANSHEI BRISK D'LITAH, 274 Keap St., built in 1876, is the oldest shule in the area. It was also known as "Keap Street Shule."
CONG. ARUGATH HABOSEM, 559 Bedford Ave.
CONG. ATZEI CHAIM, 152 Jewes St.
CONG. BETH HAKNESETH CHOFETZ CHAIM, 284 Rodney St.
CONG. BETH JACOB OHEV SHALOM, 284 Rodney St.
CONG. BETH YEHUDA, 904-8 Bedford Ave.
CONG. OHEL MOSHE CHEVRA THILIM, 569 Willoughby Ave.
CONG. SHTIPANESHTER KALUS NUSSACH SFARD, 355 Keap St.
CONG. TIFERETH ISRAEL, 491 Bedford Ave.
CONG. ZEMACH DAVID CHASIDE SQUARE, 571 Bedford Ave.
SHOTZER SASSOWER CONG., 143 Rodney St.
YOUNG ISRAEL OF BROOKLYN, 563 Bedford Ave.
YOUNG ISRAEL OF WILLIAMSBURG, 730 Willoughby Ave.

In the midst of these synagogues is the only Jewish Community Center in the area, the YM & YWHA of Williamsburg, 575 Bedford Ave.

There are also many separate Hasidic religious schools for boys and girls. Numerous other schools are located all along Bedford Avenue and other streets in the area. The children in these schools attend classes from early morning to evening. There is a strong emphasis on the beliefs, rituals, and practices of Hasidism in addition to their secular studies.

LUBAVITCHER HIGH SCHOOL, 770 Eastern Parkway (Crown Heights), is also the office of the United Lubavitcher Yeshivoth and the Lubavitch World Headquarters.

YESHIVAH TORAH VODAATH AND MESIVTA, 425 E. 9th St. (Flatbush), is a preparatory school. The seminary, students' hall, alumni association, and executive offices of the organization are also at this address.

The kosher butcher shops and catering establishments in Williamsburg may look the same to the visitor as they do elsewhere, but they, too, are different. The meat must be *glatt* kosher (kosher beyond a doubt); the butcher must be a Hasid himself (no one else is trusted). Most of the *glatt* kosher butcher stores carry the name of the sponsoring rebbe or of the rebbe's organization, and avow that its net profit goes for the maintenance of the religious school.

KAHAL ARUGAT HABOSEM (Zehlimer Butcher Store), 61 Lee Avenue.
KAHAL TORAT HAIM (Wisnitzer Butcher Store), Ross St.
KAHAL YETEV LEV D'SATMAR, 174 Rodney St.
YITZHAK LEVY'S MEHADRIN GLATT KOSHER COMPANY, is a *glatt* kosher sausage factory.

Glatt kosher catering establishments not only serve *glatt* kosher meats but also have a room where a skylight can be opened above the canopy during wedding ceremonies.
BETH RACHEL HALL, Heyward St. near Bedford Ave.
THE CONTINENTAL, Rutledge St. near Wythe St.
KINGS TERRACE, Rutledge St. near Bedford Ave.

The Williamsburg area is dotted with stores that sell a variety of merchandise. There are numerous *shmura* matzo bakeries producing handmade matzos that have been guarded from the time of harvesting (the "most zealous of the zealous" will eat only handmade matzo that has been so guarded). Stores specializing in wigs and turbans for women to keep their hair covered, Hasidic dairy companies, *mikvahs*, Hasidic clothing shops, religious objects, hardware stores carrying kosher ritual baths for dishes and other objects, can be seen in this neighborhood. Among some of the more interesting are:

APPEL'S EGG MARKET, advertises unwashed eggs for Passover, which assures the buyer that the eggs were not washed in solutions containing *hometz* (leaven).
SUKKAT SHALOM WOODWORKING, 175 Lee Ave., sells portable *sukkahs*.
TIV-TOV HARDWARE STORE, 125 Lee Ave., sells *shabbos zeigers* used for turning house appliances on or off on the Sabbath.
WELHELM'S, 157 Division Ave., sells *shabbos zeigers* and other interesting religious items.
ZEIGER AND FARKAS CORP., 181 Marcy Ave., sells portable *sukkahs*.

A number of Hasidim have left Williamsburg for better sections of the city, the suburbs, uncrowded areas in New Jersey, and Israel. Physically, many parts of the area are slums. The high-rise housing developments pose a problem to the Hasidim, who refuse to ride elevators on the Sabbath. Those who do live in these new developments will only rent apartments on the lower floors.
The visitor to Williamsburg will sense the spirit that pervades the area, especially on such holidays as Purim, Simhas Torah, or just before Passover. On Purim, the young children masquerade either as characters in the Purim story, prominent personalities of today, or figures out of fairy

tales. Hasidic men hurry arm in arm, carrying *shaloach manos* (Purim gifts), of food, including *hamantaschen*, or other items for their relatives, friends or others who are poorer than they. On Simhas Torah, streets are closed off for a gay celebration, with the Hasidim dancing and singing in the streets. Just before Passover, one can visit a matzo bakery and see how *shmura* matzo is made.

Another unusual occasion is a Hasidishe wedding. After the ceremony itself, the festivities start out slowly, gradually building up to an almost overwhelming crescendo of dancing, singing, clapping, and laughing. Men and women do not touch each other; even the bride and groom dance apart, each holding the end of a handkerchief between them. At all Hasidic festivals, men dance and dine with men, and women with women; a screen or wall generally separates the two sexes.

In the 1920s and 1930s the Williamsburg area was predominantly Jewish. Bedford Avenue was the main street for strollers to show off their finery. Jewish people from the Lower East Side moved to Williamsburg as a step upward on the social ladder. Starting in the 1940s, the Jewish people who prospered, began to move to Borough Park and Bensonhurst. The building of the Brooklyn-Queens Expressway in 1957 destroyed many houses and displaced hundreds of people in Williamsburg who then moved to Crown Heights and adjacent areas. The empty apartments that remained were taken over by many ultra-Orthodox Jews who had arrived from Hungary in the 1940s. These are the Williamsburg Hasidim of today.

Whether one goes to Williamsburg on special occasions or just at ordinary times, the visitor will be impressed with the inner religious spirit and joy rather than with the outer form; this is what the Hasidim themselves emphasize, and it is so.

SYNAGOGUES (Brooklyn—General)

ORTHODOX

AHI EZER CONG., 1885 Ocean Parkway.

CONG. BETH-EL OF BORO PARK, 4802 15th Ave., has a magnificent domed structure, with the lights on the inside of the dome forming the pattern of a Star of David.

CONG. ZICHRON RABBI ELIEZER MESKIN, 725 Crown St., was founded by black Jews, with the cooperation of white Jews, and is open to all.

MAGEN DAVID COMMUNITY CENTER, 34 Avenue P, is the center of cultural and social activities of the Syrian Jews.

CONSERVATIVE

BROOKLYN JEWISH CENTER, 667 Eastern Parkway, is one of the two oldest synagogue-centers in the country. Its $1 million structure has been a Brooklyn landmark since 1920. It was the first synagogue in Brooklyn with complete facilities for cultural, social,. educational, and athletic activities, and its program set the pattern for the establishment of other large synagogue-centers.

BOULEVARD JEWISH CENTER, 1380 Linden Blvd., has a unified interior and exterior design with the milk-and-honey theme of the Bible as the motif. Over the entrance to the synagogue is a stylized 16-foot-high, seven-branched candelabrum, tipped by soft lights, as symbolic of both the ritual and of the motto that in unity there is strength.

CONGREGATION BAITH ISRAEL Anshei Emes, 236 Kane St., was organized by 12 men who, according to legend, grew tired of rowing across the river to Manhattan every Friday afternoon to attend Sabbath services. In 1862 they built the first synagogue in Brooklyn, at State and Boerum. It was near a stable of race horses, and soon there were complaints about "that loud praying from the synagogue" disturbing the horses. The minutes kept by the congregation reflect its changing nature. The first minutes were in English, written by Jews of Dutch and Portuguese descent. Later, they were written in German, after the wave of immigration from Germany. The German gave way to Yiddish, reflecting the flood of immigrants from Eastern Europe. Prior to the turn of the century, the minutes were again written in English, and have been since. The synagogue's congregation was originally Orthodox, but became Conservative during the Civil War. In 1905 the synagogue acquired its present building on Kane Street near Court. The high ceiling of the interior is painted almost white, and has finely wrought columns, an organ loft, balcony, and stained glass windows. It was originally built as a Dutch Reformed Church in 1846.

EAST MIDWOOD JEWISH CENTER, 1625 Ocean Ave., contains a tablet honoring the memory of the six million Jewish victims of Nazism. The tablet, measuring 8½ by 20 feet, is made of Italian marble with brass lettering; six lamps burn constantly at its base. It was the gift of Paul Lewis, a building contractor of Dallas, Texas, who has given similar memorials to other synagogues. The tablet is on the wall of the synagogue's lobby.

REFORM

CONG. BETH ELOHIM, 8th Ave. & Garfield Place, is popularly known as the Garfield Place Temple. It was founded in 1861 as Brooklyn's first Reform congregation by dissenters from Cong. Beth Israel.

PROGRESSIVE SYNAGOGUE, 1395 Ocean Ave., has a stained glass window which memorializes the six million Jews slain by the Nazis. The window design, executed by A. Raymond Katz, incorporates a figure representing a concentration camp survivor, the Nazi crematoria, and chimneys topped by the four freedoms in Hebrew.

UNION TEMPLE, 17 Eastern Parkway, is a 12-story building—possibly the tallest synagogue in the world. The temple is a union of Temple Israel of Lafayette and Bedford Aves., with Temple Beth Elohim (Keap Street Temple), as well as a union of the Reform Jews of the Williamsburg and Bedford sections. The temple contains, in addition to its sanctuary, an auditorium with a frescoed ceiling, social rooms, classrooms, and athletic facilities. The ceiling depicts the history of the synagogue, beginning with the Tabernacle in the Wilderness.

CEMETERIES

MOUNT CARMEL CEMETERY, Cypress Hill St. and Cypress Hill Ave., Workmen's Circle section, is a pantheon for outstanding figures in Jewish labor and Yiddish literary circles. Among those buried here are Sholom Aleichem, the Yiddish humorist; Meyer London, Congressman; B. Charney Vladeck, general manager of the *Jewish Daily Forward* and member of the first New York City Housing Authority; Abraham Cahan, noted editor of the *Forward;* Benjamin Schlesinger, founder of the International Ladies Garment Workers' Union; Max Pine, secretary of the United Hebrew Trades and a founder of the American Jewish Joint Distribution Committee (JDC); Abraham Shiplacoff, general manager of the Joint Board of the Amalgamated Clothing Workers of America; Morris Rosenfeld, Yiddish poet; and A. Litwak (Hayim Helfand), journalist and author. Before he died, Sholom Aleichem had said, "Let me be buried among the poor, that their graves may shine on mine and mine on theirs." His name in Hebrew is above the Yiddish poem he wrote for his own tombstone:

Here lies a simple-hearted Jew
Whose Yiddish womenfolk delighted;
All the common people, too,
Enjoyed the stories he recited.
Life to him was but a jest,
He poked fun at all that mattered;
When other men were happiest,
His heart alone was bruised and shattered.

TEMPLE BETH EL OF BORO PARK CEMETERY, near the Workmen's Circle section of the New Mt. Carmel Cemetery, has the grave of Mendel Beilis, who was accused of having murdered a Christian boy to use his blood for Passover. Beilis' trial took place in Kiev in 1913. Although the Czarist government fabricated evidence against Beilis, he was acquitted. Beilis settled in the United States in 1922 and died 12 years later.

UNION FIELDS CEMETERY, Jamaica Ave. and Crescent St. On August 3, 1851, Congregation Shearith Israel consecrated a tract of nearly seven acres on the heights of Cypress Hills overlooking Jamaica Bay, not far from Cypress Hills Cemetery. The following day, Abigail, the 80-year-old daughter of Aaron Lopez of Newport, R. I., and widow of Isaac Gomez, Jr., was the first to be buried there. The cemetery was chartered by the Legislature in 1853. A monument to Jewish soldiers in the Civil War was erected in the 1890s by the Hebrew Union Veterans Association, forerunner of the Jewish War Veterans. Buried in this cemetery are such Jewish notables as: Justice Benjamin Cardozo, Jacob de Haas, Bernard Hart, Emanuel B. Hart, Naphtali Judah, Israel Baer Kursheedt, Emma Lazarus, Commodore Uriah P. Levy, Dr. Judah L. Magnes, Benjamin Franklin Peixotto, and Adolphus S. Solomons. A plague with the words of *The New Colossus* is at the grave of Emma Lazarus.

MUSEUMS

BROOKLYN MUSEUM, Eastern Parkway and Washington Ave., has five symbolic statues representing Hebrew culture in a frieze on the outside of the left front of the building. The statues are not portraits, but representations of the "Hebrew Lawgiver," the "Hebrew Psalmist," the "Hebrew Prophet," and the "Hebrew Apostle." The names of Moses, David, Jeremiah, and Isaiah are cut in below the frieze. ●The Edward C. Blum Industrial Design Laboratory is a memorial to the late president of Federated Department Stores. ●The Frieda Schiff Warburg Memorial Sculpture Garden is named for the noted philanthropist. ●The museum has busts of comedians Alan King and Danny Kaye. ●The Worgelt Study, an extraordinary Art Deco room-within-a-room, is named in memory of Ethel Worgelt, who commissioned the room.

SCHOOLS AND SEMINARIES

SHOLOM ALEICHEM FOLK SHUL, 5013 10th Ave.
BETH EL TALMUDIC INSTITUTE, 1219 Ave. T.
BETH JACOB OF BORO PARK, 1371 46th St.
BETH JACOB TEACHERS SEMINARY OF AMERICA, 132 S. 8th St.
BIALIK SCHOOL, 500 Church Ave.
ISAAC BILDERSEE SCHOOL, 966 East 82nd St., is named for one of the Jews to be appointed a district school superintendent.
BOBOVER YESHIVA, 1533 48th St.
CENTER FOR HOLOCAUST STUDIES, 1605 Ave. J, has tapes of interviews, slides, movies, diaries, letters, posters, photographs, and clothing—all relating to the Holocaust. It was founded and is directed by Dr. Yaffa Eliach, professor of Judaic Studies at Brooklyn College—herself a survivor of the Holocaust.
CENTRAL YESHIVA BETH JOSEPH RABBINICAL SEMINARY, 1427 49th St.

FIRST HEBREW DAY NURSERY AND NEIGHBORHOOD HOUSE, 321 Roebling St.

GEORGE GERSHWIN THEATRE, Walt Whitman Hall, Brooklyn College.

GUR ARYEH INSTITUTE FOR ADVANCED JEWISH SCHOLARSHIP, 1373 President.

HARRY HERSKOWITZ INSTITUTE of Mesivta Torah Vodaath, 425 E. 9th St., at Cortelyou Rd., is an Orthodox rabbinic academy. The institute's two buildings, erected at a cost of $4 million, includes a residence hall, four libraries, an auditorium, outdoor and indoor gymnasiums, 35 classrooms, and two science laboratories. Harry Herskowitz, for whom the institute is named, was a prominent tax expert and educational philanthropist who died in 1954.

KAHAL KENESSETH SCHOOL, 723 Eastern Parkway.

KAMENITZER YESHIVA U'MESIVTA, 960 49th St.

MEYER LEVIN SCHOOL, 5909 Beverly Rd., is named for one of the first heroes of World War II.

LONG ISLAND UNIVERSITY EXTENSION, 385 Flatbush Ave. Nathan Jonas, lawyer and philanthropist, was one of the principal founders of L.I.U. in 1926, his gift of $500,000 constituting its original endowment. The university's first board chairman, he also played a major role in the creation of the Brooklyn branch of City College which became Brooklyn College. Jonas gave $1,000,000 in 1930 to make possible the merger of the Brooklyn and New York Jewish Federations of Philanthropies.

MACHZIKE TALMUD TORAH SCHOOL OF BORO PARK, 4622 14th Ave.

COL. DAVID MARCUS SCHOOL, 210 Chester St., is named for an eminent public servant and World War II intelligence officer who helped create Israel's army.

MESIVTA RABBI CHAIM BERLIN, 321 Ave. N.

MIRRER YESHIVA CENTRAL INSTITUTE, 1791 Ocean Parkway.

NER ISRAEL RABBINICAL COLLEGE, 599 Empire Blvd.

NEW HEBREW SCHOOL, 461 Empire Blvd.

DAVID PINSKY'S HEBREW FOLK SCHOOL, 1180 Brighton Beach Ave.

SIMON ROTHSCHILD SCHOOL, 300 Adelphi St., is named for one of the founders of the Abraham & Straus department store, who was one of Brooklyn's leading communal figures.

SHULAMITH SCHOOL FOR GIRLS, 1353 50th St.

STONE AVENUE TALMUD TORAH AND HEBREW FREE SCHOOL, 400 Stone Ave.

YESHIVA UNIVERSITY HIGH SCHOOL FOR BOYS, Church and Bedford Aves.

195 — BROOKLYN, NEW YORK CITY

YESHIVA UNIVERSITY HIGH SCHOOL FOR GIRLS, 2301 Snyder Ave.

UNITED LUBAVITCHER YESHIVOTH, 770 Eastern Parkway.

HILLEL FOUNDATION

BROOKLYN COLLEGE, 2901 Campus Rd. This unit occupies the Abe Stark House, named for a former Brooklyn borough president.

JEWISH COMMUNITY CENTERS

EAST FLATBUSH-RUGBY YM & YWHA, 555 Remsen Ave., has the Henry Kaufmann Building, which offers an expanded program to a highly congested area with limited play space for children.

HEBREW EDUCATIONAL SOCIETY, 9502 Seaview Ave., is the oldest Jewish Community Center in Brooklyn, having been founded as a social and cultural center for newly-arrived immigrants who had settled in Brownsville. The Society organized the first reading room in the neighborhood; a penny provident fund; a kindergarten; and classes in English, citizenship, sewing, and music. The H.E.S.'s Young Peoples Fellowship is housed in an attractive colonial-style building at 1212 East New York Ave.

HENRIETTA AND STUARD HIRSCHMAN BUILDING of the YM & YWHA of Coney Island, 3330 Surf Ave. The Shorefront YM & YWHA is at 330 Coney Island Ave. The Kings Bay YM & YWHA, 3643 Nostrand Avenue.

JEWISH COMMUNITY HOUSE OF BENSONHURST, 7802 Bay Parkway, has been a hub of communal activity since it was established in 1906. It has been in its present building since 1927.

YM & YWHA OF BORO PARK, 4912 14th Ave.

YM & YWHA OF WILLIAMSBURG, 575 Bedford Ave.

HOMES AND HOSPITALS

BROOKDALE HOSPITAL MEDICAL CENTER, Linden Blvd. and Rockaway Parkway, has, in its Theodore Shapiro Residence Hall, a bronze plaque that was cast from the sculpted reproduction of *The Oath of Maimonides*.

BROOKLYN WOMEN'S HOSPITAL, 1395 Eastern Parkway.

FIRST UNITED LEMBERGER HOME FOR AGED, 8629 Bay Parkway.

INFANTS HOME OF BROOKLYN, 1358 56th St.

JEWISH CHRONIC DISEASE HOSPITAL, now known as Kingsbrook Jewish Medical Center, 86 E. 49th St.

JEWISH HOSPITAL AND MEDICAL CENTER OF BROOKLYN, 555 Prospect Pl., was the first Jewish medical institution established in Brooklyn. It was an outgrowth of the Hebrew Hospital Dispensary, which was founded in Williamsburg in 1895.

LONG ISLAND COLLEGE HOSPITAL, Henry and Pacific Sts.,

has a memorial room dedicated to Edward C. Blum, well-known Brooklyn merchant and civic leader.

MAIMONIDES MEDICAL CENTER, 4802 10th Ave., is Brooklyn's largest voluntary general hospital. The hospital also has a mental health center and a community services center.

MENORAH HOME AND HOSPITAL FOR AGED AND INFIRM, 871 Bushwick Ave.

SEPHARDIC HOME FOR THE AGED, 2266 Cropsey Ave.

UNITY HOSPITAL, 1534 St. Johns Pl.

HOUSING PROJECTS

SCHEUER HOUSE, 3601 Surf Ave., Coney Island, is a housing community for senior citizens developed by the Jewish Association for Services for the Aged, a member agency of the Federation of Jewish Philanthropies. It is named for S. H. Scheuer and family.

STARRETT CITY, a huge middle income 46-building development built on 150 acres of former marshes and landfill along Jamaica Bay in southeastern Brooklyn, has a large Jewish population among its 25,000 residents. A number of synagogues have been established and several national Jewish organizations have branches here.

COORDINATING AGENCIES

BORO PARK JEWISH COMMUNITY COUNCIL, 4910 14th Ave.

BROOKLYN JEWISH COMMUNITY COUNCIL, 16 Court St.

CROWN HEIGHTS JEWISH COMMUNITY COUNCIL, 387 Kingston Ave.

JEWISH WAR VETERANS MEMORIAL HALL, 220 Sullivan Pl.

ENGLISH-JEWISH PRESS

The Brooklyn Jewish Journal, 16 Court St.

The Jewish Press, 338 3rd Ave., is an Orthodox newspaper in the English language. It contains a wealth of Jewish educational material.

PARKS AND RECREATION AREAS

MONROE COHEN PARK, in area bounded by East 102nd and East 104th Sts., and Seaview Ave., is named for the late member of the City Council who represented the Canarsie area.

HERMAN DOLGIN PLAYGROUND, in Sheepshead Bay Housing Project, is named for a World War II hero.

FOX SQUARE, Flatbush Ave., Nevins St., Fulton St., and Flatbush Ave. Extension, is named for William Fox, movie tycoon and the theatre he opened here in 1931.

LOEW SQ., at intersection of Pitkin and Barrett St., in Brownsville, is named for Marcus Loew, pioneer movie producer and theatre owner, who opened one of the first penny arcades showing films in Brownsville.

COLONEL MARCUS PLAYGROUND, Ocean Pky. and Ave. P, is named for Col. David "Mickey" Marcus (see West Point, N. Y.).

PROSPECT PARK has the Michael Friedsam Memorial Merry-Go-Round at the Empire Blvd. entrance, a memorial to the noted merchant and philanthropist. In the Music Grove there is a eucalyptus tree that was flown from Israel in 1953 and planted in the park on the fifth anniversary of Israel's independence.

SHIPLACOFF PARK AND PLAYGROUND, Sackman and Powell Sts., is named for Abraham J. Shiplacoff, one-time sweatshop worker, who became labor editor of the *Jewish Daily Forward*, secretary of the United Hebrew Trades, and the first Socialist ever elected to the N. Y. State Assembly (from Brownsville) in 1916. He led the 1921-22 clothing workers strike.

LOUIS SOBEL PARK, Lee and Division Aves. and Roebling St., in the Williamsburg section is named for a World War I hero.

PUBLIC PLACES

EMANUEL CELLER FEDERAL COURTHOUSE, 225 Cadman Plaza East, is named for former Rep. Emanuel Celler, who served in Congress from a Brooklyn district for 49 years and 63 days, from 1923 to 1972. He was chairman of the House Judiciary Committee for 23 years in which capacity his name appears on four amendments to the Constitution and on nearly 400 bills that became law, including every major civil rights bill since 1940. In the lobby of the courthouse there is a bust of Celler.

MANHATTAN BRIDGE, completed in 1909 as the third span linking Brooklyn and Manhattan, was designed and built by Leon S. Moisseiff, a Russian-born, Yiddish-speaking engineer.

RESTAURANTS

MEAT

BERGER'S, 1427 Coney Island Ave. (*glatt* kosher).

BUFFET BY THE SEA, 2815 Flatbush Ave. (dining and entertainment).

CHAPANOSH, E. 15th St., corner of Ave. M (Flatbush) and 5413 New Utrecht Ave. (Borough Park).

CROWN GLATT KOSHER CATERERS AND RESTAURANT, 4904 13th Ave.

GOTTLIEB'S RESTAURANT, 352 Roebling St. (*glatt* kosher).

GREIFER'S KOSHER RESTAURANT AND DELICATESSEN, 4904 13th Ave.

GUTTMAN'S, 53rd St. and 13th Ave.

HY-TULIP DELICATESSEN AND RESTAURANT, 1980 86th St.

ISRAEL KOSHER RESTAURANT, 1412 Coney Island Ave. (closed Saturday).

JAFFA, 4210 18th Ave.

KOSHER COUNTRY, 1501 Surf Ave. and Whitehead Hall, Brooklyn College.

LANDAU'S DELICATESSEN AND RESTAURANT, 65 Lee Ave. (*glatt* kosher).

MOSHE PEKING II, 1760 Utica Ave. (Kosher Chinese cuisine—closed Friday and Saturday).

NATHAN PINCUS' KOSHER DELICATESSEN, 1405 Nostrand Ave.

PRUZANSKY'S GLATT KOSHER RESTAURANT AND DELICATESSEN, 954 Eastern Parkway. (Open daily and Sunday, 10 A.M. to midnight.) Special *parve* dinners are served during the period of abstinence (when observant Jews eat no meat), and sorrow commemorating the breaching of the walls of the Temple by the Romans.

ROSENBLOOM AND ROSETTI, 4127 18th Ave., is a *glatt* kosher Italian restaurant.

S & G KOSHER RESTAURANT, 306 Brighton Beach Ave.

SCHNEIDER'S KOSHER DELICATESSEN, 226 Roebling St.

SHANG-CHAI, 2189 Flatbush Ave., is a kosher Chinese restaurant.

ISRAEL SKILOWITZ & SONS, 4914 13th Ave.

TEL AVIV CATERERS, 2915 Ocean Parkway.

DAIRY

FAMOUS DAIRY RESTAURANT, 13th Ave. and 48th St.

WEISS' DAIRY RESTAURANT, Coney Island Ave. between Ave. J and K. *Cholov Yisroel. Shomer Shabbos.*

PIZZERIAS (KOSHER)

CHAIM'S KOSHER PIZZA, 954 Nostrand Ave., features kosher pizza and Israeli *falafel*. The owner, Chaim Najjar, a Yemenite Jew, was raised in Israel and came to America in 1952. While working in a bakery, he took note of the American penchant for pizza. He also noticed that Orthodox Jewish areas did not have any restaurants serving these exotic foods. He opened a pizza parlor in 1959 at 5113 13th Ave., featuring a kosher kitchen.

L & M RESTAURANT, 1817 Ave. M, features pizza, knishes, cookies—all kosher.

LEE AVENUE KOSHER PIZZA SHOP, 108 Lee Ave., features pizza, falafel, knishes, and french fries.

NATHAN'S FAMOUS, Surf and Stilwell Aves. A list of Brooklyn's Jewish eateries would not be complete without sampling the food at the world's largest and most celebrated hot dog stand. Called the "spiritual home of the American hot dog," Nathan's sells more than eight million frankfurters a year. The founder, Nathan Handwerker, came to America from Poland in 1912 and four years later opened his hot dog stand at Coney Island with a capital of $300. Nathan's also sells sea food and Orthodox Jews will not eat there.

ENTERTAINMENT

JEWISH THEATRE CO., housed in Temple Beth Abraham, 301 Seabreeze Ave., Brighton Beach, is an ensemble company presenting Yiddish and English language plays on Jewish themes.

SHOPPING

ABRAHAM & STRAUS, 420 Fulton St., carries items for some of the holidays—Seder trays and plates, *Haggadahs*, bagel holders and cutters, as well as many items from Israel.

REBECCA BENNET PUBLICATIONS, INC., 5409 18th Ave., specializes in the Babylonian Talmud in Hebrew and English, with complete or individual tractates.

CENTER OF JEWISH BOOKS, 1660 Ocean Parkway.

CROWN HEIGHTS HEBREW BOOK STORE, 382 Kingston Ave.

FRANKEL'S HEBREW BOOK STORE, 4904 16th Ave.

MILLER'S HEBREW BOOK STORE, 349 Utica Ave.

THE BRONX

Historically "the top of the escalator" on which successive waves of New York Jews "rose from the cheap slum housing on the East Side," The Bronx was for a generation, the symbol of the Jewish lower middle-class to the millions of Americans who listened to Bronx-bred Gertrude Berg describe *The Rise of the Goldbergs* on network radio. In the 1930s, when Brooklyn had the largest Jewish population, there were sections of The Bronx as solidly Jewish as the old East Side and Brownsville had once been.

The Jewish population of The Bronx reached a peak of 585,000 in 1930 when it accounted for 48 percent of all Jews in the city. Since then it has lost

Jewish population steadily. From 538,000 in 1940, the Jewish population fell to 493,000 in 1957, and to 396,000 in 1960. It was then the borough with fewer Jews than any other except Staten Island, although it contained 22 percent of the city's total Jewish population and accounted for 38 percent of the total population of The Bronx. The decline continued into the 1970s when there were only 143,000 Jews in The Bronx, or slightly less than 12 percent of the total population.

Jewish settlement in The Bronx began in the 1840s. The first arrivals were German and Hungarian storekeepers, artisans, and peddlers who came in the wake of Irish immigrants as they moved in to work on the construction of the Harlem and Hudson River Railroads and the stone High Bridge that carried the Croton Aqueduct across the Harlem River.

Individual Jews, however, had business connections in what is now The Bronx before 1700. Jewish traders from New York who did business in Connecticut as early as 1670 traveled there via the Boston Post Road, a principal highway to New England that passed through the east Bronx. This was the road taken by the leaders of New York's Congregation Shearith Israel during the American Revolution when they closed the synagogue and carried the Torah Scrolls to the safety of Stratford, Connecticut. Jewish merchants who developed important commercial ties in northern New York State a decade before the Revolution, journeyed via the Albany Post Road through the west Bronx.

There is no evidence that any of these travelers through The Bronx ever lived there, even temporarily. Neither did the descendants of Jewish farmers and merchants who settled in Westchester County in the 18th century, although they may have been 19th century property owners in the independent southern Westchester villages that later became The Bronx.

The railroad that first linked downtown New York with Westchester County gradually changed from a sparsely populated farming region to one of the city's earliest suburbs and stimulated the settlement of artisans and tradesmen. Isaac Blumenstiel, a shoemaker who acquired some lots in 1849 in Morrisania, also owned a house and shop on Fordham Avenue. Joseph Loewenstein, a peddler, and Daniel Eichler, tailor, were located on the same street. Jacob S. Abrams, merchant, and Leopold Lehman, clockmaker, were in business on Fulton Avenue.

The Morrisania directory for 1853-54, which listed establishments in the area now embraced by Hunts Point, Mott Haven, Kingsbridge, West Farms, Tremont, and Jerome Avenues, and the Grand Concourse south of Fordham Road, included a number of Jewish names. Jacob Cohen, one of New York's first Jewish real estate speculators, who in 1871 had published a short-lived Yiddish paper in support of his campaign for supervisor, owned Karl's 23rd Ward Park, a popular Bronx summer garden, in the 1860s. The 1872 directory for the same area listed new Jewish names: Julius Epstein, clerk; Louis Falk, builder and fire department trustee; H. Friedman, liquors; Angus Goldstein, pianomaker; Selig Hecht, tailor; Isadore Isaacs, restaurant owner; Richard Kohn, peddler; Henry Levy, fancy store; Gustavus Levy, lawyer; and Israel Ritter and Samuel Sandstein, cigarmakers. There was no synagogue included in the 1872 directory's roster of 22 houses of worship. The early Jewish settlers belonged to congregations in Manhattan until a Jewish community began growing up in Morrisania, Kingsbridge, and West Farms after 1874 when these townships were annexed to New York City. The first considerable number of Jews settled in The Bronx in the late 1880s and early 1890s, following the extension of the elevated line from Harlem, the completion of bridges linking Harlem with the lower Bronx, and the inclusion of all of The Bronx in New York City.

J. Clarence Davies, who organized the Bronx Board of Trade in 1893, probably sold more Bronx real estate for housing purposes than any other man. Henry Morgenthau, Sr., who founded the Bronx House in 1911 as a Jewish settlement house, became wealthy through the sale of Bronx parcels on which vast stretches of apartment houses were erected at the turn of the century. Before Williamsbridge in the northeast Bronx became part of New York City, Abraham Mogilesky was selling building sites there.

Temple Adath Israel, organized on East 169th Street by German Jews in 1889 and for two generations a landmark on the Grand Concourse (it was sold to blacks in the 1970s), is believed to have been the first Jewish organization in The Bronx. Beth Hamedrash Hagodol Adath Jeshurun was founded in 1892. Lebanon Hospital and Congregation Bachurim Anshei Hungary were organized in 1893. Congregation Zichron Israel (1894), Congregation B'nai Jacob (1895), and Congregation Hand-in-Hand (1895) were other pioneer institutions in the Mott Haven and Prospect Avenue areas.

In his *Memories of an American Jew*, Philip Cowen, editor and communal worker, whose father was Newman Cowen, the first Russian Jew of influence in New York, touched on the beginnings of the Jewish community in the Mount Hope section around Tremont Avenue. Among the first Jewish residents there were Mr. and Mrs. Joseph Herzog (the latter a sister of Dr. Cyrus Adler, the second president of the Jewish Theological Seminary of America). The nearest Jewish religious school was at Congregation Hand-in-Hand and many of the scattered Jewish residents in Mount Hope were sending their children to nearby Christian Sunday schools.

When Cowen moved in 1896 to Mott Haven and 149th Street, at the lower end of what is now the Grand Concourse, he organized a free Hebrew school in rented quarters on Washington Avenue and 177th Street. A grant of $300 from New York's Congregation Shearith Israel helped the school get started. One of the first teachers was Mordecai M. Kaplan, later celebrated as the founder of Reconstructionism. The Baron de Hirsch Fund encouraged Jewish settlement in The Bronx in 1898. As part of a plan to get Jews out of the crowded East Side, the Fund bought 16 lots for $69,000 on 137th and 138th Streets, between Willis and Bronx Place, facing St. Mary's Park (now the heart of a Puerto Rican slum area), as the proposed site of model tenements and clothing factories. The scheme failed but it helped to enlarge the Jewish population of the borough.

By the turn of the century, more than a dozen synagogues were clustered around the Tremont, Mott Haven, and Mount Hope areas. Opening of the first subway line to The Bronx in 1904 set off a mass migration of Jews from the Lower East Side and Harlem to the lower Bronx, Tremont and Fordham sections. Later population tides moved to the Grand Concourse and University Heights, where Jewish builders erected block after block of apartment houses right after World War I. Between 1916 and 1925, four of the city's most populous Jewish neighborhoods were in The Bronx. The Tremont section was then nearly 96 percent Jewish. The Bronx YM-YWHA, oldest in the borough, moved to the Grand Concourse in the 1950s from its original site on Fulton Avenue, where it was founded in 1909.

New subway lines opened in the 1930s and 1940s gave impetus to large-scale public and private housing developments in new areas and caused a major movement of Jews to Pelham Bay Park, Edenwald, Wakefield, Gun Hill Road, Williamsbridge, Olinville, Eastchester, Unionport, Throggs Neck, and Woodlawn. The Parkchester development, erected in the 1930s by the Metropolitan Life Insurance Co., was long heavily tenanted by Jews. It occupies the site of the old Catholic Protectory Oval, where Hank Greenberg, the first Jew elected to baseball's Hall of Fame, started his career playing for James Monroe High School. Bess Myerson, whose parents came to The Bronx before World War II, is the only New York girl and the only Jew to be chosen Miss America (1945). Al Schacht, the clown prince of baseball, was born a stone's throw from Yankee Stadium. Sammy and Joe Renick, who never knew horses were used for anything but delivering milk when they went to a Bronx Hebrew school, became the country's leading jockeys.

There have been comparatively few Jews of note in the political life of The Bronx where Jewish voters have traditionally aligned themselves with the majority Democratic party. Bernard S. Deutsch, a Democrat, was elected president of the Board of Aldermen in 1933 on the LaGuardia Fusion ticket. Isidore Dollinger and Burton Roberts, both Democrats, served as district attorneys of Bronx County. Robert Abrams was twice elected Borough President, and in 1976 was serving his second term. In 1974, Abrams ran a close race for state attorney general against the incumbent Republican, Louis Lefkowitz.

New York University, whose main campus used to be in the University Heights section of The Bronx (it is now the site of Bronx Community College), had Jews among its founders and benefactors. The Guggenheim School of Aeronautics, established on the New York University campus by Daniel Guggenheim, was the first in the United States. •Julius Silver Residential Hall is named for the chairman of the Polaroid Corporation's board, who was graduated from New York University with scholarship aid.

The only Bronx monument to a Jew is a bas-relief portrait of Heinrich Heine on the Lorelei Fountain in Joyce Kilmer Park, Grand Concourse and 164th Street. Rice Stadium in Pelham Bay Park is a memorial to Isaac L. Rice, inventor of the opening in chess known as Rice's Gambit, who was a successful industrialist, lawyer, and editor. Alexander's Department store on Fordham Road is the borough's best known retail establishment. One of its owners, Mrs. Ruth Farkas, served as United States Ambassador to Luxembourg from 1973-76. The late Dr. Morris Meister founded the famed Bronx High School of Science, which has graduated many leading space age scientists, and also the Bronx Community College, of which he was the first president.

Two of the city's major medical institutions are in The Bronx: the Albert Einstein Medical College of Yeshiva University and Montefiore Hospital.

The most remarkable aspect of Jewish history in The Bronx in the last 25 years has been the mass exodus of the Jewish population. As the earliest sections of the south Bronx became overcrowded, Jewish families who could afford it, left for Pelham Bay Parkway, Williamsbridge, Wakefield, and the Grand Concourse—that wide tree-lined boulevard became *the* social address for lower and middle-class Jews. The great depression of the 1930s and the years of World War II brought almost a complete halt to house building. As the cheap tenements erected in the 1920s or earlier became run-down and their Jewish tenants left, they were replaced by working-class blacks and Puerto Ricans. The latter were attracted to the south Bronx from Harlem by cheap housing and proximity to jobs in Manhattan—the same advantages that had attracted the earlier groups of the Irish, Jews, and Italians. As the suburban housing boom got under way in the 1940s, there was an almost mass exit of Jews from the south Bronx and later from the Tremont, Morrisania, Hunts Point, and Intervale areas. By the 1960s the east Tremont and south Bronx areas were among some of the city's worst slums. One after another old established synagogues began to close as the Jewish exodus left them with greatly reduced memberships. The number of synagogues dropped from 125 to less than 70.

The Grand Concourse, lined with squat, solid apartment houses for 4½ miles from east 138th Street to Mosholu Parkway, sparked a massive building boom when it opened in 1909. The opening of the Jerome Avenue and Concourse subway lines in the 1930s gave further impetus to building, and by World War II, the Concourse south of Fordham Road was an almost solid Jewish neighborhood. In the 1970s, however, the Concourse south of Tremont Avenue had become an urban slum occupied mostly by blacks and Puerto Ricans who replaced the departing Jews. The same trend occurred in the University Heights area and further east in the Hunts Point, Morrisania, and Intervale sections. The well-known Intervale Jewish Center, built in the 1920s by the father of Herman Wouk, the novelist, was cut down to one story. Twenty aged Jews worship there on Saturdays, surrounded by deteriorating buildings where 100,000 Jews once lived. What is left of the synagogue looks like a fortress, with double locked steel doors and wire hatches protecting its windows. The 10,000 people, mostly Jews, who lived in five and six-story tenements on East Tremont Avenue, were forced to find new homes when many houses were torn down to make way for the Cross Bronx Expressway. This enforced Jewish migration is believed by many to have touched off the Jewish exodus from The Bronx.

The Sephardic Jews left The Bronx en masse when their center was sold to blacks and migrated to Queens in 1973 and 1974 where a new center is being built. The Hebrew Institute of The Bronx, on University Heights, closed its doors in the early 1970s. The brand new $3,000,000 Salanter-Akiba-Riverdale Academy, which opened in 1975 in Riverdale, is a merger of three day schools from the east Bronx. The Bronx YMHA has opened a branch in Riverdale where it will ultimately move its main building, now on the Grand Concourse.

Federation maintains a service center at the Y to seek out the more than 3,000 elderly Jewish poor who have resisted moving from deteriorated neighborhoods where they have spent much of their lives. The city's second largest pocket of Jewish poverty is in The Bronx. The aged Jewish poor, many of them widows, who still remain in the Morrisania and Tremont areas, are often beaten, robbed, and occasionally murdered.

The continuing exodus of lower middle-class Jews from once stable neighborhoods gave rise to the new Jewish community in Co-Op City, a huge cooperative housing development whose 35 apartment towers cover 210 acres in the northeast Bronx and house some 75,000 people, nearly 75 percent of them Jews. Almost all of Co-Op City's residents are middle and lower income families headed by teachers, civil service employees, small businessmen, hospital personnel, skilled craftsmen, a sprinkling of doctors, lawyers, dentists, and accountants, and a large proportion of retirees, widows, and widowers living on fixed incomes.

Long before the first tenants moved into Co-Op City in 1968, neighboring synagogues had planned on moving into quarters provided by the management which is closely related to the labor movement. In the mid-1970s, Co-Op City had six synagogues on the premises and one or more units of virtually every major national Jewish organization. Federation provides coordinated services through an on-the-spot office maintained by the Jewish Family Service. The nearby Bronx House, on Pelham Bay Parkway, sponsors a coordinated program with and for the Jewish residents of Co-Op City. The Montefiore Medical Center, an affiliate of Montefiore Hospital, has its own clinic in Co-Op City. The two weekly newspapers that serve Co-Op City (one a private enterprise), are packed with news about Jewish programs, projects, meetings, and fundraising. The Co-Op City Jews constitute a Jewish community larger than those in Denver, Cincinnati, Houston, Berlin, Rome, Vienna, and Amsterdam. There is an active Jewish Community Council and fundraising campaigns for the Joint Campaign of the

UJA-Federation, Hadassah, ORT, Histadrut, Jewish War Veterans, Farband, and B'nai B'rith. Co-Op City siphoned off thousands of Jews who were ready to leave older Bronx neighborhoods but who could not or would not settle in the suburbs. Most could not afford the more expensive apartments and houses in Riverdale, the upper middle-class area in the northwest corner of the borough.

The Jewish settlement in Riverdale dates from the years following World War I when a few Jewish families from Yonkers, in adjacent Westchester County, began moving in. Riverdale was then a rural corner of The Bronx of mostly palatial estates, some large houses, and private schools. In the 1970s it was the home of Manhattan College and the College of St. Vincent (both Catholic), the Hebrew Home for the Aged, several well-known private elementary and secondary schools, and the Salanter-Akiba-Riverdale Academy, which occupies the site of the former Arturo Toscanini estate.

The high percentage of synagogue affiliation that developed in other new Jewish communities in Greater New York or those which grew rapidly on the base of older settlements was missing in Riverdale. The Jewish population was estimated in the 1970s to be between 40,000 and 60,000 out of a total of some 92,000. Whichever figure is accepted, Riverdale has more Jews than all but a dozen or so American Jewish communities. All but 20 percent of them live in high rise apartment houses, although large segments of the community are strictly zoned for detached private homes. When the first apartment houses were built in the 1950s, the home owners resented them because they diluted the semirural environment for which Riverdale is noted. A bitter zoning fight erupted when the Bronx YM-YWHA sought to build its main headquarters in Riverdale. At the end of 1975 the Y still lacked an approved site, although the community raised no objections to the erection of a Soviet residential compound in the area. Few of Riverdale's residents like to admit that they live in The Bronx, but since a separate post office was established, mail must now be addressed Bronx, New York, with an appropriate Riverdale zip code.

Riverdale's first Jewish settlers were well-to-do businessmen, manufacturers, officeholders, and professionals who wanted rural living within the city limits. The first Jewish worship services were held in 1924 at 61 Marble Hill Avenue in the home of Morris Nacht in the Kingsbridge area, once an independent town of which Riverdale was a part. An Orthodox group broke away in 1934 and formed Kenneseth Israel of Riverdale in 1938. A Reform group broke away in 1933. In Riverdale proper, the Riverdale Temple (Reform) was founded in 1946 although a Sunday school had been established in 1941. The Conservative Synagogue of Riverdale dates from 1954, and the Riverdale Jewish Center (Orthodox) was organized in the same year. The Hebrew Tabernacle of Washington Heights (in northern Manhattan) maintains a Sunday school in Riverdale for children of its members who have settled there, and is discussing the possibility of moving to Riverdale.

The opening of the Salanter-Akiba-Riverdale Academy attracted a growing number of Orthodox Jews who belong to the Beth Midrash Horeb Congregation, the Ahavath Tsedek Congregation in Kingsbridge, the Young Israel of Riverdale, Congregation Levi Isaac Riverdale Torah Center, and Ohel Torah, which moved to Riverdale from the Bronx in 1967. Despite the large number of congregations, their regular membership represented less than 10 percent of the total Jewish population in the 1970s.

The Pelham Bay Park area contained some 50,000 Jews in 1976, living in well-kept apartment houses and private houses between Bronx Park and Williamsbridge Road and between Waring Avenue and Bronxdale Road. This section has some of the characteristics of the one-time close-knit Jewish neighborhoods that have been abandoned. A number of Russian Jewish refugees have settled in the neighborhood which has many synagogues and yeshivas. Bronx House, the principal communal Jewish institution in the area, has created a Russian American Neighborhood Action Committee as well as programs for the many Yiddish-speaking older residents in the neighborhood. The Mosholu Parkway area had a large Jewish settlement in the 1970s, sharing the five and six-story apartment houses with the Irish, Italians, and a growing number of blacks who work at the nearby Montefiore Medical Center. Jews have been leaving this area in growing numbers because of their fear that the quality of the neighborhood and public schools is declining. Some interracial violence in the schools stimulated younger families to move to Westchester and Rockland Counties.

The 100 or more synagogues that dotted The Bronx in 1964 have been reduced to about 70, many of them occupying old and deteriorating buildings or store front quarters. In 1976 most of the remaining congregations were Orthodox, however, there were still ten Conservative and eight Reform congregations in the borough.

* * * * *

SYNAGOGUES

ORTHODOX

B'NAI ISRAEL OF EDENWALD, 1014 E. 227th St.
CHOTIMER JEWISH CENTER, 2256 Bronx Park E.
CONG. ANSHE AMAS, 713 E. 222nd St.
CONG. B'NAI ISRAEL, 1570 Walton Ave.
CONG. MOUNT HOREB, Falasha Synagogue, 1042 Stebbins Ave.
JEWISH CENTER OF WAKEFIELD & EDENWALD, 641 E. 233rd Street.
KINGSBRIDGE CENTER OF ISRAEL, 3115 Corlear Ave.
KINGSBRIDGE HEIGHTS JEWISH CENTER, 124 Eames Pl.
MOSHOLU JEWISH CENTER, 3044 Hull Ave.

RIVERDALE JEWISH CENTER, 3700 Independence Ave., has an ultra-modern structure. The congregation was launched with the aid of Yeshiva University, which assigned a "rabbinical Daniel Boone" to the Riverdale area with no more than a slip of paper bearing the names of five local residents who had contacted Yeshiva for aid.

SEPHARDIC, SHA-RE RAHAMIM, 100 Co-Op City Blvd.

YOUNG ISRAEL MESILATH YESHURIM, 1921 Walton Ave.

YOUNG ISRAEL OF ASTOR GARDENS, 1328 Allerton Ave.

YOUNG ISRAEL OF CO-OP CITY, 147-1 Dreiser La.

YOUNG ISRAEL OF KINGSBRIDGE, 2620 University Ave.

YOUNG ISRAEL OF MOSHOLU PKWY., 100 E. 208th St.

YOUNG ISRAEL OF PARKCHESTER, 1375 Virginia Ave.

YOUNG ISRAEL OF PELHAM PARKWAY, Barnes and Lydig Aves.

YOUNG ISRAEL OF RIVERDALE, 547 West 239th St.

YOUNG ISRAEL OF THE CONCOURSE, Grand Concourse at 165th St.

CONSERVATIVE

CONG. AHAVATH TSEDEK, 3425 Kingsbridge Ave.

CONSERVATIVE SYNAGOGUE OF RIVERDALE, 250th St. & Henry Hudson Pkwy.

CO-OP CITY JEWISH CENTER, 900 Co-Op City Blvd.

PELHAM PARKWAY JEWISH CENTER, 900 Pelham Pkwy. S.

JACOB H. SCHIFF CENTER, 2510 Valentine Ave.

SHIELD OF DAVID INSTITUTE, 1800 Andrews Ave.

TEMPLE EMANUEL AT PARKCHESTER, 2000 Benedict Ave.

REFORM

RIVERDALE TEMPLE, 246th St. & Independence Ave., has a chapel made of four components—wood, stone, glass, and metal. One side of the chapel is made up of great stones reminiscent of those of the wall of Jerusalem; on the opposite side are large windows. The pulpit has a mosaic wall in multi-colors of Jewish ceremonial symbols in Venetian glass. The symbols are a Torah Crown, a ram, phylacteries, a *kiddush* cup, a fish and a Torah. In the center of the wall is the Ark with doors about 12 feet high in the form of the Tablets of the Law hammered in sterling silver; the Ten Commandments are in 22 carat gold Hebrew letters. Over the Ark is the Eternal Light in the form of a Star of David with the word *Shaddai* (The Almighty), in its center. Under the Ark the mosaic is black and white, suggestive of the *talis*. A modern Menorah graces the pulpit, in front of which are boxes for plants and flowers. The doors leading into the chapel are beautifully carved with reproductions of the open Torah and other religious symbols. Every phase of the temple was executed by the architect, Simon B. Zelnik.

SINAI CONGREGATION OF THE BRONX, 2011 Grand Concourse.

TEMPLE JUDEA, 615 Reiss Place.

TREMONT TEMPLE BETH-EL OF CO-OP CITY BRANCH, 920 Baychester Ave.

TREMONT TEMPLE—CENTER OF MERCY, 2064 Grand Concourse.

SCHOOLS AND OTHER EDUCATIONAL INSTITUTIONS

BETH JACOB-BETH LEAH SCHOOL FOR GIRLS, 1779 E. 172nd Street.

BETH JACOB-BETH MIRIAM SCHOOL, 1570 Walton Ave.

BETH JACOB SCHOOL FOR GIRLS, 2126 Barnes Ave.

ALBERT EINSTEIN COLLEGE OF MEDICINE of Yeshiva University, Eastchester Rd. and Morris Park Ave., is the first medical school established under Jewish auspices in America (founded in 1955). The main building is a ten-story, glass-faced structure of contemporary design. ●The three-story D. Samuel Gottesman Library, which has room for 200,000 volumes, is adjacent to the college's nine-story science building. One side of the entire length of the library's reading room is glass and faces the main campus and the white brick, seven-story Abraham Mazer Student Residence Hall. ●The ten-story, twelve-sided, tower-like building at Morris Park and Newport Aves. is the Ullmann Research Center for Health Sciences. ●Among the other facilities are the fan-shaped Mary and Karl Robbins Auditorium and the Max L. and Sadie Friedman Student-Faculty Lounge.

The college is named for the famous physicist, mathematician, and Nobel Prize winner. An original 20-page manuscript by Einstein containing one of his early attempts to find a unified field theory is among the important Einstein papers in the Gottesman Library. Although the college is under Jewish auspices, it is nonsectarian and selects students and faculty solely on the basis of scholarship and ability.

The college is the heart of a $100 million medical center that includes a $40 million hospital center constructed by the City of New York and a $45 million psychiatric hospital established by the State of New York. The hospital center includes the Abraham Jacobi Hospital, named for Dr. Abraham Jacobi, famous for his contributions to the science of pediatrics. He opened the first pediatric clinic, invented the laryngoscope, and was elected president of the American Medical Association on his 80th birthday in 1910. Although visitors are welcome at the campus, the Albert Einstein College of Medicine is not open to the public. ☐

209 — THE BRONX, NEW YORK CITY

SAMUEL GOMPERS VOCATIONAL HIGH SCHOOL, 455 Southern Blvd., is named for the founder and first president of the American Federation of Labor.

GOULD MEMORIAL LIBRARY, on campus of Bronx Community College, has over the entrance to its main hall, a Hebrew inscription which translated reads: "The beginning of wisdom is the fear of the Lord" (Psalm 111:10). The same saying appears on the wall in six other languages. In the Library's reading room there are Hebrew inscriptions from the Torah, Maimonides, and Isaiah.

GUGGENHEIM SCHOOL OF AERONAUTICS, the first in the U.S., founded by Daniel Guggenheim, is on the campus of Bronx Community College.

HERBERT LEHMAN COLLEGE of City University, Bedford Park Blvd. and Goulden Ave.

HEBREW INSTITUTE AT RIVERDALE, 3333 Henry Hudson Pkwy., W.

SALANTER AKIBA RIVERDALE ACADEMY, 655 W. 254th St.

LUBAVITCHER YESHIVA ACHEI TMIMIM, 3415 Olinville Ave.

YESHIVA TORAH V'EMUNAH, INC., 1779 E. 172nd St.

JEWISH COMMUNITY CENTERS

BRONX HOUSE, 990 Pelham Pkwy., S., was founded in 1911 by Henry Morgenthau, Sr., as a neighborhood settlement.

BRONX RIVERDALE YM-YWHA, 450 West 250th St.

BRONX YM & YWHA, 1130 Grand Concourse.

MOSHOLU-MONTEFIORE COMMUNITY CENTER of the Associated YM & YWHAs of Greater New York, 3450 DeKalb Ave., is on the grounds of Montefiore Hospital. In addition to its regular program of social group work with people of all ages, the Center conducts a variety of projects with the hospital. One outstanding example is its work with orthopedically handicapped children. The Center has a permanent art exhibit, a roof playground, and a nursery school.

PELHAM PARKWAY BRANCH OF BRONX HOUSE, 2222 Wallace Ave.

HOMES AND HOSPITALS

BETH ABRAHAM HOME FOR THE CHRONICALLY ILL, 612 Allerton Ave., is one of the largest homes of its kind. Beth Abraham Hospital is at the same address.

BRONX HOME FOR SONS AND DAUGHTERS OF MOSES, 990 College Ave.

BRONX-LEBANON HOSPITAL CENTER, Grand Concourse and East Mt. Eden Ave.

EDENWALD SCHOOL FOR BOYS AND GIRLS of Jewish Child Care Association, 1250 East 229th St.

ANDREW FREEDMAN HOME, 1125 Grand Concourse, is a home for the aged founded in 1916 by Andrew Freedman, subway contractor and one-time owner of the New York Giants.

HENRY ITTLESON CENTER FOR CHILD RESEARCH, 5050 Iselin Ave., an affiliate of the Jewish Board of Guardians, studies causes of severe childhood emotional and psychological disorders.

HEBREW HOME FOR THE AGED, 5901 Palisade Ave.

HEBREW HOME FOR THE CHRONIC SICK-CHEVRA MISH-NAIS, 1776 Clay Ave.

MONTEFIORE HOSPITAL AND MEDICAL CENTER, 210th St. and Bainbridge Ave., was founded in 1884 on the centennial of the birth of Sir Moses Montefiore, famous Anglo-Jewish leader and philanthropist. It was originally a home for incurable invalids, but it has since become the nation's largest privately-supported general hospital for the scientific treatment of prolonged illnesses, and it is now a great medical center. The hospital's vast medical complex includes the Henry L. Moses Research Institute, an expanded Solomon and Betty Loeb Memorial Center for intensive post-hospital nursing care, an ambulatory services building, an emergency suite, a diagnostic and treatment center, and basic science laboratories. It was at Montefiore Hospital that cobalt 60 (radioactive isotopes) was first used early in 1953 in the fight against cancer.

WORKMEN'S CIRCLE HOME FOR THE AGED, 3155 Grace Ave.

HILLEL FOUNDATION
LEHMAN COLLEGE, 55 Rudolph Terrace, Yonkers.

HOUSING DEVELOPMENTS
AMALGAMATED APARTMENTS, 8 Van Cortlandt South, is a cooperative project erected in 1927-32 by the Amalgamated Clothing Workers of America, then an almost solidly Jewish union. The buildings were the first low-rent apartments built and operated under the New York State Housing Law.

CO-OP CITY, the world's largest cooperative housing development, in northeast Bronx, where the New England Thruway and the Hutchinson River Parkway intersect, has as many Jewish residents as Atlanta or Indianapolis, and more than New Orleans, Des Moines, and Wilmington, Delaware, put together. It is virtually a community unto itself, with eight synagogues on the premises, one or more branches of virtually every national Jewish organization, and offices of local Jewish welfare, family service, and child care agencies. A large proportion of the Jewish residents are elderly people, living on pensions and social security, while others are lower middle class, many of whom moved from the older decaying areas of The Bronx.

RESTAURANTS
SCHWELLER'S KOSHER RESTAURANT AND DELICATES-
SEN, 3411 Jerome Ave.

SHOPPING
PELHAM PARKWAY HEBREW BOOK STORE, 781 Lydig Ave.

PUBLIC PLACES
HALL OF FAME FOR GREAT AMERICANS, on campus of Bronx Community College, has busts of noted American Jews elected by public ballot every five years—Rabbi Isaac Mayer Wise, father of Reform Judaism in America; Louis D. Brandeis, first Jew named to the U.S. Supreme Court; Dr. Albert Michelson, physicist and first American to win the Nobel Prize in physics; and Lillian D. Wald, founder of Henry Street Settlement and pioneer of public nursing service.

LORELEI FOUNTAIN, recalling the legendary siren of Heinrich Heine's *Die Lorelei*, is located in Joyce Kilmer Park, Grand Concourse and 164th St. On the south side of the fountain is a bas-relief fountain of Heine, the great German Jewish poet. Completed in 1893 as a gift to Duesseldorf, Heine's birthplace, it was refused by the German government. German-Americans in New York then purchased the fountain and presented it to the city.

ISAAC L. RICE STADIUM in Pelham Bay Park, was established with a $1,000,000 gift from the widow of Isaac L. Rice, a musician, editor, inventor, lawyer, industrialist, and chess master. Rice organized railroads, lectured at Columbia University Law School, invented the opening in chess known as Rice's Gambit, founded electric storage battery and boat companies, and developed many inventions in the electric, rubber, and transportation fields.

SOCIAL SERVICE AGENCIES
ALTRO WORKSHOP, 3600 Jerome Ave., a non-sectarian rehabilitation center for patients cured of cardiac diseases where they are helped to return to productive life. It is an affiliate of the Federation of Jewish Philanthropies.

STREETS AND PARKS
DEUTSCH PLAZA, University Ave., just south of Tremont Ave., is named for Bernard S. Deutsch, who was elected president of the N.Y.C. Board of Aldermen in 1933 in the election triumph of Fiorello H. LaGuardia as mayor. Deutsch served as president of the American Jewish Congress. He died in 1935.

CPL. IRWIN FISCHER PL., south of W. 170th St., bet. Nelson and Shakespeare Aves., was named in 1949 for a soldier killed in World War II.

GLADSTONE SQ., at Westchester Ave. and Southern Blvd., is

named for Benjamin Gladstone, a member of the New York State Assembly, who served in World War I.

LATKIN SQ., at intersection of East 169th St., Home St., Intervale Ave., and Tiffany St., is named for David Latkin who was killed in World War I.

QUEENS

The 379,000 Jews who live in the borough of Queens constitute the fourth largest aggregation of Jews in any county of the United States with only Kings (Brooklyn), Nassau, and Los Angeles Counties having more Jews. Queens and Staten Island are the only two boroughs in which the Jewish population has shown some growth. The rise of the Queens Jewish community is one of the most remarkable aspects of the historic Jewish population shifts in New York City.

At the end of World War I, when Queens had barely 400,000 people, its Jewish population was 10,000. This rose to 50,000 in 1923, more than doubled to 115,000 in 1940, and almost doubled again by 1950 when it reached 223,000. The heaviest increase, reflecting the post-World War II exodus from Brooklyn, Manhattan, and The Bronx, occurred between 1950 and 1957. In the latter year Queens passed Manhattan as the borough with the third largest Jewish population. Growth slowed somewhat in the 1960s when Queens passed The Bronx as the borough with the second largest Jewish population, topped only by Brooklyn.

Individual Jews lived in what is now Queens before the Revolution and were doing business in Jamaica, Flushing, and Newtown more than a century before these villages were incorporated into the City of New York. There is a record of at least four Jewish merchants in Queens between 1759 and 1770. The firm of Hart Aaron and Jacob Cohen had branches in Jamaica, Flushing, and Newtown in 1759 and 1760. Levy Moses and Isaac Isaacs, both with families, were in business in Jamaica in the 1760s.

Isaacs' sons, Joseph and Henry, were born in Jamaica and circumcised there by Abraham I. Abrahams, the most popular *mohel* in the New York area in the mid-18th century. Abrahams' registry of circumcisions performed from June, 1756 to January, 1781 shows that he officiated three times in the Jamaica prison. In each instance the occasion was the birth of one of the sons of Levy Moses, who was regularly jailed for debt.

A Jewish community did not develop, however, until after the Civil War when Jewish peddlers, storekeepers, and a few farmers began settling in the Long Island villages that were annexed to New York City in 1898. One section of Forest Hills stands on what was once known as Goldberg's Dairy Farm in the early 1870s. Among the first Jewish arrivals were the Miller and Exiner families, who established themselves in Jamaica in 1868. The Worms, Frank, and Brandon families came to Newtown, now known as Jackson Heights, in the early 1880s. Emanuel Brandon owned a cigar factory and was elected judge of the Court of County Sessions. Samuel Worms served as one of Newtown's first excise commissioners. The earliest known Jewish institution in Queens was the Hebrew Sanitarium, established in Far Rockaway in 1876.

German-Jewish vacationers who began spending summers in the seaside villages on the Rockaway Peninsula in the 1880s organized what was probably the first Jewish worship services in Queens. An Orthodox congregation was formed in Hammels around 1890, while the summer service held over the drygoods store of A. Louis Nebenzahl, who had peddled all over Long Island from 1879-1882, grew into Temple Israel in 1900.

Astoria's Congregation Mishkan Israel was founded in 1894 by a group of Jewish storekeepers. Two years later, Flushing's Gates of Prayer was formed by merchants who had been in business in Flushing since the 1880s. Jamaica's Congregation Ahavas Israel, organized in 1900, originated with a *minyan* that began meeting in the home of Emil Spitzer in the 1890s. Other early Jewish settlements were made in Corona (1900), Maspeth (1904), Long Island City (1904), Middle Village (1908), Richmond Hill (1909), and Ridgewood (1910). Some of these communities were created by peddlers turned storekeepers who had crossed from the Jewish neighborhoods in Brownsville and East New York in Brooklyn.

The opening of the Queensboro Bridge in 1909 brought the first sizable influx of Jews who established new communities in Ozone Park, Woodhaven, Woodside, Queens Village, and Hollis. The first subway lines to reach Queens during the 1920s gave impetus to Jewish settlement in Sunnyside and Jackson Heights, particularly in the newly-built two-family homes erected by the Metropolitan Life Insurance Co. to meet the post-World War I housing shortage. The late Clarence S. Stein, chairman of the New York State Housing and Regional Planning Commission, planned the Sunnyside Gardens development which was occupied in the 1930s by many Jewish newlyweds.

The first large Jewish concentration of Jews in Queens developed in the Rockaways, which accounted for nearly 36 percent of the borough's Jewish population in 1923. Separate communities grew up in Far Rockaway, Averne, Edgemere, Belle Harbor, Neponsit, and Rockaway Beach, each with its own synagogues and societies. In the 1930s, the Rockaways were still the most populous Jewish neighborhood and the only one where Jews represented more than 40 percent of the population.

Once a model community and a popular summer resort for lower middle-income families, the Rockaways were described as a disaster area in 1964 by its Congressman. Huge housing developments that attracted low income welfare families, a decaying beachfront, and the razing of wooden bungalows and old hotels as part of some future urban renewal project, created slum conditions. The population, however, increased from 68,000 in the 1960s to over 100,000 in the 1970s. Some of the population increase came from the residents of nursing homes. In the 1970s, 40 percent of all the nursing homes in Queens and ten percent of those in New York City were in the Rockaways. The nursing homes were the biggest employer on the Rockaway Peninsula. The Rockaways became a dumping ground for infirm elderly persons and discharged mental patients in nursing homes, while many of the new high rise apartment houses were occupied by poor blacks and Puerto Ricans.

Many of the elderly residents of the Rockaways were poor Jews who were often attacked by anti-Semitic hoodlums. The Anti-Defamation League recruited auxiliary police to increase the safety and security of the Jewish population in the housing developments. Edgemere and Rockaway Beach established units of the Maccabees to protect Jews. In the 1970s there was occasional fighting between Black Panthers and members of the Jewish Defense League. Federation has opened a center for the aged in Far Rockaway. The Jewish Association for Service to the Aged, has built a 22-story apartment house for 547 aged families. Others are planned.

In Far Rockaway, which adjoins the village of Lawrence, in Nassau County, there is a growing Orthodox Jewish community of some 2,500 families. The first of them arrived in the 1950s. They now maintain ten synagogues, several yeshivas and day schools, and support numerous kosher food stores. In 1975 they completed an *eruv*—a halachically-approved enclosure by means of wires atop telephone poles—bounded by the L.I.R.R. tracks on the north, Rockaway Turnpike on the east, the ocean on the south, and Beach 19th St. on the west. This enclosure permits them to carry items within the area, thus getting around the halachic ban on carrying any parcel from one domain or *eruv* to another on the Sabbath.

By the end of the 1930s, Sunnyside began to lose its Jewish population, as did some of the other older Jewish settlements, while new middle-class settlements began to develop in Jamaica, Laurelton, Springfield Gardens, and St. Albans. These four neighborhoods were almost 20 percent Jewish by the 1940s. A decade later Springfield Gardens and St. Albans had become predominantly black while the first signs of change became evident in Jamaica. Laurelton, on the edge of Nassau County, was an all-white community until the mid-1960s. Blockbusting by unscrupulous real estate brokers created a panic and by 1966 Laurelton had become 20 percent black as Jewish families began leaving, as did other white families. The Jewish Community Council in Laurelton and the local synagogue struggled to maintain the delicate racial balance by an intensive effort to bring in new Jewish families. Many of the Jewish families who refused to abandon Laurelton favored an integrated community. The Jewish Council of Southeast Queens, representing the synagogues in Cambria Heights, Laurelton, Rosedale, and Queens Village sought to attract new Jewish families by offering potential buyers who lacked enough cash for down payments, interest-free loans of up to $3,000 payable in three years. In exchange for the loans, provided by the Hebrew Free Loan Society, the buyers were expected to become synagogue members as part of the effort to strengthen Jewish institutions.

This undertaking was only partly successful. The Federation of Jewish Philanthropies gave the Laurelton Jewish Community Council a $10,000 grant to fight panic selling and to help preserve the Jewish community. A series of open houses to which potential new Jewish residents were invited was held and the Council set up a home finding service. Nevertheless, the Jewish population of Laurelton, which had accounted for 90 percent of all residents in 1954, declined to 40 percent in 1974.

Rochdale Village, in southeast Queens, had a similar experience. Among the original 24,000 residents of the 20 identical 14-story buildings, were thousands of middle-income Jews but they, like many other whites, have moved out, largely because of crime and dissatisfaction with local schools. Jackson Heights, one of the older areas of Jewish settlement, still has a considerable Jewish community, but there too, in a neighborhood of apartment houses and private houses, an organized effort to attract younger Jewish families was undertaken in the 1970s. Many of the Jewish residents were older families while many of the newcomers to Jackson Heights were Hispanics.

The big change in the Jewish residential pattern in Queens began after World War II when the new rapid transit lines and automobile parkways made it easy to reach Queens from the older sections of Manhattan, Brooklyn, and The Bronx. Many Jews from the older Jewish neighborhoods in the other boroughs had first visited Queens during the 1939 World's Fair and found it appealing. When returning Jewish war veterans found a housing shortage in their home neighborhoods, they poured into the new apartment houses that had begun to rise in Queens.

Instant Jewish neighborhoods were born as Jews moved from the Jewish sections of Brooklyn, The Bronx, and from older areas of Queens. Miles of new high rise apartment houses along the main avenues, boulevards, and streets, as well as garden apartments and private houses were rented and bought by Jews of all economic levels in Fresh Meadows, Bayside, Queens Village, Elmhurst, Jamaica, Flushing, Long Island City, College Point, Whitestone, Rosedale, Douglaston, Little Neck, Rego Park, Kew Gardens, and Forest Hills. The Forest Hills-Rego Park area, which had less than 500 Jews in the 1920s when most apartments there were closed to them, was less than two percent Jewish in the 1930s. Douglaston and Little Neck, bordering Great Neck in Nassau County, had virtually no Jews in the 1920s and 1930s.

By the end of the 1950s, the Forest Hills-Rego Park area was more than half Jewish and had superseded the Rockaways as the principal Jewish neighborhood.The South Flushing and Fresh Meadows sections were each nearly 40 percent Jewish. The Laurelton-Rosedale neighborhood was still 30 percent Jewish, but Astoria, Ridgewood, Maspeth, Richmond Hill, Ozone Park, and Corona had become minor Jewish concentrations. In the Rockaways, where hotels and clubs which had refused to admit Jews in the early 1900s later became all-Jewish establishments. A new year-round Jewish middle-class community developed in the high rise apartments erected along the seashore in the 1960s. In 1976, over 65 percent of all the Jews in Queens lived in six neighborhoods: Forest Hills-Rego Park, Kew Gardens and Kew Gardens Hills, South Flushing-Fresh Meadows, Bayside-Oakland Gardens, Douglaston-Little Neck, and the Rockaways. At the end of 1975 a new Jewish community sprang up on Roosevelt Island in the middle of the East River where the first Jewish residents in a massive new housing complex organized the Congregation of Roosevelt Island.

Most of the immense postwar growth of the Queens Jewish population consisted of younger families who had not been previously affiliated with synagogues. In the new child-centered life that developed in Queens in the 1950s and 1960s, these families flocked to the synagogue in tremendous numbers. Because the existing congregations could not accommodate the newcomers, new synagogues were established in every neighborhood. Some of the older congregations erected new buildings or additions. All of the new congregations embarked on construction programs. Millions of dollars were raised and spent in Queens for new synagogues and religious schools between 1948 and 1960. In 1963 there were 110 synagogues in Queens—56 Orthodox, 43 Conservative, and 11 Reform. The comparable 1976 figures were 78 Orthodox, 45 Conservative, and 12 Reform.

Some of the Orthodox congregations from Brooklyn and The Bronx have moved to Queens, which is dotted with Hebrew day schools and yeshivas. Kew Gardens Hills has had a special attraction for the Orthodox. In 1976 it had eight Orthodox synagogues, a number of glatt kosher butchers, a couple of kosher restaurants, and kosher bakeries and pizza parlors. In 1951 when Young Israel organized in Kew Gardens Hills, the neighborhood was 20 percent Jewish but it was nearly 80 percent in 1976, and half of that is accounted for by Orthodox Jews. More Orthodox Jews are being attracted to the area because it now has an eruv, a network of pole-strung wires that marks off a given area and binds it to the household of its residents, thus enabling Orthodox Jews to push baby carriages on the Sabbath and to engage in activities which would not otherwise be permitted except within the bounds of their own homes. The Hillcrest-Flushing area also has an eruv.

Because so many Israelis live in Queens—an estimated 75 percent of all the 100,000 Israelis in New York City—the borough has been dubbed "the fourth city of Israel." Queens Boulevard is virtually a Jewish promenade. Hebrew newspapers are on sale at newsstands. Israeli foods are available in the supermarkets. There is a proliferation of Israeli restaurants and retail establishments owned by Israelis. Some local merchants speak Hebrew. The Bank Leumi has a branch in Queens. The 1970 census showed that Queens had the highest proportion of residents of foreign origin in the city. Half of its over 2,000,000 people were either born abroad or had one foreign-born parent. Most of the borough's foreign-born are concentrated in Forest Hills-Rego Park, Jackson Heights, and Flushing. The third largest group comes from Russia, which usually means Jews, and the fourth largest comes from Germany and Austria, which reflects the large number of German-Jewish refugees in the area. A substantial majority of the 100,000 people in Forest Hills and the 25,000 in Rego Park are Jewish.

Most Forest Hills Jews are refugees from other parts of the city who fled to Queens when the influx of low-income minorities and welfare families led to an increase in crime and violence, lowered school standards, and a deterioration of neighborhoods. The move to Forest Hills, Rego Park, and Kew Gardens was a search for safety in the streets, schools, elevators, and corridors. Queens Boulevard is lined with tall apartment houses that became the dominant feature of Queens housing when the type of building shifted from single family houses and six-story apartment houses. The largest housing development in Queens is the $150 million Lefrak City, built by Samuel Lefrak. It houses 25,000 people, many of them Jews, in 5,000 apartments in 20 duplicate brick structures spread out over 40 acres. Lefrak City has two synagogues and among its security guards are some who speak Yiddish.

Lefrak City's tenants are typical of the polyglot populace of the Rego Park-Forest Hills area. Besides the tens of thousands of Israelis, the neighborhood has colonies of Yemenite, Russian, Egyptian, Yugoslavian, Moroccan, and Bokharan Jews. In the mid-1970s, the area became an important center for Sephardic Jews who moved from Brooklyn and The Bronx. Many Greek and Turkish Jews who had resided in The Bronx moved to Queens in anticipation of the relocation of the Sephardic Jewish Center of The Bronx, which sold its building and moved to Forest Hills-Rego Park. Pizza shops run by Yemenite Jews in the area are popular gathering places for Israelis. The East New York YM-YWHA disposed of its building in 1972 in Brooklyn and moved to Queens. It was renamed the Central Queens YMHA. It conducts branch programs in Lefrak City, Howard Beach, and Rego Park pending the erection of a large main building in the Forest Hills area.

In 1972, the largely middle-class Jewish community of Forest Hills exploded in anger and bitterness over the city's plan to erect three 24-story buildings containing 840 apartments in Rego Park which were to be occupied largely, if not entirely, by low income and welfare families. The huge complex was designed to establish low income housing for minorities within a middle-class neighborhood and away from ghetto areas—the so-called scatter housing approach. Fearing an influx of poor blacks with the resultant strain on neighborhood schools, traffic, police, fire, and health facilities, and the likelihood of a major change in the neighborhood, a large majority of the area's Jews lined up against the project. When construction began there were inflammatory speeches, sit-downs on Long Island Expressway, and confrontations between Jews and blacks on opposite sides of the street at the project site.

The Jewish fight against the housing project was ostensibly aimed at the environmental dangers it threatened. In effect, however, they were saying by their opposition that Forest Hills-Rego Park was a secure place to live and they did not want welfare cases and minorities undermining that sense of safety. The older residents remembered the neighborhoods they had built in Brooklyn and The Bronx and from which they had fled as those areas deteriorated from increased crime and squalor. The fight created wide division in the Jewish community. A minority, including some rabbis, supported the project, but the bulk of the Jewish population—residents, businessmen, public officials, and employees of various enterprises—fiercely opposed the project. The rabbinate too, was divided, with the majority opposed, reflecting the view of their congregants. One synagogue whose rabbi supported the housing development was invaded by congregants of a neighboring synagogue who interrupted the service and threatened the rabbi.

The major national Jewish community relations agencies became involved in the controversy because their Forest Hills members were involved. The American Jewish Committee opened an office in Forest Hills to help allay fears, to develop a senior citizens tenants association, and to undertake a variety of educational programs for use when the project opened. The Queens Jewish Community Council was born out of the conflict. It openly charged the Lindsay administration with trying to destroy the Forest Hills Jewish community. The Council was backed by the Orthodox Rabbinical Association of Queens which called on all rabbis to denounce the project from the pulpit during the High Holy Days. Pro-project rabbis received threatening calls and letters after some of them had called attention to the irony of Jews opposing the admission of minorities in an area where Jews themselves had once had to fight housing restrictions. Oddly enough, the first Chasidic families who settled in Forest Hills and Rego Park also encountered some opposition from Jewish residents who feared another Williamsburg might develop.

The controversy led to many Jewish families moving out of the Forest Hills-Rego Park neighborhood but the majority that remained were finally resigned to the project. In a compromise, the project plans were reduced to three buildings of 12 stories, with a total of 430 apartments. The entire complex was converted into a low income cooperative with some 40 percent of the occupants being low income aged, which in practice would mean elderly Jews already living in the area. At the end of 1975 when the first tenants moved in, there was a vestige of fear over the potentially negative impact on the neighborhood. These fears were intensified when the Board of Education began busing black and Puerto Rican students from other areas into Forest Hills High School.

Notwithstanding its size, Queens Jewry developed no independent borough-wide Jewish institutions until the housing fight gave rise to the Queens Jewish Community Council. There are borough-wide federations of local units of national Jewish organizations and temporary committees that conduct area appeals for the Joint Campaign of the United Jewish Appeal of Greater New York-Federation of Jewish Philanthropies. The Associated YM & YWHAs of Greater New York has established branch Ys in Far Rockaway and the Douglaston-Little Neck section. Long Island Jewish-Hillside Medical Center, on the Queens-Nassau border, a merger of Hillside Hospital and Long Island Jewish Hospital, is a major Federation agency. The Federation-supported Long Island Jewish Community Services and the Federation Employment and Guidance Service also operate in Queens. At John F. Kennedy International Airport, the New York Board of Rabbis maintains the International Synagogue.

A good deal of the heavy residential construction that has changed the face of Queens was accomplished by Jewish builders. The biggest of these is Samuel J. Lefrak, who boasts that one out of every 16 New Yorkers lives in a Lefrak-built apartment house. He is the largest single property owner in Queens and the borough's single biggest taxpayer. In addition to Lefrak City, he has blueprinted Satellite City, to be erected over the Sunnyside yards of the Long Island Railroad, where he would move the entire garment industry and provide housing for 17,000 families. He already owns twin 20-story apartment towers that straddle the railroad tracks at Kew Gardens. He also built large housing projects in Seaside and Hammels on the Rockaway Peninsula.

The Jamaica, Flushing, and Queens Boulevard retail shopping areas were also largely the creation of Jewish businessmen. The Gertz department store, largest in Queens, was founded in Jamaica by Benjamin Gertz at the turn of the century, and now has branches in the suburbs. The ten-block area of Rego Park, just west of Forest Hills, has been converted into central Queens' "downtown" area. Within walking distance of the Long Island Expressway, this new shopping center has office buildings, luxury condominiums, and branch stores of Alexander's, Korvette's, Macy's, and Ohrbach's. In downtown Jamaica there are Macy's and May stores in addition to Gertz's.

The large Jewish population helped change Queen's political complexion from solidly Republican to Democratic, and considerable support for the Liberal party. Since the 1950s, Jewish voters who used to help pile up huge Democratic majorities in Brooklyn and The Bronx, have greatly strengthened the Democrats in Queens County. The first Jew to attain borough-wide political status was a Republican, Benjamin Marvin, a municipal court judge in the 1920s. He owned the *Long Island Daily Press*, now known as the *Long Island Press*, one of the links in the nationwide newspaper chain owned by Samuel Newhouse. The two Jews elected to Congress from Queens in the 1950s and 1960s won with Liberal Party backing, although one was a Democrat (Benjamin Rosenthal) and the other a Republican (Seymour Halpern). Halpern did not run for reelection in 1974 but Rosenthal was still in the House in 1976, together with another Democrat, Lester Wolff, whose district includes a slice of eastern Queens and the Great Neck area of Nassau County.

In 1963, the Democrats were the first major party to designate a Jew as county leader, Moses Weinstein. Melvin Klein and Sidney S. Hein were Republican county leaders. Queens has had two Jewish Borough Presidents, Sidney Leviss and Donald Manes. In 1975 the Queens Interfaith Clergy Council chose a rabbi as its first Jewish president. David Katz was the founder of the Queens Chamber of Commerce. Queens College, the borough's major higher educational institution, has a Yiddish section in its Paul Klapper library, named for its first president, offers courses in Yiddish, and is the home of the semiannual magazine, *Yiddish*.

*****

SYNAGOGUES

ORTHODOX

CONG. AHAVATH SHOLOM, 75-02 113th St., Forest Hills.
CONG. CHOFETZ CHAIM, 92-15 69th Ave., Forest Hills.
CONG. EMUNA SHLEIMA, 69-69 Main St.
CONG. KNESETH ISRAEL, 728 Empire Ave., Far Rockaway, familiarly known as "the White Shule." At one time it numbered among its congregants about 35 ordained, non-pulpit rabbis. The congregation has no *hazzan*. Instead it uses a battery of its own unusually gifted *baaley tefilah*, who work in rotation.
CONG. SHAARAY TEFILA, 1295 Central Ave., Far Rockaway. Both this congregation and Cong. Kneseth Israel help make Far Rockaway a unique Jewish community—predominantly Orthodox. Traffic on the Sabbath and Jewish holidays virtually ceases on some streets, where Jewish all-day schools are common (the best known is Hi-Li—the Hebrew Institute of Long Island). It is not unusual to see bearded men in Hasidic garb and boys with side-locks. The community has a high proportion of religiously-educated

laymen. The building is designed in the tradition of New York's Spanish and Portuguese Synagogue and is geared more to the entire Jewish community than to the Jewishly-educated. All told, there are 19 synagogues and nine yeshivas in Far Rockaway. There are also *eruvs* in the Wavecrest-Bayswater area and the eastern-most section, enabling the Orthodox to carry on the Sabbath and wheel carriages without violating the sanctity of the Sabbath.

CONG. SONS OF ISRAEL, 33-21 Crescent St., Long Island City.

CONG. TIFARETH AL-OZER V'YESHIVAS DEGEL-HATORAH, 82-61 Beverly Rd., Kew Gardens.

KEW GARDENS SYNAGOGUE-ADATH YESHURUN, 82-17 Lefferts Blvd., Kew Gardens.

MASPETH JEWISH CENTER, 66-64 Grand Ave.

QUEENS JEWISH CENTER AND TALMUD TORAH, 66-05 108th St.

SEPHARDIC JEWISH CONGREGATION AND CENTER, 101-17 67 Drive, Forest Hills.

TIFERETH ISRAEL OF JACKSON HEIGHTS, 88th St. & 32nd Avenue.

YOUNG ISRAEL OF FOREST HILLS, Yellowstone Blvd. & Burns Street.

YOUNG ISRAEL OF HILLCREST, 169-07 Jewel Ave.

YOUNG ISRAEL OF JACKSON HEIGHTS, 86-15 37th Ave.

YOUNG ISRAEL OF KEW GARDENS HILLS, 150-01 70th Rd.

YOUNG ISRAEL OF SUNNYSIDE, 41-12 45th St.

CONSERVATIVE

BAYSIDE JEWISH CENTER, 203-05 32nd Ave.

BAYSIDE-OAKS JEWISH CENTER, 56-40 231st St.

BAYSWATER JEWISH CENTER, 2355 Healy Avenue, Far Rockaway.

BAY TERRACE JEWISH CENTER, 209th St. & Willets Point Boulevard.

BELLEROSE JEWISH CENTER, 254-04 Union Turnpike.

BELL PARK JEWISH CENTER, 231-10 Hillside Ave.

CLEARVIEW JEWISH CENTER, 16-50 Utopia Parkway, Whitestone.

FOREST HILLS JEWISH CENTER, 106-06 Queens Blvd., has an Ark designed by Arthur Szyk in the form of a *tzitz* (the breastplate of a Torah Scroll). The pattern includes the symbols of the Jewish festivals, the emblems of the Twelve Tribes, and a series of 39 jewels representing the 39 books of the Bible. The borders carry Biblical verses praising the Torah. The whole majestic design rises to a peak that forms the two tablets of the Ten Commandments, and these are capped by the Crown of the Torah.

HILLCREST JEWISH CENTER, 183-02 Union Turnpike, Flushing, has for its façade a mural executed in ceramic tile consisting of five eight-foot-high panels, each expressing a particular theme: the Sabbath, peace, the fruitful life, righteousness, and eternity. A mural in the lobby, *Jacob's Dream*, depicts the Twelve Tribes in stars. Both the exterior and the lobby murals were designed by Anton Refregier, a non-Jewish artist. On the doors of the Ark in the sanctuary there is a charming miniature mosaic by A. Raymond Katz blending a few traditional motifs into its largely abstract play. The sanctuary itself is intimate, and one structural detail that contributes to this intimacy is a niche behind the Ark that broadens upward and outward to become a kind of canopy. The hung ceiling has a large glass panel bearing a wooden Star of David.

JAMAICA ESTATES HEBREW CENTER, 182-69 Wexford Terrace.

JEWISH CENTER OF JACKSON HEIGHTS, 34-25 82nd St., has a chapel dedicated to the memory of the six million victims of Nazism.

JEWISH CENTER OF KEW GARDENS HILLS, 71-25 Main St., Flushing.

REGO PARK JEWISH CENTER, 97-30 Queens Blvd., has a 6 by 36-foot mosaic panel over its main entrance executed in Venetian glass. The motifs in the panel are of the nine Jewish festivals and the symbols of the name of G-d. The fingers of a hand holding a ram's horn also form the letter *shin* (standing for *Shaddai*, the Almighty). A huge Star of David hangs above the mosaic. A. Raymond Katz, who designed the mosaic, also designed the synagogue's two sets of stained glass windows, one of which represents the ethical, religious, and national significance of the three Patriarchs— Abraham, Isaac, and Jacob. The Ark and its setting are an elaborate composition in wood and marble.

SUNNYSIDE JEWISH CENTER, 45-46 43rd St.

TEMPLE GATES OF PRAYER, 38-20 Parsons Blvd.

REFORM

CONG. BETH HILLEL OF JACKSON HEIGHTS, 23-38 81st St.

FREE SYNAGOGUE OF FLUSHING, 136 Sanford Ave., has in its building some marble from the dismantled Vanderbilt mansion on 5th Ave. The congregation's community house was originally the home of a Long Island railroad executive and its designer was the famous architect, Stanford White.

ROOSEVELT JEWISH CONG., serves the Jewish residents of the

housing developments on Roosevelt Island, which is located in the middle of the East River.

TEMPLE BETH-AM, 120-43 166th St.

TEMPLE BETH SHOLOM, 171-39 Northern Blvd., Flushing.

TEMPLE EMANU-EL OF FAR ROCKAWAY, 1526 Central Ave.

TEMPLE EMANU-EL OF QUEENS, 91-15 Corona Avenue, Elmhurst.

TEMPLE ISAIAH, 75-24 Grand Central Pkwy., Forest Hills, has etched in stone on the left side of the façade, the famous quotation from Micah: "What does the Lord require of thee? Only to do justly, love mercy, and walk humbly with thy G-d." Above the entrance the words "The righteous lives by his faith" are inscribed in Hebrew and English. In the sanctuary the Ark doors are handcarved by Milton Horn, well-known sculptor. Stained glass windows on each side wall depict the various Jewish festivals. An innovation at Temple Isaiah is the closed circuit televised High Holy Day services in the auxiliary sanctuary.

TEMPLE ISRAEL OF JAMAICA, 188-15 McLoughlin Ave., was designed by Percival Goodman. There is a mosaic in the west wall designed by Goodman and an outstanding oil-burning Menorah and Eternal Lamp designed by Arnold Bergier.

TEMPLE JUDEA, 82-17 153rd Ave.

TEMPLE SHOLOM, 263-10 Union Turnpike.

TEMPLE OR OF THE DEAF, holds services in the sign language for the deaf in Temple Israel, 188 Grand Central Pkwy., Hollis.

SCHOOLS AND SEMINARIES

BENJAMIN CARDOZO HIGH SCHOOL, 57-20 223rd St., Bayside, named for Supreme Court Justice Benjamin N. Cardozo, has a monument of Cardozo on its front lawn.

ISRAEL MEYER HA-COHEN RABBINICAL SEMINARY OF AMERICA, 92-15 69th Ave., Forest Hills.

HEBREW ACADEMY OF WEST QUEENS, 86-15 37th Ave.

MAX AND ROSE HELLER HEBREW ACADEMY, 203-05 32nd Ave., Bayside.

LEXINGTON SCHOOL FOR THE DEAF, 30th Ave. and 75th St., Jackson Heights, is a $6 million center on a seven-acre tract. The center includes a school for 300 deaf students, a graduate studies institute, facilities for research, and an out-patient hearing and speech clinic. The first school in America to teach the deaf to speak and to read lips, the Lexington School is one of many affiliates of the Federation of Jewish Philanthropies. In addition to the wide variety of vocational shops, training facilities, and courses, the school is planning a treatment and diagnostic center.

SOLOMON SCHECHTER SCHOOL, 76-16 Parsons Blvd. Flushing.
BENJAMIN SCHLESINGER PUBLIC SCHOOL, 133-25 New
York Blvd., Jamaica, is named for an eminent leader of the labor movement.
YESHIVA OF FLUSHING, 71-50 Parsons Blvd.
YESHIVA RABBI DOV REVEL OF FOREST HILLS, 71-02 113th
Street.
YESHIVA TIFERETH MOSHE, 83-06 Abingdon Road, Kew
Gardens.

JEWISH COMMUNITY CENTERS
CENTRAL QUEENS YM & YWHA, 108-05 68th Rd., Forest Hills.
GUSTAVE HARTMAN YM & YWHA OF THE ROCKAWAYS,
Hartman La. and Beach Channel Drive, Far Rockaway.
NORTH HILLS YM & YWHA (Samuel Field Bldg.), 58th Ave. and
Little Neck Parkway, Little Neck.
SEPHARDIC JEWISH CENTER, 62-67 108th St., Forest Hills,
was under construction in 1976, replacing a building in The Bronx.
YM & YWHA OF GREATER FLUSHING (Abraham and Dora Felt
Bldg.), 45-35 Kissena Blvd.

HILLEL FOUNDATION
QUEENS COLLEGE, 152-45 Melbourne Ave., Flushing.

HOUSING PROJECTS
BROOKDALE VILLAGE, Beach 119th St., bet. Seagirt Blvd. and
the Boardwalk, the largest non-profit senior citizen housing complex in New
York State, is sponsored and operated by the Jewish Association for
Services for the Aged. A retirement community of 1,600 residents,
Brookdale Village comprises four high-rise apartment towers and an
adjoining community center.

COORDINATING AGENCIES
JEWISH COMMUNITY SERVICES OF LONG ISLAND, 97-45
Queens Blvd., Rego Park.
QUEENS JEWISH COMMUNITY COUNCIL, 86-82 Palo Alto St.,
Holliswood.

HOMES AND HOSPITALS
Goldwater Memorial Hospital, Welfare Island, is named for Dr.
Sigismund S. Goldwater, hospital administrator and public health authority.
Goldwater was the New York City Commissioner of Hospitals from
1934-1940. Earlier he had been superintendent of Mount Sinai Hospital and
Health Commissioner of New York City.

MISCELLANEOUS

HOROWITZ BROS. & MARGARETEN (kosher foods), 29-00 Review Ave., Long Island City
LONG ISLAND ZIONIST HOUSE, 132-32nd Ave., Kew Gardens.

MUSEUMS AND LIBRARIES

KLAPPER MEMORIAL LIBRARY at Queens College, 65-30 Kissena Blvd., Flushing, honors Dr. Paul Klapper, the college's first president and believed to be the first unconverted Jew to be named president of any non-rabbinical institution of higher learning. An immigrant from Romania, he rose to be dean of City College's School of Education and became president of Queens in 1937, serving until 1948. He helped lay the ground work for the establishment of the State University of New York.

RESTAURANTS AND NIGHTCLUBS

ARELE'S, Long Island Expressway at 162nd St., is a nightclub under rabbinical supervision featuring dining, dancing, and floor shows.

CAFE BABA OF ISRAEL, 91-33 63rd Drive, is a *glatt* kosher nightclub.

THE FLAME LAPID, 97-04 Queens Blvd., serves Israeli food.

LUIGI GOLDSTEIN'S, 72-24 Main Street, is a kosher Italian restaurant.

JERUSALEM WEST, 117-18 Queens Blvd., is a kosher Chinese restaurant.

KARMEL'S KOSHER BURGERS, 19-03 Cornaga Avenue, Far Rockaway.

KOSHER CHEF, 17-29 Seagirt Blvd., Far Rockaway.

KOSHER KORNER, 67-03 Main St., Flushing.

KOSHER PIZZA-FALAFEL, 71-24 Main St.

LEVY'S KOSHER PIZZA & ISRAELI FALAFEL, 68-28 Main St. (*Shomer Shabbat*).

LINDEN HILL KOSHER DELICATESSEN AND RESTAURANT, 29-22 Union Turnpike, Flushing.

NEW FOREST RESTAURANT, 64-20 108th St. Forest Hills.

PATIO KOSHER DELICATESSEN & RESTAURANT, 78-16A Linden Blvd., Howard Beach.

PHIL'S BROADWAY KOSHER DELICATESSEN & RESTAURANT, 30-05 Broadway, Astoria.

SHOPPING

CONTINENTAL ART GALLERY, 72-21 Austin St., sells works of Israeli artists.

GIFT WORLD, 72-20 Main St., sells books of Jewish interest.

HOUSE OF ISRAEL, 90-05 150th St., Jamaica.

THE JONATHAN DAVID CO., 68-22 Eliot Ave., Middle Village, publishes books of sermons and commentaries on various aspects of Judaism, books of instruction and psychology, some fiction and juvenile works, and sells numerous items for use in synagogues and religious schools. Among the articles to be found here are medals, charms, pins, plaques, certificates, albums inscribed with a Magen David, and just about everything for the synagogue, including furniture.

JOHN F. KENNEDY INTERNATIONAL AIRPORT

Opened in April, 1964, the International Synagogue at the airport is part of Chapel Plaza, located on a lagoon in the central area of International Park adjoining the Protestant and Catholic chapels. The plaza is the first tri-faith chapel development at an American airport. The main sanctuary of the synagogue is modeled after the first synagogue built in America. A museum containing religious objects from Jewish communities throughout the world, a Jewish information center, and a library reading room have been set up within the synagogue, which is sponsored by the New York Board of Rabbis. The structure is dominated by the two tablets of the Ten Commandments, which rise 40 feet from their base in the lagoon. The tablets are flanked on both sides by sculptured stained glass windows depicting the Twelve Tribes of Israel. The foyer of the synagogue contains a tablet of states, on which the sponsoring congregations and individuals from the 50 states have been inscribed.

Among the items displayed in the International Museum are replicas of famous copper plates given by the ruling Hindu king to Joseph Rabban, the leader of the Cochin Indian Jewish community; a 200-year old *shofar*, serpentine in shape and about two feet long; two reed-like leaves on which is inscribed in Malayan a contract between a money-lender and a synagogue that borrowed 1,000 rupees; and other interesting articles. The copper plates, engraved in old Tamil script, were made sometime between 379 B.C.E. and the 9th or 10th century C.E.

Inside the imposing arched concourse of the International Arrivals Building is a large, gray-black marble plaque bearing a raised torch with an excerpt from the same poem by Emma Lazarus that is etched into the base of the Statue of Liberty:

> . . . *Give me your tired, your poor,*
> *Your huddled masses yearning to breathe free*
> . . .
> *Send these, the homeless, tempest-tost to me,*
> *I lift my lamp beside the golden door!*

One line of the poem was omitted: "The wretched refuse of your teeming shore," on orders of Austin J. Tobin, executive director of the New York Port Authority, which operates the airfield. Tobin said the deleted line "had meaning during the mass migrations of the nineteenth century, but it has no meaning now and might be offensive to the fine people of Europe—they might not regard themselves as 'wretched refuse,' " Inside the building the flag of Israel hangs alongside the flags of other nations.

The east wall of the EL AL Airlines Terminal is covered with a mural *Man's Aspiration of Flight*, by Zvi Gali, one of Israel's leading artists. It uses the Italian Renaissance technique of *sgraffito*, which gives the mural a sculptured effect. On the opposite wall, Bezalel Schatz, another Israeli artist, used simple bars of silver to profile capitals served by EL AL and to show their time by silver clock arms.

STATEN ISLAND

Although the Jewish population of the borough of Richmond is growing faster than the general population, fewer Jews lived there in 1976 than in three or four of the giant apartment house developments in The Bronx, Brooklyn, and Queens. In 1963 there were 11,000 Jews on Staten Island, about half of one percent of the total population. In 1975 the Jewish population was 21,000 out of a total of some 350,000. Most of the Jews live in St. George and Port Richmond but there are also sizeable settlements in New Dorp, Tompkinsville, Castleton Corners, New Brighton, Tottenville, Roseville, Stapleton, and South Beach.

Geography and limited transportation facilities have kept Staten Island and its Jewish community small. The opening of the Verrazano Narrows Bridge from Brooklyn to Staten Island in 1965 brought a building boom to Staten Island and a considerable influx of new residents, including Jews. But in 1976 there were no indications that the Staten Island Jewish community would assume the proportions of the older settlements in Queens and Brooklyn.

Though the first white settlers occupied Staten Island in 1661, there is no trace of Jewish residents or even property-owners and merchants before the 1850s. Moses Greenwald, a German immigrant, is believed to have been the earliest Jewish resident. His son, Abram, was born on Staten Island in the 1860s. Several other families established themselves at St. George, Tompkinsville, Port Richmond, and New Brighton before 1880.

Among the first European Jewish settlers were the Kiviats, who arrived from the East Side in 1892, bringing with them a six-month old boy named Abel. Abel Kiviat, who learned to run in the open fields of Staten Island, became one of the great track and field stars of the country, winning national titles in the 600 and 1,000 yard runs, the mile, and cross-country racing from 1910-1915. He was a close contender in the 1912 Olympic 1,500-meter race.

Jewish religious services were first held around 1882 in the home of Simon Raunes, 7 Richmond Turnpike, now 49 Victory Boulevard. Congregation B'nai Jeshurun was the pioneer synagogue, having been founded in Tompkinsville in 1888. The Chevrah Agudath Chesed Shel Emeth, a charitable society, was organized in 1889. A second congregation, Agudath Achim Ansche Chesed, was formed at New Brighton in 1900, and Temple Emanu-El was organized in 1907. In 1916, when there were somewhat more than 3,500 Jews, a fourth congregation, Temple Tifereth Israel, was founded at Stapleton. In 1976 there were nine congregations, as well as a Jewish Community Center and a cluster of local branches of national Jewish organizations.

The Federation of Jewish Philanthropies maintains one of its Henry Kaufmann Campgrounds on Staten Island. It also sponsors a home for unmarried mothers.

The first substantial influx of Jewish residents began after World War II when white collar workers were attracted by the low-cost of new one-family homes. Some Jewish business and professional men from the heavily industrialized area around Bayonne, New Jersey also settled on Staten Island because they found homes there easily accessible. To reach Manhattan or Brooklyn without driving a car, Staten Island residents must take a ferryboat, and the lack of direct transportation links other than the Verrazano Bridge has discouraged mass migration to Staten Island.

*****

SYNAGOGUES

ORTHODOX

CONG. AGUDATH ACHIM ANSHE CHESED, 641 Delafield Ave., is the second oldest congregation on the island.

229 — STATEN ISLAND, NEW YORK CITY

SYNAGOGUE OF THE YESHIVA OF STATEN ISLAND, 1870
Drumboole Rd., E.
YOUNG ISRAEL OF STATEN ISLAND, 835 Forest Hill Rd.

CONSERVATIVE

CONG. AHAVATH ISRAEL, 59 Sequine Ave.
CONG. B'NAI ISRAEL, 45 Twombley Ave.
CONG. B'NAI JESHURUN, 19 Martling Ave., is the oldest congre-
gation on the island.
TEMPLE EMANU-EL, 984 Post Ave., is the third oldest congrega-
tion on the island.
TEMPLE TIFERETH ISRAEL, 119 Wright St.

REFORM

TEMPLE ISRAEL, 315 Forest Ave.

COMMUNITY CENTER
JEWISH COMMUNITY CENTER, 475 Victory Blvd.

SCHOOLS AND SEMINARIES
RABBI JACOB JOSEPH SCHOOL, 3495 Richmond Rd. This school
was formerly located on the Lower East Side for over 76 years. It is an all-
day school and is named after the only Chief Rabbi that New York City ever
had.
YESHIVA OF STATEN ISLAND, 1870 Drumboole Rd., E.
YESHIVA TIFERET SCHMUEL EZRA-JEWISH FOUNDA-
TION SCHOOL, 20 Park Hill Circle.

MISCELLANEOUS
BERNSTEIN INTERMEDIATE SCHOOL, Hylan Blvd. and
Huguenot Ave., is named for a prominent local communal leader.

FLORA HAAS SITE of the Henry Kaufmann Campgrounds, 1131 Manor Rd., is a Federation agency which has a permanent day camping site for children from other borough community centers.

ABRAHAM LEVY MEMORIAL PARK, cor. Jewett and Castleton Aves., memorializes the first Staten Island soldier to die in World War I.

JEWISH FAMILY SERVICE, 114 Central Ave.

RICHMOND MEMORIAL HOSPITAL, 375 Sequine Ave., is a voluntary non-profit, general hospital located in a building donated by Berta E. Dreyfus as a memorial to her husband. Portraits of Dr. and Mrs. Louis A. (Berta) Dreyfus are in the lobby.

WAGNER COLLEGE, Grimes Hill, has a plaque in the lobby of its main administration building recording the establishment of its biological laboratories in 1940 in memory of Dr. Louis A. Dreyfus.

RESTAURANTS

WEINSTEIN DELICATESSEN, 816 Forest Ave.

NASSAU and
SUFFOLK COUNTIES

Nassau and Suffolk Counties, New York City's largest suburb, have more Jews than any one of New York City's five boroughs, and, together, constitute the third largest Jewish community in the United States. Only New York City as a whole and Los Angeles County have more Jews.

In the 1930s, the two cities and 54 towns and villages of Nassau and Suffolk Counties counted barely 18,000 Jews. By 1963, however, there were 352,000 in Nassau County and 38,000 in Suffolk County. When the total population of the two counties reached the 2,000,000 mark for the first time at the end of 1962, Jews constituted about 20 percent of the total. In the 1970s, the Jewish population had grown to 605,000 (Nassau, 455,000, and Suffolk, 150,000), or about 22½ percent of the total population of the 2,715,000 in the two-county area.

Although a large percentage of the working residents of Nassau and Suffolk Counties actually work in the counties, the Long Island Railroad, mindful that a considerable number of its daily commuters to New York are Jews, uses a Hebrew calendar to make certain changes in its schedule. On the eve of the High Holy days and Passover, the railroad always adds extra trains to accommodate Jewish commuters homeward bound at an earlier time than usual. School principals and teachers consult the Hebrew calendar in setting dates for major school events, final examinations, school openings, and graduations.

The largest Jewish concentration is in the Town of Hempstead, which is made up of 33 villages and the city of Long Beach, where 275,000 Jews represent about 40 percent of the total population. This is the area that includes Levittown, Oceanside, Rockville Centre, Valley Stream, East Meadow, Westbury, Hempstead, West Hempstead, Wantagh, and the Five

231

Towns (Lawrence, Cedarhurst, Hewlett, Woodmere, and Inwood). The town of North Hempstead, which embraces the major North Shore communities of Great Neck, Manhasset, Port Washington, Roslyn, and the city of Glen Cove, had 100,000 Jews in the 1970s. In the town of Oyster Bay, which includes the villages of Bethpage, Jericho, Hicksville, Massapequa, Plainedge, Plainview, Syosset, and Westbury, there were 80,000 Jews. In Suffolk County, 90,000 Jews lived in the western segment, the one closest to New York; 50,000 in the central portion; and 10,000 in the eastern tip.

New York was still New Amsterdam when Jews were doing business in all three counties of Colonial Long Island—Kings (Brooklyn), Queens, which once included all of Nassau County, and Suffolk. "The whole island was familiar country to Colonial Jewry," Dr. Jacob R. Marcus points out in his book, *Early American Jewry*.

As early as the 1660s Jewish merchants had found their way to that part of Long Island beyond the New York City limits. The ubiquitous Asser Levy of New Amsterdam owned property on Long Island and, after his death, his family moved there in 1730. Oyster Bay's town records contain a document dated January 19, 1745 listing the sale of 19 acres by the widow of Samuel Myers Cohen. A former president of New York's Congregation Shearith Israel, Cohen had acquired the property in 1741 or even earlier. Hart Aaron and Jacob Cohen had stores at Islip and Jericho between 1759 and 1760. Levy Michael lived at South Haven in 1760 when his son, Michael, was circumcised there by Abraham I. Abrahams of New York. Joseph Jacobs came to Southampton in 1760. Isaac Moses and Isaac Isaacs, whose home was in Jamaica, also had business interests on Long Island before the Revolution.

The best known of the handful of Jewish residents on Long Island before 1800 was Aaron Isaacs, who settled at East Hampton around 1750. Isaacs, who had been a member of Shearith Israel, was one of Long Island's most prominent merchants and shipowners in the middle of the 18th century. He owned property in Montauk and East Hampton and was part-owner of a wharf at Sag Harbor. During the Revolution, when the British controlled Long Island, Isaacs fled to Connecticut with other patriots. In 1750, he married a Christian. All of his eleven children were baptized. One daughter became the mother of John Howard Payne who wrote *Home Sweet Home*, based on the memory of his grandfather's house. The "Home Sweet Home" is still one of East Hampton's landmarks. The salt-box house sits not far from where Isaacs is buried, in a Christian cemetery.

A scattering of Jews lived on Long Island in the first half of the 19th century, but they were never numerous enough to acquire even the smallest burial ground or to conduct Jewish religious services. Between 1870 and 1890, Jewish peddlers, storekeepers, and factory workers from New York City began establishing themselves in the principal trading villages— Lindenhurst, Sag Harbor, Greenport, Riverhead, Southampton, Jericho, Lynbrook, Hempstead, Bay Shore, Babylon, Rockville Centre, Glen Cove, and Port Washington. Simultaneously, well-to-do Jews from Brooklyn and New York started coming to Long Island for summer ocean breezes. Some of the latter acquired substantial estates which were later converted into parks. Belmont State Park was once the estate and horse farm of August Belmont, Jewish-born banker, diplomat, and one of the founders of American horse racing. The Guggenheims, Schiffs, and Kahns also built Long Island mansions. Some of the vacationers who became permanent residents joined forces with the resident Jewish merchants to establish the first Jewish communities east of the New York City line.

Adolph Levy, an immigrant from Russia, began peddling among the clam diggers in the waterfront shacks from Baldwin to Massapequa in the late 1880s. He used to spend the nights in an old hotel in Seaford. Tired of walking, he made the hotel his base of operations and later bought it. There he played host to other traveling salesmen before moving to Freeport where he opened a men's clothing store at the turn of the century. His oldest son, David, was elected the first Jewish councilman on the Hempstead Town Board in the 1930s. Another son, George Morton Levy, became one of Nassau County's best known lawyers and founder of Roosevelt Raceway.

In the early 1880s, Harry Goldstein and his brother set up their peddling operation in an Eastport farmhouse. In 1885 Harry opened a little store in town. The Goldstein brothers and their sons also did business from a horse and wagon with the farmers from Riverhead to East Hampton, bringing new appliances as they came on the market. The Goldstein Department Store is still in business, but some of the third generation Goldsteins changed their name to Gerard. A second generation Goldstein, Lawrence, recalled how he and his brothers met the train from New York every Thursday because it brought a package of kosher meat bought by their grandmother in New York.

The first of these was probably in Lindenhurst in the 1870s when that village was still known as Breslau. The Jewish residents peddled in the nearby villages or worked in a local button factory. The families took turns going into New York by train and trolley to buy kosher meat. In 1875 these early Lindenhurst Jews opened a synagogue and built a *mikveh*. This settlement did not endure; the present Lindenhurst Jewish community dates from 1912.

The oldest Jewish community in continuous existence is in Sag Harbor where the United Hebrew Brethren was organized in 1883. The death of a child in 1889 and the lack of a local burial place led to the formation of the Hebrew Cemetery Association out of which evolved Temple Adas Israel, Long Island's oldest congregation. A synagogue was erected in 1898 when the congregation had 50 members. A quarrel between Russian and Hungarian Jews led the latter to form their own congregation and to acquire their own cemetery. The dissidents came back in 1918 and together established Temple Adas Israel. The two cemeteries, however, still exist side by side just off the highway between Sag Harbor and East Hampton, separated only by an iron railing. "Schmerel" Heller, the first *shochet* in Suffolk County, ran a boarding house for peddlers. Morris Simon, the cantor of the congregation, sold tea and coffee in Heller's home, and later opened a crockery store before moving to Patchogue. Among the early Jewish families in Sag Harbor were the Spodicks, Max Ollswang, the Eisenbergs, Morris Meyer, T. Thomashefsky, of the famed family of Yiddish actors, Sam Rosenberg, and a German Jew who was the village policeman. Eisenberg opened the village's kosher butcher shop. "Schmerel" Heller was the congregation's fundraiser who went to New York City to raise money for the first synagogue building and came back with a donation from Jacob H. Schiff. Many of the first Jewish settlers in Sag Habor were brought there by Joseph Fahy, a non-Jewish manufacturer who imported 40 to 50 Jewish families directly from the Castle Garden immigrant station for work in his watchcase factory.

Congregation Tifereth Israel in Glen Cove and the United Hebrew Benevolent Society in Bay Shore were both founded in 1897. The Glen Cove congregation met in private homes until 1900 when it bought a building known as the "opera house," which it used as a synagogue until 1925 when its present sanctuary was dedicated. This is the synagogue that has served as the focal point for demonstrations, sit-ins, and pray-ins at the nearby Soviet residential compound. The North Shore Jewish Center, located in Port Jefferson Station since the 1970s, was established in East Setauket in 1893. Greenport held worship services in the 1890s in the home of Fannie Levine and Congregation Tifereth Israel was founded there in 1900 and a synagogue was opened in 1904 under the leadership of Nathan Kaplan, for whom one of the village's principal thoroughfares is named.

Barnett Salke, a Civil War veteran who came to Hempstead in the 1870s, was one of the group that joined Dr. Adolph Rosenthal in 1901 in an unsuccessful attempt to establish a congregation there. Failing in that, the town's Jewish merchants, like their contemporaries all over Long Island, traveled to New York or Brooklyn for the High Holy days. Mrs. Lester Appel, who was born in Hempstead in the late 1890s, a decade after her parents settled there, recalled that they had owned the village's first hotel, known as Roth's Hotel, a popular gathering place for Long Island society. The general store opened by Isaac Jacobson in Lynbrook in 1896 was closed by his daughter-in-law in 1971. He had been a peddler in the area since 1891. Sam Patiky, whose parents, Jennie and Elias, settled in Kings Park in the late 1890s and opened a small department store, was one of the founders of the Kings Park Jewish Center.

There were Jews in Huntington in 1900 and they organized a *minyan* in the home of William Teich. The first High Holy day services were held in an old fire house on Main Street, where Isaac Levenbron was fire chief. Eight men founded the Brotherhood of Jewish Men in Huntington in 1906 which became the Huntington Hebrew Center a year later. A cemetery was opened in 1908 and the first synagogue was dedicated in 1911 on Church Street. It drew members from Northport, Kings Park, and other nearby communities who stayed with local families for the holidays so they could walk to synagogue. Rabbi Mayer Israel Herman, who came to Huntington in 1930, is believed to have been the first ordained rabbi to officiate in Suffolk County. Prior to World War I, there were also synagogues in Patchogue (1903), Rockville Centre (1907), Hempstead (1908), Riverhead (1911), Great Neck, (1912), and Lindenhurst (1912). Long Beach, Cedarhurst, and Lawrence, to which Jews first came as summer residents, had no permanent congregation until the 1920s. Temple Israel, Lawrence's oldest synagogue, moved from Far Rockaway in 1930.

A few of the first 20th century Jewish settlers came originally as farmers. In 1905, the Jewish Agricultural Society opened a test farm at Kings Park, where 60 Jewish immigrants learned elementary agricultural skills. Some of these students later became farmers at Farmingdale, Riverhead, Center Moriches, Calverton and East Islip. In the 1970s, there were still a number of Suffolk Jews engaged in dairy and poultry farming and tobacco growing as well as some who handled farm produce on a wholesale basis. Harry B. Goldstein of East Islip was in the dairy and cattle business for 55 years. Great Neck, where some 60 percent of the 43,000 residents of the seven villages included in the general area are Jewish, traces its Jewish beginnings to Avram Wolf, a tailor. He was brought from New York in 1875 by W. R. Grace, the shipping magnate, because he wanted his tailor close by. Wolf later went into the real estate and insurance business. Because the Great Neck Playhouse, now a movie theatre, was a major theatrical tryout house in the 1920s, many stage celebrities made their homes there, among them Eddie Cantor and Groucho Marx. Some of the Great Neck villages openly barred Jewish homeowners until the 1930s. Kings Point, Great Neck's wealthy suburb, has a substantial Jewish population.

World War I introduced large numbers of Jews to Long Island for the first time and provided some of them with a reason for moving there. It was at Camps Yaphank and Upton, both near Patchogue, that thousands of Jewish draftees from the New York area received their military training in 1917 and 1918. Tired of the long weekend visiting trip to Patchogue, some of the draftees' families settled down in nearby towns for the duration. Many became permanent residents, as did numbers of the returning Jewish doughboys who recalled the pleasant homes and business opportunities they had seen on Long Island.

Meanwhile, permanent Jewish communities were growing up in Long Beach, when summer residents decided to stay permanently, and in Great Neck and the Five Towns, where successful Broadway personalities, wealthy garment manufacturers, and other businessmen built lavish homes. One of the latter was Charles A. Levine, "the flying junkman from Brooklyn," who invested part of the fortune he had made in salvaging World War I equipment in financing Clarence Chamberlain's nonstop flight from Roosevelt Field on Long Island to Germany in 1927. Flying with Chamberlain, Levine was the first transAtlantic airplane passenger. Dr. Henry

Walden, a Jewish dentist who designed and piloted the first American monoplane, flew it from Mineola in 1909.

Long before there was the "miracle mile" shopping area on the Manhasset segment of Northern Boulevard, Jaffe's department store was a North Shore landmark. Benjamin Jaffe, who came to Manhasset in the early 1890s, opened branch stores in Glen Cove, Locust Valley, and Valley Stream. His grandsons operated the business until 1975 when it closed. In 1920 a Zionist group was founded in Greenport, a forerunner of the present Eastern Suffolk Zionist District. Four years later, Israel Kramer bought a tract of land in West Babylon with the intention of establishing a Zionist colony there. He placed ads in all the Yiddish newspapers and rented buses to take prospects from the Lindenhurst station of the Long Island Railroad to the property. But there were no buyers. Ezra Park, the name given to the area by Kramer, is now populated largely by people of Italian origin, but the neighborhood's main street is called Herzel (sic) Boulevard. One of the first post-World War II synagogues on Long Island was erected in Riverhead in 1947. There had been a congregation called Beth Haknesses Anshe Riverhead for a number of years and in 1924, as Temple Israel, it built a one-room synagogue. During the war, when Rabbi Simon Reznikoff, now of Temple Gates of Prayer, Valley Stream, was a chaplain at the Suffolk County Army Air Field in Westhampton, he encouraged the community to plan for a new building.

After World War II, thousands of returning veterans from New York City began the mass Jewish movement to the suburbs. Attracted by the low-cost one-family houses on Long Island that sprang up like mushrooms in huge developments, young Jewish families of limited means poured into Nassau County. It was William J. Levitt and his sons who started to change the face of Long Island from potato farms to large scale housing. The Levitts built houses on belt lines, like ships and planes had been built during the war. The day the Levitts' sales office opened on March 7, 1949, there were more than 1,000 couples waiting in line. Some had been there three or four days and nights, living on coffee and doughnuts. When the doors opened, it was like the Oklahoma land rush of 1889, so eager were the young married couples to be among the first to buy one of the basic four-room houses for $6,990 or to rent one at $60 a month. Many of the buyers were Jews. A makeshift synagogue was opened in an abandoned airplane hangar. Land for Levittown's Israel Community Center was donated by the Levitts but its members did much of the work involved in the building. Ultimately, the Levitts built 18,000 single-family houses on 4,000 acres.

As new housing developments opened up, Jewish families became the first settlers in many of them, creating instant Jewish communities overnight or greatly enlarging older settlements. A second wave of Jewish migration from New York in the early 1950s carried the Jewish population to the North Shore, the far edges of Nassau County, and into the western part of Suffolk County. In 1952 there were only nine Jewish congregations in

Suffolk County. By 1963 there were 20, as Jewish settlements reached Montauk Point, the most eastern tip of Long Island.

As Jewish families climbed the success ladder, many of them began to leave the smaller, mass-designed houses in Levittown, Hicksville, Valley Stream, and East Meadow for more expensive individually-built homes on the North Shore and the Five Towns. In Levittown, where the total population was 65,000 in the 1970s, only 11,000 were Jews, and only 11 percent of these were affiliated with the local synagogue. Growth continued in newer areas of Nassau and Suffolk Counties until the mid-1960s as newcomers from New York bought the older houses or pushed on to the newer developments.

By the 1960s a new trend set in. Nassau County had run out of land for large scale housing developments but garden and cooperative apartments were beginning to sprout. Older families that had roots on Long Island and preferred to stay in the suburbs eagerly became renters once again. The concept of an apartment in the sun in the beach areas also attracted former Jewish homeowners to the new high rise apartments in Long Beach and to cooperative residences that went up in the larger villages. At the same time, communities that were once heavily Jewish became less so. Rockville Centre, which developed into a major Catholic community when it became the diocesan headquarters of a bishop, lost Jewish population. Other communities have had similar experiences. As Jewish families with grown children departed for the city, suburban apartments, or Florida and Arizona, and were replaced by non-Jews, synagogue membership on Long Island, once numbering 80 percent of the total Jewish population, began to fall off. Massive declines in elementary and secondary school enrollments were matched by a falling off in the number of students in Jewish religious schools.

The postwar influx of Jews had touched off a massive boom in synagogue construction. At first the newer congregations formed in every town and village met in fire houses, schools, churches, Masonic halls, and even stores. Most of the older Orthodox congregations changed to Conservative and Reform and almost none of the new congregations founded in the 1950s were Orthodox. In the 1960s and 1970s, however, a number of Young Israel congregations came into being. In 1963 there were 109 congregations in Nassau County, all with full-time rabbis and their own buildings, many with substantial school buildings and recreational facilities as well, and 20 in Suffolk County. In the 1970s there were 130 in Nassau County and 32 in Suffolk County, including one each at Fire Island and Mastic Beach. Synagogue membership, however, began to decline in the 1970s. Enrollment in Jewish schools, which had almost tripled to 40,460 between 1945 and 1968, experienced an 8 percent decline in the early 1970s and further declines were expected before the end of the decade. The biggest decline was in the one-day-a-week schools whose enrollment dropped from 20,000 to 14,700, reflecting a steady shrinkage in Long Island's school age population and the falling Jewish birthrate. Enrollment in Hebrew day schools rose from 1,050 to 2,600 and the number of such schools increased to 11. The Hebrew Academy of Nassau County, founded in 1953, was the first Long Island Hebrew day school.

In other phases of communal life, the Jews of Nassau and Suffolk Counties are closely tied to New York City. The Joint Campaign of the United Jewish Appeal and Federation of Jewish Philanthropies and the New York-based national Jewish organizations conduct intensive drives on Long Island and reach out there for leadership. There are several hundred branches on Long Island of the various national Jewish organizations, a Long Island Board of Rabbis, a Long Island Rabbinical Council (Orthodox), a Long Island branch of the teachers' institute of Hebrew Union College-Jewish Institute of Religion, a Long Island Committee for Soviet Jewry, a public affairs council of Reform synagogues, and Long Island councils of local units of national Jewish organizations. The United Jewish Ys of Long Island promote support for the five existing YM-YWHAs in Nassau County and encourage the establishment of new ones. There are a number of local and regional Jewish Community Councils.

The Federation of Jewish Philanthropies, of which the five Ys and the United Jewish Ys are beneficiaries, also maintains Long Island offices of its Jewish Association for Service to the Aged and Jewish Community Services, and Federation Employment and Guidance Service. The Board of Jewish Education serves over 100 religious schools on Long Island. Federation conducts a day camp for Long Island and New York YMHAs at the Henry Kaufmann Campgrounds and sponsors the Usdan Center for Creative and Performing Arts, both at Wyandanch. There is a Long Island Division of Federation's Commission on Synagogue Relations. The Long Island Jewish-Hillside Medical Center and its affiliated Jewish Institute for Geriatric Care are also Federation affiliates. In West Hempstead, the Orthodox Jews have created an eruv, an enclave of strung wires that permits Sabbath-observing Jews to engage in a variety of activities within its boundaries that they would not otherwise be permitted on the Sabbath, except in their own homes. A plan of the Long Island Jewish Hospital-Medical Center to move its South Shore Division, the former St. Joseph's Hospital, from Far Rockaway in New York City, to Lawrence, in Nassau County, ran into strong opposition from the residents of Lawrence and the plan was dropped. Efforts of Far Rockaway's Temple Shaaray Zedek, an Orthodox congregation, to move across the city line into Lawrence were balked by the opposition of Lawrence residents, many of them Jews.

Kosher butchers are easy to find on Long Island. Newsday, the Long Island Daily founded by the late Alicia Patterson and her late husband, Harry Guggenheim, carries numerous ads for the fundraising bazaars conducted by synagogues and Jewish women's organizations throughout Long Island. Chanukah menorahs in banks and at shopping malls, Chanukah greetings in Long Island Railroad stations, public libraries, and Chanukah clubs in banks are commonplace. The Nassau County Police have enough

Jews to warrant an organization called Magen (shield), with a rabbi as its chaplain. A number of Jewish organizations provide volunteers for social, recreational, and religious programs for Jewish patients at some of Long Island's 76 nursing homes.

In some Long Island communities zoning ordinances were invoked in futile efforts to bar the construction of synagogues. In some villages it took Jews quite a while to break through unwritten restrictions and narrowly interpreted zoning regulations. Some of this opposition was a carry-over from the days when Long Island was a hotbed of anti-Semitic feeling and Ku Klux Klan activity. During the 1940s and early 1950s, synagogue building sites were regularly desecrated by anti-Semitic vandals. As late as 1975, a new congregation in Seaford encountered difficulty in its effort to establish a synagogue because of zoning regulations. Anti-Semitic incidents in the schools were reported periodically to the Long Island offices of the Anti-Defamation League, American Jewish Committee, and American Jewish Congress.

When A. T. Stewart, the department store magnate, laid out Garden City in 1869 as a model village, he specifically barred Jews from buying homes there, but this ban has long since been lifted. As recently as 1915, Long Beach, now about 40 percent Jewish, had clubs and hotels that refused to admit Jews. Virtually none of the golf, country, and yachting clubs on Long Island used to admit Jews. In 1971 there were 60 such clubs for non-Jews, 20 for Jews, and one had a 50-50 membership. Long Island's leading yacht club, which always excluded Jews, changed its policy just in time to enable its first Jewish member to pilot the yacht that carried the United States to victory in the 1962 America Cup race with Great Britain. In the 1970s some Jewish merchants fell afoul of old Sunday closing laws when they kept their establishments open on Sunday to test the validity of the laws.

Coming largely from all-Jewish neighborhoods in New York City, the postwar Jewish settlers on Long Island found their first social contacts with Jewish neighbors or in the activities of synagogues and other Jewish organizations. Gradually, the Jewish residents developed relationships with non-Jews through PTAs, scouting, volunteer fire departments, public libraries, chambers of commerce, youth organizations, civic associations, and common concern with neighborhood improvements and rising taxes.

In the 1950s and 1960s, there was a good deal of excitement in some communities over the display of Christological symbols in public places, Christmas observances, and Bible reading in the schools. While Jews were in the vanguard of Long Island's struggle over school and housing integration, many resisted it. They had left New York City for the suburbs because their old neighborhoods were in or near the edge of growing black and Puerto Rican communities. The South Shore village of Roosevelt lost its entire Jewish population when it became 95 percent black in the late 1960s. Some Jewish businessmen and professionals remain but the Jewish Center was sold and the proceeds used to buy life memberships in other synagogues for the older members. In Freeport, also on the South Shore, where Jews constitute 10 percent of the 41,000 residents, Congregation B'nai Israel, oldest of the village's two synagogues, took the lead in a campaign to encourage Jews to move to Freeport. The synagogue membership raised a special fund to underwrite the effort which included a home-finding service to stem a Jewish exodus as the village's black population increased.

The Jewish Association for Service to the Aged reported in the 1970s that there were some 30,000 Jewish aged on Long Island, including 4,500 Jewish poor in Long Beach. JASA operates the Brookdale JASA Senior Citizens Center at Temple Beth El, Long Beach, and is engaged in a variety of projects for the Jewish aged. Long Island's first golden age club was founded in 1950 in the Five Towns by the Peninsula Section of the National Council of Jewish Women.

While most of the postwar Jewish settlers on Long Island earned their livelihoods in New York City, a substantial change developed in the 1950s and 1960s when a growing number of Long Island Jews went into business on the island as retailers, manufacturers of electronic components, and plastics; as store managers in the newly opened department store branches and retail shops that filled the massive new shopping centers. Others were employed at Brookhaven National Laboratories, as engineers, technicians, scientists, and aerospace specialists in the aviation plants. They became owners or executives in the printing, industrial, chemical, and pharmaceutical plants that dot Nassau and Suffolk Counties. Many were engaged in the expanding service industries required to meet the growing needs of more than 2,500,000 people, in the professions, and in public service as employees of the county, state, and Federal governments. Jews were well represented on the faculties of the state and private universities in Nassau and Suffolk Counties. The network of parkways, expressways, public parks, and beaches that made Long Island attractive to home owners, businessmen, and vacationers is a monument to the vision of Robert Moses, for years president of the Long Island State Park Commission.

The more than 30-fold increase in the Jewish population since the 1930s made Jewish voters a political factor for the first time on Long Island. Prior to 1940, Jewish officeholders on any level were rare. Cedarhurst had Jewish mayors from 1928-1937, and Long Beach elected four Jewish mayors between 1929 and 1941. Glen Cove had a Jewish mayor, and Morton Stein was mayor of Malverne in 1963. Several of the Great Neck and Five Towns villages also had Jewish mayors. At first the city-bred Jews who were expected to reduce the overwhelmingly Republican majorities disappointed the Democrats by voting as their new neighbors did. But since the 1950s the margin between Republicans and Democrats has been narrowing, largely because of new Jewish voters from New York.

Election of Jews to village boards of trustees and school boards has become fairly widespread. A number of villages have had Jewish presidents of school boards and boards of trustees. There have been quite a few Jewish county judges in both Nassau and Suffolk Counties. Nearly a fourth of the State Supreme Court Justices on Long Island were Jews in the 1970s including one woman. Two Jewish women served as county judges in Nassau. Two Jews served as district attorneys in Nassau. Three Jews have been elected to Congress from Nassau County, Herbert Tenzer, Allard Lowenstein, and Lester Wolff, who was in Congress in 1976. When Suffolk County adopted the county legislature form of government, one of the members elected was Jewish. The first woman elected to the State Senate from Long Island was a Jew. Three Jews have served as head of the Nassau County Democratic Committee. Sol Wachtler, now a justice of the State Court of Appeals, lost a close race as the Republican candidate for Nassau County Executive. Norman Blackman, a retired real estate developer, who ran unsuccessfully for County Executive in 1973 as an independent, is the founder of Aware, a watchdog agency that keeps an eye on political wrong doing.

Highly civic-minded, Long Island's Jews are in the vanguard of many island-wide cultural and educational enterprises. Jews serve on the boards of trustees of Hofstra and Adelphi Universities; a Jew was president of the Nassau-Suffolk YMCA; George Morton Levy, a prominent attorney who grew up in Freeport, was the chief developer of Roosevelt Raceway. Leo Kopelman is the director of the Nassau-Suffolk Regional Planning Board. Robert Bernstein is chairman of the Association of Nassau County Art Organizations, and Martin Drewitz is director of the Long Island Youth Orchestra. Seymour Lipkin has been conductor of the Long Island Symphony since 1963, and Oscar Chudinowsky has operated, since 1929, Oscar's Literary Emporium in Huntington, the island's largest book store. Three Jews served on the panel of 19 civic leaders that created the design for a Nassau County legislature. David Laventhol is editor of *Newsday*, Long Island's influential daily paper. When *Newsday* drew up a list of the 50 people who run Long Island, it included ten Jews prominent in real estate, law, politics, city planning, and social service.

*****

AMITYVILLE

Beth Sholom Center of Amityville and the Massapequas, 79 County Line Rd.

Temple Sinai (see Massapequa).

ATLANTIC BEACH

Jewish Center of Atlantic Beach, 100 Nassau Ave. and Park St., is the only Jewish institution in this suburban village between Long Beach and Far Rockaway, which has a Jewish population of about 1,000, half of the 2,000 year-round residents. During the summer the village caters to tens of thousands who come to the local beach clubs.

BABYLON

Belmont Lake State Park, one of the largest of the L.I. state parks, covers about a third of what was once the country estate and horse farm of August Belmont, Jewish-born banker, diplomat, and one of the founders of American horse racing. Born in Germany in 1816, Belmont was first employed by the House of Rothschild in Frankfurt-am-Main, Germany, and later in Naples. He came to the U.S. in 1837 as an agent of the Rothschilds but soon established his own banking firm. A leader of and one of the financial supporters of the Democratic Party from 1844 on, Belmont was appointed U.S. chargé d'affaires at The Hague in 1853 by President Franklin Pierce. A year later he was promoted to the rank of minister-resident—probably the first Jew to hold this rank in the American diplomatic service. He served until 1857. During the Civil War, Belmont took a leading part in financing the war loans of the Federal government through his European banking connections. He also raised and equipped a regiment of German-born troops from New York. Although Belmont separated himself from the Jewish community, his Jewish origin was repeatedly used by anti-Semitic writers to attack him, especially in the Southern papers during the Civil War. From 1860-1884 Belmont was a member of the National Democratic Committee and served as its chairman for several years. Owner of a famous racing stable (Belmont Park in New York City's Borough of Queens is named for him), Belmont headed the American Jockey Club for many years. He married the daughter of Commodore Matthew C. Perry, who was responsible for opening Japan to the West. This marriage made Belmont a nephew of Commodore Oliver Hazard Perry, victor of the naval Battle of Lake Erie with the British in 1813. His marriage to a Christian gave rise to the rumor that he had been converted. There is no proof of this, although he is buried in a Christian cemetery in Newport, R.I. Some writers have said that Belmont's family name was originally Schoenberg and that Belmont is the Gallic form of Schoenberg. Belmont's oldest son, Perry, was twice elected to Congress from the town of Babylon, the only person sent to Congress from that part of New York up to 1953.

Cong. Beth Sholom, 441 Deer Park Ave.

Robert Moses State Park is named for Robert F. Moses, creator of Long Island's network of parks and connecting parkways. As president of the Long Island State Park Commission, Moses was responsible for acquiring the sites for every one of Long Island's state parks and for converting them into beautiful recreation spots. Moses was also president of the 1939 New York World's Fair. He masterminded New York City's network of new bridges, parkways, tunnels, shorefront parks, and initiated and supervised the development of Jones Beach. Descended from an old Sephardic family, Moses was secretary of state of New York in 1927 and the losing Republican candidate for governor in 1934 when he was defeated by Herbert H. Lehman.

Babylon was once proposed as the site of a Zionist training colony. In

1924, Israel Kramer bought a large tract in West Babylon with the intention of forming a Zionist colony there. This effort proved unsuccessful. Later, Kramer built one-family houses in the area which he named Ezra Park. The wide main street of the development has a sign that reads, "Herzel (sic) Boulevard."

BALDWIN
Baldwin Jewish Centre, 885 East Seaman Ave.
South Baldwin Jewish Center, 2959 Grand Ave.
South Shore YM & YWHA, 806 Merrick Rd.

BAY SHORE
Jewish Center, 34 N. Clinton St.
Sinai Reform Temple, 39 Brentwood Rd.

BELLMORE
Bellmore Jewish Center, 2550 S. Centre Ave.
East Bay Reform Temple, 2569 Merrick Rd.
Temple Beth-El, 1373 Bellmore Rd. (North Bellmore).

BETHPAGE
Hebrew Academy of Nassau County, 42 Locust Ave.
Jewish Center, 600 Broadway.
Society of Jewish Science, Round Swamp Rd. and Claremont Ave., has an unusual Torah inscribed in 1791 and used by Jews in Asiatic Russia. The Torah is enclosed in an elaborate silver and wood case. It is of Oriental origin and came originally from Bokhara in central Russia. It is made of leather rather than the usual parchment and uses a type of Oriental script. The society's services are similar to those held by the Society of Jewish Science in Manhattan. Services are held Friday evening and Saturday morning.

BRENTWOOD
Jewish Center, 28 Sixth Ave.

BROOKVILLE
Benjamin Abrams Communication Center, C.W. Post College of Long Island University, Northern Blvd., is named for the president of the Emerson Radio and Phonograph Corp., a trustee of the university.
Charles and Gertrude Merinoff Center of Association for the Help of Retarded Children, 189 Wheatly Rd., honors a husband and wife team that made many important contributions to the Nassau County chapter of the association.

CEDARHURST

Abraham Adelberg Monument, in the village park facing Cedarhurst Ave., near the L. I. Railroad station, is a memorial to the man who was one of the developers of the village and its mayor from 1928 until his death in 1932. Erected by public subscription, the monument is a large boulder to which is affixed a bas-relief portrait of Adelberg and the inscription: "To the memory of a beloved citizen unselfish in his devotion to community betterment."

Sephardic Temple, Branch Blvd.

Temple Beth El United Community Center, Broadway and Locust Ave.

Young Israel of Lawrence-Cedarhurst, 26 Columbia Ave.

CENTER MORICHES

Jewish Center of Moriches, Main St. This congregation is an outgrowth of a program of social and welfare services provided by Center Moriches residents to GIs from Camp Upton and the East Moriches Coast Guard Station from 1939 until the end of World War II. Leaders of this service established a men's club after the war and this became the nucleus of the congregation.

CENTRAL ISLIP

Temple Etz Chayim, 312 E. Suffolk Ave.

COLD SPRING HARBOR

Kehillath Sholom, 58 Goose Hill Rd.

COMMACK

Jewish Center, 83 Shirley Ct.

Temple Beth David, 100 Hauppauge Rd.

DEER PARK

Suffolk Jewish Center, 330 Central Ave.

DIX HILLS

Jewish Center, Deer Park Ave., has in its sanctuary a ceiling whose beams are interlaced to form Stars of David.

I. L. Peretz School, Timburr Lane Day School, Burr's Lane.

Temple Beth Torah, 158 Carman Rd.

EAST HAMPTON

Home, Sweet Home Museum, on the east side of the village green next to the church, was the birthplace, in 1791, of John Howard Payne, author of the words to the famed song, *Home, Sweet Home*, and grandson of Aaron Isaacs, one of the first Jewish settlers on Long Island. Some of the property Isaacs once owned is now part of the extensive lands in East Hampton owned by Evan Manning Frankel, a product of New York's Lower East Side, who retired as a millionaire in 1952 and settled down in East Hampton. In 1975 he was said to own more than 1,000 acres of choice residential property in addition to his 15-acre estate, Brigadoon.

Jewish Center of the Hamptons, 44 Woods Lane.

EAST HILLS
Traditional Cong. of Roslyn-Kehilath Masoret.

EAST MEADOW
East Meadow Jewish Center, 1400 Prospect Ave.

Israel Grove, in the Carillon area of Eisenhower Park, a stand of 27 trees, one for each year of Israel's existence and one as a memorial to those who fell in her defense, was dedicated in 1974 by David Rivlin, Israel Consul General in New York.

Long Island Advisory Board of Anti-Defamation League of B'nai B'rith, 2310 Hempstead Tpke.

Memorial to the 6,000,000, a marble block set in stone in the lake area of Eisenhower Park, honors those murdered by the Nazis. Affixed to the block is a bronze tablet inscribed, "a living remembrance to the Six Million Jews." The memorial was originally dedicated in 1968 by Temple Beth El, Bellmore; Bellmore Jewish Center; Merrick Jewish Center; Cong. B'nai Israel, Freeport; South Baldwin Jewish Center; and Wantagh Jewish Center. It was rededicated in 1973 on the 30th anniversary of the Warsaw Ghetto Uprising, together with a memorial tree.

I. L. Peretz Jewish School, 574 Newbridge Ave.

Suburban Park Jewish Center, 400 Old Westbury Rd.

Temple Emanu-El, 123 Merrick Ave.

EAST NORTHPORT
East Northport Jewish Center, 328 Elwood Rd., has a sanctuary covered by an airy A-framed roof, representing the tent used by ancient Hebrews.

EAST ROCKAWAY
Hewlett-East Rockaway Jewish Center, 295 Main St., has in its main lobby a Holocaust memorial depicting the burning bush with six pointed flames symbolizing the 6 million martyrs. The flames are of various sizes to symbolize children, adults, and the elderly, and the contorted shapes recall the tortuous experience of these victims.

ELMONT
Belmont Park, the famous race track opened in 1905, is named for

August Belmont, Jewish-born horse breeder, diplomat, and banker.
Jewish Center, 500 Elmont Rd. and Cerenzia Blvd., has five stained glass windows depicting the First Five Books of Moses.
Temple B'nai Israel, Elmont Rd. and Baylis Ave.

FARMINGDALE
Jewish Center, 425 Fulton St., has a 25 by 17 foot mural composed of two dozen separate panels dominated by a painting of Moses and the burning bush. Two inscriptions in Hebrew frame the painting—"Thou shalt love thy God and "Love thy neighbor as thyself." Depicted in the mural are the signs of zodiac, major Jewish Holy days, and the names of the 12 tribes of Israel.

FIRE ISLAND
Fire Island Synagogue, Midway and C Street., Seaview, was founded by Herman Wouk, the author, and Joseph S. Gershman.
Robert F. Moses Beach is named for the man who conceived the idea of developing the South Shore barrier beaches off Long Island. The bridge over Fire Island Inlet is also named for him.

FLORAL PARK
Bellerose Jewish Center, 254-04 Union Turnpike.
Floral Park Jewish Center, 26 N. Tyson Ave.
Temple Sholom, 263-10 Union Turnpike.

FRANKLIN SQUARE
Central Nassau YM & YWHA, 276 Franklin Ave.
Jewish Center, Pacific and Lloyd Sts.

FREEPORT
Cong. B'nai Israel, 91 N. Bayview Ave.
Union Reform Temple, 475 N. Brookside Ave.

GARDEN CITY
Hillel Foundation at Adelphi University, Religious Center, South Ave.
Jewish Center, 168 Nassau Blvd.

GLEN COVE
Cong. Tifereth Israel, Hill Dr. and Landing Rd., is one of the oldest congregations on Long Island, having been founded in 1897.
Denis Park, at foot of Town Path, Glen St., now called Heritage Park, flies the flag of every nation represented by descendants of immigrants in the

very ethnic city of Glen Cove, including the flag of Israel.
North Country Reform Temple, Crescent Beach Rd.

GREAT NECK
American Jewish Congress, North Shore Division, 98 Cutter Mill Rd.
Cong. Shomrei Hadat, 558 Middle Neck Rd.
Great Neck Synagogue, 26 Old Mill Rd.
North Shore Hebrew Academy, 26 Old Mill Rd.
Reconstructionist Synagogue, 2 Park Circle.
Temple Beth El, 5 Old Mill Rd., is the oldest of the eight synagogues in Great Neck, which has one of the largest Jewish communities on Long Island. Of the 44,000 people who reside in the nine incorporated villages (Great Neck, Great Neck Estates, Great Neck Plaza, Kensington, Kings Point, Lake Success, Russell Gardens, Saddle Rock, and Thomaston) and a small unincorporated area that make up what is generally known as Great Neck, 60 percent are Jewish. Beth El has a stunning stark white bimah, wall, and ark created by sculptress Louise Nevelson, a symbolic portrayal of a white flame to memorialize the 6,000,000 Jewish victims of the Holocaust. The nonobjective sculpture, consisting of white boxes of wood that break up light and shadow, is 55 feet wide and 15 feet high, and includes a design for the Ark and the Eternal Light. Eight of the Torahs in the Ark are dressed in handsewn mantles designed by Mrs. Ina Golub, and produced by a committee of 20 women. The mantles use word concepts rather than representative design. The words depicted are: *tzedakah*, light; *chesed*, loving kindness; *mishpat*, justice; *kedusha*, holiness; *shalom*, peace; *simcha*, joy; and *emet*, truth. Beth El has an excellent collection of Hebraic art and ceremonial objects. Among the latter is a Vienna brass Menorah which was smuggled out of Austria during the Nazi era by refugees. The huge synagogue doors depict a profusion of Biblical themes in 36 panels wrought in silver, 18 on each side.
Temple Beth Joseph, 1 Linden Pl.
Temple Emanuel, 150 Hicks Lane.
Temple Isaiah, 35 Bond St.
Temple Israel, 108 Old Mill Rd. A glass-enclosed corridor linking old and new buildings serves as a museum. One wall displays ancient Judaic relics and artifacts from Jewish communities of the past.

GREENPORT
Kaplan Avenue is named for Nathan Kaplan, an early settler here.
Temple Tifereth Israel, 4th St.

GREENVALE
B. Davis Schwartz Memorial Library of the C. W. Post Center of Long Island University, Greenvale Campus, is named for a benefactor of the college and former trustee, who was active in a variety of Jewish causes. The

NASSAU AND SUFFOLK COUNTIES — 248

$6 million structure has a capacity of one million volumes. The library houses the Cassirer Collection of Minerals, contributed by Fred Cassirer, a world-famous German-born mineralogist. The college's Interfaith Chapel, a $1.2 million structure, is one of two such chapels on Long Island, the other being at the U. S. Merchant Marine Academy at Kings Point.

HAUPPAUGE
Hebrew Academy of Suffolk, 525 Veteran's Memorial Highway, has a 20-foot Menorah in front of its building. The Rabbi Joseph Lief Library is a memorial to the late Jewish chaplain at the Veterans Administration Hospital at Northport.

Temple Beth Chai, Townline Rd.

HEMPSTEAD
American Jewish Committee, Long Island Chapter, 134 Jackson St.

Cong. Beth Israel, 94 Fulton Ave.

Hillel Foundation at Hofstra University, 100 Fulton St., has a tree outside its main door planted in memory of President Harry S. Truman in a *Tu Beshvat* ceremony.

Jewish Community Services of Long Island, 50 Clinton St.

George Morton Levy, Sr., Law Library at Hofstra University Law School, is named for the prominent attorney, and president and founder of Roosevelt Raceway.

Long Island Jewish Week, 156 N. Franklin St.

Paul Radin Memorial, a bas relief portrait of the famed anthropologist, is in the Hofstra University Library's Paul Radin Collection of 5,500 items that include Radin's own writings and those of Dr. Franz Boas, under whom he studied. The 9th floor of the Library is the David Filderman Gallery of Art.

Howard L. and Muriel Weingrow Fine Arts Library, which occupies one floor of the Hofstra University Library, on Hempstead Turnpike, is a major research collection of 4,000 books, documents, manuscripts, graphics, and prints relating to the foundations of modern art movements. Weingrow, who bought the collection from Philip Kaplan, has been a trustee of Hofstra University, an advisor to President Lyndon Johnson in the Office of Economic Opportunity, and served as treasurer of the Democratic National Committee in 1972.

HEWLETT
American Jewish Congress, South Shore Division, 301 Mill Rd.

Cong. Beth Emeth, 36 Franklin Ave.

Yeshiva Toras Chaim, 1170 William St.

HICKSVILLE

Theodore S. Cinnamon Ltd., 420 Jerusalem Ave., is a Judaica bookseller and publisher.

Cong. Shaarei Zedek, New South Rd. and Old Country Rd.

"Gates of Paradise," massive bronze doors whose ten panels depict famous episodes from the Hebrew Bible, are the entrance to Trinity Evangelical Lutheran Church, 40 West Nicholai St. They are exact replicas of the famed doors which Lorenzo Ghiberti fashioned in the early 1400s in Florence, Italy, for the Baptistery of the Cathedral of San Giovanni Battista. During World War II, sculptor Bruno Bearzi of Florence removed the famous sculptures to conceal them from the Nazis. While they were in his possession, he made molds from them—the molds from which he later cast the Hicksville replicas. The scenes depicted are Creation, Cain and Abel, Noah and the Ark, Abraham, Isaac and Jacob, Joseph, Moses on the way up Mt. Sinai, Joshua crossing the Jordan, David slaying Goliath, and Solomon welcoming the Queen of Sheba.

Jewish Center, Maglie Dr. and Jerusalem Ave.

Jewish Community Services of Long Island, 76 N. Broadway.

Pioneer Women, Nassau-Suffolk Council, 386 Oyster Bay Rd.

Temple Beth Elohim, RFD 1.

HUNTINGTON

Church St. is said to have acquired its name from the fact that the town's first synagogue was built at 11A Church St. Shorn of any Jewish symbolism, this building still stands as an apartment dwelling.

Dix Hills Jewish Center, 900 Walt Whitman Rd.

Huntington Jewish Center, 510 Park Ave. A chapel dedicated in 1976 memorializes the late Rabbi Joseph H. Lief, the Jewish chaplain at the Northport Veterans Administration Hospital, who led the daily *minyan* at the Center for many years.

Mt. Golda is one of the oldest Jewish cemeteries on Long Island.

Temple Beth El, 660 Park Ave.

HUNTINGTON STATION

Sholem Aleichem Folk Shule, Lincoln School, East 9th St.

South Huntington Jewish Center, 2600 New York Ave.

Temple Beth Torah, 660 Park Ave.

INWOOD

Jewish Community Center, Bayswater Blvd. and Elm Rd.

ISLAND PARK

Cong. Beth Emeth Jewish Center, 191 Long Beach Rd.

JERICHO
Jewish Center, North Broadway and Jericho Rd. Its building is said to have been the first religious structure erected by any faith in Jericho since 1788. There is a seating area for 1,500 people.
Temple Or-Elohim, 18 Tobie Lane.
Women's American ORT, North Shore Division, 50 Jericho Tpke.

JONES BEACH
Sidney Shapiro Memorial, in the Jones Beach Theatre, Gate D lobby, is a bronze plaque honoring the late chief engineer and general manager of the Long Island State Park Commission, who designed and built Jones Beach State Park and other parks, parkways, and bridges during a 46-year career with the commission.

KINGS PARK
Jewish Center, Route 25A, East Main St.
Patiky Street is named for the late Sam Patiky, his father and brothers, who settled on a farm in nearby Elwood at the turn of the century. The Patikys were founders of the Jewish Brotherhood in 1907—the original name of the Jewish Center.

KINGS POINT
U.S. Merchant Marine Academy has an interfaith chapel where Jewish services are held for Jewish cadets. The Torah was a gift of Chaplain and Mrs. Joshua L. Goldberg in 1962 on the centennial of the Jewish military chaplaincy.

LAKE GROVE
Markman's Center, 2842 Middle Country Rd., handles Judaica and Israeli gifts.

LAKE RONKONKOMA
Cong. Ohr Torah-Jewish Center, 821 Hawkins Ave. (Lake Grove).

LAKE SUCCESS
Jewish Center, 354 Lakeville Rd.

LAWRENCE
Brandeis School, 25 Frost Lane.
Cong. Beth Sholom, 390 Broadway.
Hillel School, 33 Washington Ave.
Temple Israel, 140 Central Ave., is a large synagogue shaped like a Magen David.

Temple Sinai, 131 Washington Ave., has a procession of stained glass windows in its sanctuary. The theme was inspired by the Biblical account of the Jews in the Sinai Desert.

The Source, 307 Central Ave., is a Judaica bookstore.

LEVITTOWN

This preplanned community of 60,000 was carved out of a stretch of potato fields, later renamed Levittown in honor of Abraham Levitt and his son, William, who built the town. When the Levitts opened the town's first section in 1947, returning veterans, desperate for housing, queued up in lines to rent the first 150 two-bedroom Cape Cods at $60 a month. Later the Levitts built more houses for rental or purchase—some selling as low as $6,990. By the end of 1951 there were 18,000 houses dotting the one-time potato fields.

Israel Community Center, 3235 Hempstead Tpke., the only Jewish institution in Levittown, stands on land donated by the Levitts. Construction began with much of the manual labor done by the members. There are 11,000 Jews in Levittown which has a total population of 65,000.

LIDO BEACH

Lido Beach Jewish Center, Fairway Rd.

LINDENHURST

Lindenhurst Hebrew Cong., 225 N. 4th St.

LONG BEACH

Once a summer resort for affluent Jewish New Yorkers, Long Beach began to decline in the 1960s, as the vacation habits of middle-class Jews shifted. Some of the beach clubs that dotted the Long Beach shore were taken over by Nassau County. Many of the large private homes have been converted to retirement and nursing homes. A good many of the year-round Jewish residents who had settled down in one-family homes built in newer sections of the city, have left, owing to the changing social conditions in the community. Nevertheless, 65 percent of the total population of 33,000 is Jewish, making Long Beach the only city north of Miami Beach with a Jewish majority.

Al's Kosher Delicatessen and Restaurant, 897 W. Beech.

Beach YM & YWHA, 405 Long Beach Rd.

Cong. Bachurei Chemed, 210 Edwards Blvd., is a Jewish youth congregation, probably the only one of its kind in the United States. In 1946, a group of young people, dissatisfied with the religious observance of their parents, organized a congregation of their own, with the assistance and advice of their Hebrew teacher, Simon Solomon. Three years later, thirteen adults who had gathered after Hosha'ana Rabbah services decided to launch a campaign for funds for a synagogue for the Orthodox Jewish youth congregation. The synagogue is small but complete. In the center is a modern square *bimah* with Jewish symbols in its design. The Ark is in the form of two giant tablets of the Ten Commandments. There is a balcony for girls and women. Although adults attend services quite regularly and are given the honor of being called up to the Torah, the entire service is conducted by the youth; it is not, however, a junior congregation since nothing in the service is omitted. The entire service is in Hebrew; eight boys serve as readers of the Torah and four serve as cantors.

Cong. Beth Sholom, 700 East Park Ave.

Edwards Boulevard is named for Louis F. Edwards, who was mayor of Long Beach from 1937-1939 when he was murdered. Edwards was one of four Jews who have been mayor of this seashore city.

Hebrew Academy of Long Beach, 530 West Broadway.

Jewish Association for Services to the Aged, 74 West Park Ave., a branch of an agency of the Federation of Jewish Philanthropies of New York, serves many of the estimated 8,500 older Jewish residents who live in fading hotels, retirement homes, nursing homes, or in apartments. These residents represent the largest number of low-income Jews in the county.

Komanoff Extended Care Facility of Long Beach Memorial Hospital, 455 E. Bay Rd., honors Mrs. Isidore Komanoff, the first woman to be elected to the Nassau Board of Supervisors, and her husband, who were among the city's leading civic leaders for 30 years.

Lido Beach Jewish Center, 1 Fairway Rd.

Lido Hotel, opened in 1928 as a Riviera resort close to home for New York socialites, rigidly barred Jews until 1940 when it passed into Jewish ownership. Today the hotel is a *glatt* kosher establishment that caters to middle-aged well-to-do Jews.

Marron's Kosher Delicatessen Restaurant, 17 E. Park Ave.

Rabbinical College of Long Island, 205 West Beech St.

Sephardic Congregation of Long Beach, 161 Lafayette Blvd.

Tel Aviv Kosher Delicatessen and Restaurant, 51 E. Park Ave.

Temple Beth El, 570 West Walnut St., houses JASA-Brookdale Senior Citizens Center.

Temple Emanu-El, 455 Neptune Blvd.

Temple Israel, Riverdale Blvd. and Walnut St.

Temple Zion, 62 Maryland Ave.

YM & YWHA of Long Beach, 405 Long Beach Rd.

Young Israel, 158 Long Beach Rd.

LYNBROOK

Cong. Beth David, 188 Vincent Ave.

Temple Emanu-El, Ross Plaza.

Women's American ORT, South Shore Division, 381 Sunrise Hwy.

MALVERNE
Jewish Center, 1 Norwood Lane.

MANHASSET
Levitt Clinic of North Shore University Hospital, 300 Community Drive, a five-story diagnostic center serving as a referral center for Long Island's 4,500 physicians, is named for William I. Levitt, the noted builder and philanthropist, who contributed $1 million toward the $9 million cost.

Reconstructionist Synagogue, Friends Meeting House, Northern Blvd. and Shelter Rock Rd. When and if zoning problems are cleared up, the congregation will move to Glenwood Rd., Roslyn Harbor.

Temple Judea, 333 Searington Rd.

MASSAPEQUA
Cong. Beth El, 99 Jerusalem Ave.

Hillel Hebrew Academy, 1066 Hicksville Rd.

Temple Judea, Jerusalem and Central Aves., has a 3 by 10 foot multicolored tapestry depicting the Jewish holiday symbols. Created by members of the sisterhood, the needlepoint piece adorns a second story wall.

Temple Sinai, 270 Clocks Blvd.

MASTIC BEACH
Hebrew Center, Neighborhood Rd.

MELVILLE
L.I. Jewish World, Windsor Pl.

Temple Beth Torah, Bagatelle Rd.

MERRICK
Cong. Ohav Sholom, 145 S. Merrick Ave.

Mama Liga's Kosher Steakhouse, 2035 Merrick Rd.

Merrick Jewish Center, 225 Fox Blvd.

Temple Beth Am, Kirkwood and Merrick Aves.

Temple Israel of S. Merrick, 2655 Clubhouse Rd.

MIDDLE ISLAND
Stones with Hebrew lettering, on west side of Miller Place—Yaphank Rd., about 3 miles north of Middle Country Rd., used as a protection barrier on a sod farm, are not pieces of Jewish gravestones. They are old cemetery stones—not gravestones—that were once part of posts or arches erected many years ago by individuals or congregations to mark the entrances or boundaries of their plots in Mount Carmel Cemetery, Brooklyn. The stones were removed some years ago, with the permission of the owners, to allow for easier maintenance of the cemetery. The owner of the sod farm acquired large chunks of granite and cement from the cemetery. One large stone that

was probably used as an archway is inscribed, "Cong. Kehilath Jeshurun, East 85th St., N. Y." Some of the stones have names on them and others have Hebrew carvings.

MINEOLA
Cong. Beth Sholom, 261 Willis Ave.
Court House of N.Y. State Supreme Court, Trial Term Part One, displays portraits of retired Supreme Court Justices Bernard Meyer and Manuel Levine.
Jewish Association for Services to Aged, 158 3rd St.
Jewish Community Services of L.I., 158 3rd St.

NEW HYDE PARK
Jewish Community Center, 100 Lakeville Rd.
L.I. Institute for Jewish Studies (Hineni House), 76-48 26th St.
Long Island Jewish-Hillside Medical Center, 271-11 76th Ave., the largest voluntary hospital in Nassau County, is a merger of the Long Island Jewish Medical Center and Hillside Hospital, both agencies of the Federation of Jewish Philanthropies. Adjacent to the medical center and attached to it by an underpass, is the $25 million Jewish Institute for Geriatric Care, also a Federation agency, which was the nation's first medical-geriatric-psychiatric complex. On the grounds of the medical center is the metropolitan New York area's first major children's hospital.
Temple Emanuel, 3315 Hillside Ave.
Young Israel, 264-15 77th Ave.

NORTH BELLMORE
Temple Beth El, 1373 Bellmore Rd.
Young Israel of North Bellmore, 2428 Hamilton Rd.

NORTHPORT
Rube Goldberg's desk, at which the famed cartoonist did much of his work from 1940 until his death in 1971, is one of the prized possessions of the Department of Adult Education of the Northport Public Schools, 66 Laurel Rd. Goldberg lived at Asharoken in the Northport school district for many years and often shared his art for community causes. It was bequeathed by his widow to the Department.

NORTH WOODMERE
Cong. Ohr Torah, 410 Hungry Harbor Rd. This is also the headquarters of Hineni, a Jewish evangelistic organization led by Mrs. Esther Jungreis, wife of the congregation's rabbi. The congregation has the first Holocaust Museum on Long Island, housing artifacts and memorabilia of concentration camps, including items that were used or worn by survivors.

OAKDALE
B'nai Israel Reform Temple, Biltmore Ave. and Idle Hour Blvd.

OCEANSIDE
Sholem Aleichem School, 3980 Weidener Ave.
Cong. B'nai Torah, Oceanside Rd.
Cong. Shaar Hashamayim, 3309 Skillman Ave.
Jewish Center of Ocean Harbor, Weidner and Royal Aves.
Oceanside Jewish Center, 2860 Brower Ave.
Temple Avodah, 3050 Oceanside Rd.
Young Israel, 150 Waukena Ave.

OLD BETHPAGE
Synagogue of Jewish Science, 825 Round Swamp Rd.
Temple Beth Elohim, 926 Round Swamp Rd.

OLD WESTBURY
Westbury Hebrew Cong., 21 Old Westbury Rd.

OYSTER BAY
Jewish Center, Marion St.
Sagamore Hill National Historic Site, Cove Neck Rd., the former home of President Theodore Roosevelt, has on exhibit in the North Room, a pair of seven-branched Menorahs, a gift to the Roosevelts from a family friend.

PATCHOGUE
Temple Beth El, 45 Oak St.
Young Israel of Patchogue, 28 Mowbray St.

PLAINEDGE
Dr. Gerald Greenberg Museum in the Northedge Elementary School, Stewart Ave., north of Hempstead Tpke., is named for the school's late principal who helped create the museum.

PLAINVIEW
Jewish Center, 95 Floral Dr.
Malka's Jerusalem, 1103 Old Country Rd., is an Israeli nightclub.
Manetto Hill Jewish Center, 244 Manetto Hill Rd.
Mid-Island YMHA, Orchard St. (old Fern Place School).
 Ruby's Delicatessen and Restaurant, 387 S. Oyster Bay Rd.
Young Israel of Plainview, 115 Northern Pkwy.

PORT JEFFERSON STATION
North Shore Jewish Center, 385 Old Town Rd.

PORT WASHINGTON

Community Synagogue, 150 Middle Neck Rd. (Sands Point). One of the synagogue's two buildings looks like a medieval castle. It was once part of the estate of former Gov. Averell Harriman. The congregation's Antique Judaica Museum contains 95 important ceremonial objects.

Daniel and Florence Guggenheim Elementary School, Port Washington Blvd., is named for the noted Jewish philanthropists.

Port Jewish Center, 1515 Middle Neck Rd. (United Methodist Church), had as its rabbi in 1974-75 Michal Seserman who was ordained in 1975 as the third woman rabbi in the United States.

Temple Beth Israel, Temple Dr. A tapestry composed of 161,280 knots hooked by 318 persons hanging in the sanctuary, illustrates the concepts of the Sabbath as "the culmination of creation." At the base of the exterior of the building, a tower that forms an extension of the bimah area, is a framed window containing an illuminated Menorah. The building was designed by the well-known architect, Percival Goodman.

RIVERHEAD

Suffolk County Historical Society, 300 W. Main St., has on exhibit the famous John Hulbert Flag, said to be the first American flag with stars and stripes, which also contains 13 six-pointed white stars on a field of blue. Made a year before the Betsy Ross emblem, the Hulbert Flag was carried by Capt. John Hulbert of Bridgehampton and his company of Minute Men during the first year of the Revolutionary War.

Temple Israel, 490 Northville Tpke.

ROCKVILLE CENTRE

Barasch Memorial Field, a part of Lister Park on Sunrise Highway, is named for Samuel Barasch, who was the village's recreation director from 1940-1952.

Central Synagogue of Nassau County, 430 DeMott Ave.

Hebrew Union College—Jewish Institute of Religion School of Religion Extension, 430 DeMott Ave.

Temple B'nai Sholom, 100 Hempstead Ave.

ROOSEVELT FIELD

A 16-foot Menorah, on the Fountain Mall, South End, of this well-known area, is lighted daily during Chanukah.

ROSLYN

Lincoln Kosher Delicatessen, Inc., 29 Lincoln Ave.

Solomon Schechter Day School, Roslyn Rd., (Roslyn Heights).

Shelter Rock Jewish Center, Shelter Rock and Searingtown Rds.

Temple Beth Sholom, Roslyn Rd. and Northern State Pkwy. (Roslyn Heights).

Temple Sinai, 425 Roslyn Rd., (Roslyn Heights), has a junior chapel dedicated to the memory of Anne Frank, the celebrated Jewish martyr and diarist.

ROSLYN HARBOR
Reconstructionist Synagogue of North Shore, plans to occupy its own building on Glenwood Rd. when and if it can overcome present zoning problems.

SAG HARBOR
Temple Adas Israel, Elizabeth St. and Atlantic Ave., is believed to worship in the oldest existing synagogue building on Long Island, its sanctuary having been erected in 1898. Its old cemetery is on Route 114, on the way to East Hampton.

SANDS POINT
Benjamin and Rita Kaufman Learning Center of the Maimonides Institute.

Sands Point Park and Preserve is a 200-acre Nassau County nature preserve bequeathed to the public by Harry Guggenheim in 1971. Scion of the famous family of industrialists, mining tycoons, and philanthropists, Guggenheim was an aviator in World Wars I and II, served as U.S. Ambassador to Cuba, and was cofounder and publisher of *Newsday*, the famous L.I. daily newspaper. "Falaise," a 26-room Norman mansion containing many art treasures, was also bequeathed by Guggenheim. Hempstead House, Guggenheim's former residence, houses exhibits on Daniel Guggenheim, Harry's father. In this house Charles A. Lindbergh found refuge after his historic flight in 1927, and where he and other noted fliers were often guests. Harry Guggenheim was one of the chief supporters of the rocket and astronautic experiments of Dr. Robert Goddard. Among the exhibits in Hempstead House are some of Harry Guggenheim's uniforms and the horseracing trophies he won.

SAYVILLE
Temple Shalom, 225 Greeley Ave.

SEAFORD
Jewish Center, 2343 S. Seamen's Neck Rd.
Mid-Island YMHA, 3833 Jerusalem Ave., is a branch of the main building in Plainview.

SETAUKET
Hillel Foundation at State University of New York at Stony Brook, 75 Sheep Pasture Rd.

SMITHTOWN
Hebrew Academy of Suffolk County, 525 Veterans Highway.
Jewish Community Services of L.I., 22 Lawrence Ave.
Suffolk County Institute of Jewish Studies, meets weekly in St. Anthony's High School, St. John Ave.
Temple Beth Shalom, Edgewood Ave. and River Rd.
The Melting Pot, Hillside Shopping Plaza, Route 111, is a Kosher-style restaurant.
West Suffolk YM-YWHA, 22 Lawrence Ave.

STONY BROOK
Hillel Foundation, State University, (see Setauket).
L. I. Hall of Fame, a sculpture garden in the Stony Brook Museum, has a smiling bronze likeness of Robert F. Moses, who was among the first three Long Islanders elected to the Hall of Fame.
State University of New York at Stony Brook has a Benjamin N. Cardozo College for Men, named for the late justice of the U. S. Supreme Court (see Albany, New York); ●Ruth Benedict College honoring the late anthropologist who trained Margaret Mead; ●a dormitory named for Bernard M. Baruch, adviser to Presidents; ●and the Roth Quadrangle, named for Emery Roth, Jr., the noted architect.
Temple Isaiah, 1404 Stony Brook Rd.

SYOSSET
Central Hebrew High School, 330 S. Oyster Bay Rd.
East Nassau Hebrew Cong., 310A South Oyster Bay Rd., has two giant stained glass windows, each 32 feet high by 30 feet wide, on the entire eastern wall of the sanctuary, that depict the Ten Commandments. Superimposed are huge flames that leap up and around the letters, representing the Burning Bush, as a symbol of eternal religious freedom. The windows are framed in tiny blue tiles that glow at night on the Northern Pkwy. Two huge arches frame the windows on the outside, representing the Tablets of the Law. On the synagogue grounds is an apple tree that is pruned into the shape of a Menorah.
Midway Jewish Center, 330 South Oyster Bay Rd.
North Shore Synagogue, 83 Muttontown Rd.

UNIONDALE
Hebrew Academy of Nassau County, 215 Oak St., occupies a site that was once part of Mitchell Field.
Jewish Center, 760 Jerusalem Ave.

UPTON

Brookhaven National Laboratory, the largest atomic laboratory in the nation, is dedicated to basic research on the peaceful uses of atomic energy. Among the founders was Dr. I. L. Rabi, Columbia University Nobel laureate in physics.

VALLEY STREAM

Gertrude Wachtler Cohen Hearing and Vertigo Center at Franklin General Hospital, 900 Franklin Ave.

Cong. Beth Sholom (Sunrise Jewish Center), 550 Rockaway Ave.

Jewish Center of Alden Terrace (Cong. Tree of Life), 502 N. Central Ave.

Temple Gates of Zion, 322 N. Corona Ave.

Temple Hillel (Southside Jewish Center), 1000 Rosedale Rd.

Temple Judea, 195 Rockaway Ave.

WANTAGH

Federation Employment & Guidance Service, 3521 Jerusalem Ave.

Jewish Center, 3710 Woodbine Ave.

Jewish Community Services, 3521 Jerusalem Ave.

L. I. Pedagogic Center of N. Y. Board of Jewish Education, 3521 Jerusalem Ave.

South Shore YM & YWHA, 806 Merrick Rd.

Suburban Temple, 2900 Jerusalem Ave.

United Jewish Ys of L. I., 3521 Jerusalem Ave.

WESTBURY

Community Reform Temple (Temple Beth Avodah), 275 Ellison Ave.

Israeli Doll Collection, among a collection of more than 1,000 dolls, is on view in the home of Mr. and Mrs. Alfred Marcus, 17 Lace Lane.

Temple Beth Torah, 243 Cantiague Rd.

Temple Sholom, 675 Brookside Court.

WEST HEMPSTEAD

Hebrew Academy of Nassau County 609 Hempstead Ave.

Jewish Community Center, 711 Dogwood Ave.

Nassau Community Temple, 240 Hempstead Ave.

Young Israel, 640 Hempstead Ave., paid $1 to Francis T. Purcell, a Catholic who was presiding supervisor of the town of Hempstead, for a 20-year lease to a square mile of West Hempstead as "common ground for the purpose of carrying." The synagogue is within that mile square area and its Orthodox members are permitted to carry prayerbooks, talethim, and other items to and from the synagogue on the Sabbath. This "fenced in" area is known as an *eruv*. The Talmud bars such carrying except on common ground surrounded by a wall, in this case an encirclement of telephone poles.

WOODMERE

Cong. Sons of Israel, 111 Irving Pl., has a series of five stained glass windows depicting the first five books of the Hebrew Bible.

Young Israel, 859 Peninsula Blvd.

WOODSBURGH

An almost all-Jewish village of 830 residents in 217 houses, tucked away among the better known Five Towns villages of Hewlett, Woodmere, and Cedarhurst, has only five known non-Jewish residents.

WYANDANCH

Usdan Center for the Creative and Performing Arts, 185 Colonial Springs Rd., named for Suzanne and Nathaniel Usdan, and the Alice N. Proskauer Site of the Henry Kaufmann Campgrounds are situated on 231 acres of woodlands and rolling hills on one of the highest elevation points on Long Island. This country day camp is equipped to serve 2,400 children daily from the Jewish Community Centers and YMHAs of New York City, Nassau, and Suffolk Counties. The first multi-agency country day camp to be developed on the outskirts of New York City with permanent structures, the Henry Kaufmann Campgrounds provide city youngsters with a true camping experience in a natural, rustic environment. Sponsored by the Federation of Jewish Philanthropies of New York, the Henry Kaufmann Campgrounds has pioneered the fast-growing trend of country day camping during the last decade.

WESTCHESTER COUNTY

Westchester County was the first suburban area in which Jews from New York City settled, probably because it could be reached by land via The Bronx, the only one of the five boroughs that is not an island. In the 1930s, when Westchester's Jews numbered 30,000, all but a handful lived in Mount Vernon, Yonkers, New Rochelle, and White Plains, the business centers of the county. Most of the heads of Jewish families were in retail trade, the professions, or self-employed artisans; only a few commuted to New York. A number of wealthy Jews—notably, the Lehmans, the Warburgs, and the Ochses—owned extensive estates in the hilly area and along Long Island Sound. When the established golf and yacht clubs barred even the most influential Jews, Westchester became the site of some of the earliest Jewish golf and country clubs. Houses and apartments in some sections of the county also excluded Jews. Bronxville was the last holdout.

In the 1970s, Westchester had 165,000 Jews, almost as many as in Manhattan and more than those in The Bronx, from which many Westchester Jews came. Nearly half of all Westchester Jews live in White Plains, New Rochelle, Mount Vernon, and Yonkers. The other half is widely scattered, with substantial concentrations in Larchmont, Scarsdale, Port Chester, Rye, Mamaroneck, Tuckahoe, Pelham, Tarrytown, Harrison, and smaller but growing communities in Yorktown Heights, Chappaqua, Purchase, Hastings-On-Hudson, and Ardsley. In the 1970s, Jews represented nearly 16 percent of the county's total population. Further increase is expected in the next decade as more middle and upper middle-income Jewish families leave New York City.

Jewish beginnings in Westchester date back to the decade between 1715 and 1725 when Moses Levy, a leading New York City merchant, was a

261

substantial property owner in what is now Rye. The first known Jewish residents in the county were the six sons of Michael Hays, a Dutch Jew, who settled near New Rochelle in 1720. They are said to have come in their own ship, bringing with them servants, cattle, seeds, and tools. The Hays brothers, who established themselves as farmers and merchants, had extensive holdings around Rye and Mount Pleasant (Pleasantville). One brother, Jacob, founded a family identified with Westchester County for more than 150 years. Judah Hays lived in Rye until about 1730 when he moved to New York, where his brothers, Solomon, Isaac, and Abraham, had preceded him. All members of New York's Congregation Shearith Israel, they became the forebears of a long line of Jewish notables.

Jacob's sons, Michael and David, Jr., were born in Pleasantville in the 1730s. The latter served with George Washington's forces in the French and Indian War and is said to have been present when the French defeated General Braddock in western Pennsylvania. Michael Hays was a farmer and merchant at Northcastle on the eve of the American Revolution. Tories drove him from his farm in 1776 and captured supplies he had assembled for the American army. After the Revolution he became active in politics. He is said to have helped draft the first constitution of New York State. In 1788 he was elected assessor of Pleasantville.

Asser Etting, father-in-law of David Hays, Sr., one of the original six Hays brothers, was in business at Northcastle in 1752, about the same time that Ralph Jacobs engaged in farming at Rye, and Meyer Benjamin at Yonkers. Abraham I. Abrahams, the most popular *mohel* in New York during the mid-18th century, recorded that he had officiated at the circumcision of Benjamin's son in 1758 at Yonkers. While David Hays, Sr., was serving with the American forces at the Battle of Long Island, Tories burned his farm house at Bedford. Mrs. Hays was in bed with a newborn infant when her Tory neighbors put her house to the torch. She had refused to disclose the hideout of a party of patriots attempting to drive cattle through the enemy lines to the American encampment at White Plains. Her seven-year old son, Jacob, later to become New York City's police chief, was one of those engaged in this hazardous foray.

The infant Hays was Benjamin Etting Hays, who lived in Pleasantville for nearly 75 years. An observant Jew and a qualified ritual slaughterer, he was known to his neighbors as "Uncle Ben the Jew, the best Christian in Westchester County." He donated the land on which Pleasantville's first high school was built. Benjamin's son, David, who owned a kosher hotel at Pleasantville in the 1840s, was the maternal grandfather of the late Arthur Hays Sulzberger, publisher of *The New York Times*.

Since all of these early Westchester Jewish settlers were members of Congregation Shearith Israel in New York, the synagogue leaders worried over the fact that because they lived so far away, they might be less inclined to pay their assessments. In 1736, Shearith Israel adopted a resolution pointing out that the cost of maintaining the synagogue required the assistance of "our brethren living in the country, even if their business and residence was not in the city." Twenty years later another resolution cautioned Westchester members against laxity in ritual and Sabbath observances.

Long before Westchester County became the seat of a number of important Jewish child care, medical, and old age institutions, a son-in-law of David Hays, Sr., put forth a scheme to establish in Pleasantville "the American Jewish Asylum," a sort of combined orphan home and trade school for Jewish boys and girls from all parts of the world. In the 1820s, Jacob S. Solis, who had married Charity Hays in Pleasantville in 1811, sent out a circular announcing his plan, but it never progressed beyond that stage.

Other Jewish families settled in Westchester County—Solomon Levy lived in Peekskill in the early 1800s, Samson Simson, one of the wealthiest and most prominent New York City Jews, exiled himself to Yonkers in 1813 after being injured in a street assault. In the late 18th century, Simson's father had acquired an estate that extended from Palisade Avenue to what is now the Saw Mill River Parkway. To that barony the son retired, living there with his sister and two grandchildren until 1846. He established his own kosher kitchen, matzoth bakery, and synagogue, but kept aloof from the Jews of the city. He also took part in prison reform, Westchester politics, and charity. When Simson returned to New York, he became one of the chief founders of Mount Sinai Hospital in 1852. That same year he organized the Jewish Theological and Scientific Institution as a rabbinical seminary. Hoping to see it established in Westchester County, he contributed several lots in Yonkers. However, nothing came of his plan, and the property was converted into the first assets of the Jewish Theological Seminary of America.

The first permanent Jewish community in Westchester came into being in Yonkers. An item in a Yonkers newspaper in 1870 reported that "the Hebrews of Yonkers have leased and fitted up for a synagogue the entire fourth story of Anderson's building on Getty Square and the Reverend M. Bernstein has been engaged to minister to them." There is a record of another service in 1875 in the home of Herman Lyons. Public High Holy Day services were held in 1887 in the hall of the Young Women's Christian Temperance Union on North Broadway. Out of this service came Congregation Oheb Zedek, which was chartered in 1903. The chief founders were Aaron Rabinowitz and Adolph Klein. The latter, a Hungarian Jew who settled in Yonkers in 1884, recruited Jewish workers for the Alexander Smith Carpet Company, which moved from The Bronx to Yonkers in the early 1890s. In 1890, the Hebrew Benevolent Society of Yonkers bought Teutonia Hall as the city's first synagogue.

The first Jew to settle in Mount Vernon was Moritz Lowenstein, a Civil War veteran who lost a leg on the battlefield. An employee at the U.S. Customs Office in New York City, Levy commuted daily to his job for 40 years, and may well have been the first Jewish commuter. Between 1869 and

1885 other Jewish Civil War veterans, tradesmen, artisans, and peddlers established themselves in Mount Vernon, New Rochelle, Port Chester, Tarrytown, Ossining, Mamaroneck, and White Plains. Mount Vernon's first *minyan* met in the home of Louis Subitzky in 1882, residents of Wakefield, Woodlawn, and Kingsbridge having been invited to complete the *minyan*. This *minyan* became Congregation Brothers of Israel in 1891 when there were 50 Jewish families in Mount Vernon. Congregation Sons of Israel in Ossining also dates from 1891. Port Chester had a synagogue in 1892 and a year later there was one in Tarrytown. New Rochelle's oldest congregation, Anshe Sholom, goes back to 1898. In the early 1900s there were also small settlements with congregations in Hastings-on-Hudson, Mt. Kisco, Peekskill, Tuckahoe, and Mamaroneck. Yonkers had a YMHA in 1900, and Mount Vernon established one in 1909.

Virtually all of the first congregations were Orthodox. In the 1960s, there were 46 synagogues in Westchester County—11 Orthodox, 21 Conservative, and 14 Reform congregations. Fifteen years later, the comparable figures were 25 Reform, 25 Conservative, and 10 Orthodox. The post-World War II building boom throughout Westchester brought a large influx of Jews who established new synagogues and synagogue-centers, Hebrew schools, and other Jewish institutions.

At the end of the 1960s, the county's major cities began to lose population to the fast-growing towns in the county and to the newly-built areas in other parts of the county. Between 1960 and 1965, 8,000 residents of Mount Vernon left the city to escape racial tensions, crime and narcotics in the schools, and the influx of blacks. Many of the migrating families were Jews. In 1954 there were 25,000 Jews in Mount Vernon, and they comprised one-third of the city's population. By 1969 there were only 12,000 Jews, the others having moved to Riverdale in The Bronx, to Scarsdale, Larchmont, and other Westchester communities, or to Rockland County and Connecticut. The city's synagogues were hard hit by the migration. Mount Vernon's Sinai Temple declined from 1,200 families in 1959 to 250 a decade later. Many of the Jewish families that left were young parents who did not want to send their children to the Mount Vernon public schools, the very same schools that had first attracted these families in the 1930s. The Jews who left the county's four big cities were often the builders of new Jewish communities in as yet undeveloped areas of the county. In 1948, Yorktown Heights had four Jewish families, two of whom—Jack Schaffer and Samson Solomon—were farmers. In the 1970s there were 400 Jewish families in the area out of a total of 5,000.

The principal national Jewish organizations are represented by chapters in every Westchester town and city. Some of them have created countywide councils. Each community conducts an annual drive for the Joint Campaign of the United Jewish Appeal-Federation of Jewish Philanthropies. There are a Westchester Board of Rabbis, a Westchester Jewish Conference that serves as a county clearing house and provides information, a Westchester task force of Federation's Commission on Synagogue Relations, and a number of Federation agencies. The Westchester Jewish Community Services, Federation's family service agency, has branches in Yonkers, New Rochelle, Mount Vernon, and White Plains. There are three Jewish newspapers in the county, *The Mosaic*, published by the Mount Vernon Jewish Community Council; *The Jewish Chronicle*, published by the Yonkers Jewish Community Council, and *The Jewish Tribune*, a private enterprise. The Mid-Westchester YM-YWHA in Scarsdale is affiliated with the Associated YM-YWHAs of Greater New York. There are independent YMHAs in Yonkers, Mount Vernon, and Port Chester, and a Hillel Counselorship at Pace College, served by the rabbi of the Community Synagogue in Rye.

The influx of thousands of Jewish voters from New York City where they had usually supported Democratic candidates, made a small dent in the political complexion of Westchester County, which has long been solidly Republican. Jewish officeholders on the county wide level are rare in Westchester. In 1975, Samuel Fredman was elected chairman of the County Democratic Committee. Some of the county villages have had Jewish mayors. Eugene H. Lehman was mayor of Tarrytown in 1931, and H. S. Green succeeded him two years later. Monroe Steiner was mayor of Larchmont in 1930. In 1974, Richard Maas was acting-mayor of White Plains. State Supreme Court Justice Alvin R. Ruskin served as a judge of the County Family Court.

*****

ARMONK

Anita Louise Ehrman Recreation Center, High St., Byran Hill Rd. and Cox Ave., an 11-acre site donated to the town of North Castle by Mr. and Mrs. Frederick L. Ehrman, is a memorial to their daughter, Anita Louise.

BREWSTER

Temple Beth Elohim, Route 22.

BRIARCLIFF MANOR

Cong. Sons of Israel, 1666 Pleasantville Rd.

BRONXVILLE

Walter Rothschild House at Sarah Lawrence College is named for the former president of the Abraham & Straus stores.

CHAPPAQUA

Temple Beth El of Northern Westchester, 222 S. Bedford Rd.

CROTON-ON-HUDSON
Temple Israel of Northern Westchester, Glengary Rd.

DOBBS FERRY
Greenburgh Hebrew Center, 515 Broadway.

HARRISON
Louis M. Klein Middle School, Nelson and Union Aves., is named for a former superintendent of schools.

Temple Emanu-El (Jewish Community Center), Union Ave., features a splendid circular sanctuary 62 feet in diameter.

HASTINGS-ON-HUDSON
Temple Beth Shalom, 740 N. Broadway.

Westchester Hills Cemetery, 400 Saw Mill River Rd., has the unusual mausoleum in which showman Billy Rose is buried. Three stained glass windows depict a pen, a telephone, and the notes of songs to trace his career. On one of the windows there is a map of Israel and musical notes from the song *Without a Song*, for which Rose wrote the lyrics. The center window shows a copy of a medal given to Rose by Israel after he had donated $1 million worth of art for the Billy Rose Art Museum in Jerusalem, now part of the Israel Museum. The word "wolf " is written in Hebrew on the window, an affectionate term that David Ben-Gurion used for Rose. The granite structure overlooking the entrance to the cemetery is directly opposite the mausoleum of famed composer George Gershwin, and the grave of singer Judy Holliday.

HAWTHORNE
Cedar Knolls School of New York Board of Jewish Guardians, 226 Linda Ave.

LAKE CARMEL
Jewish Center, Yorktown Rd.

LARCHMONT
Cong. Beth Emeth, 2111 Boston Post Rd.
Larchmont Temple, 75 Larchmont Ave.

MAHOPAC
Jewish Center of the Mahopacs, Route 6.
Temple Beth Shalom, Croton Falls Rd.

MAMARONECK
Westchester Jewish Center, Palmer and Rockland Aves., has an unusual free standing Ark in hardwood flanked on each side by Menorah stands joined to the Ark, and a circular exterior sculpture and Menorah.

Westchester Religious Institute and Day School, 856 Orienta Ave.

MOHEGAN LAKE
Martha Guinsberg Pavilion, a public recreation center, is named for the wife of a prominent resident.

Mohegan Park Jewish Center, Decatur Rd.

MOUNT KISCO
Cong. Beth Medrash Chemed, Pines Bridge Rd.

Cong. Bet Torah, 60 Smith Ave.

Training Farm of Nitra Yeshiva, Pines Bridge Rd., is a training center for Orthodox teenagers planning to settle on Orthodox kibbutzim in Israel.

MOUNT VERNON
Cong. Brothers of Israel, 10 S. 8th Ave.

Emanu-El Jewish Center, 261 Lincoln Ave.

Fleetwood Synagogue, 11 E. Broad St.

Free Synagogue of Westchester, 500 N. Columbus Ave.

Jewish Center of Mount Vernon, 230 S. Columbus Ave.

Jewish Community Council, 30 Oakley Ave.

The Mosaic, 30 Oakley Ave.

Residence of Jewish Child Care Assoc. of N.Y., 163 Esplanade.

St. Paul's Episcopal Church, 897 Columbus Ave., a national shrine of the Bill of Rights, has a pair of eight-branched brass candlesticks and a pewter sanctuary lamp which were once the property of the synagogue in Landau, Germany. They were brought to the U.S. by Joseph Levy, maternal grandfather of Adolph S. Ochs, late publisher of The New York Times, and presented to the church by Ochs' son-in-law and daughter, Mr. and Mrs. Arthur Hays Sulzberger, as a memorial to Ochs. St. Paul's Episcopal Church is associated with John Peter Zenger's struggle for freedom of the press in Colonial days. His accurate report in 1733 of a fraudulent election on the village green, where the church now stands, resulted in his arrest for libel and subsequent acquittal, an event which was a landmark in the battle for a free press.

Shalom Nursing Home, is a strictly kosher institution sponsored by the National Council of Young Israel, Clairemont Ave.

Temple Sinai, 132 Crary Ave.

Westchester Jewish Community Services, 2 Gramatan Ave.

Westchester Jewish Tribune, 113 S. 3rd Ave.

Y.M.H.A. of Lower Westchester, 30 Oakley Ave.

NEW CASTLE
Warburg Park, used by the town of New Castle as a public park and

recreation area, is a memorial to the late Felix Warburg, the noted Jewish philanthropist. The 37 acre site was donated by James N. and Bessie H. Rosenberg.

NEW ROCHELLE

Beth El Synagogue-Center, Northfield Rd. at North Ave., has a frontal view emphasizing a 50-foot tall column of limestone incised with a golden Menorah and the Ten Commandments. A Sukkot garden and terraced meditation park are also part of the exterior. The two stained glass windows that run the full height of the structure, represent the Biblical story of Joachim and Boaz and the two beacons of light guiding the Children of Israel, one by day and one by night. In the main foyer there hangs a sculpture, *The Living Star of David*, created by the Israeli artist, Yaakov Agam. The bimah chairs for the rabbi and other dignitaries are upholstered seats incorporated into a stone base, an idea adapted from the Seat of Moses in the ancient synagogue at Hazor. The *Wall of the Martyrs*, a monumental bronze sculpture by Luise Kaish, said to be the first work of such scope and dimension commissioned by an American synagogue, is a symbolic representation of Jewish martyrdom through the ages. It hangs in the synagogue's Hall of Martyrs. It was endowed by Mr. and Mrs. Harry Platt. The Menorah in the synagogue is an exact copy of the Menorah in the Second Temple in Jerusalem. In the upper lobby are 61 panels containing English translations of the 54 regular weekly portions of the Torah and seven double portions. It is claimed that this display is the only one of its kind in a synagogue.

Cong. Anshe Sholom, 50 North Ave.

Raizen Memorial Plaza, between Main and Huguenot Sts., honors the late Charles S. Raizen, a former president of Temple Israel, who was one of the city's leading civic leaders and philanthropists. A bronze sculpture of Raizen set in a fountain of water stands in the plaza.

Temple Israel, 1000 Pinebrook Blvd.

United Home for Aged Hebrews, 60 Willow Dr.

Westchester Jewish Community Services, 271 North Ave.

Young Israel of Westchester, 1228 North Ave.

OSSINING

Cong. Anshe Dorshe Emes Reconstructionist Synagogue, Albany Post Rd.

PEEKSKILL

First Hebrew Cong., 1821 E. Main St.

Hebrew Day School of Northern Westchester and Putnam County, 1821 E. Main St.

Temple Israel of Putnam Valley, Lake Dr.

Valeria Home, Furnace Dock Rd., a vacation resort "for people of education and refinement, belonging to the middle class who would not be justified in asking for or accepting charity, but who are, nevertheless, not able to pay the prices exacted for a sojourn in the usual health resorts or sanitaria," was founded in 1914 with a $4 million endowment by Jacob Langloth, German-Jewish banker, and named for his wife, Valeria.

Young Israel, Pinelake Park.

PELHAM MANOR
Jewish Center, 451 Esplanade.

PLEASANTVILLE
Pleasantville Cottage School of Jewish Child Care Association, Broadway.

PORT CHESTER
Cong. Kneses Tifereth Israel, 575 King St., is a rectangular synagogue set against an ellipse. The entrance is within the ellipse, and the sanctuary and other parts are within the rectangle. The first rises only part way against the facade, so that the two units do not compete for attention—the sanctuary is dominant. The synagogue is sheathed in an off-white pre-cast stone. Jewel-like colored glass is set into its slit masonry walls. These narrow panels, each of a luminous color, are distributed in five tiers across the facade.

Jewish Center of Port Chester and Town of Rye, 258 Willett Ave., displays in its lobby an oil painting entitled *Torah, Chuppa and Good Deeds.*

POUND RIDGE
Hiram Halle Memorial Library, Route 124, is named for the Jewish financier who donated the land and original building in which the library is housed.

PURCHASE
Roy R. Neuberger Museum at State University of New York, College at Purchase, Lincoln Ave. and Anderson Hill Rd., houses the multimillion dollar collection of 20th century American art contributed by Neuberger to the University's art center. The museum, which was the college's first building, houses Neuberger's collection of paintings and sculptures, as well as the Elaine and Raphael Malsin Collection of Oceanic Art, and the Aimee and Eliot Hirshberg Collection of African Art.

Pforzheimer Memorial Building, Purchase St., the home of the Westchester Academy of Medicine, is named for Mr. and Mrs. Carl Pforzheimer, philanthropists and bibliophiles, whose son, Carl, Jr., presented the mansion and ten acres as a memorial to his parents. The building and grounds were formerly the estate of the late Gov. Herbert H. Lehman.

The Peter Lehman Post of the Purchase American Legion is named for Lehman's son, who was killed in World War II while flying with the Royal Air Force.

PUTNAM
Reform Temple of Putnam Valley, Church Rd.

RYE
Community Synagogue, 200 Forest Ave.
Cong. Emanu-El of Westchester, Westchester Ave. and Kenilworth Rd.

SCARSDALE
Scarsdale Synagogue, 2 Ogden Rd.
Westchester Children's Schule, Greenville Community Church, Ardsley Rd. near Central Ave.
Westchester Reform Temple, 255 Mamaroneck Rd. The main wing of the building is shaped like a Star of David. The walls of the sanctuary building are of fieldstone and are twenty feet high. A 12-foot high triangular lobby extends from the building toward a driveway.
Y.M. & Y.W.H.A. of Mid-Westchester, 999 Wilmot Rd.
Young Israel of Scarsdale, 43 Barand Rd.

SHENEROCK
Hebrew Cong. of Somers, Cypress Lane.

SHRUB OAK
Workmen's Circle Jewish Culture School, United Methodist Church, E. Main St.

TARRYTOWN
Marc Chagall Windows (nine), in the Union Church of Pocantico Hills, 555 Bedford Rd., N. Tarrytown, illustrate passages from the Book of Genesis and the Prophets.
Sleepy Hollow Cemetery, 540 N. Broadway, made famous by Washington Irving's stories, is the last resting place of Samuel Gompers, founder and for two generations, president of the American Federation of Labor (see District of Columbia).
Temple Beth Abraham, 25 Leroy Ave., has a tall sculpture at its entrance which reaches from roof line toward the sky and can be seen at a great distance. A pylon whose design incorporates in bronze, steel, and stained glass, The Tablets of the Law, is based on two columns. The steel columns turn into two ladders as they pierce the roof, recalling the ladder of Jacob. They terminate in the curves of the Tablets of the Law which are topped by a series of opposing curves forming the Menorah.

271 — WESTCHESTER COUNTY

TUCKAHOE
Genesis Hebrew Center, 25 Oakland Ave.

VALHALLA
Blythedale Children's Hospital, Bradhurst Ave.

WHITE PLAINS
Cong. Beth Am Shalom, 295 Soundview Ave.
Hebrew Institute, 20 Greenridge Ave.
Jewish Community Center, 252 Soundview Ave., a synagogue
despite its name, is housed in a parabolic structure outside of which stands an
abstract bronze sculpture.
Solomon Schechter Day School, 280 Old Mamaroneck Rd.
Temple Israel Center, 280 Old Mamaroneck Rd.
Westchester Jewish Community Services, 172 S. Broadway.
Woodlands Community Temple, 50 Worthington Rd.

YONKERS
Cong. Agudas Achim, 21 Hudson St., has a chapel named for the
parents of Sid Caesar, stage and television star, who attended Hebrew
school here and celebrated his bar mitzvah here.
Cong. Ohab Zedek, 7 Prospect St. and 63 Hamilton Ave.
Cong. Sons of Israel, 105 Radford St.
Greystone Jewish Center, 600 N. Broadway.
Hebrew Academy High School, 700 McLean Ave.
Hebrew Academy High School of Lincoln Park, 311 Central Park
Ave.
Jewish Chronicle, 122 S. Broadway.
Jewish Community Center, 122 S. Broadway.
Jewish Community Council, 122 S. Broadway
Jewish Guild for the Blind Home, 75 Stratton Ave.
Lincoln Park Jewish Center, 311 Central Park Ave.
Mesivta of Yonkers, 63 Hamilton Ave.
Midchester Jewish Center, 236 Grandview Blvd., has on an exterior
wall a huge bronze Menorah designed as a memorial to the 6,000,000 victims
of the Nazi Holocaust. It was a gift of Mr. and Mrs. Fred Silberman.
Neustadter Convalescent Center of Mount Sinai Hospital, 700
McLean Ave.
Northeast Jewish Center, 11 Salisbury Rd.
Smith-O'Hara-Levine Park, Lawrence and Wolffe Sts., is named in
part for Pfc. Daniel Ira Levine, who was killed in action in 1944 in France
during World War II.
Temple Emanu-El, 306 Ramsey Rd.
Untermyer Park and Gardens, 919 N. Broadway, is a public park
maintained by the city and named for the late Samuel J. Untermyer, the

noted lawyer. Once part of Untermyer's palatial estate and gardens known as Greystone, the park was bequeathed to the city in 1940 by Untermyer. It includes a Greek garden and theatre and part of what was once the largest private gardens in the U. S. Son of a Confederate veteran, Untermyer, a native of Lynchburg, Va., practiced law in New York for 61 years. He handled thousands of cases involving corporate matters, defended labor unions, acted for various committees of Congress and the New York State Legislature in exposing the money trust, housing scandals, the New York Stock Exchange, and in unifying the New York City transit system. The public investigations to which Untermyer was counsel led to the creation of the Federal Reserve System, the Federal Trade Commission, and the Securities and Exchange Commission. A law partner of Louis Marshall (see Syracuse, N. Y.), Untermyer once headed the Palestine Foundation Fund (Keren Hayesod). Counsel to Herman Bernstein in the first suit brought against Henry Ford for his libelous statements about the Jewish people, Untermyer in his last years became the leader of the movement to boycott German goods after the advent of Hitlerism in 1933. He donated the Minnie Untermyer Memorial Theatre to the Hebrew University in memory of his wife.

United Home for Aged Hebrews, 60 Willow Dr.

United Talmud Torah, P.O.B. 203.

Westchester Jewish Community Services, 20 S. Broadway and 598 Tuckahoe Rd.

Yonkers Sports Hall of Fame Room, in the Administrative Building of the Department of Parks, Recreation, and Conservation, is dedicated to Abe Cohen, who originated the Hall of Fame.

YORKTOWN HEIGHTS
Jewish Center, 2966 Crompond Rd.

Temple Beth Am, 203 Church Pl.

AROUND THE
JEWISH CALENDAR

SEPTEMBER-OCTOBER

Annually, there is a ceremony at the flagpole at State and Whitehall Sts. in lower Manhattan, commemorating the landing of the first group of 23 Jewish settlers in America. The ceremony is co-sponsored by the Jewish Historical Society of New York and the American Jewish Historical Society.

Tashlich, the custom of the first day of *Rosh Hashanah* of casting bread crumbs into a body of water and reciting prayers, may be observed at various spots along the Hudson River, and in Brooklyn, at the Williamsburg Bridge, Botanic Gardens, Prospect Park, Brighton Beach, and Coney Island. The custom symbolizes the casting off of sins.

On *Yom Kippur*, most Orthodox and Hasidic Jews wear a *kittle*—a long white robe-like garment, to symbolize purity (and the purification) of our sins.

Prior to *Sukkot*, it is interesting to go to the Lower East Side to see the brisk business in *s'chach*, the greenery for the *Sukkah* and *lulovim* and *esrogim* on Canal Street between Essex or Orchard Streets. A number of restaurants build *Sukkahs* for the holiday where people can eat their meals. The Jewish Theological Seminary of America, 3080 Broadway, builds a very large and beautiful *Sukkah* decorated with pines. Congregation Shearith Israel and Yeshiva University also erect *Sukkot*. On the roof of the 50-story Monsanto Building, 43 W. 42nd St., a *Sukkah* is erected. Called the "*Sukkah* in the Sky," the custom was started by Jack Weiler, realtor and philanthropist.

On *Simhas Torah* night, thousands of people from all parts of the city are attracted to the Satmar Rebbe's synagogue on Rodney St. (between Bedford and Lee Aves.), in Williamsburg. Police are often on hand to control

273

the curious visitors waiting for the early morning *hakafos* (procession), to parade, swaying, clapping, and chanting right into the middle of the street, which has been cordoned off for the occasion. Other colorful *Simhas Torah* celebrations include the ones at Lubavitcher Yeshivoth, 770 Eastern Parkway (Crown Heights section of Brooklyn); Bobover Yeshiva, in Borough Park, Brooklyn; the Mesivta Rabbi Chaim Berlin Yeshiva, Ave. N. (Flatbush section of Brooklyn); the Machzike Talmud Torah School of Borough Park, 4622 14th Ave. (Brooklyn); and the Mirrer Yeshiva Central Institute, 1791 Ocean Parkway (Flatbush section of Brooklyn). (See also: section on Brooklyn.)

NOVEMBER

Services for Thanksgiving Day have been a custom at Congregation Shearith Israel (Spanish and Portuguese Synagogue), Central Park West at 70th St., since 1871. The Metropolitan Synagogue, 10 Park Ave., conducts a joint Thanksgiving service with the Community Church.

DECEMBER

Chanukah celebrations consist of the kindling of lights on Menorahs (candelabra) for eight consecutive days. The celebration begins with the first day with one candle and thereafter increased one each day for the remainder of the Chanukah period. Synagogues and Jewish Community Centers throughout New York City and its suburbs conduct programs to mark the Maccabean festival. The largest of these celebrations is at the 92nd St. YM-YWHA and Brooklyn College.

FEBRUARY

February is the special month for brotherhood, and a number of synagogues and churches in New York sponsor joint programs to mark the occasion. One of the most notable is the *Brotherhood Service* conducted by the Metropolitan Synagogue Choir and the Choir of the Church of the Master.

MARCH

As *Purim* usually falls during this month (occasionally the last week in February), there is a Jewish Music Festival, held from *Purim* to Passover under the national auspices of the Jewish Music Council of the National Jewish Welfare Board (JWB), and a number of events in New York, as well as throughout the country, to mark this occasion. The Sephardic Cultural Program of Yeshiva University and the Workmen's Circle sponsor music festivals also. The Israeli Dance Festival is also held in New York in March. It is during this month (also part of February and of April), that many groups tour the Streit Matzoth factory in lower Manhattan and the Horowitz Margareten Kosher Foods Co., in Queens, to see how matzo is made.

During the *Purim* celebration in Williamsburg, Brooklyn, the visitor will see small boys with *payot* masquerading in the streets as grown-up Hasidim, with beards made from absorbent cotton, or little girls pretending that they are Queen Esther. Purim in Williamsburg is a joyous time for young and old alike. In the evening at the Satmar Rebbe's (Rodney St.), the singing is ecstatic and wild. At the Lubavitcher Rebbe's synagogue, 770 Eastern Parkway (Crown Heights, Brooklyn), the singing is somewhat more subdued. Later, the Rebbe talks on a subject related to *Purim*, then lifts up his cup of wine—a signal for his followers to lift theirs, and they all drink, and the singing and swaying begin again, lasting far into the night.

For the *megillah*-reading, the visitor should go to Congregation Shearith Israel, Central Park West and 70th St. The National Council of Young Israel, 3 West 16th St., conducts an annual *Purim* program for children. The 92nd Street YM & YWHA conducts a *Purim* carnival, as do many Jewish Community Centers, synagogues, and Jewish schools.

A number of synagogues and Centers mark the Jewish Music Festival, including the Metropolitan Synagogue, 10 Park Ave.; the 92nd Street Y; and Temple Emanu-El.

APRIL

This is usually the month of Passover, and the services at Congregation Shearith Israel are among those especially worth attending. Particularly beautiful are the portions of the service when both congregation and choir join with the Reader in the chanting of prayers set in poetic form.

The making of *shmura* matzoh in Williamsburg may be seen by arranging in advance with a matzoh bakery. Jewish schools can take their students on this kind of tour to see how this strictly guarded handmade matzoh is made. The Satmar Matzoh Bakery, 427 Broadway, Brooklyn, will conduct tours of groups. The Streit Matzoth Co., 150 Rivington St. and the Horowitz-Margareten Kosher Foods Co., 29-00 Review Ave., Long Island City, Queens, will also conduct tours of groups. These, however, are not *shmura* matzos.

MAY

Festivities, parades, and picnics mark *Lag B'Omer* at Lubavitcher world headquarters in Brooklyn. Thousands of yeshiva, Hebrew, and public school children march side by side along Eastern Parkway in Crown Heights, to the beat of drums and gay music. The Parkway, lined with thousands of spectators, is cordoned off by the police for the occasion.

Shavuot, during May or June, is the feast of the first fruits. The entire synagogue of Congregation Shearith Israel is bedecked with greens. The steps leading to the holy Ark are covered with many beautiful and colorful flowers that symbolize the fruits that were brought as offerings in Temple days. An additional service takes place during the afternoon of *Shavuot* preceding *Mincha*. The *Azharoth* are chanted, and this is followed by the reading of the Book of Ruth. On the first day, the traditional 248 positive

JEWISH CALENDAR — 276

commandments of the Torah, in the poem composed by Solomon ibn Gabirol, are read, and then the first half of the Book of Ruth is cantillated. On the second day, the 365 negative commandments are read, after which the second half of the Book of Ruth is read. Both the *Azharoth* and the Bible are read by all the congregants present, each consecutively reading a single verse.

Every year on Memorial Day, Congregation Shearith Israel marks the graves of soldiers and other patriots of the American Revolution in its historic cemetery on St. James Place below Chatham Square, in its cemetery on West 21st St., and in its graveyard on West 11th St. (see HISTORIC CEMETERIES).

JUNE

Israel Independence Day, observed on the 5th of Iyar in the Hebrew calendar, is usually marked by the Salute to Israel Parade early in June, under the auspices of the American Zionist Youth Foundation.

JULY

On the black fast day of *Tisha B'Av*, which falls in July or August, Congregation Shearith Israel is draped in black and the services are not read from the *tebah*, the reading desk from which every service is read during the entire year, but, as a sign of sadness and mourning, from a table set low in front of the *tebah*. This table is also draped in black and has chairs for the *hazzanim* and the presiding officer. The 12 white tapers that surround the reading desk are covered in black, and the Ark also has a black covering. Everything is shrouded in darkness to commemorate one of the most tragic events in Jewish history—the destruction of the Temple in Jerusalem.

The *hazzan* begins the service with the chant of Psalm 137, "By the rivers of Babylon there we sat, yea, we also wept. . ." The sorrowful melody sets the mood for the entire service. The chant is solemn and mournful and permeated with the sound of lamentation. Following the *Amidah*, the service continues with a *kinah*, a dirge. Then the Book of Lamentations is read. The first chapter is read by the *hazzan*, and after that each chapter is read either by another *hazzan* or a member of the congregation. After the Book of Lamentations is finished, other dirges are sung, each of which has a melancholy and touching melody of its own. One of the unusual and interesting aspects of this part of the service is that often the accentuation in the reading is purposely incorrect. This is to emphasize the unusually sorrowful occasion and the fact that everything is changed for the worse on this sad day. Before the closing *kinah* is read, the Reader announces the number of years that have passed since the destruction of the Temple. The final chapter in the evening liturgy is then read, beginning with the words, "For the sake of my Temple and for the glory of Zion, the renowned city, will I weep day and night." The words, "May our prayer be accepted with loving favor," are omitted. On the following day, even the Torah Scroll is covered in black, and the beautiful silver bells that usually adorn the scroll are replaced with two black coverings.

AUGUST

Though there is little activity during this month of specific Jewish interest (unless *Tisha B'Av* occurs during August, see above), the *shofar* is blown at the end of morning devotions during daily services. This custom is performed during the month of *Elul* preceding Rosh Hashanah.

There are other activities of Jewish interest held throughout the year. For a more comprehensive listing, consult *The Jewish Week*, which also includes radio and TV programs of special interest to Jews.

Index

Abrahams, Abraham I., 212, 232, 262
Abrams, Robert, 78, 202
Abzug, Bella, 186
Adler, Dr. Cyrus, 36, 201
Adler, Felix, 79, 91, 92, 176
Agencies for the handicapped, 156
Agencies related to Israel, 40-41, 107, 146-148, 151-152-170-171, 205, 249
Agudath Israel of America, 148, 157
Aguilar, Grace, 134
Aleichem, Sholom, 90, 98, 104-105, 131, 134, 139, 176, 192
Algemeiner Journal, 149
Altman, Benjamin, 64, 105, 134
American Association for Jewish Education, 150
American Committee for Weizmann Institute, 151
American Federation of Jewish Fighters, Camp Inmates, and Nazi Victims, 145
American Friends of Bar-Ilan University, 151
American Friends of Ben-Gurion University of the Negev, 151
American Friends of Haifa University, 151
American Friends of Hebrew University, 151
American Friends of Tel Aviv University, 151
American Hebrew, 88, 103
American Israel Cultural Foundation, 146
American Jewish Committee, 39, 56, 108, 145, 173, 218, 239, 248
American Jewish Congress, 38, 40, 56, 108, 145, 160, 211, 239, 247-248
American Jewish Joint Distribution Committee, 39-41, 146, 192
American Jewish League for Israel, 146
American Jewish tercentenary, 101
American Jewish Year Book, 144-145
American Jews in World War II, 93
American Mizrachi Women, 137, 146
American Museum of Immigration, 103
American Organization Directory, 144
American ORT Federation, 25, 153
American Society for Technion-Israel Institute of Technology, 151
American Zionist Federation, 146
American Zionist Youth Foundation, 146
Anti-Defamation League, 56, 145, 179, 214, 239, 245
Artists, 34, 86, 104, 115, 122

Assistance with personal and family problems, 157, 158
Association of Jewish Center Workers, 153
Atran Center for Jewish Culture, 150
Aufbau, 149

Baeck, Leo Institute, 135
Barsimon, Jacob, 92
Baruch, Bernard M., 86 79, 144, 159, 171, 258
Baruch College, 144
Baruch, Simon, 79, 159, 171
Beame, Mayor Abraham, 75, 79, 106, 181, 185
Beecher, Rev. Henry Ward, 177
Belkin, Dr. Samuel, 37
Belmont, August, 54, 233, 242, 246
Ben-Gurion, David, 266
Benjamin, Judah, 54
Berger, Meyer, 181
Berlin, Irving, 84, 95
Bernstein, Leonard, 120
Beth Israel Hospital, 154
Beth Jacob Schools, 150
Beyond the Melting Pot, 19
"Bintel Brief," 89, 149
Blaustein, Jacob, 173
B'nai B'rith, 30, 54, 56, 105, 144-145, 165, 179, 105, 245
Bnai Zion, 146
Board of Jewish Education, 16, 44-46, 150, 161, 238, 259
Borg Child Guidance Institute, 155
"Borscht Belt," 25, 97
Bramson ORT Trade School, 153
Brandeis, Justice Louis D., 41, 68, 132, 159, 171, 176, 211
Brandeis University House, 151
Brith Abraham, 146, 152
Brooklyn Jewish Federation, 42
Brooklyn Jewish Journal, 196
Buchanan, President James, 31

Cahan, Ab, 67-68, 89, 99, 149, 192
Cardozo, Justice Benjamin F., 81, 103, 137, 143, 176, 193, 223, 258
Castle Garden, 33
Celler, Emanuel, 185-196, 197
Central Bureau for the Jewish Aged, 154
Central Conference of American Rabbis, 158
Central Synagogue, 118-119

Central Yiddish Culture Organization, 150
Chasidic Community, (Brooklyn; see also Lubavitcher movement), 183; food and catering, 188-189; schools, 188, 195, 209; shopping, 189,190; shules, 188
Chatham Square Cemetery, 26, 106, 135-136
Cherne, Leo, 92
Child care institutions, 155-156
Child Development Center, 155
City University of N.Y., 144
Cohen, Benjamin V., 57
Cohen, Morris Raphael, 34, 80, 104, 133
Commentary, 87, 145
committees for institutions of higher learning, 151
community centers: Brooklyn, 195; Bronx, 209; Manhattan, 153-154; Queens, 223-224; Staten Island, 229
community relations agencies, 145-146
Conference of Presidents of Major American Jewish Organizations, 152
Cong. B'nai Jeshurun, 27-28, 31, 38, 49, 62, 91, 115-116, 124
Cong. Shearith Israel, 26-31, 41, 49, 54, 61-62, 73, 91, 93, 101-102, 106, 109-112, 134-127, 135-136, 138, 143, 174, 176, 192, 200-201, 232, 262-263
Congress for Jewish Culture, 150
Congress House, 145-146
Congressional Medal of Honor, 93
Consulate General of Israel, 146
coordinating agencies: Brooklyn, 196; Bronx, 211; Manhattan, 152-153; Queens, 224; Staten Island, 230
Corbin, Austin, 177-178
Council of Jewish Federations and Welfare Funds, 152
Council of Jewish Organizations in Civil Service, 152
Czarist pogroms, 23, 38, 40, 56, 75, 103, 179

Day, The, 89-90
de Hirsch, Baron Maurice, 34, 180, 201
de Leon, Daniel, 67-68
de Lucena, Abraham, 22, 53, 58, 101
development of Hebrew day schools, 45-46
Downtown Talmud Torah, 150
Dubinsky, David, 57, 69

Early American Jewry, 232
early benevolent societies, 29-30, 32-33
early Zionist movements, 37-38
Educational Alliance, 33-35, 38, 51, 104-105, 153, 160, 180
Educators Assembly, 158
Eichanan, Isaac, Rabbinical Seminary, 37, 46-47, 136-137
Einhorn, Rabbi David, 35-36
Einstein, Dr. Albert, 80, 132, 144, 203, 208
Einstein, Albert, College of Medicine, 203, 208
Eisendrath, Dr. Maurice, 37
Eisenhower, President Dwight D., 144
Eisenstein, Judah D., 90
Ellis Island, 25, 33, 65, 99, 103
Encyclopedia Judaica, 99
entertainment: Brooklyn, 199; Manhattan, 160-169; Queens, 225
Epistles to the Hebrews, 103
Epstein, Sir Jacob, 34, 86, 104, 134
Ethical Culture Society, 38, 79, 176

Farband, 147, 205
Federation Employment and Guidance Service, 153, 219, 238
Federation of American Zionists, 37-38, 41
Federation of Jewish Philanthropies, 16-18, 32, 42-45, 60, 144, 148, 152-153, 170, 181, 185, 194, 196, 205, 211, 214-215, 219, 223, 228, 230, 238, 252, 259, 264
Feller, Abraham, 173
Finkelstein, Dr. Louis, 36, 180
Fischel, Rev. Arnold, 54
Flexner, Dr. Simon, 142
Frankfurter, Justice Felix, 80
Franks, Benjamin, 61
Franks, Jacob, 27, 61, 174
Franks, Rebecca, 101
fraternal orders, 152
Free Sons of Israel, 152
Free Synagogue, 38, 49, 92, 120-122
Freiheit, 90
Friedsam, Michael, 44, 134, 169, 197

Gershwin, George, 84, 170, 194, 266
Glazer, Nathan, 19, 87
Goldberg, Justice Arthur J., 77
Goldmark, Dr. Joseph, 176
Goldstein, Rabbi Israel, 116
Gomez, Dr. Horatio, 110
Gompers, Samuel, 39, 67, 159, 209, 270

United Synagogue of America, 37, 46, 158
United Synagogue Youth, 158
"University in Exile," 81, 141
Untermeyer, Samuel J., 76, 271-272

Van Buren, President Martin, 31, 73
vocational agencies, 153

Waksman, Dr. Selman A., 80
Wald, Lillian D., 91, 105-106, 160, 172, 211
Warburg, Mr. and Mrs. Felix M., 39-40, 101, 109, 138, 154, 193, 268
Warburg, Paul, 101
Washington, President George, 92, 101, 262
Washington Jewish Cemetery, 176
Westchester County, 261-272
Westchester County Board of Rabbis, 264
Westchester County Jewish Community Services, 264
Westchester County Jewish Conference, 264
Westchester Jewish Tribune, 267
Wilson, President Woodrow, 64, 76, 140
Wise Congress House, 108
Wise, Rabbi Isaac Mayer, 35, 117-119, 140, 166, 211
Wise, Jonah B., 119, 140
Wise, Louise, Services, 158
Wise, Rabbi Stephen S., 37-38, 77, 91-92, 108, 116, 120-123, 145, 158, 160, 175
Wolff, Lester, 241
Women's American ORT, 153, 159, 205, 250, 252
Women's League for Israel, 148
women's organizations, 158-159

Workmen's Circle, 51, 68, 98, 149, 152, 176, 210, 270
World Bureau for Jewish Education, 150
World Confederation of YMHAs and Jewish Community Centers, 154
World Jewish Congress, 38, 160
World Over, 150
World Zionist Organization, 148
Wright, Frank Lloyd, 109
writers and poets, 33-34, 62, 85-87, 89-90, 99, 101-103, 143, 176, 181, 186, 193, 227

Yeshiva Heichal Hatalmud of Tel Aviv, 151
Yeshiva Heichal Hatorah, 151
Yeshiva Ohr Torah, 151
Yeshiva Rabbi Moses Soloveichik, 151
Yeshiva Rabbi Samson Raphael Hirsch, 151
Yeshiva University, 47, 52, 80, 134-138, 165, 207-208
Yiddish Folkszeitung, 67
Yiddish theatre, 39, 82-84, 99, 160-161
Yiddish theatre stars, 82-83
YIVO Institute for Jewish Research, 108-109, 130-131
YMHA-YWHA, 16, 30, 32-34, 38, 42, 50, 52, 86, 96, 153-154, 161, 179, 194-185, 188, 195, 202, 204-205, 209, 217, 219, 224, 238, 243, 246, 251-252, 255, 257, 260, 264-265, 267, 270
Yulee, David Levy, 54

Zeckendorf, William, 71, 81, 186
Zionist Archives and Library, 132, 148
Zionist Organization of America, 41, 148